Separation
A Ukrainian WWII Survival Memoir

by Stepan Fedenko
translated by Damian Oleksiuk

Dedicated to my dearest parents,
Ivan and Fevronia Fedenko

~~~~~~~~

This book was translated from Ukrainian to English by my grandson, Damian Oleksiuk. He'll use the profits to take his first trip to Ukraine and film a documentary about his journey, following my footsteps through Ukraine, Poland, and Germany.

We appreciate your support. Thank you.

~~~~~~~~

From Damian: I found that translating the memoir word for word directly created a clunky feel to the sentence structure and story, so some passages have been altered from the original manuscript in order to create a more readable copy of the book.

~~~~~~~~

If you would like to reach Stepan or Damian, please email Damian at <u>dnoflows@gmail.com</u>.

CHAPTER ONE

History

The next few pages give an overview of Ukraine's struggle for freedom during the 1930s and '40s. If you'd like to skip the history and move on to my story, jump ahead to Chapter 2 (pg. 14). More information about terms marked by an asterisk can be found at the end of the book prior to the "About the Author" page.

Autumn 1939 brings us to Galicia, the region of Western Ukraine that holds our dear village of Uherci, along with the nearby town of Horodok, and a bit further northeast, the colorful city of Lviv. My name is Stepan Fedenko and at the time I was twelve years old and living with my Mama, Tato(Ukrainian for father), my brothers Volodymyr, Oleh, and Michael, along with my sister Maria. Unfortunately, Soviet so-called "Liberators" were storming through Ukraine from the East, led by the Red Army* and the terrifying NKVD*, which was Joseph Stalin's Soviet secret police whose main motivation was political repression.

Under this Soviet rule, our lives had become increasingly more difficult and dangerous. Any freedom we had under the previous Polish rule was snatched from our grasp. What food could still be bought was ripped off our shelves. Furthermore, under previous Polish rule, we could at least speak and write and defend what was Ukrainian. We could protest the government as well as protect our culture and folk customs. But under the Soviets, speaking out was strictly prohibited and considered a betrayal of "the motherland." Death or deportation was expected soon thereafter.

What kind of country is this? Certainly not Ukrainian. But I was convinced that it wasn't Russian either, because Russia was never home for me.

As the Soviets tightened their grip, the Communist system gained more power. Union farms were created, and the stronger Ukrainian workers were ripped away from their homes. Russia took everything, including our fertile land, which was handed down from generation to generation. There was no compensation for the families. Fear and unprecedented terror spread through our villages, homes, and minds.

Trains nicknamed "Black Ravens" swooped in on city tracks carrying NKVD officers. Local farmers gave them this nickname, because, like ravens who kidnapped chickens, this NKVD kidnapped our people, entire families even. They mostly did it at night, all within about two hours, sometimes even in the rain or snow, corralling and exporting whoever they pleased. The rest of the village slept, laying just as vulnerable to a potential kidnapping the next week or even that same night. The kidnapped were taken to the dirty, unheated commodity cars of these "Black Ravens," and like cattle they were transported deep into the distant ice-hell of Soviet Siberia. There they were imprisoned without trial and without true guilt and were forced to work for an alien nation.

And why? For what? Why threaten us? Why label us as "sinners," just for being Ukrainian born? Who has the power to decide where they're born? Weren't these the same Russians fighting against the Germans who were doing the exact same to the Jews? How was this any different? What did the Jews do? Just as Ukrainians, they were simply born. Who did they hurt? Who did we hurt? Who invented this first such abuse? Who created such law?

And how many people perished on the road to Siberia? How many actually made it? Which outcome was better? Many were never seen from again. And many weren't remembered either. *What happened to these innocent people? This is what the Russians called the Ukrainian "liberation" from Poland?*

This Ukrainian Soviet Republic looked simply like "Ukraine" to the outside world. But underneath that mask festered and ruled the cruel communist dictatorship: Stalin, his NKVD hit-men, along with Russian as well as Ukrainian traitors. This insane system, forced onto Galicia by these so-called "liberators," led to the destruction of Ukraine's children, language, culture, tradition, dignity, and to add to that, we were forced to *praise* these "liberators" as well.

So we weren't ordered to simply rip apart our own culture, but we were also forced to show gratitude to those that brought upon this unbearable pain. They bullied us Ukrainians to live a lie, and to cry loudly of their Soviet Paradise... "I know none other than this country, where man he breathes so free!"

They warned us that even if we had a single *thought* of freedom, they would immediately label us as enemies of the "motherland" and deportation to distant Siberia would soon follow. Deported Ukrainians were then forced to build roads and pipelines... and for the benefit of who? The Soviets! And only those involved with this mess, us and these Soviets, knew any of this was happening. The rest of the world was blind.

In schools, young children were brainwashed and ordered to tattle on relatives who criticized the communist regime or spoke of Ukrainian freedom. The Soviets hounded these children, beating into their brains ideas against religion and God, calling it the opium of the people. This was evil genius on the part of the Soviets - infiltrating the most vulnerable of Ukrainians leading to deep changes lasting generations instead of trying to convert their parents who knew better.

The worst was on Christmas, when the "liberation" authorities ordered us to go to school like it was any other day. They replaced Christmas with, well, nothing that meant anything to us - a "Grandpa Frost" and the "New Year." *Why celebrate a new year when there was no Christmas? This year wasn't done yet!* As a young boy, this change was a major disappointment. *Who did Christmas hurt?*

So I dragged my feet to school that not-so-Christmas day, head hung low, just a twelve year old with a terrible cold at that. But I had to. I didn't want to raise any suspicion against my family.

These Soviets wanted our minds to read: "We are liberated!"

Which was so far from the truth.

What really scared me was the memory of a play I had seen before the war, depicting a Ukrainian village during the artificially induced famine of the 1930s. Whole villages of people died of hunger while living on Ukrainian soil as fertile as any on great Mother Earth. Millions died in total. Food was taken from these starving villagers and either given to Soviets or simply thrown away. And the outside world didn't hear our cries for help either, for Soviet propaganda filtered out any news of famine trying to leak its way out of Ukraine. I wanted no repeat of this here in Galicia. But we needed help. We couldn't do this alone. *When would the rest of the world hear our cries?*

So this was our new life under the Soviet regime. The loss of our people, either those transported to Siberia or murdered in prisons or otherwise, spoke loudly to us Ukrainians. Even if the devil himself had taken over, or even pure evil itself, it wouldn't be any worse than Russian Communism.

These putrid conditions brought us to June 1941 when German planes dropped bombs onto the Soviet-occupied town of Horodok. Transportation was immediately interrupted. The road to the city was covered with tanks and military machines. Also, in Lviv, in the underground cellar prison called Brygidki, Germans found hoards of innocent Ukrainians murdered by Soviets.

Thus, the Germans were gaining power and a change was in the works. We heard that they had sympathy towards our situation and wanted to be our *new* liberators. So we started asking ourselves, "Can these Germans help us out?"

Because we needed a break from Russian rule. We

wouldn't last otherwise. If our farmers worked harder, the Soviets just took more crop. And we didn't have a stable enough or unifying collaborative force to fight behind. There was no joint movement. There was no communication. We couldn't fight them off, because we couldn't come together.

But we desperately wanted freedom.

So we thought maybe Russia and Germany would rip each other apart. Then Ukraine, minding its own business, could slip out from under broken rule and live free.

So in true Ukrainian spirit, which was "survive today, hope for tomorrow," our nation's leadership, without the consent of the Soviets or Nazis, declared independence within the initial week of World War II, on June 30, 1941.

Survive today, hope for tomorrow.

Ukrainian leadership then decided that it would be easier to fight alongside Germany versus the Soviets, because those Ukrainian soldiers enlisted in the Soviet's Red Army would hopefully desert en masse when hearing of this all-in push for freedom, *especially* if the Germans would tolerate our independence in exchange for our cooperation. This could be a big shift in our favor.

We also picked Germany because Russia wanted our resources *so badly*. Russia's options were either cold, desolate Siberia or the vast fertile plains and mild temperate of Ukraine.

"They have what we want, and we can take it."

We heard nothing of the Germans wanting to tear our country apart like the Soviets did, so we really had no choice.

Unfortunately, us Ukrainians were alone in daring to

believe in a free Ukraine. Germany immediately took a stance against our freedom, threatening our newly independent state. These Germans were clear in their focus and a free Ukraine had nothing to do with it.

They ordered us to immediately withdraw our proclamation of independence. Otherwise, they'd incarcerate every Ukrainian leader. But the newly created Ukrainian government didn't succumb to German threats. They held their ground.

But this plan fell through within a breathe of Ukraine's declared stance. Germans fulfilled their promise, and within a month, almost all members of the Ukrainian government were arrested, amongst them Yaroslav Stetsko* and Stepan Bandera*, two Ukrainian leaders whose mere names mentioned stirred excitement for freedom. They were all deported to concentration camps, deep into Germany. It was a crippling blow to our already disjointed leadership.

And just like that, Germany's sympathy towards Ukraine, and their stance as these "new liberators," had vanished. Those non-arrested members of the government then dove into one of Ukraine's two Underground organizations with the understanding that Ukraine could no longer wait for the foreign aide that wasn't coming and should best organize themselves and their own efforts to break free from this ugly oppression.

So how did I fit into all this?

As a young boy, the Underground* made a great

impression on me. I was more than ecstatic to read and re-read all of their literature. Their slogan, "Freedom of Nations and Freedom of People," couldn't have sounded any better in those dark times of war. I passed these books around to all of my most trusted friends, but none of them became as entrenched as I did.

Through Tato, I also got to connect with leaders of the Underground personally. I listened intently to their conversations as they spoke of plans to regain control of the country they loved so dearly.

The most gripping topic for me was always how the Second World War would end. *Who's going to win? Who takes control and why? What could put us on the side of victory?* Interestingly, the Underground leaders, at a time when Germany had just seized Leningrad and was now approaching Moscow, felt that Germany would still lose. But they also maintained that the Soviets would collapse as well. And how could both happen? They somehow implicitly believed that our allies from the West would help Russia, but only to the point of destroying Germany.

They claimed that the war wouldn't end when the German demon was slain. Instead, they believed that England and America, as well as the rest of the world, would finally be acquainted with and conscious of Russian Imperialists and their brutal prison system, Siberian concentration camps, and their hope that this terrifying form of communism would "save" all of Europe and beyond.

So the Underground hoped that this light on their lies would provide proof enough to overthrow the Soviet's stronghold on the lives of the helpless innocent. The Undergrounders figured that these Soviets wouldn't have the Polish or Baltic support either, because both of those countries had previously been devastated by the German Ribbentrop* *and* Russian Molotov*. The Allies would then defeat them both!

This was the Underground's hope, at least. A hope which manifested a grassroots plan of getting armed through stealing from Germans and getting involved in Black Market trading. Ukraine would give the Allies any little push it could, from our simple but passionate hands.

But the most important part of our plan, even more important than putting arms in our young warriors' hands, was to inform and spread consciousness among the Ukrainian people, to let them know that the only fear worth holding onto was the fear of not being free. Nobody would drop freedom on our doorstep, and we needed to be ready when that sliver of opportunity arose.

In this great time of war and turmoil, the Underground members explained that this might just be the best opportunity in our entire history for freedom and independence.

So this brings us to the Spring of 1944. Russians and Germans were taking advantage of our weaknesses and storming through us, pillaging and destroying our villages.

And like cornered dogs, Ukrainian youths lashed out. Our fear of oppression became stronger than our fear of death. We were fed up with always being in third or fourth place of who actually owned our nation. It became a culture of nothing to lose, so the youth unhesitatingly sacrificed their normal lives and voluntarily went to train and take up arms, even joining the German army with the sole purpose of getting trained, stealing weapons, and preparing to betray at a moment's notice. They were sick of being ruled.

We weren't free, and there's nothing we wanted more.

CHAPTER TWO

THE SIEGE - APRIL 25TH, 1944

This brings us to the Fall of 1944. I was a seventeen year old, 5'2" electrical engineering student visiting my family for Easter. Our modest home sat nestled in Uherci, a village of 400 plots lying southwest of Lviv in Western Ukraine. Nightingales chirped and corvine cawed from their perches in oak trees by our home, my hardworking Tato(Ukrainian for father) held work as a blacksmith, and my loving Mama made sure our family went to church every Sunday. If only it were that simple.

Ukraine's constant claw for freedom from the Soviets had been dragging on for generations, and the Germans too now pillaged what little we had left, an immutable reminder that our beloved Ukraine was not, and may never be, truly ours.

It was also time for my sister Maria and me to go back to school. The night before our first day, our younger brother Michael had trouble sleeping and complained all night, awaking early to shuffling outside our window. His job that morning was to wagon us to nearby Horodok, where we'd take the train to school in Lviv. He worried about us being late and made sure to keep his eyes on the slow-moving clock throughout the night.

When the morning came and Michael finally got up and went outside to check the weather, he burst back into our rooms, shook us and said, "The village is full of German troops! Woman and children are crying! They're taking all the men!"

Maria and I, along with our brothers Oleh and Volodymyr, sprung out our beds and scurried to the window to check for ourselves. Michael liked to joke around.

But this was no joke. Across the road, German troops were escorting our uncle out of his house. Meanwhile, Tato crept into our room and grabbed me.

"Shhh. Come with me," he said, and I snuck out the door with him.

We hunched down behind the wooden fence in our front yard and watched German guards snatch villagemen from their homes and crying families, escorting them down the road. Every man was taken.

We scurried back into the house and awaited our turn, knowing that any chance of escape was suicide. Our family would never make it, with my little siblings and my mother. Tato and I would never leave them. That choice never faltered - we'd never separate.

I thought back to what Tato had said one day when we were working on our cellar and I had asked him about fleeing: "We stay to defend our land and the weak."

But nobody showed up at our door - a miracle! The Germans were gone. We stared at each other in disbelief.

Did they make a mistake? Maybe they missed us?

Tato told Maria and I to keep getting ready for school, so we wouldn't cause any unnecessary suspicion. We understood the need for normalcy in crisis, but then a thought hit Tato and he grabbed my arm.

"I almost forgot!" he said. "There's a rifle hidden under the furnace. Stepan, hide it better, down in the gutter. Use whatever's under there - ashes, kindling... hurry!"

I ran to the furnace, dropped to my knees and found the rifle wrapped in paper and tightly woven string. I got as deep underneath the furnace as I could and jammed the rifle down into the little gutter. I leveled the soil out over the rifle to conceal my work. I spread ashes and other small logs around, trying to make it look natural and normal and not like someone had just hidden a rifle.

The Oleh, my ten year old brother, startled me: "What are you hiding?"

!

I didn't want to scare him or let him see the rifle.

"Oleh," I whispered, "Come here!" and he did and I said, "Don't tell anybody you saw me doing this. Don't touch anything down here! If you listen to me ever, listen to me now. Ok?"

He ran back to Tato.

I put the last of the logs in place, like they were being set out to dry and went back into our living room where I found out that apparently my brother Michael had ran off.

Worry hit Tato's face. "If the Germans do show, they'll ask about him."

SEPARATION

When the Germans first came to power in our village, the authorities issued a law stating that each home needed an occupancy register, of which the list had to be confirmed by the village council. It was nailed to our front door. Michael was on that list. This was not good.

Where could you have gone? How do we explain your absence?!

And then it hit me - I'd been living in Lviv the last two years, and I wouldn't be on the list.

"Tato! I'm not on the list," I said. "If they come, I can be Michael. They'll count the names. They'll count us. We'll be fine." That settled his nerves a bit.

Maria and I finished getting ready for school. I'd never packed my bag so fast. Everything except our driver was in place.

I snuck back outside to see what was going on.

But it was a ghost town. Completely empty. No villagemen. No crying women and children. *Where did they take everybody? Did they really forget about us? Or did they make a mistake?*

Then I looked out the window past Sonia's house, where just last night she had kissed me goodbye, and saw our grade-school's headmaster, Krupa, walking out of the schoolhouse followed by twenty or so German officers dressed in long leather coats and military hats. I shot back behind the fence.

Why the school? And why so many officers for Krupa? He's not working the Underground.

I crouched and crawled back into the house and told Tato what I saw. We all scurried to the window to see what came next. But Krupa wasn't being led by the Germans like the other men were. *He* was leading *them*.

"They must have come for retribution... for the shooting," Tato said as he sat back with a look of disbelief on his face. German officers were shot at a few days earlier outside our village during a mission that went poorly. I was a part of that mission.

Tato added, "Now let happen, the will of God."

I wondered what kind of retribution they'd bring. This had never happened before. It could be anything.

Then Krupa and the guards stopped in front of... *our* house.

We froze. We couldn't run. Fleeing could bring an even bigger German wrath than the one we were about to get.

Krupa walked into our yard followed by all twenty or so of these German officers. They immediately surrounded our house.

Terror enveloped our family. The Germans didn't forget about us - we were their main target.

I'd heard countless stories like this from Underground meetings, but the thought of Germans surrounding *our* house never crossed my mind.

Maybe they were waiting for us to react after taking the other men. Maybe they thought we'd run. Either way now they had us surrounded.

The lead officer gave some direction and a few others searched our hedges. Another group approached a pile of bricks in our yard, which Tato had recently bought to build us a new home. The officers moved the house-load of bricks and tried digging with their iron shovels. But Tato put these bricks there for a reason - not because he was hiding anything, but because it was good, solid ground to put a house-load of bricks on.

After some time, they were convinced of the same and stopped their search. Someone must have told them that we were hiding weapons there.

Then a group of officers, led by a tall, pot-bellied, red-in-the-face German Commander, walked unannounced through our door. There was no knock or permission granted.

In front of the Nazis stood schoolmaster Krupa. He looked utterly confused and out of place. He had walked into our home plenty of times. He was always smiling, often joking with Tato, and he treated me well. His son and daughter went to school with me in Lviv, and we'd often help each other with our homework. We helped each other make friends too.

But at this moment, Krupa was different - distraught, pale, and his mannerisms and posture were that of an ashamed, feeble man.

He, with all confidence depleted, raised his head a bit and greeted us in a trembling voice. Krupa didn't utter us another word, turned back to the paunchy Commander and in German asked, "Can I leave?"

The German agreed and Krupa left silently from our home, probably returning to his own family. That would be the last time I would ever see schoolmaster Krupa.

"Line up. Against the wall," one of the officers ordered us in German. "You too," he said, pointing to my youngest brother Volodymyr, who at the time was only nine. He was sitting on the stovetop shaking, terrified. Poor Volodymyr. We were all shocked and didn't move. Mama couldn't hold back.

She burst into tears.

"Line up!" shouted the officer, this time in Polish. He walked over to the house registry poster and read over the details. *Please don't ask.* I really didn't want to lie.

The officer counted us, confirming what he saw on the card. Six on the card, six in the house. Mama, Tato, Volodymyr, Oleh, Maria, and me for Michael. Maria has been studying in Lviv with me too, but she left a year later and the register hadn't been updated yet. All seemed ok so far.

The Germans showed no initial suspicion, but I started to worry about where Michael was.

Are you in the barn?

He loved hiding out in the haystacks. I pictured the Germans searching the stacks with their long and sharp bayonets, stabbing a terrified Michael in the process. I couldn't picture anywhere else he'd go. I felt sick.

We then heard shuffles and movements below us, in our cellar - the Germans were throwing about all our storage. My heart skipped as every wooden board clanked. Probably searching for weapons. Luckily, there was nothing down there.

But the red-faced German wasn't satisfied with his raid. With every report of clean room after clean room, he rumbled and grumbled more and more angrily, becoming less and less human and more and more a snarling beast.

"Well then fine! I'll do it myself!" he yelled.

It seemed like he wouldn't rest until he found *something*. I thought of the rifle.

After tossing about some things, the red-faced German paused and his eyes found the pictures hanging up on our wall.

"Aaaahh," he said, with a sort of evil satisfaction. For a long time he peered at these pictures, portraits of Taras Shevchenko, Ivan Franko, Father Markian Shashkevych and Symon Petliura. They were all patriotic symbols of Ukraine's fight for freedom. Many of them were locked up, for their activities were stamped "illegal" by the Soviets or Germans.

This pot-bellied beast lingered longer in front of Simon Petliura's picture. Petliura was the Head of the Ukrainian State from 1918-1920. He rose to power on ideals of rebellion and freedom from all those who oppressed Ukraine. He had also granted Jews more rights in Ukraine than any other European government had and was assassinated by a Ukrainian-born Jewish anarchist in 1926.

The red-faced German then unsheathed his long bayonet and cracked the frame's glass face. Then he sliced through the middle of the picture.

He proudly said to himself, "Simon Petliura... bandit." Then, as if that hadn't satisfied him enough, he ordered Tato and I to separate from the rest of the family.

"The girl too?" one of his assistants said of Maria.

The Commander nodded a yes. "And search the house again - all of it! Every room, every crevice, every trunk of clothing! Documents, papers, books, notebooks! Everything!"

He stormed out the house, leaving two of his remaining deputies. They whispered to each other and nodded in understanding.

"Get us some milk," one said to Maria.

She gladly agreed, went out and milked the cow, and

brought back two glasses. When she returned, she stood with Mama and my two brothers, instead of with Tato and me.

It was easy to see that if one of our two groups was in danger, it was Tato and mine. Neither of the Germans ordered Maria back in our group, and in the end, this probably saved her life.

We heard the paunchy Commander cursing his assistants because they couldn't find a thing.

He ordered them to search a third time, but this time with incredible detail. They wanted to rationalize searching our home. They didn't want to fail. They wanted to figure us out. He ordered one of his men to dig again under the bricks where no digging was actually possible.

Maybe they won't find a thing. Maybe they'll leave us alone. Please, just leave. Go away. You have no reason to be here.

We again heard soldiers tossing hay bales in the barn, combing it from head to toe, even more thorough than before. With each new order from the Commander, I became more worried.

I thought about the rifle under the furnace. I thought about wherever Michael could be. Because the Germans insisted so dearly on finding *something* suspicious, I figured that we were probably the most punished house in the village. They were setting an example for others. Someone must have ratted us out. But what they said, I didn't know.

Then one of the officers told Oleh to crawl underneath the oven and remove all the boards and any chopped wood. My heart skipped a beat. Oleh knew that *something* was down there, but I didn't tell him what it was. My family's anxiety tightened.

With the officer watching closely, Oleh nervously got down and tossed about a few logs of firewood, but mostly he just re-arranged them back and forth, moving them side to side.

Yes Oleh! Good.

Unfortunately for Oleh, Mama had just baked bread that morning, so that heat plus his anxiety put him into a heavy sweat. He did not want to go any deeper.

Luckily, the German who had been tracing Oleh's every move, couldn't bend down any longer and stood up, rubbing his lower back. Oleh finished searching around, and the German seemed satisfied. Oleh had even leveled out the ground better than I had, really making it look like nothing was down there. I figured we were in the clear.

But then the German gave Oleh his bayonet. "Keep poking around," he said. *Ah! Oleh will be just as surprised by this rifle as the German!* Oleh did as he was told, poking about nimbly. What agony!

After a few minutes, the German ordered Oleh out from underneath that hellacious furnace heat. His face was covered in ashes, dirt, and sweat. As the German shined his flashlight underneath the furnace, Tato and I waited impatiently. Satisfied, the German ordered Oleh to toss the logs back underneath the stove, and we quietly let our breathes out. I quickly thanked God but then my head swiveled towards the other soldiers, who'd began searching our kitchen. Next to the kitchen window there hung a wooden shelf filled with bowls, plates, and glazed clay jugs, and on the end sat a "masnychka," a small wooden churn in which Mama sometimes made butter.

Last time Tato went to the store, he bought a larger masnychka, so Mama wasn't using this smaller one anymore. Seeing this little masnychka on the shelf sent shivers through my body. My legs became rubber and stuck to the floor. I could hardly move.

I had hidden a magazine for a revolver in that masnychka, which I had brought home from Lviv several weeks back. I had coaxed an Uherci-raised Ukrainian policeman named Yosef to sell it to me. In general, Lviv's Police Force had ties to the Melnyk* branch of the Underground movement, so most policemen would never sell weapons to a village boy like me. But most of Lviv's Police Force wasn't infatuated with my sister Maria like Yosef was. Seeing Ukraine's freedom movement separated into chunks like this with no real central leadership was so frustrating, but Tato and I had to take what we could get however we could get it.

So Yosef sold me a gun and two magazines and I snuck them back on the train from Lviv to Horodok and then home and gave Tato one load and the revolver. I put the other load in the masnychka, thinking I'd give it to him when I got another gun.

And before the Germans barged in today, Tato and I Nazi-proofed every corner of our home. We even burned our copies of Underground literature. But I completely forgot about the bullets hidden in the masnychka!

Nobody else in the family knew about these bullets. Not even Tato. *So we're going down because of me? How did I forget? How could I be so stupid?*

Peering at these Germans, who were carefully searching the shelf, bowl by bowl, my self-hate turned to fear. I knew that as soon as the Germans found the magazine, Tato would be berated for the location of the accompanying revolver.

"Where's the gun!?"

"Where'd you get the bullets!?"

I couldn't think of a good answer. I wanted all the blame. I worried that Tato would take all of *my* guilt. Tato would never let me take that fall.

I wanted so badly to talk to him, but I couldn't. The guard was right next to us *and* ordered us not to talk. I racked my mind of how I could distract the Germans, but nothing came, so I did the only thing left I could do - pray.

Please God, don't let them search the masnychka. Don't let them search the masnychka.

One of the guards searched the last bowl before the masnychka.

And then, suddenly, something happened that I myself truly can not explain. Perhaps it *was* the grace of God, the grace for our family.

I heard a hysterical snort come from a German who had been outside searching our porch.

He cried out to the others, "Come quick and see what I've found!"

The German guard next to the masnychka turned and shouted, "What's so funny over there?"

"Get over here and see for yourself!" he replied, still unable to control his shrieks.

To my amazement, the German left the masnychka and

24

walked outside to see what his fellow soldier had found so funny. A moment later, they both walked back into the house with little bunny rabbits in their hands.

Michael had cherished playing with these rabbits in the stables, where their burrows were. The Germans must have ran them out of the barn, through their little tunnels, and into the porch wall.

These frightened rabbits, looking for safer ground, ended up landing in soldiers' hands and being softly caressed by the same German mitts that had just ransacked our home.

What luck!

But thankfully, neither German returned to the masnychka. They just kept showing off rabbits to one another.

Next, the commander ordered a guard to review all the notes and books that I had brought home from school. He carefully peered over every page. Apparently he could read Ukrainian.

Sandwiched in the pages of the books, he found my little notes, addresses of friends from school, a few jokes, and lyrics to songs that I hadn't yet learned by heart. The German seemed a little too curious shuffling through it all. He lingered on a page which I had written down the lyrics to a Ukrainian Underground Army song. The German then stood up from his chair, opened the window, and called the other officers inside. They came in and he translated my notes into German for them. The lyrics were all about rebellion and the freedom of our dear Ukraine.

One verse went like so:

The UPA* is the armed force,

SEPARATION

That re-baptizes its enemies.
Judgement still comes
And the Ukrainian people will be free!
Another, like so:
Glory to Ukraine, the homeland,
Glory to its heroes, the OUN*.
Glory to our trident and Bandera*,
Freedom for all nations!

I started singing them in my head, but I was too terrified to remember the melody. Singing was an incredibly important part of the Ukrainian culture. It brought people and voices together... but at that moment, with my notes, it felt more like it was about to tear us apart.

The Commander then called off the search and told the officer to bring him the notebook. Only the notebook. Apparently, they had found what they were looking for, as little as it was. My guilt, lost in the rifle and butter churner, had found itself now attached to my notebook.

My fault? Again? How could this be? I should have known that they could read Ukrainian!

At least with my notebook they could put all the blame on me, and not on anyone else in my family. Tato couldn't take this one.

Mama also seemed to realize that this long of a search couldn't end well. Her face hung heavy with anxiety. She knew the Germans would arrest Tato and me.

Mama paced through our home, as if searching for something, probably worrying about how she would fair alone with the family, how she could keep it running. There was no way to store food in our home long term, and already we were in dire need of money.

And because I planned on heading to school that morning, I was dressed in my best outfit and new boots that I had just picked up from the shoemaker. These were so-called "English boots," made of real red leather. They were quite fashionable in our area, and I wanted to brag to my friends, especially to the girls.

Looking at Mama, I instantly felt regret in wearing these clothes and wanted to change. Mama needed to sell them back. She needed the money.

Mama read my mind and regretfully yet courageously asked me, "Could you change into something else, if the Germans wouldn't mind?" It might have been the hardest thing she'd ever asked of me.

The Germans were busy, so I quickly changed back into some old clothes and then the Commander walked in, followed by several officers.

After a short conversation, the red-faced Commander ordered Tato and me out of the house. They said nothing to my sister Maria, who stood by and supported my tearful Mama. My youngest brother, Volodymyr, who was lying back on top of the stove, cried too. To shut him up, one German snapped his arm with a whip, immediately ceasing Vlad's moans. I felt queasy.

I stood up to make sure Volodymyr was ok, but the same German who whipped him kicked my hip with his military boot and pushed me out the door.

Tato and I were escorted down the road by a pack of

German soldiers. I pictured gallows and figured that both of us would be hanging by day's end.

At that moment, as we walked by Sonia's house, she slipped out her door and saw Tato and I surrounded by troops. She buried her face into her hands and immediately ran back inside. *Would this be the last time I see you?*

The guards led us to the field on the far end of the village, which was covered with German soldiers armed with machine guns ready to fire. The gallows I'd first imagined were thankfully not there, giving me hope that maybe these Germans wouldn't punish anyone publicly.

Tato and I were led to all the other men sitting in long rows, densely packed, waiting for whatever the Germans might do to us. We were quickly separated, and before I could protest, I was stuck into a row of five and an officer walked along our flank and counted us.

I hope these Germans don't randomly pick out hostages. They had done so recently in a nearby village. I distracted myself from this thought by looking for my brother Michael, who remained unseen.

Then I noticed that I was easily the youngest of the men. Loneliness crept in.

Not far from our field, a group of courageous women from the village gathered, worried about what these Germans might do to their husbands or son. With tears in their eyes and babies in their arms, they tried getting closer but were blockaded by the German troops. Everyone waited in silence.

After the German officers congregated, the paunchy Commander, who headed the "audit" of our home, ordered his lead officer to explain why we were gathered here today.

His officer opened up a leather notebook and withdrew a sheet of paper. Then, in Ukrainian, he said, "If I call your name, line up before me."

This wasn't a gathering of random hostages. This was a premeditated arrest.

He read three names:

"Michael Dyachok."

"Jakuba Hryhorij."

"Yosef Mazur."

And then two more:

"Ivan Fedenko."

"Stepan Fedenko."

My heart dropped.

The officer hid his notes and said, "During today's search of your little village, we were very easy on you. Right now, we are only arresting these five. We've been informed that these people are engaged in unauthorized employment, and that their work is detrimental to the German Reich."

My heart sank even further.

"We want to verify," he said, "that these denunciations are true. This is our first order of business. And secondly, not far from here, in *your very forest*, Colonel Otto Linka and his secretary Kashuba were wounded. We still don't know who shot them. Linka believes that they may have been deserting Germans, but we think that you five will tell us who did it."

How much do they know?

"And when we uncover that these five are not guilty, we'll promptly release them home. Let this be an example to you all. You must respect us Germans. No one here will tell us how and what to do. And, at this moment, there are no crimes attributed to your village, so today we'll only arrest these five suspicious people," he said.

Suspicious people? I knew that my work wasn't in line with the Reich, but who told them? And what did they say?

"Let this be a warning for the future too. If another shooting happens or if we're attacked by guerrillas in the forest, we'll line up the rest of you and shoot you on the spot," he said and then added, "Once again, if we see that these arrested are not guilty, then you'll have them back soon. You'll see."

The irony dripped from his lips. *They knew.*

These words comforted the other villagemen and their attentive women. Many of them rejoiced getting back their relatives, initially expecting something terrible.

But there *was* something terrible. Tato and I got caught.

Most of the un-arrested villagers crept away, as if one wrong move might change their fate. The Germans ordered them out of the way, not to disrupt the traffic. A few of the villagers bravely hung around, standing at the side of the road, looking back at us with compassion. Many of them knew exactly why we were being arrested - we worked for the Underground.

Meanwhile, two military freight trucks covered in tarps drove up to the square. Us five arrested were led to the one filled with waiting German soldiers. I found it impossible to move my heavy feet, hoping maybe roots could grow into the ground and I wouldn't have to leave.

The guards escorted us into the truck and we sat down on the metal floor. The guards themselves sat up on benches, favorable perches to keep eyes on us *suspicious* people. The soldiers who participated in the raid went off to the other car.

Just then, about a dozen daring village women ran up to our truck to say their goodbyes, to grab our hands, to weep. They tried to comfort us, saying they'd pray for our quick release. Mama and Maria appeared, as well as some of our neighbors. The crying grew heavier as the fearful realization of the moment sunk into their hearts.

Some villagers promised to take care of our family. This made my heart a little lighter. Mama was strong, maybe too strong. She'd try to shoulder the burden of providing, so it was a sliver of good hope to hear that others would help.

The trucks jolted forward and the women ran after us, trying to get one more moment with their kin. Mama grabbed the tailgate of our truck. She begged in vain, "Release them! Release them or take me with you!"

The truck outran the other women and it was just Mama left sprinting, hands latched onto the tailgate. I couldn't believe it. I knew she was strong, but not like this.

One guard then stood up and kicked Mama off the gate with his military boot and she tumbled into the middle of the road. The women behind her caught up and pulled her aside just as the second truck of the convoy barreled through, nearly running her over and adding more tragedy. I stared in disbelief. That final moment with my Mama burned into my memory. I would never forget it.

She once told me that she wanted my head to rest against

her when she died. *Would I ever get that chance?*

I stared at the German who kicked her. I hated him.

Why did you have to kick her?

Was it not enough for you to take us away from her?

She would have fallen off sooner or later - why kick her off?!

Mama disappeared into the dust shuffled up by the second convoy. Little did I know that this would be the last time I'd ever see her in person. A devastated Tato sat silently, watching the German who kicked Mama as though he'd pounce in retribution at any moment.

"Tato..." I started to say but a German swiftly lined up his rifle right between my eyes and shouted, "No talking!"

I had never been on that end of a rifle before.

The convoy didn't go far. It turned and arrived at the other end of our village at the castle of Count Nyezabitosky, which was now occupied by the Wehrmacht, the German armed forces. Most of the soldiers got out of the trucks and we were ordered to stay put. It was probably lunch time.

They left us with two guards in the truck and two more patrolling the ground. They once again reiterated to us, "No talking!" They probably didn't know Ukrainian and wanted to avoid us plotting against them.

After these four guards were relieved and the rest of the soldiers returned, they laid out on benches and I figured that they might at least let us use a toilet. But they didn't.

Coming out of the castle last was the paunchy Commander. His face was somehow redder. I figured him exiting last was directly related to how much time he spent stuffing himself.

He joked loudly, and everyone laughed but us prisoners. He satisfyingly got into his small personal car, chauffeur waiting, and then he gave the signal and we drove further down the road. Behind the personal car drove two more cars, and then the two convoys, one with us and one with the soldiers who raided Uherci.

I became more and more disgusted looking at these arrogant Germans. They seemed to have eaten plenty enough... and drank enough too, for they were all loudly yelling amongst themselves.

You could do whatever you want, whether anyone liked it or not, couldn't you?

They paid almost no attention to us. It's like we weren't even there.

I looked back down the road, through my arched tarpaulin window. This road led straight to Horodok so I figured that they were taking us to the prison there. For almost two years I walked this road to school and back, twice a day. I knew every ditch. If the weather was nice, it was a good forty five minutes, and there were snowy days when it took double.

And I used to complain about that cold! If I only knew then what today would bring... would I have complained? Now I was being driven... and I'm still complaining! Would I ever walk this road again? My mind sprung into action.

Could I flee? I know every one of these roads. The jump from the car isn't too high, and I'm not that far from home.

But then I thought of Tato. *What would happen to him? Or what if I got hurt running? Twist my ankle maybe?* They'd catch me and have no use for me. I'd surely be executed.

SEPARATION

We arrived in Horodok, passing by my old school on Skitnyk road, the Horodok market, and then kept moving further east. Staying in Horodok wouldn't be too bad, because Mama could easily visit and bring us food, clothing, and anything else we needed. But we kept moving and moving and before I knew it those plans were spoiled and our transports were out past the city limits.

We weren't being questioned in Horodok. We were headed northeast, towards Lviv, another 30 km further. At that moment I realized that they were taking us wherever they pleased, and I couldn't change a thing.

CHAPTER THREE

EASTER

Easter Saturday in the village, 10 days prior.

The villagers of Uherci donned traditional Ukrainian festive attire, clean white shirts lined with colorfully embroidered trim. Thrown across their shoulders, in white canvas bags, men carried gigantic Easter loafs called Paska, which were topped with intricate designs resembling a young girl's braids or the crown of a Roman king. Women and children followed carrying baskets filled with golden butter, hard-boiled eggs, hearty sausage, swollen bread rolls, and cheese, all glowing by the light of a single lit candle, resting against the basket's rim.

A "Christ is risen!" belted from the collective breast of these rural people as a priest walked through two long rows of us villagers. He blessed the beautiful spreads by meticulously flicking holy water, which trickled along the crevices of our Paskas. When the priest finished blessing the Easter baskets, and for this he was gifted several of the more impressively decorated eggs, he wished everyone a happy holidays and moved on further through the village.

The villagers then walked amongst themselves, wishing each other a happy holidays. They admired the wives' work of baking the best and most grandiose Paska. Some of them grew so large that the villagers couldn't pull them from the mouths of their ovens, so they broke the bread into pieces just so they could still be enjoyed. The hopes and failures of baking the biggest Paska were shared and laughed at.

The weather on this Easter Saturday was beautiful, sunny, and warm. During these times of turmoil, it was these simple joys that made life a little more pleasant.

But my mind wasn't here. It was on the war. I was clouded with fear of Stalin's reign. I was worried about Hitler's takeover of Europe. And on top of that, earlier this morning, Tato told me that two members of the Ukrainian Underground would be arriving soon. They needed a local to lead them to their next checkpoint.

"Tato," I replied, "This time - don't ask anyone else - I'll gladly do it myself."

Tato was pleased that his son was following in his footsteps as a believer in a truly free Ukraine, a fight our people have been fighting for hundreds of years. Tato had given all but his life to the movement. I was moving towards doing the same.

So this mission started with me meeting the two Undergrounders at the edge of the forest that stretched alongside the village.

"The password is 'kraj sela'(village edge)," Tato said.

My task was to escort them through the thicket to the Undergrounders living at the other end of Uherci. From there, they'd be escorted with horses over to the next village.

I knew this job well. I'd been running these routes for two years now, since I was fifteen. Sometimes, when we're rushed, I'm forced to cut right through the village instead of sleeking through the woods. Sometimes we'd run into my friends who'd ask about the new faces.

"Friends from school," I'd say, while leading younger members.

"Professors from Lviv," I'd say, with the older ones.

But it always went smoothly. They always believed me. I was going to school about 36 kilometers away in Lviv, so they wouldn't recognize these men anyway. I didn't like lying, but I needed them to believe me. Ukraine was crawling with Polish and Soviet and now German spies, and they scoured for Underground activity, ratting out and arresting anyone who carried but a sniff of suspicion.

Because of this, Tato was always very careful with his Underground work. Everything he could do on his own, he did. He needed to keep the circle small, so that he could protect his family, himself, and the village as well. That, on top of being a blacksmith, made me wonder how he ever found time to sleep.

He also didn't seek his own glory. There was no room for it. He always put the Ukrainian people first. And now that the second World War burned throughout Ukraine, his duty was more important than ever. He never spoke of his OUN* (Organization of Ukrainian Nationals) affiliation with my sister or either of my three brothers. Just Mama and I exclusively.

At this point, Ukraine had almost always been ruled by

someone else. Poland, Moscow, Germany, and now Moscow again... Tato was determined to help break Ukraine free from this pattern.

After Easter talk died down and a short break at home, I walked out into our yard to get some air and noticed an unknown man and woman riding horseback on the road in front of our home. Both were well dressed in nice civilian clothing, happy, and loudly yammering to each other in German. I didn't pay them much attention, because this was a common sight; I figured they were part of the local German Wehrmacht Garrison, a military unit staying at the former Polish nobleman Nezabitovski's agricultural castle which was overtaken by Nazi force.

I took light note of them and went about my day.

Later that evening, I walked to the forest to meet the visiting Undergrounders. Tato warned me repeatedly to be extra careful not to raise any unnecessary suspicion. Polish families around the village could easily track me if I wasn't mindful. Oftentimes, these families would rat out Underground members to the Germans in return for better treatment.

After receiving one such tip from a Polish family, the German military planted itself within the city district of nearby Horodok. They called out the head of our village, Dennis Chornenkyj, telling him that they have information of Ukrainian insurgents passing through his neighborhood.

"If we find this to be true," a German soldier explained to

him, "then we'll arrest you for not telling us first. And, since we're so understanding, we have another choice for you - you can arrest them yourself."

Dennis, pulling double-duty as a member of the Underground, would never take this second option. Risking prison was his only choice, because a free Ukraine was his only goal. All he could do was let Tato know of the situation and hope for no slip ups. Both the Ukrainians and local Poles would rather just live in harmony, but since freedom and resources were scarce, people almost always chose their own family's needs over keeping quiet.

A few weeks back, a Ukrainian woman, who was married to a Pole, told my parents that Polish underground warriors, called the Country Army, snaked through our village. She overheard her husband's conversation that Poland was getting ready, when the time was right, to overtake Western Ukraine, including the nearby city of Lviv.

So our geography with these local Poles might have been shared, but the objectives of our double-lives were not.

(Ukrainians fighting for freedom were part of the Ukrainian People's Self-defense, later on called the OUN and the UPA. The OUN was the Organization of Ukrainian Nationals*, which was the entire movement of Ukraine fighting for freedom. The UPA, or Ukrainian Povstanska Armya*, was the OUN's army, which translates best to the Ukrainian Insurgent Army.)

So peaceful times seemed no where near - the German front was also approaching and rumors of conflict spread.

As I traced the edge of the forest, my mind came back to

the mission. *Who will I meet today? And what could be so important that this gets done on Easter Saturday? Is the UPA recruiting us? To join them to train in the Carpathian Mountains?*

Sometimes members of the OUN would come through and distribute educational pamphlets explaining what we could do for the movement. Ukraine's people were very passionate about freedom, but its collective push for this freedom was disjointed. This information would hopefully help unite her.

Throughout my childhood, this literature, Tato's recaps of Underground meetings, and even my personal meetings with Undergrounders gave me the courage, the hope, and the willingness to further imbed myself into the Underground. Although I was still a kid, I was brought up breathing a thick Ukrainian spirit, and because I saw those around me suffer for the betterment of alien nations - I felt the need to contribute. Hearing that other nations were being plundered and used... "colonized" they'd say... I'd regret it if I didn't do everything I could to prevent Ukraine from falling deeper into that hole. *Maybe I could help it climb out?*

Tato recently told me a story about two young Ukrainian leaders in their thirties, Bilas and Danylysh, who were snatched and imprisoned just for being *rumored* as Underground members. When they were both hung in Lviv's Brygidki Prison, I also realized that my inclusion in the Underground potentially meant the worst of consequences, even to those too young to really grasp their severity.

In our home, Tato and I often spoke of the Polish Army's pacification of Ukrainian villages in 1933. They stormed in and shattered all Ukrainian education, killed Ukrainian-conscious peasants, even Greek-Catholic Priests. Before my eyes was a wretched image of overworked Ukrainian peasants, slaving from sunrise to way past sunset to feed Poland and then their own families as well. After long winters, even though the men had worked round the clock, other family members were forced by hunger to beg. They'd travel to villages where they hoped not to be recognized. Scrounging for charity in Ukraine was a deeply embarrassing act at that time. It was often confronted with real anger and shame.

And for any children seeking a better life through school, secondary Ukrainian education became plagued with high costs and Polish governmental hurdles, discouraging kids from gaining any knowledge that could improve their own fortune. So after dropping out of school, children left their native Ukraine and traveled to Poland and were forced to work to keep their families in Ukraine afloat. These children were plagued with harassment, forced to forget their native language, and most families fell under great pressure from local authorities to switch from a Greek-Catholic ritual of having their own head of the church to the Roman-Catholic faith, which was led by the Pope in Rome. This was a gigantic deal in Ukraine, where so much pain had been caused by outside reign.

Belief was what got us through the day. Belief kept us afloat and hopeful. So how could I sit still when the surrounding nations were not only taking our hard-earned grains but our freedom to choose which power to thank for those grains as well?

SEPARATION

Every thought brought me closer to my rendezvous with the Underground. My curiosity grew with every step. During the last mission, I met a connoisseur of music, who taught me song lyrics of the rebellion. I memorized them and taught my friends too. One went like so:

Executioners come running, entering every home.
Ripping friends away for labor.
Twice a day, they bring water,
But more often, we're whipped.

"Isn't it time for me to join the UPA?" I asked Tato after one Underground meeting. This was the aforementioned Ukrainian Insurgent Army, the Underground military who fought for Ukraine's independence.

"You're still too young. You're needed here at home for local Underground work. And our nation requires smart leadership, so you must keep learning, keep studying. Force, yes, is necessary," Tato said sternly, "but a sharp mind to know where to put that strength is even more important," he said and then added with a smile, "And they probably wouldn't take you anyway."

Even though I respected Tato's judgement and I was only seventeen, I still itched to fight. I decided that I would ask a couple enlistment questions at this upcoming forest meeting. Slim chance Tato would find out and I couldn't help myself.

As I was lost in daydreams of the UPA, a triad of bullets whizzed over my head like wasps. I hit the dirt. Instincts took over and I crawled to the nearest thicket, hiding wide-eyed in prickly thorns.

What was that?! Gunfire?!

Hugging the ground, I heard a lively clop-de-clop of horses, galloping like lightening across the path I almost just took. I looked up. *The German military couple from the village!* They were grasping the horses' necks for dear life, knuckles white and chests violently colliding with the horses' manes.

They're fleeing! What are they running from? Did they see me?

Unarmed and full of fear but more-so curiosity, I crouched and snuck forward toward the origin of the shots. I really had no choice. There was a mission at stake. About 50 meters away, through the thicket, I spotted a horse-drawn carriage, manned by a driver and accompanied by two German soldiers.

Germans running from Germans?! Germans shooting at Germans? Something wasn't right.

The soldiers hopped off the hay seats of the carriage and ordered the driver, in Ukrainian, to turn the horses back and lay low. *Ukrainians!*

The driver hastily turned his horses back, and the soldiers quickly dove into the depths of the forest. *So they're either undercover Ukrainians or Ukrainians working for the Germans.* That second option didn't make sense, shots fired considered.

My fear subsided. I didn't realize at first that these two could be the Underground members I was supposed to meet, but nothing else made sense.

Without further delay, still hidden, I exclaimed the first part of the password, "Kraj sela!" and they suddenly stopped, spun their heads in my direction, and responded with

"Zustrinemo sebe!" (Meet us). It was them. Only then did I run out of the bushes and stand on the trail before them.

"Boy are we glad to see you," said one of the two smiling soldiers, as I greeted and shook hands with both. We kept our names to ourselves. Better to keep them buried, if possible.

"What happened?" I asked.

"Let's get a move on, and we'll explain," he said. We got their things together and started moving.

"We're only a kilometer and a half from the local German garrison, and those two Germans were moving that way, so we have to move now," I said hurriedly, still spooked by the shots.

No way I would chance running into Germans while moving the Undergrounders, especially with shots fired. There was a company of maybe 200 soldiers staying at the castle. The Germans could be raiding the forest at any moment.

Tato had mentioned to me that the Undergrounders' guide would be leading them to the next village over, called Hodvyshnia, which was about four kilometers away. Four kilometers along the road of course. We'd have to steer clear of any true path to lay low.

"I know where you need to go," I said.

"Can you take us?" asked one of them. Both these soldiers seemed to me still quite young, in their 30s, and healthy too, so I decided we'd be able to disappear quickly enough. That, and they were traveling light with a leather briefcase and a small military knapsack. There was no better option than to move along with them. I agreed.

So the plans had changed. We wouldn't be meeting with the horses anymore, or their guide for that matter. Too dangerous. We couldn't bring that attention to the innocence of Uherci.

No horse and I was now their guide.

But I wasn't worried - I knew these woods as well as anyone. They were my home. And Tato raised me to track. As long as these two can keep quiet, we should be fine. I made a note not to get so lost in thought this time, and we bee-lined through the woods. It'd be dark before we got in. No time to waste.

As we trudged, we had to dive into the woods once, for an unknown man passed us by. Drifter maybe, but we didn't care to find out and he walked on. Time passed and we arrived at the valley that led to Hodvyshnia. We stopped at the treeline and rested and waited for full nightfall, so we could pass under the cover of darkness.

"So what happened back there?" I asked.

"Two people on horseback appeared right in front of us on the road. Our driver wanted to steer clear, but it was too late. They turned out to be Germans and came up to us and immediately started questioning about where we were going. A man and a woman. The man was really cocky too. We told him we were going to Horodok, but for whatever reason, this answer didn't satisfy him, and he asked us what regiment we belonged to. Before we could answer that one, he whipped out his revolver and ordered us to show him our military documents. Looked kinda like he wanted to be a hero in front of his girlfriend. So we had no choice - we gave him our fake papers and figured we were about to be caught by this overly pompous officer. Our crappy German tongue didn't help either, so we were cooked. I gave him my papers and as he pulled out his briefcase to check these papers against his, my friend here whipped out his pistol and fired a shot towards the soldier and another towards his girlfriend. The German's confidence flushed out his feet and his horse reared up without him. He even dropped his revolver! The lady's horse did the same when it heard her screech - she got hit. They then jumped on their horses and ran off. We shot at them a couple more times, but didn't want to kill them. We just wanted them gone," one soldier explained.

"We're sorry we had to bring such dirty work to your village, especially on Holy Saturday. We didn't expect it, but it was the only thing we could do. They would have taken us in otherwise," said the other.

I nodded. We decided that the chances of German retaliation on the village were probably slim anyways. The couple would be too embarrassed to tell their higher-ups that they were tricked and overpowered. There was also no way the couple could tell whether these two Undergrounders were German deserters, undercover Ukrainians, or otherwise.

But then again, our fate resided in the hands of Germans, and that hadn't served Ukraine well lately.

A few hours later, we made it to Hodvyshnia, and I decided it'd be best for me to sneak over to the District Representative's home alone. Two presumably German officers sneaking about would cause quite a bit more alarm than a young Ukrainian boy.

So I walked up to the house, gave the door a knock, and a surprised DR appeared, rushing me into the house and quickly shutting the door behind me.

"Why so late? Where are your horses?" he asked. Hiccups aren't welcomed in Underground activity. With Soviets and Germans exporting Underground members to camps, fear was an overwhelming dictator of emotion as of late.

"And why aren't you home?" he asked, offering me a cup of water.

I explained everything, from the shooting to the re-route.

"As soon as the sky turned, I knew something was wrong," he said. Ukrainians have a funny premonition when things go awry.

"We were extra careful coming in. Nobody noticed us," I said.

I *hoped* nobody noticed us.

"The rebels will tell you everything else. I need to hurry home," I said. *I don't make it back from a routine mission by sundown? Tato must be worried.*

"Oh, and don't be fooled - they're in German uniform," I said, as I led him to the two Underground soldiers in the forest.

"Every day, something new," he said, a little more amused than worried.

After turning the rebels over to the District Representative, we said our quick farewells, and the DR gave me a note for Tato that I thrust into my boot, in case I was searched. I was off.

As I entered the meadow, my mind sprung forward to

what could be happening back at the village.

Will the German couple talk? What are their ranks? Officers, maybe? How could *they keep quiet? Keep a story like that to themselves? How will the German military react? A raid? Would they surround and isolate the village?*

My focus then fell into myself. *Would I run into their ambush? Find myself behind enemy lines?* I pictured myself sitting and watching Uherci getting ransacked.

I thought of heading back to spend the night at the District Representative's home and return to Uherci in the morning, but staying would only create more worry for my family and I'd be missing from the Easter celebration, causing the villagers to stir. I decided to return gently. No one would notice.

My mind wandered to those who weren't with their families. I felt sad for those two Undergrounders who would be spending Easter in a foreign village, celebrating with those whom fate had dictated. There was no day off in the fight for independence. We could not let up. Even on Easter.

I took an even less-traveled route home, through fields and gardens, to insure no unnecessary run-ins. Low, black clouds had stolen my moonlight, leading me to twist and tweak my ankles and knees in plow ditches. I found myself lost a couple times too, but then I finally saw a faint flickering of light, like a distant lighthouse. That became my guide, along with dogs barking in the village.

As I got edge of Uherci, I scanned its modest homes for movement. No Germans. No raid. Just peace. Most families should have been sound asleep by the time I came in for tomorrow was a big day - Easter Sunday. Tomorrow, like the ancient oil bearers of Jerusalem, our village would rise before dawn to celebrate.

I crept through a few neighboring vegetable gardens before ending up back home. Everything was calm, and coming up to my doorstep, anxiety subsided and relief flooded in. I had survived.

I opened the door and wasn't surprised to find Tato waiting up for me. He immediately pulled me in, so as not to cause any unnecessary attention. Suspicion alone was all the Germans needed to arrest us.

"Tato, I went through the gardens, like you said, and was so careful and nobody saw me or could have thought that I was even gone," I said hurriedly.

"I saw two Germans fleeing through the village on horseback," said Tato. "Others saw them too, saying they were both injured, leaving a trail of blood behind them. Others said they saw blood stains on the whites of their shirts. We all heard shots from the forest. I was so worried. I thought something terrible had happened.

"I didn't tell anyone about you being out there," he said. "And I couldn't go after you. That would have caused alarm, and if I had told someone else to get you, he would just be another mouth that could spill when the Germans came around."

After I explained my story, Tato told me that plenty of curious neighbors came by to ask whether he knew anything about the shooting in the woods. He replied that he knew as much as they did - just that shots were fired. He hoped that the villagers wouldn't dream up all sorts of fantasies that night. Easter was only a few hours away, so Tato and I hoped that the villagers would be preoccupied enough with the holiday not to gossip.

But then there was the local German military unit. We hoped they'd keep their mouths shut, but chances were slim. Those Germans needed patching up. *Where else would they go besides their own doctors?*

I gave Tato the letter from the District Representative, which wished Tato a Happy Easter and an apology for the shooting.

"A good gesture," said Tato, but the expression on his face was regret. He didn't like that Easter might be spoiled by last night's shooting. Germans aren't so easy to let go of a shooting of their own. Recently, the Germans avenged a death in a nearby village by lining up the villagemen and hanging every tenth one. They left those men hanging in the middle of the village, a reminder of who was in charge in our country.

We finished up our conversation and went to bed. We had to be at the church at five, which was now only a few hours away.

"Jesus rose before the sun came up. So will we," I pictured Mama saying, as I lay in bed.

Mama's name was Fevronia and she was very devout. She got us to church every Sunday, and in her spare time she'd read missionary magazines to us children. There were plenty of times I wanted to go play with my friends, but she'd insist on me listening to "just a little bit more" before I left.

In order to miss a Sunday mass, one of us would have to be deathly ill, which had never actually happened. Our parents knew no other excuse, and we children followed suit. God was their belief, and it was ours too.

From a young age, I sang hymns with the church choir, which was led by our village mayor, Ivan Chornenkyj. I'd follow their every breathe and sing heartily and feel true freedom.

In those times, being part of the village choir was a great achievement and honor. The older members of the choir influenced me greatly, and the younger choir gathered on Fridays, Saturdays, and Sunday evenings. We'd sing about faith, national happenings, and the Ukrainian spirit. Sometimes the energy was so electric that we sung way past midnight, weaving among us feelings of destiny, joy, and sorrow. It was a wonderful escape from times of war and a lovely image to fall asleep to.

Soon-after, I dozed.

Although last to go to bed, Mama awoke us all the next morning. We quickly washed up, got dressed in our Sunday best, walked out the door and found ourselves under a blanket of a million stars. An accompanying golden moon lit our pathway to the chapel. *Those storm clouds must have parted last night - a good omen for today's celebration.*

Along the road we met up with other families hurrying to

church, and although some of them had to travel about four kilometers, they still went by foot, leaving their horses and buggies behind. A small sacrifice to embody their strength and hardened spirit. If Jesus suffered on the cross, they could leave their horses at home. These distances didn't keep people from their faith.

Villagers approached Tato with questions about last night.

"Ivan, what'd you hear about the shots in the forest?" one asked. Tato always had answers, and they expected one now more than ever.

"Did someone get shot?" one asked.

"I heard someone was killed!" another hushed.

Tato answered every inquiry at once:

"I too heard these rumors, but I wasn't there. And neither were you, so you don't know either. Please stop spreading them, for none of us know the truth. Don't create unnecessary panic in our village. I could start a rumor that the Germans accidentally shot at each other, which would leave our village out of it. There's no cause for alarm, so just enjoy today, for it's Easter Sunday. Be calm and happy and grateful for this day."

They all turned their heads away and continued on. Tato's wise words held integrity throughout the village. And although he hated lying, he knew what needed to be done. Ukraine's freedom, as well as our family's safety, was on the line.

We arrived at the church to a gathering of festively dressed people. Tato drew my attention to a nearby neighbor who had never before attended a religious service. War had apparently drawn out his desperation. Everybody, on initial glance, looked like they were attending any normal Easter celebration, but a closer look showed scrunched brows and heavy faces giving away their underlying anxiety...

Who shot who?

Are the Russians invading?

Will the Germans seize control?

Where will we find our next week's meals?

Women and children gathered near the bell tower that belted joy throughout our land every Easter Sunday morning. But this year, people waited for the ringing in vain. There were no bells. Germans had confiscated them, climbing up ladders to steal the closest thing we had to Heaven. Rumors said that they were deported for use in ammunition factories. It also doubled as a dampening of our hope.

But German intentions were oftentimes predicted by Tato, and one morning, before the bells were confiscated, members of the Underground took down the two larger bells and buried them in the field next to the bell tower. To deceive the Germans, they replaced them with the old bells, one that wasn't bronze and another that didn't ring anymore.

After the Germans took these old bells, Tato told me, "When we hid the new bells, we promised each other to put them back up when Ukraine gained its freedom." Tato was convinced that this would happen during his lifetime.

Another one of our traditions was to fire three rifle shots in honor of Christ's Rise. But the Germans outlawed that too, saying it could somehow benefit the Underground. Their logic didn't seem quite sound, because then wouldn't we be wasting bullets? Bullets that then wouldn't hit their soldiers? But it brought down our spirits, so it worked out for them nonetheless. Gunfire meant power. But we were just looking to celebrate.

Our procession then walked three times around the church and sang the traditional hymn "Christ is risen." We settled down outside the church, and the priest greeted us with another "Christ is risen!" His voice was hearty, thick and powerful. I let it sink into me, to fuel my hope for a better tomorrow. But the familiar gunfire that should have followed was missed.

Why must even the simplest of joys be snatched away?

As we all walked into the church, most heads were drooped lower than usual, another sign of the sadness and uncertainty of this dampened celebration.

What waits for us tomorrow?

The frozen bowels of Siberia?

The labor camps of Germany?

Any chance of freedom?

Most families prayed longer than usual. Everyone at that time feared the menacing fronts, sounds of gunfire, injuries and imported illnesses as well. Ukraine was being sandwiched by its two worst nightmares, Nazi Germany and Soviet Russia, and nobody was sure which one to fear more.

Apparently the Germans had given Division Galicia the word that they would soon be butting heads with the Soviet Red Army. The Division Galicia was made up of Ukrainians trained by Germans to fight the Soviets. But what the Germans didn't know was that many of these Ukrainians were really just trying to get an upper hand in Ukrainian liberation, learning how to fight and getting armed, waiting for the opportunity to desert en masse and retaliate. Villagers prayed for these young soldiers, hoping that their sacrifices didn't end in failure.

"Dearest faithful," began the priest, "I can see the pain your faces. But now is not the time to panic or falter in your faith. Keep your spirits strong. Pray passionately! We are not alone! Christ is with us and let us rise with him now stronger than ever. He suffered, was persecuted, beaten, even crucified, but on the third day he conquered his death and rose from his grave."

He was right. Our bells may be buried, but our faith still lives on. *It would just be a little easier to remember that if those bells would ring.* I thought back to contests among the men of who could ring the bell with the clearest and deepest vibration. Most ended up with rope burns in their armpits, but a select few momentarily owned the hearts of the village, their tug of war with the thunderous bells a success.

The priest went on: "They punish, enslave, and starve us to death! They plant us in their prisons! But we keep fighting! We keep living. And now, we look forward to our resurrection! Do not fall into despondency. Celebrate Easter as it was celebrated by our grandfathers and great-grandfathers, with joy and peace and ancient customs in hand!"

I took in the priests words and prayed. The rest of the day went by without a hitch.

SEPARATION

The next day was Easter Monday. Our family walked back towards the church and to the cemetery, "to honor the Sichovey Riflemen, for these time are uncertain," the priest had said. The Sichovey Riflemen were young Ukrainians who sacrificed their lives so that Ukraine could come one step closer to her freedom.

When we got to the graves, we sang. I stared at one grave that stood twice as high as the others, signifying a rifleman who'd died too soon, probably in his teens.

My body then opened to the deep bass of the village men. I always wanted to sing bass, but with me still being seventeen and having such a small stature, I probably never would.

I tried anyway.

After we quieted down, the priest honored our soldiers: "In this world, there is no greater sacrifice than to give your life for your friends. Here in these graves rest young men who gave their lives to make ours better."

He then gave a nod to Tato, who walked onto a raised platform beside the riflemen's tombs and began to speak.

"We've all experienced tragedy. And *this* war may be our greatest. But we've survived the past, and we will survive this as well. Our Jerusalem is burning and belligerent fronts plunge deep into our beloved country. Bombs fall. The rip-roar of gunfire surrounds us. But let those fronts destroy themselves and let us take advantage, taking our own selves up with arms, keeping order within our homes, even if we too have to make the greatest sacrifice - our very own lives," Tato said.

His powerful voice shook the villagers' hearts, pleading to

unify their spirits. The villagers intently listened on.

"Others will not hand us our independence. Others are banding together to take our precious soil, so *we* must come together to manifest *our own* freedom, to become the sole owners of our own native land! These alien nations have hung on our necks for too long, dragging us closer and closer to our graves. So we must do this ourselves. Just as we build our own homes, we must build our own nation. And let us look up to these young heroes buried here below us. They gave up their chance to grow old for our right to freedom. And how many of these graves are now scattered throughout Ukraine? And how many more are hidden in the Far Eastern lands of frozen Siberia? Those soldiers deserved to be buried *here* - in *their* own land!"

Tato's speech energized me.

"So let's look to these heroes, for it's better to be buried and rest in these graves than to rot imprisoned. It's time for us to take the chains off our wrists and ankles. Soon our nation will rise just as Christ was resurrected himself!" Tato said.

Tears fell from one woman's eyes.

"In some of us, there's concern about tomorrow's uncertainty. In others, there's joy and hope for a better tomorrow. And some of you have even sacrificed your own children to fight..."

A shout interrupted Tato from the woods outside the cemetery:

"Poland has not yet perished!" hollered two boys from the treeline.

A group of our Ukrainian boys sprinted over to those

bushes, but the Poles fled on bikes towards the German village Studilky.

Our attention was successfully dismantled. Tato had just energized us, motivated us. And these cowards had to ruin the holiday mood. Just another reminder that Ukraine was always being picked on. *Can't just one part of this holiday run without a hitch?*

The villagers broke the sunken mood by starting to sing again, which brought my mind back to the celebration. Tato said no more and the priest finished the ceremony with a couple small rituals for families who'd lost their loved ones. I was so proud of Tato for his bold words and fluid delivery, and that throughout the village, he was loved and respected. That day's vividness would be implanted in my memory forever.

But there was another reason I felt so emboldened that day - a girl. Like me, her family sent her to school in Lviv, but up until now I never had the courage to talk to her. Her family also kept her cooped up inside and very rarely let her outside the house for fun. Her parents let her really only do two things: read and study.

On this third day of Easter, my eyes caught her standing with a friend. I'd never been this close to her before, and she became more and more beautiful with every step I took towards her. My plan was to catch her after the ceremony and say a few words. *What should I say?*

But that plan quickly failed. Her parents came out of nowhere and swooped her away. As she was leaving, she looked back at me and smiled. I was stunned and wondered if I should smile back, but it was too late, for she had already turned away.

The next day I dragged my friends around her house to see if she was around, without actually letting them know what we were doing. They complained that "there was nothing to do around here!" but I kept my crush a secret, because I didn't want any of them to get jealous. But I couldn't find her.

A week went by like that with heavy disenchantment - I had no school work, so I had plenty of free time to talk with her, but she was nowhere to be seen. I really wanted to ask her about where she lived in Lviv. *Maybe I'd visit you one evening? Maybe you'd go with me to the theatre? Of course, you'd immediately agree!* So much was said in one look!

But then I ran into one of her friends who told me that she'd gone to the next village over to take care for her sick grandmother. My plans were ruined again and I was filled with disappointment.

On top of not seeing her, I watched Soviet aircrafts drop fiery missiles over our dear city of Lviv. And at only 36 kilometers away, I could feel the rumbles of the bombs hitting the ground. The Russians looked as though they were trying to win back Lviv, whatever would be left of her, anyway. Our buildings were crumbling and our people were dying.

With the frequency of these bombings, Tato and I reinforced our cellar, halfway hidden underneath the house, so that we could find safety if the Germans and Soviets decided to bring their fight to Uherci.

While we were working, I told Tato, "I heard at school,

from my friends, that many of our distinguished people and church activists are fleeing west, because the Russians from the east would use even more brutality against Ukrainian patriots this time around and Nazi Germany seemed like a less gruesome option. Tato, what have you heard?"

Tato looked up from his work bench and stoically said, "Let those go who *need* to go. Let the cowards go as well."

I perked up.

"We stay here. On *our* land. We have to stay and defend her. If we left, who would defend our poor? Our weak? Unless I'm forced, I won't leave the village. Our fight is here. We stay here," he finished.

I never bothered Tato with this question again, and he didn't need to repeat himself.

We would stay. Tato knew best. His steadfastness to Ukrainian freedom came from *his* tato, my Dido Petro. In the 30's, when Poland was still in control of our land, Polish police increasingly tried finding guilt against Tato and threatened to arrest him if he kept opposing Polish authorities in order to further Ukrainianization. Tato kept pushing the idea that Ukraine was being treated unjustly. He kept prodding against the pacification by the Poles. Poland agreed autonomy to Galicia after the First World War, but without free speech, where truly was this autonomy?

So one day, the local Polish Police Commandant, who our village nicknamed "Fats," entered our house when Dido Petro was sitting calmly weaving canvas. The Commandant called Tato from his smithy and threatened him with arrest. He invented all sorts of reasons to lock him up, saying the fence wasn't painted, that the dog wasn't tied up, that our house has a hole in it that wasn't made by regulations.

But Dido Petro and his walrus mustache wouldn't hear any more of this criticism against his son and stood up tall, approached the Commandant and firmly and loudly said, "Get out of MY house! MY house. MY dog. MY hole. Say this to ME. Not my son. Leave at once! Get out of MY house and bring me a complaint on paper, or I'll break your legs, because here in MY house, you have no rights."

The Commandant was startled back and weakly threatened: "This is not over! I'll be back with another officer." Luckily, his plan failed, because the Polish-German war broke just after. The Commandant fled from our village and none of us ever saw him again.

So was I scared? Yes. Tato's confidence helped, but the rumbling of the bombs increased moment by moment. It was only a matter of time before *someone* arrived in our village. I just hoped that somehow it wouldn't end up being the Germans or the Soviets.

That Sunday, the village went back to church. No one had to be convinced to pray. Many were scared. War and hardship plagued their minds. Some villagers were missing. Many had fled.

But my mind wasn't on the war. Or the priest. I was scanning for Sonia.

My eyes found her amongst the congregation. She was paying attention to the priest and his sermon. I could hear the priest talking, but the words weren't registering. Her radiance took up every nook of my mind.

And her taking up my mind instead of the war made for a very happy me. After the sermon, I walked out of the church, looking for my friends and family but secretly hoping that this girl would float out of the church as well.

But once again, it didn't happen as I imagined. She walked out the side door, towed by her family, and I watched as they immediately walked home.

How did I miss her again?! I realized then that a chance meeting wasn't going to happen. I had to make it happen. I had to go to her house. It was decided.

Throughout the week, my friends kept bugging me to hang out.

"Vacation's almost done! Come out and play, Stepan! We haven't see you all week!"

But I kept dismissing them, sitting at home and hoping that I'd garner up the courage to go to her house. Instead, I was stalling - trying to read and prepare for school and it was no use. She wouldn't leave my mind.

So one day I found the courage to walk by, around, and then near her house. It was awful! So tough! But again, I didn't see her. I left dejected and came home to an early dinner from Mama and knew I had to go back afterwards. *But the first time was such agony! Could I really go again? What if her parents find me first? What would they say? Would they tell my parents?* The custom in our neighborhood was that before any man could approach a daughter, he'd have to run it by her father first.

I skipped that part.

But I went anyway, leaving half my dinner on the table, full of courage that immediately escaped me when I saw her house.

How could she say no? turned into *Her dad's going to let me have it!*

But I took step after step after step, and I got to her front gate and stopped.

No way. Not possible. I can't.

I couldn't move. My legs were filled with bricks.

What if her tato answers? Is he an angry man? Would he chase me out? Would he tell mine?

Then a dream appeared in her doorway.

I came closer to this dream. She was smiling and said hello.

"Would you like to take a walk, sometime?" I said.

"Sure, but I can't for long, because my parents are waiting for me. They want me to get ready for school tomorrow," she said.

We were all leaving for Lviv in the morning.

"I'll get scolded otherwise. Let's get moving," she said.

I pictured her getting yelled at and almost turned her back inside but kept my mouth shut.

"I'm Sonia," she said.

"Stepan," I replied.

"Let's skip the formal stuff," she said and smiled.

This caught me off guard. Courting was very formal in Uherci, but I guess I skipped a pretty important part too. I liked her even more.

SEPARATION

Sonia started to talk about living at her grandmother's for the holidays.

"It's really boring," she said. "I miss my friends and barely know any of the youth over there."

How could you not make friends? You're wonderful.

We talked about school, our hangouts in Lviv, friends, and other pleasantries. She even lived close by in Lviv! We quickly melted into each other, catching up like old friends.

"I promise... I'll visit you in Lviv this week, and maybe we can go to the cinema... or to the theatre!" I was so excited. She was too. But then our carefree plan-making turned to the war.

"But what will happen in Lviv?" she asked. "My mama almost banned me from heading out tomorrow, because of the bombing."

"Well..." I wasn't sure how to put a positive spin on that one. *What* will *happen in Lviv? Should we go? Maybe we should run! Away from this war!* But my mind quickly settled, and I said, "Your parents love you very much. They're just being extra careful. You're their only one."

She smiled and our walk came to an abrupt end. The conversation was over quicker than it started and it was time to go our separate ways. We grabbed each other's hands and stared into each other's eyes and before I knew it, she planted a quick kiss on my lips and snuck inside, the door shutting in my face.

I was blissfully dumbfounded.

I walked home floating. There was no terrible war, bombing, Germans, Russians, or otherwise. I felt like a hero.

I came home, met up with my brothers and started trading stories. The topic of women sprung up. They harassed me, hoping to pry open the secret I couldn't keep my face from showing. But I was too embarrassed to talk about Sonia. It was all still too fresh. I stalled and stalled and then Tato came to the rescue.

"I want to talk to you about what you need to take on the road tomorrow," he said.

Perfect timing! I didn't want to lie to my brothers. I hated lying.

Tato pulled me aside and said nothing of school. His face was stern. I knew this was important. "Don't be brave without a true cause... in school, or in Lviv. When the Soviets start their offensive on Lviv, come home as soon as you can. You'll be much safer here."

And just like that, my joy disappeared. The war was back.

"Don't talk to anyone about the shooting. Trust no one. We might not be out of the clear just yet," he said.

Mama entered the room, and said, "Everything is packed for tomorrow." Her voice was heavy.

I came close to her, kissed her cheek, thanked her for everything she has done for the family. Nothing was more important to her than me. She always had my stuff packed, ready, and carefully organized so I could have a smooth trip to Lviv. And she never complained about how hard she had to work for us. Or that Tato, heavily engaged in Ukrainian consciousness, helped her so little. It seemed to me that they both loved each other so very much and well understood what their roles were in taking care of our family, because in my seventeen years experiencing them together, I never saw them fight. No anger, no arguments, not once.

"Maybe it would be better if you stayed home," Mama said, tearing up, "The city is so dangerous..." She didn't mention the bombs or the people being killed.

Tato explained that he had prepared me. "They're both reasonable, Fevronia. If it's not right, they'll know. They'll come back." My sister Maria was going too.

Tato knew best how to calmly wrap up a conversation. He always did. Mama didn't argue.

That being said, I went to bed that night with my mind racing.

Thoughts of Sonia, thoughts of the Underground, thoughts of the war.

Reflecting on all these events, I somehow fell asleep, firmly and quietly.

The next morning Nazis stormed Uherci. Tato and I were arrested and driven further and further from home on a German truck in which rode the soldier wearing the boot that kicked Mama out of my life forever.

CHAPTER FOUR

LVIV

The 33 kilometer road from Horodok to Lviv was the same one Tato had first carted me up to enroll in mechanical school. That day back in 1942, the surrounding landscape was beautiful, smooth, and captivating, interspersed with villages and forests.

But today I rode down this road as a prisoner. I prayed that maybe Ukrainian freedom fighters of the UPA sat perched in these woods, ready to rescue us. I fantasized a wonderful raid, Ukrainians with rifles springing from the bushes to break us free. We would sprint back to Uherci and rescue the family and move west!

But these naive thoughts quickly subsided as we arrived in Lviv.

We drove down the familiar streets of Horodots'ka and Kazymyrivska. We passed by the tall spire of the Polish church St. Elizabeth, and a bit further, in all his majestic power, we passed the Cathedral of St. George. Kazymyrivska Street is well known to Ukrainians, for on it sat the famous prison of Brygidky. *Is that where we're going? Or maybe Lontsky?*

SEPARATION

One night, two weeks before this arrest, I was walking down Kazymyrivska street to the Odeon theatre with my friends. As we passed by Lontsky Prison, prisoners hollered at me. But I paid no attention to them. First off, there were always German guards around, but secondly, each and every prisoner planted inside was a criminal who'd committed serious injustices. They dragged no sympathy out of me.

But now I was riding down this street as a "criminal," and I realized that innocent people have been rotting in Lontsky all along. They weren't all wrong-doers... They hadn't all been malicious... They may have even been patriots!

We arrived at Lontsky's gate, surrounded by its thick walls and iron-barred windows. Not far from here was the mechanical school that I was supposed to be at today.

Tato encouraged me to study electrical engineering. While he worked in his smithy, he would ask himself, "Why should we heat this iron with dirty coal? It takes so long! It would be much faster and cleaner with electric current." He said that I had to unravel this dilemma. His wish was that I mastered electricity. *Would I ever get that chance?*

Sitting in front of the prison gates, it was impossible for me to accept that I was about to be on the other side of these walls. I was no longer free to walk these streets of Lviv, these streets with memories so dear to me.

We entered Lontsky's gates and our convoy settled in the small prison yard paved with little jagged stones. The guards jumped down from the truck bed and ordered us out. After sitting for so many hours in the same position, my legs were wood. Tato could barely straighten his out. Hunched over, he asked me in a whisper if I needed a bathroom, because he really needed to go.

The guards told us to stay put: "A prison official will be with you shortly to sign you in, assign you a number, and bring you to a cell."

Out of us five, I was the only one who knew German, so I translated everything for the others.

Please Lord, don't separate me from Tato. I wanted so badly to talk to him - We needed to agree on a story before we were taken in for questioning.

But my hopes were interrupted by the prison door suddenly opening and a guard calling me in first.

Me first?

The doors shut behind me. My eyes adjusted to the darkness of the room and before me appeared a table with three middle-aged officers.

"What is your name?" one asked, in German.

"Stepan Fedenko," I replied.

He pulled some notes out of his backpack and quietly whispered and deliberated with the other officers.

What do you know?

An officer, in Ukrainian, asked me to remove everything from my pockets. I did and laid my things carefully on the table. I feared making a wrong move. He took what little I had and hid it in the bag.

"When you're free," he said, "all these things will be returned." His Ukrainian was good, but his accent was heavy.

SEPARATION

On officer noticed that I had yet another pocket and told me to check it. I had purposely skipped this one, hoping that they wouldn't say anything, because I was holding onto pictures of our family and friends. Maria had slipped them to me as we were saying goodbye in the village.

"Sorry. I forgot," I said nervously and gave him the pictures.

While examining these pictures, the chairman asked me my age, height, date of birth, religious affiliation and then recorded it all in his documents. He slipped my photos into the bag with my things and sent me to the next room. No one closed these doors behind me. In this new room I saw an open toilet and asked no one's permission to use it. I realized that I hadn't gone since last night.

From the other room I heard Tato being questioned. He didn't know German, so they used Ukrainian to question him: "You carry the same last name as the boy. Are you his father?"

He replied yes, and the rest of his questions came as mine, and they made him empty his pockets. They searched him and then they ordered him into the room I was in. He was so grateful to see me but maybe even more grateful because I introduced him to the toilet.

When he finished, seeing that no one else was near, he pulled me in tight, like we hadn't seen each other in years. This was the first opportunity we had to talk to each other, and he said, "Don't worry. We may still have a miracle on our side, because the Russian front isn't far. So who knows how long these Germans will hold power. When the front gets here, we'll be seen as enemies of the Germans and be freed."

Could we really rely on the Russians for freedom?

"And if these Germans have nothing to learn from us, then they'll let us out," he said.

Such were Tato's hopes. He was trying his best to comfort me, and I really wanted to believe what he said, but to me it felt like consolation. *The Germans brought us here for a reason, and after bringing us this far, why would they release us so quickly?*

Then Tato whispered words that I did not expect, "I'll never admit my guilt, even if they threaten to kill me."

"So remember," he said, "when you're questioned and beaten and bruised and battered and they tell you to confess, because your Tato has - 'He admitted to being a member of the OUN!' - do not believe them! I will never confess. They'll never beat it out of me."

I took Tato's stance as well.

"They won't learn a thing from me either. I'll tell them I have no interests but school and that's why I'd never heard of the Underground."

"As for the Underground songs in my notebook," I told Tato, "I'll tell them I jotted them down on a train coming home from Lviv, where I met some young Ukrainian students on their way to train for Germany's Division Galicia. I could tell the Germans that these boys were singing songs, urging me to write down the words. They were so excited! How could I not? And if they ask about the UPAs, UCDs, or OUNs written in my book, I'll fake-guess that they're Division units, right?" Hopefully that would suffice.

Tato immediately agreed and said, "And when they ask me about the UPA, I'll tell them that I've heard of it, but that they were supposed to be off somewhere in Volhynia(NW of Lviv), far from us and that I know no more. If the Germans follow that rabbit hole, I'll say I heard about it in Horodok, from migrating traders. Who they were, I don't remember. All sorts of people arrive in Horodok."

I was so grateful to spend these few moments alone with Tato to agree on our stories. Just then the three other villagemen entered the room and scurried over to the lone toilet.

Finding ourselves finally alone, we each tried to guess why the Germans arrested us five and not the others.

Tato warned us and said, "Stop this nonsense, because no one actually knows why, and they can listen in to everything we say. With this pointless talk, they could suspect all of us innocent villagers to be criminals and just for that suspicion, we'd be punished, I'm sure."

Then, in a whisper, he said, "I know nothing and won't talk at any cost. You should all do the same."

Tato's words were understood by all, and everyone immediately hushed.

Then he spoke up, "I have no idea why I was arrested. I'm innocent. And I'm not interested in anything else but taking care of my family and my church. That's all we care about and that's all we know." He said it loud enough for the Germans to overhear.

I know nothing. I'm just a villager. I know nothing. I'm just a schoolboy.

Then all three interrogating officers walked in and two thoroughly searched us, feeling us head to toe, making sure they didn't miss anything.

Satisfied, they pushed us through a large iron door and into a long prison corridor, divided by several iron partitions. One officer led as the others tailed us. The roaring of their heavy German boots echoed loudly, like we were walking through a cave.

They escorted us up two flights of steep, narrow, wooden stairs. They squeaked with every step, an eery reminder that I wasn't in Uherci anymore. We were led through another iron door and into another hallway.

Lontsky didn't look this big to me from the outside.

With every step, the prison seemed to grow. The hallway left me scared, deflated, and surrounded by cold, locked-up cells lining my sides. Tiny windows were carved into each door, so that Germans could check on their captives.

At least we're still together. That was the only thing I could hold on to at that moment.

They led us into a second corridor, this one littered with prisoner voices and guards sitting at the other end of the hall loudly laughing and mocking their captives. The echoes of the guards voices added to our fear.

They stopped us in front of cell 37 and the guard unlocked it. Immediately a pale prisoner came out and announced in German, "Cell #37. 54 prisoners. We're healthy and have no other problems."

The German paid him no attention.

Peeking inside this cell, I saw some curious faces start to appear from the dark. The lead guard said, "Adding five. There should be plenty of room."

They shoved us into the chamber and slammed the door closed behind us. My eyes adjusted and I saw that this cell was full of people. Most of them stood, aside from a few elders leaning against the walls. They immediately started complaining about how we were all going to fit on the floor that night.

Taking a closer look, I saw that this room had only one toilet and a water valve.

Some prisoners came up to us and started asking questions.

"Where'd you come from?"

"What did they arrest you for?"

The prisoner who reported at the door excitedly embraced Tato with both arms and asked, "What are you doing here, Ivan?! How'd you get here?" This chance meeting between friends surprised them both. He rattled off questions about news in Horodok, the nearby fronts, but mostly about the rising arrest rate of Ukrainians.

Tato introduced us. His name was Kostecki.

"So young!" he said, embracing me. "This is not a place for you yet." He must have been 40-45 years old, like Tato. But he was a lot skinnier than Tato. "We have to look out for each other if we want to leave this place alive," Kostecki said.

"You see, I've been in this crowded cell for seven weeks now. Someone ratted me out, saying I was the District Leader of Horodok and that I belong to the Underground, 'the forbidden OUN.' But it seems to me that they've got no solid evidence, which is why I've just been sitting here."

Seven weeks? Aren't Tato and I in the same situation? Does that give us seven weeks too? That means I'd miss this semester of school!

"New prisoners are brought almost every day here to room 37, and after that they're usually moved to another cell after being questioned, depending on the severity of the accusation. Then they're judged and either remain in prison or deported into Germany. Some are dismissed too," he added.

So how does somebody get dismissed?

"I worry about what this means for me, because they've kept me here for so long. Maybe they forgot about me?" he said.

Being so tightly packed into this cell, I could see how someone could be forgotten. *So then what do I do? Be memorable so they don't forget about me? Or lay low and blend in?* Kostecki gave the roll call, so if *he* was forgotten, I worried about how easy it could be to get lost in the sea of prisoners.

He and Tato talked for some time. They only knew one another and no one else. Later on Tato told me that he indeed was an Undergrounder from Horodok, and that's how they're so well acquainted. During these seven weeks, Kostecki was only summoned to one investigation and otherwise left to spoil.

I caught up the other three from our village with what I learned from Kostecki. Then I pulled away from them in order to orient myself with the prison. I looked out the window and realized our chamber faced north and right below us was Kazymyrivska. The realization that I was now on this side of the wall made me feel awful for prisoners who I had previously ignored.

Kostecki then interrupted his conversation with Tato, informing everybody that it was time to smoke. *Really? They searched us. They took everything. Smoking was strictly prohibited. And even if you got cigarettes into here, how would you light one?*

"How is that possible?" I asked.

"One prisoner, who was a heavy smoker, snuck tobacco in a secretly sewn pocket in his underwear. He decided to share it with all of us, as long as someone else figured out how to light it. Another prisoner got tooth powder from his family, and in that powder? A hidden stone," one prisoner replied.

I watched attentively as Kostecki delicately pulled a rolling paper from his pocket. Another prisoner pulled a bit of tobacco from his own, gave it to Kostecki, and Kostecki carefully rolled a cigarette, making sure every last piece of tobacco made it in.

Kostecki then whipped out a hidden spoon, which had been sharpened. Using that sharp end, he scraped tiny shavings from the end of a toothbrush, laying them delicately in one pile.

He took the cigarette to his lips and methodically twisted it. Then he bent over, with it still in his mouth, and rested the tip of the cigarette on the toothbrush shavings. From another pocket he pulled out two stones and started striking them, creating sparks that danced into the pile of shavings.

A larger spark finally lit the shavings, which flamed up and just as quickly flamed out. I thought he'd have to try again but to my dismay, Kostecki rose with a lit cigarette. The smokers had by then lined up, and the cigarette was passed, each of them taking one lone drag. Each prisoner cherished his pull, most closing their eyes, probably dreaming of anything other than here.

This was the happiest I'd see any of these smokers while in prison. It was also the first time I'd realized how strong of a habit smoking was. I I decided then never to pick it up.

Kostecki, satisfied with his success, came close to Tato again and asked him if we'd eaten today. Tato said no, and Kostecki quickly replied that dinner had been served and no more food would come today. My stomach must have heard Kostecki, because I felt a sudden pang. I hadn't eaten all day, but I knew I could hold off until tomorrow. I'd gone hungry before.

My thoughts then wandered into the world outside the bars. *How is Mama? And the rest of the family? Maria? Oleh? Volodymyr? Michael? And now I'm in here... what will these Germans do with us? Maybe keep us alive... release us even!* My hopes were somewhat high.

These thoughts were interrupted by one of the older prisoners, saying it was time for prayer. He knelt first and the rest followed.

Each of the prisoners crossed themselves and spoke in a full voice, a rumble unlike any I'd ever heard. Very clearly, slowly, and devoutly, we said the Lord's Prayer and then Hail Mary. I'd spent all my life going to church, but I'd never felt a prayer so deeply as I did then. *Had I ever been around people that so strongly felt their prayers?*

And because it was Easter, the older man continued with song. His melodious voice started "Christ is Risen," and every other prisoner joined. Their singing was so sincere, so attentive, so present, like this was their last chance to connect with God. I instantly knew that this was a moment I'd never forget. These prayers ended suitably... "God merciful... forgive our sins." Tears streamed down the checks of many.

I imagined every prisoner dreaming of sitting with their family in a field of tall grass or in the front yard of their home... their wife, children, their most cherished friends surrounding them, once again reunited with the people they loved most.

A prisoner saw me admiring the sincerity of the prayer, and told me that of the 59 prisoners, eight were Polish. "They came from nearby villages and could speak and pray in Ukrainian. They kneel *with* us," he said. I looked about, realizing that I had no idea Poles were among us. *The Polish have been trying to take Ukraine over for years and now they're praying with us?*

It was a pleasant shock amongst the awful circumstance of being imprisoned. So *this* could bring us together. Prison, for a moment, was beautiful. *This is what daily prayer should be like.* I knew I would never forget this prayer.

I turned my attention inward. *I want to live. I want to be free. I want to see Spring... I want to smell the flowers blooming... I want to hear the nightingales singing in our grove.* Spring was my favorite time of year.

Then I looked to the man who led our prayers. "What is his profession?" I asked another prisoner.

"A Ukrainian priest. The Germans arrested him a week before Easter," he said. I pictured the village he came from, trying to celebrate Easter without a priest.

Suddenly, the door of our chamber swung open and in its mouth appeared three soldiers. One stepped in, pushed through prisoners, and hurriedly searched every corner of the room - even the toilet. Kostecki greeted him while he was searching but he paid Kostecki no attention. The soldier wrote something down in his notebook, and without saying a thing, he turned back and left the chamber proudly, chest to the ceiling.

"Inspection," said a prisoner. "Happens twice a day. Once in the morning, once before bed."

After the inspection, the prisoners all tried to find themselves a cranny of floor space to spend the night, with most of us forced to sleep sitting up, knees bent and legs cramped. None of us had a change of clothes, so we laid down in the ones we wore, shoes too. It was cold enough to keep my shoes on, and I didn't want anyone to "trade" with me tomorrow morning. Mine were well-broken into my feet and wanted to make sure no one else tried to take them.

As Tato was trying to help me get more comfortable, Kostecki loudly asked me, "How old are you?"

"Seventeen," I replied and immediately felt uncomfortable, because I realized that he wanted collect pity from the others, to get me a bigger sleeping spot.

"My son and I will be fine," Tato interjected, sensing my discomfort. "We won't be bothering anyone." It was nice to have him at my side - I didn't want any special treatment.

Kostecki then settled against the door, and seeing that all prisoners had found a spot, he turned out the light, said goodnight, and the chamber grew quiet.

SEPARATION

Many prisoners quickly dozed off, but sleep didn't come as easily to me. One by one, prisoners started snoring, getting louder as the night deepened. Their roaring throats transformed into a mighty strange and funny orchestra.

How could anyone sleep like this?

I exhaled, shifted my weight, and saw that Tato had similar troubles. I figured prison wouldn't be easy, but I never pictured sleeping sitting up while my unconsciousness fought against a snoring orchestra.

Prisoners entered a careless sleep, their nervous tremors rattling their neighbors, causing grumbles and whines. The good intentions from prayer earlier were now nowhere to be seen, yet most found a way to accept this disadvantage.

How long do we have to live like this? How long can *we live like this?*

"Put your head on my chest," Tato said, coming to the rescue.

My body got comfortable, but his hot and heavy breathe on my head made it impossible to relax. Although the prison wasn't heated, the collective breathe and crammed bodies of these 59 prisoners kept everything way too warm. No one else came to our chamber that night, but I sensed a flashlight shine through the door's window every few hours, another thing that kept me from fully falling into real rest.

The next morning, a few officers came into the chamber and read off the names of us five from Uherci. The guards ordered us to take our things, but they had already taken them.

I guess we're not returning...

Kostecki approached Tato, shook his hand, and wished him a speedy release.

"And if you're out soon, please find my family in Horodok, and tell them that I'm well, that the investigation is still ongoing, and that I'll be released soon," said Kostecki. Tato agreed, but it seemed to me like Kostecki didn't quite believe his own words.

The guards led us down to the second floor and introduced us to our new home, chamber 22. They pushed us in and said nothing more and locked the door behind us.

There were only two other prisoners in this chamber, as opposed to 54 in the last. The cell itself was half the size of the one prior. Sitting close to the ceiling was a small window, with three iron bars and a wood sill that blocked part of the already minuscule sliver of daylight peering in. The room was furnished like the other, with a toilet and tap to wash.

I had an ugly feeling that this move meant we weren't leaving Lontsky anytime soon.

One of these two prisoners walked up to us and in Polish asked, "Where are you from? Are you Polish? What language do you speak?"

As we answered, I noticed the other prisoner - tall, solidly built... and he didn't bother budging off the floor. He just stared at the ceiling and our presence didn't interest him at all.

"My name is Zbyshek," the first prisoner said. "I come from a Polish family, and I've been in this chamber for three weeks. There were six Ukrainians sitting in here with me, but they were taken out yesterday by the guards. Released to Germany... sent home... I don't know. Shame they were taken too! The Ukrainian Relief Committee donated clothes to these prisoners once a week on Tuesdays - and a bread roll too!"

The Ukrainian Relief Committee? Who's that? And why weren't we getting any rolls? Do they know we're here? Does Mama know we're here? I suddenly realized that no one knew where we were.

"Those rolls were fantastic! I can't praise the Ukrainian sincerity enough. These prisoners shared their bread every time, though indeed they themselves were starving and didn't have to give me a thing."

First - Poles praying with Ukrainians? Now - a Pole praising Ukrainians? I wondered about this new camaraderie as we took off our coats and laid them where we'd probably sleep that night.

Zbyshek continued walking about the chamber, asking himself whether the Committee would bring us bread today, because it was indeed Tuesday. It looked to me that our new acquaintance was very hungry, which meant the prison food was meager. He seemed a bit kooky too.

Tato drew Zbyshek's attention, saying, "We were arrested yesterday morning, and they've yet to feed us." Zbyshek stopped his pacing and his complaining and gave us a pitying look. Then he asked a bunch of questions:

"Where in Ukraine are you from?"

"Why did the Germans arrest you?"

"What's new with the war?"

"When will the Russians get to Lviv?"

And on and on.

For each of his questions, we responded. But for every one we asked him, he immediately twisted it around and didn't answer, never saying a thing about himself.

"Be careful with him," Tato whispered.

Who is this Zbyshek? What is he hiding?

So we treaded lightly with our answers, keeping a curious eye on his movements.

Two guards then appeared at the door with two prisoners carrying a boiler of black coffee and bowl of bread rolls.

I hadn't even *seen* food in over a day.

The guard ordered us to stand in a row. We each were given a tin of coffee and a piece of bread. We were ordered to drink and eat it all at once, which wasn't a problem, because we were starving.

The coffee was bitter, but warm, and the bread was stale, but it was food nonetheless. What surprised me most was that Tato ate the slowest.

"I'm not even hungry," he said. "Here, take mine."

But his generosity stirred me.

I denied and quietly asked him not to do that anymore. I felt ashamed in front of all the prisoners. Tato quickly realized that I wanted to feel like an equal and no longer tried to convince me that he wasn't hungry.

After breakfast, the well-built prisoner we initially saw lying on the chamber floor began nervously pacing back and forth across the chamber. In broken Ukrainian and Polish he asked if any of us spoke German.

I responded that I did and he said, "There's a rule here,

that when the officers come in for their morning and evening checks, one of the prisoners has to inform them of the number of prisoners in the cell, whether we're healthy, and whether everything is in order..."

The prisoners all looked at me, for I knew German the best. For whatever reason, I agreed.

Later that day, Zbyshek told me that the well-built prisoner who brought up the rule actually knows German well, but he was too terrified to take the roll call job.

"He looks like a Jew," said Zbyshek. "The Ukrainians that left yesterday thought so too." *He was too scared to do it - should I be scared too?*

It seemed like these Germans weren't yet pinning any guilt on the Poles or us Ukrainians, but if they found out that this man was a Jew, then by their standards, they needed no reason to do away with him.

So I thought back to Kostecki, calling roll every morning and evening and taking true charge of the cell. *It's either the guy who might be a Jew or me - someone has to do it.* I decided not to second guess myself.

Later that morning, a couple officers entered our chamber. I called roll, they looked at me attentively, made no reply, and then said:

"Ivan Fedenko - follow us."

Why is he first? For whatever reason, I expected myself to go first. But in a funny way, his sudden call gave me hope - *Maybe these Germans will simply make sure we're innocent and when we pass their tests we'll certainly be released! They promised us this in the village - if we weren't guilty, we'd be free!*

But as the guards took Tato away, my hope soon turned to fear. Uncertainty crept in. *What will they ask him? Will they force him to admit who shot the Germans? Will they beat him, abuse him? Will they ask about the Underground? Is he gonna come back?*

Just last night, Tato and I tried strengthening our stories, but we couldn't do any better than before. Ignorance would hopefully work. We convinced ourselves that if one of us broke and confessed, that there would be no chance for pardon and they'd kill us both, or worse, we'd be left to rot. Our only choice was to forget life or death and cling to our stories, with thoughts of each other as motivation.

But the longer Tato was gone, the more nervous I became. My mind couldn't gauge how long he was gone. Every minute was an hour.

"Zbyshek, were other prisoners punished? Beaten? Abused? Zbyshek?!" I asked.

My concern was impossible to hide.

"Don't worry. It's only his first investigation. They're very polite the first time. They ask about everything in detail, record it all... they actually ask quite warmly."

So far so good.

"They want prisoners to talk on their own will. Less work for them. When they finish, they'll review the information and decide whether you get to go free. They might even say you've been wrongly accused," he said.

Then he leaned forward and whispered, "Don't speak on your own will. Just answer what they ask. *Only* what they ask. Others have echoed the same."

He leaned back and then continued, "And I'm sure your

Tato will return. Otherwise they would have told him to take all his things."

Zbyshek's words calmed me down, making it a little easier to hold off my impatience. He didn't seem so secretive now either. It was nice of him to comfort me. He really didn't have to.

But worry quickly sank back in. Images crept in of Tato being asked questions that we didn't cover. *What are they asking him?! Would he hesitate? Would I get a chance to talk to him when he gets back? Or would they take me right away?*

The chamber door suddenly opened and Tato walked in. He looked calm, balanced, completely normal. He smiled even, like he wanted to say something. But his intentions were interrupted:

"Stepan Fedenko. Follow us, immediately."

There was my answer.

I figured that they wouldn't call me right away - we were so close to lunch... I stepped up timidly and two guards flanked my sides - they took me up to the fourth floor and led me into a spacious room with pictures of German leaders hanging from the walls. In the middle stood an oversized portrait of Adolf Hitler.

Beneath Hitler sat a German soldier behind a desk going over documents. The bustle of street cars leaked in through a large open window, reminding me that there was still life beyond these walls. Another officer entered the room and sat down and my escorts left.

Looking out the window, for some reason I felt that if the investigators did beat me, a beating that I couldn't handle, then I might be able to jump out. It was four flights.

My thoughts were interrupted by the German: "Sitz." I sat. He pulled some notes from his briefcase and spread them across the table. Among them were my notes taken during the raid of our home.

This will be my main charge. The Underground lyrics. This is my persecuting evidence.

The investigating officer then asked the other, "Please close the window. The traffic is *so* bothersome."

He started speaking to me in Ukrainian, although his accent was off. He couldn't pronounce the hard "L," which reminded me of the nearby-to-Uherci German village Noyhofen. It was solely inhabited by Germans with this accent.

His first question was my name, slowly followed by birthday, birthplace, how much school I'd finished, what I'm currently studying, and my address in Lviv. He meticulously recorded all my answers in the register.

"You were studying in Lviv... so what were you doing in Uherci?" he asked.

Because of the slow pace of the questioning, I found a little more courage and said, "Just a week ago, according to our church calendar, it was the holiday of Christ's resurrection and I was on a holy vacation with the family."

"Were you in the village all three days?"

"Yes," I said. My hair stood on end. The lying had begun.

"And on that third day, did you go to the cemetery?"

"Yes." *Where are you going with this?*

He slowly continued: "Who spoke at the soldiers' graves?"

"The priest."

"Anyone else?"

It then became apparent that he knew about the celebration at the cemetery and I calmly answered, "My father."

He then looked me straight in the eye and asked, "Do you remember if... at any point... any of these people spoke out against the German movement?"

I immediately denied it and said, "I remember everything well. Neither the priest nor my father even mentioned the Germans." Which was true.

"*I* was told..." he paused, shifting in his seat, "that one of the speakers told the villagers to get ready for the armed uprisings against the Germans, to steal weapons and distribute among the people."

Partially true.

"Not true," I said. "I carefully listened to the speakers, was right next to them, and heard everything. Whoever made this accusation just wanted the Germans to punish us Ukrainians. When my father spoke, two Poles outside the cemetery shouted taunts and whistled, and when we ran over to check out who they were, they sped off to the village of Stodilka. Before the war, that village was filled with Germans and Poles."

"Then please, I insist, tell me everything that you remember of your father's speech," he said.

"He was worried about the hard times coming for us Ukrainians. Communist Russia had taken over most of Ukraine and drew nearer and nearer every day. He said we must be prepared for anything, to sacrifice our lives for our nation, just as the young boys of the Sichovi riflemen did, who rested in those graves before us. Tato used their sacrifice as an example, for it was them who had shown us that it is better to rest in the grave then live a life of agony," I said.

"He didn't speak for long," I continued, "Women cried for their fallen children. Then that shout from the woods interrupted him."

I was very cautious in my speech, at the same time giving him enough detail so that he'd be convinced. I repeated, "My father meant no harm against the Germans and spoke no wrongs against them. This denunciation is a vicious invention in order to somehow discredit him or to rid him from our village."

The investigator listened intently and wrote something in his notebook. That was the last inquiry about Tato, and then he picked up my notebook that the Germans snatched while searching our home and asked, "Do you recognize this book?"

"Yes. I use it to record the addresses of my school friends, exam dates, birthdays, and some new songs in it."

I made sure to say "new," as to cover myself later.

He politely continued. "What is written here in these songs?"

This was the question I waited for, the one answer I prepared and planned for with Tato.

Without any hesitation, I said, "I recently heard those songs on the train from Lviv to Horodok. I was on my way home from school, and next to me were some young men, happy and singing with joy, urging all the passengers to join in."

I hoped that I didn't sound too scripted.

"Because nobody knew the words, they encouraged us to write down their lyrics, which many travelers did, including me. These young men told us that they were off to Dębica, Poland to train in the Ukrainian Division called Galicia. These songs were composed in their honor, and they really wanted us to jot them down," I said.

"And the acronyms?" he asked.

"They said that the USD, UPA, and OUN were some kind of important parts of the Division. One of those guys sat down next to me and said, 'Write these down, because next year I'm sure you'll be joining us. We want you to be ready to sing,' and I instantly felt a connection with those young men. They were so confident, happy, and sang with such unshakeable passion. That's probably why I wrote them down," I said.

The investigator then scrunched his eyebrows, looked at me oddly, and asked, "You hadn't heard these acronyms before? In any brochures? Or leaflets?"

"Nope. I haven't seen them," I said. *Stop questioning me! Of course I've seen them elsewhere! I practically memorized those brochures!*

He was surprised by my answer, saying, "*I* was under the impression that these acronyms, the UPA and the OUN, were known by *every single Ukrainian.*"

"Never seen them before," I insisted further. "I'm still young, I come from a small village, I live alone in the city, and I'm not interested in anything but school."

But he didn't seem to buy it. I justified myself even more,

saying, "I love my family so much. And I spend all my time studying so I could start working and support them."

"So you never read any newspapers? Or went to any performances that mentioned the UPA?" he asked.

Do you see right through me? But I couldn't falter now. I knew Tato didn't. He was counting on me.

"No. All my time is dedicated to studying. I have no time for these other things," I said. "I haven't seen these acronyms anywhere else. Maybe they're from some political party or something, but I'm entirely uninterested in politics. Only school is important."

After each answer, he further recorded notes in his registry. *What is he writing?* He even started repeating questions to see if my answers would change.

Luckily, at some point, interrogations ended. My mind was cooked by his repeated requests about the Underground, but I was glad that he didn't ask me about the shooting in the woods.

I tried reading the investigator's body language to guess whether he believed what I said or not, but he was stiff as a board. My hope was that I appeared before him a simple, young man, a normal fool who saw no other world besides the classroom.

He rose and said, "We will review your case, and if all that you said appears to be true, we'll quickly release you."

Those words lit a spark of hope in me. *Maybe I'll still get out of here alive!*

The escorting guards entered the room and the investigator told them to take me back to my chamber. The investigator didn't look so scary to me anymore. He seemed young, educated, cheerful, friendly, and he showed me a sort of distant sympathy.

Maybe I could still justify my behavior? Maybe they'll believe me. But why didn't you ask about the shooting? You had the chance to ask...

The guards led me back down these same acoustic corridors, stomp-a-clacking their boots like they were on a special mission. When I got back into the chamber, Tato came to me at once.

"How it go? Did they treat you ok?"

"Yes," I said and was drained and slouched against the wall. I spent so much of today worrying - memorizing our story, thinking about Tato in questioning, then keeping my own investigation straight... thinking, thinking, thinking about how to shape my words so that Tato and I wouldn't get beaten. The prisoners who were arrested with us began discussing how they'd talk to investigators in order to portray innocence.

"The investigation was calm. The officials behaved entirely humane. No threats or scare tactics," I said. I stayed very general because I figured the less I say, the better. I wanted to protect Tato and myself first.

Quietly, Tato then told me, "Good work, son. I said all the same."

"These Germans always behave well in the first interview," butted in Zbyshek. "Wait for the second or third. This time they just wanted to get your initial story, check your reaction. At the next interrogation, things will be very different."

We both looked over at him.

"They'll push the more challenging issues. They'll lay out all the info they've got on you and make you admit everything. These investigators are different. Violent. Prepare well. This was all told to me by a fellow prisoner, who looked to me like he'd been beat up good. I await the same fate - I've had my first and they were friendly," Zbyshek said.

He'd deflated any relief my spent body had mustered.

Lunch passed by and I figured that the other three Uherci villagers would be taken in, but they never were. Not that day or the day after, so Tato and I began realizing that we were their main culprits.

I looked at the bright side - at least we had room enough to lay down that night. Tato and I slept right next to each other. I wrapped my boots up in my shirt and used them as a makeshift pillow. We laid my coat down underneath us and used Tato's as a blanket. But even pressed up against each other, his coat didn't cover us up.

That night, after the evening rounds, the prisoners all laid to rest sooner than usual. Some predicted that they'd be called the next day for questioning and wanted to be well rested and relaxed. Whether they could be so in these conditions, that was another story.

Somehow I slept well that night. Tato did too. We got through the initial investigation. *What could be next?*

The next day, three Ukrainians from a village east of Lviv were added to our chamber. Their story was similar to ours - Germans surrounded their village and arrested six under the pretense that they were part of the Ukrainian Underground. They also spent a night in the sardine-packed quarters of cell 37 before being moved in with us.

The German guards, who arrested these Ukrainians, said that they were sick of their military and police stations being ransacked for artillery, so they arrested them. The Germans were arresting various local Ukrainian leaders, because these leaders "should know who were behind these attacks" and figured that threatening violence would rectify the problem.

"Otherwise," these Germans told these new Ukrainians, "we'll destroy your leaders immediately."

And these new cell-mates of ours *were* Underground members, so they would indeed know if Ukrainians were behind these attacks, but they complained that they really had no idea who was going after these German posts.

"It might be the Soviets," one said, "pretending to be Ukrainians to provoke the Germans."

After we swapped more stories and explained what we'd learned about the prison structure here at Lontsky, Tato pulled the senior member of their group and warned him to be careful.

"These walls may have ears," Tato said.

I spoke with the others about school and plans for the Spring. None of these plans included being arrested. *Would we make it out before Spring's end? Will I ever hear my favorite birds again - those dancing nightingales with their flute-like chirps?*

After lunch we all formed a circle and started walking clockwise round the chamber to get some movement in our legs. It was the only way for us to feel somewhat alive in this hole. All of us were so used to village life - farming, walking dozens of miles, helping in the smithy. This immobility led to racing thoughts. Movement helped.

When night fell, we talked about the powerful and beautiful prayer in cell 37.

"Today, let's try some of the same," said Tato. "We're eight Ukrainian strong, and here's to hoping that we all can sing."

All of us but the two non-Ukrainians loudly recited "Our Father" and "Hail Mary" and sang "Christ has Risen." Tato's simple voice led the group and we all chipped in. Zbyshek and the giant supposed-Jew laid quietly in their places.

After prayer, we set up our coat bed and blanket and then our boot pillows and laid to rest. I quickly fell asleep and I'm not sure how long I was out but then I suddenly sprung up to loud and rapid firing.

What is that?! The front? Already?

Tato sprung up too.

"What is that?" he hurriedly asked.

Our chamber lit up, flashing bright like someone was flicking the lights on and off. I looked towards the bulb in our chamber - nothing.

Then I looked up through our tiny window and saw what could have only been roasting stars falling from heaven.

"Rocket fire!" I heard one prisoner yell.

Flames trailed these rockets and lit up the whole city of Lviv. Then bombs hit the ground and rattled our chamber. Planes were dropping targets so that the big bombers knew where to unload.

The gunfire was piercing. I cupped my ears. It must have

been the German anti-aircraft guns that were stationed at the nearby citadel. Every shot pulsated the prison walls.

German guards ran through the halls yelling. We heard them run out the corridors and lock all the gates behind them. *They must be going for underground shelter! What about us?*

We were left alone.

I imagined the bombs somehow destroying the prison but keeping us alive in the process. *Maybe they'd fall* around *us? I know this part of the city... We could flee!* And I knew the forests around Lviv as well. *We could easily disappear! They'd never find us!*

But that wasn't my only thought.

What if these bombs fell on *us? Would we get hurt? Would rescuers reach us? All the iron gates are shut! Would anybody even care to come?*

I heard the whisper of another prisoner praying in the corner of the chamber, asking God for salvation. I turned to Tato.

"Tato, be calm. Don't worry," I begged. "We'll survive."

He then began to whisper a prayer to himself. I joined him and he grabbed my hand. Suddenly the whole prison jumped.

Don't open your eyes. Keep praying.

A bomb must have hit just next to the prison. My ears were ringing. *Where's the next one?*

I clung even closer to Tato and more fervently prayed. *Please, God. Let us live, please. But if not... accept us.*

And slowly the the pa-rat-a-tat-tat and flashes of the anti-aircraft artillery went out. German spotlights searched the sky for enemy aircrafts. City sirens wailed, giving notice that the bombing had ended.

Thank you, God. Apparently, it wasn't my time yet. Iron

partitions clanked open as guards thundered back to their posts.

The bombs didn't free us. The bombs didn't kill us. Silence had won and somehow with heightened senses we all fell asleep.

With each subsequent day, our shackled life became commonplace. Three times a day, meager food rations were given. Prisoners were taken in and out for interrogation. We walked in our circle. Every day guards yelled, fierce as lions, showing us that they were the all-powerful lords of this prison.

At the end of the week, we were gifted a very interesting chamber mate. He was medium height, looked healthy, was very talkative and nothing seemed to scare him.

We asked him his nationality and he replied, "None of them. I am worldly."

But then he did tell us that he belonged to a religious group called the Jehovah's Witnesses. I did not know what this was.

He spoke Ukrainian to us Ukrainians, to the Poles, Polish, and he said he could speak other languages too, among them English and German. He showed off this skill by immediately complaining in each of these languages.

"These Germans! They arrested me without reason! I am not the enemy. My mission on Earth is to preach truth, to tell everyone that the kingdom of God is near!" the Jehovah's Witness said.

Really?

"They took away my Bible! What an injustice!"

And without asking any of us if we were believers, or belonged to any church, he immediately started converting us to his faith. We curiously watched. This Witness seemed like an educated man, spurting out all sorts of worldly events, the history of different nations, and quoting books by various authors. He'd "read and re-read!" them so I decided to give him a chance. His statement about God's kingdom drew me in too. I was interested.

"I spread the hope that all prisoners are waiting for!"

Wonderful!

"And where do I bring this news from?" he asked himself. "I've had a revelation from God himself! He told me that in two months, *just two months,* the world will end! So repent all of your sins, and for that we'll all escape the wrath of God!"

And that's when I lost him. *The end of the world? Revelation from God himself? I'm not so sure...* He kept talking like we had agreed.

"The Germans arrested me at the Krakow market in Lviv, where I'd been publicly preaching all day to the people. I told them the same I tell you - two months and the world is done. In three, Christ comes to serve as judge and hold trial for all.

"So do not sorrow here in prison! Fear nothing! All the Earthly government will soon pass away. If they hadn't taken my Bible, I could show you myself! You have a great opportunity here, being sent to jail and getting a chance to learn all this from me. When you believe, you will be saved!"

He wouldn't stop.

"I recently had a revelation from God, and it's my mission

to tell as many people as I can. These Germans arrested me because someone told them that I preach about the quickly-approaching end, and that many-a-people were following my word. I'm sure that they'll call me in promptly for investigation, because they want to know all about this as soon as possible."

I already had something to believe in. But he seemed so sure. What confounded it all was that not an hour after he predicted an investigation, two guards came in and ordered him out.

This Jehovah's Witness had certainly made his impression. All the chamber's prisoners rose in spirit too, and we were all somehow revived, even though we doubted his prophecy and this revelation. We all became a little sad that he was so quickly taken from us. I was confused.

After he left, Tato questioned his statements.

"Why would this ordinary man, and *just* him out of all the ordinary men in the whole world... why would he have the privilege to bestow the end of the world?" he said. "Why doesn't the church mention anything about this? There have been plenty of these 'saints' who were given the first right to proclaim such a thing. I read a similar story about a man who called himself a prophet and preached that in six months, the world would come to an end. He was so convinced that he would have given his head to prove it. But that was fifteen years ago. Many a-six months have passed and nothing has changed."

Although Jehovah hadn't convinced anyone to convert to his religion, we still did talk about him for some time. A couple hours later, he found himself back in our chamber.

"These Germans gathered a group of their officers!" he started enthusiastically. "They put me in a gigantic room, gave me a Bible, and then ordered me to tell them everything I preached to the people of the city."

Quite the audience.

"These officers - they listened so intently, asking me all these questions when I was done. I told them everything I'd told you. 'It's time to repent! The end of the world is near! It's two months away! If you repent your sins, you will be saved!'

"Then they ordered me to read these passages in the Bible which state that I alone am the sole holder of this news of the end of the world!"

And after reading the passages, the Germans apparently had heard enough.

"I told them 'I had a revelation! I'm obliged to tell the truth to everyone,'" Jehovah said. "The officers had a little meeting, sent me back, and told me that they'd release me soon."

"And they took my Bible again," he added.

We had no idea what to make of this man, but the crazy thing was - the next morning - they called him again!

Being released already? How does is he predicting all this? None of us could believe it.

But after our morning walk, the Jehovah's Witness was tossed back into our chamber, shoulders slumped, sad and dissatisfied.

None of us initially said a word, giving him a moment to come to, and then as if on cue, he began again - "Those officers! They called me a Russian spy! They said I was causing a riot amongst the people and that they'd beat be if I didn't cease my preaching. One of them was ready to hit me, but the other two held him back. They said they had special plans for me. They're gonna hole me up in this prison until I quit my preaching.

"But I'll never stop, even if they threaten death! Those Germans mocked me and for that they'll truly be sorry... I'm worried though, because I don't think I converted any of them," he said.

What faith this man had! After all that, he still thought he could convert them.

And then as if there wasn't enough action, our chamber doors opened and another prisoner appeared. He confidently walked in and gave a hearty Russian "Privyet!"

It looked as though prison hadn't stirred a hair on this man's head. He was tall, with oak trunk legs and spoke boldly. "Where can I spread myself out?" he asked.

One of the other prisoners tended to him while we listened on to Jehovah's Witness. Prophecy aside, he was a great preacher and had a beautiful singing voice. In order to try and rope us in, he sang some religious songs that we'd never heard before. We didn't mind. It was much better than sitting and staring at a stone wall.

One of these songs, in Polish, went like so:
Satan gathers his army
For the final fight.
But don't sympathize with him,
For Jesus is your King.

Blow hard into your trombones,
And do what God says,
Jehovah fights today, for all of his people.
And another...
When he who handcuffs the sea...
When a storm ravages out of control in the distance...
I seek protection
In the shadow of his hand
He will shelter us in a safe place,
Where without harm, we shall be.

But not all of us were happy to listen - it began to bother our new Russian cellmate. His sharp face and demeanor immediately made me think that he was some kind of Russian communist agent. Sprawled out on the floor, he said to Jehovah, "Stop all these fables and nonsensical laments!"

But this had little impact on Jehovah. He kindly and gently proceeded to tell the Russian, "You are not correct, and you should be the first person to hear more about God and religion, about Christ and how to properly prepare for the end of the world. Change that attitude and you will also be saved."

"I am a communist!" The Russian blurted. "Whether anyone likes it or not. I need know nothing about anything else."

Such a proud reply turned our chamber sour. We all started to realize that besides German authorities, we'd have to be wary of "fellow" prisoners as well.

But I thought communism was dead? Didn't the Russians proclaim the restoration of Russian Orthodoxy? Hadn't they joined forces with the

Allies?

But this man's eyes said otherwise. A pupil like this, with such passion... *he* showed me that communism was still quite strong. I started to feel awful again about *either* side winning this war... *German nazism? Soviet communism? Which evil would win out?* My slim hope laid with the Americans.

That evening, we Ukrainians prayed and sang, not caring whether someone's religious beliefs or political beliefs would get in our way. And to our surprise, Jehovah joined in, helping us sing about Christ's rise. This majority made me feel secure. At least we had some numbers.

After we sang, a thick silence laid in our cell, as if the words of our songs remained in the chamber, vibrating between the walls. We all soon dozed.

The next morning guards ordered us out of the chamber. I huddled up to Zbyshek, who'd spent the longest time in this jail, and asked if he knew where they were taking us.

"They've never taken everyone out of the chamber..." Zbyshek said.

The unknown.

"But it won't be evil. Maybe they're taking us to the showers to give us a good scrubbing," he said. His answer brought me a little comfort. *They can't interrogate all of us together, can they?*

The guards escorted us down to the first floor and out to the prison yard. It was surrounded on all sides by four stories of prison cells and masonry fence. The group of prisoners before us were corralled, and we were told that we had 15 minutes to roam.

"Get in pairs and walk," said a guard. "You are strictly forbidden to talk to anyone, especially if you meet any friends or relatives. If these rules are broken, you will be strictly punished. Be grateful that we've let you outside."

As I started to walk, I fell into a dream. Everything became incredibly vivid - even the gravel was alive. I hadn't felt sunlight in over a week. Then the nightmare crept in. *Where's my freedom? Where's my family? I'm supposed to be in school, studying to become an engineer. I'm supposed to learn about electrical current to help Tato in the smithy! What am I doing in here?!*

And as fast as our walk started, it ended.

When we got back to the chamber, the Russian prisoner, who just the day before called himself a Communist, began to tell us his story. He proudly strut from one end of the chamber to the other, while the rest of us scattered and laid to rest.

I tried tuning him out, because I was offended. So I marveled at his inability to fear instead. With such intense Communist views, he could be lining himself up for a good beating, but that didn't seem to bother him because I think he was getting high off showing us his superiority.

From time to time, he'd single one of us out, preachily harassing us about whether we had the 'opportunity' to become acquainted with world-renown Western writers.

"Who of you has read their literature?! Who of you knows their history?!"

No one answered.

"I am a Communist, and I will stay one forever! The Communist system is the best and rightly so it shall prevail throughout the entire world, including America! Everything I know was taught to me by Communism! I am a Communist, and I will stay one forever!"

We Ukrainians need only know one thing about Communism - it destroyed our people and our land. Any passionate tirade was just a flat line of words.

Without any of us asking, he started naming off Western writers. He quoted Byron, Shakespeare, Victor Hugo, Jack London, Dostoyevsky, Pushkin, Turhyneva and others.

"The Communist system is the world's best! It must seize the world! You see, the Russian Army is coming back to save us! They're not far from Lviv!" he said.

"A spy?" Tato asked me under his breathe.

Our thoughts were aligned.

"Either that... maybe a fanatic or advocate," I replied.

The Russian boasted: "I've studied in Leningrad and Moscow! I volunteered to fight for Russia and after finishing just half of my training they sent me off to defend Moscow. How about that?

"One night, my regiment was completely surrounded by Germans. We couldn't do a thing, but we would never surrender! We went into battle and they killed us all, everyone but me. I tried to flee, but the bastards caught me and now I'm here," he said.

I did not like being locked up with this Soviet.

"But do not worry," he said, as if trying to comfort us, "the front is near and soon our Red Army will free us all! We must get prepared. Let us properly welcome her!"

Tato couldn't handle this nonsense anymore.

"You have one thing... *one thing* right. The Red Army will come rescue *you*. But you can hardly imagine what will happen to us Ukrainians. The Germans arrested us, because we fight for a free Ukraine. The Red Army will do the same. The only difference being? We'll be deported to frozen Siberia to perish there instead of here."

"No, no, no," the Muscovite said. "Not true."

Tato roared back. "You consider yourself smart, no? Well then back down when I speak because none of us interrupted you. You will now hear all that *I* have to say to *you*. Now let me begin by saying I was the head of the village council when the Red Army arrived for the first time with, well, you must know them so well, their NKVD."

The NKVD was the Russian secret police, like the SS to the Nazis, who were responsible for the Soviet's dirty work, including population transfers, ethnic 'cleansing,' and mass genocide.

Tato went on. "At the time, they said they were liberating us from Polish aristocracy, as you do now from German fascism. Let's take a look at how that 'freedom' looked:

"The best of our people - the conscious Ukrainians, clergymen, farmers... they were all immediately arrested, dragged to Siberia, and were promptly murdered. Murdered! And for what, I ask you? What did we do wrong? And what right do you Russians have here in Ukraine, to tell us how we should live? Why don't you take yourselves and go to *your* Siberia, and leave us here in *our* Ukraine?"

Tato wasn't finished.

"We Ukrainians don't come to free any of you, so keep *your* Siberia for *your* criminals and do us no favors of 'liberation.' You try to enlighten us through these writers, these strangers, but why don't you praise the words of our great poet, Taras Shevchenko? He who lives here among you! But no! You falsify his work. You rip his words apart, leaving only what makes you comfortable.

"We honor your great writers, just the same as those of the West, but do you do this in return? Have you read Shevchenko? Have you read what he wrote of your Kings? Or were you not allowed? Because your Kings 'freed' him too, and then arrested him for 10 years! And I'll ask you again - for what?! I'll save you the time and answer this too - because he loved his Ukrainian people. And because he wrote that what you're doing was wrong.

"And did you hear what your Kings had to say about that? They said that Ukraine is nothing. That there is no Ukrainian language. That it was forbidden to read and write anything in our dear language. Your Kings destroyed our Kozak Ukraine, while those same Kozak hands built your city of St. Petersburg, and those Kozak bones still rot underneath it."

I had never heard Tato like this. The Communist was frozen. Tato went on:

"And have you heard of the Hetman Ivan Mazepa? Why do you still swear off his name in your churches? Shouldn't you be praying instead? Why don't you just take your culture go sit in *your* Moscow? But no - you've recently seized Lithuania, Latvia, Estonia!

"You are the same invaders and colonialists as the capitalists and fascists! Maybe even worse! We Ukrainians don't need foreign liberators and 'teachers' like you. None of you bring us any freedom or prosperity. The Ukrainian people will do it themselves and it's time for you and our 'liberators' to understand this.

"And now in closing, I ask you: were you told by your friend Stalin how many millions of Ukrainians died in the famine of 1933? Were you? No? ... You don't deserve to know."

And like that, he was done. The room vibrated with Tato's message. The answer to his question? It could be four million. Or it could be eight. Stalin made sure this number was impossible to track.

Pride swelled within me. Tato was well versed and reading all those books and journals hadn't been for nothing. Tato kept his tone balanced, but I could hear the painful sting of heavy injustice in his voice.

But he forgot his precaution to the other Ukrainians: 'Don't overspeak with strange and unknown persons!' Even this Russian could be a German agent, and that's why he so boldly praised communism. But several more prisoners felt Tato's passion as well, and they too challenged the Russian's beliefs. My worry subsided.

This Russian had probably never heard from free Ukrainians, well, free from Russian rule anyway. He might never heard from us Ukrainians about the yoke that was laid upon us for centuries by Moscow.

"Alright!" said the Muscovite, after being berated by us all.

"I admit I don't know everything. We were never taught any of this!"

Then, changing this disadvantageous subject, he said, "Well we should probably get rid of these Germans first, and that'll domino, fixing everything else!"

No one responded, and then he laid down on the floor defeated.

Tato then leaned over to me and whispered, "I still don't know with whom I was really speaking to. Is he really a Muscovite? An undercover German agent?"

"At least you didn't denounce the Germans," I replied, and I took Tato's hand and together we laid down for the night.

Early the next morning, as if the moon had reset him, the Muscovite began praising the Soviet system again. But he no longer stood up to Tato.

Another prisoner asked the Muscovite why Stalin induced an artificial famine in Ukraine. "Why kill those millions of men, women and children?"

"It's all your own invention," he said. "A straight lie."

Until now, nobody must have ever mentioned the famine to him.

"If it's really how you say it is," he said, "then I would have read about it. I've read it all and this famine isn't mentioned anywhere."

It scared me to know that so many millions could die without the rest of the world knowing it. This Russian didn't even know, and it was happening in his own country!

"You're all just a bunch of silly fascists, discouraging the development of communism," he said. But Tato's words still echoed through my mind and this Russian's words felt distant.

In the end he could only hear himself and turned out more fanatical than the Jehovah Witness and his ideas about the end of the world. We ignored the Russian for the next two days, and then the guards promptly took him away.

That same day, the prisoner who Zbyshek had assumed was a Jew was taken as well. Since we got to this chamber, the Jew spoke to no one, looked for no company, and when he was taken away, no one said goodbye.

During our second week in prison, Tato and I got clean linens from Mama through a Ukrainian Relief Committee rep. We each got a bread roll, but the rep was forbidden to talk to us.

Seeing the linens made me sad. I couldn't hold back weeping. Tato's eyes also glistened.

I pictured a crying Mama and Maria cleaning these sheets, salty tears dropping on the laundry. I wanted so desperately to thank them, but they weren't there.

We thanked them out loud anyway, a thanks we hoped they could hear. I embraced the linens and kissed them like they were Mama. *When will I see you again?*

The bread from the committee lifted our spirits a little too. We decided to only eat a quarter roll each and save the rest. But then we both felt sorry for Zbyshek and Jehovah's Witness, that they got nothing, so we gave them both a piece too. The other Ukrainians did the same.

I searched through the laundry, looking for notes, but there were none.

Zbyshek noticed me searching and said, "The Germans threatened the Committee, telling them that if they found something that wasn't permitted in the family care packages, they'd immediately ban the delivery program." This would have to do.

The rest of this second week in Lontsky passed uneventfully. Tato and I often speculated about what would come next of us. *Would they call us again to be investigated? Will we be asked about the forest shooting?* These anxious thoughts plagued our drawn out hours in jail.

Luckily, at the end of the week, we were again let out into the yard for 15 minutes. But our good fortune quickly turned into a painful realization and for the first time I saw that these Germans were not joking around.

A wooden pillar stood buried in the middle of the prison yard. A man was tied to it, half-hanging from his wrists. A German guard stood next to him, lashing him with a whip, leaving bloody rips in his clothes criss-crossed against his chest. No one told us why he was being beaten, but he probably had forgotten the yard rule of not talking. Seeing this made me sick.

He was dragged back into the prison.

This 15 minute walk wasn't as freeing as the last time and more-so a reflection of the beaten man. He was visual proof that we could be hurt here. Not just starved. Not just caged.

But broken down. Humiliated. And for what? He probably saw a relative he hadn't seen in weeks, months maybe, got excited and yelled out, and then was promptly tied to the pillar and reminded of the rule.

We returned to the chamber with worries about our own fate. In order to cope, we shared each other's stories, fears, wants, saying anything really. We had to fill up the time somehow. We had to interrupt our thoughts. Books and newspapers were forbidden, so talking was our only release.

We even started to joke. Zbyshek had so much appreciated our stance against the Soviet Moskal that we harped him: "When are they bringing you a Polish roommate? Otherwise soon you'll be one of us!"

"Not so fast! I don't speak a lick of Ukrainian, so good luck!" he said.

We also noticed that we'd been gifted a tenor with the last batch of prisoners. We heard him whisper some songs here and there, not taking much notice in him, but then as his confidence rose, so did his voice, and what a voice it was.

We were immediately interested in his singing. We pushed him to sing a little more and more each day, and then one day he quietly let his voice hit the highest of tones! We had no carpet or furniture in the chamber either, so the acoustics were huge. This singer's name was Michael Wolf.

I bet the whole prison listened when he sang. German guards would sneak closer to our chamber to listen. Nobody told him to stop.

We didn't let Wolf skip a day, singing prominent Ukrainian song after song. His favorites were "Show Yourself,

Bright Moon," "I Look to the Sky and Meditate," "Hrits, Don't go to the Evening Meetings," "Plunge into Sorrow," among others.

Then he quietly sang, just for himself, his own song, with a melody of lost hope and the lyrics of a solemn prisoner which would never leave my mind:

I sit in the dark prison barracks,
Entirely cut off from the world.
I see nothing
but a solid wall and iron bars in the windows.
I sit and think,
of how I know nothing of those at home,
Of the spring flowers blossoming,
or of how the river nimbly flows.

After his solos, we'd all sing a few songs together. Right before bed, we'd pray and continue to sing "Christ is Risen," even though Easter had passed. It was our way to rise as well. Jehovah's Witness even joined us, and out of habit, he always chimed in about his prophecy. But he stopped trying to convert us, simply rejoicing in the fact that he saw good-natured, faithful Christians.

Prisoners also started boldly discussing the Ukrainian Underground operations from back in our villages. I noticed our Polish cellmate Zbyshek often listening in, and he'd ask me the meaning of words he didn't understand. *Maybe someday he'd learn Ukrainian after all.*

At night, we continued to wake up to Soviet air raids, and were well scared of the consequences, but we slowly got used to it. The guards still scurried down into the basement, and

SEPARATION

we were left to our fate.

CHAPTER FIVE

PAIN

The days of our confinement moved at a snail's pace, so my thoughts often pulled me back to Uherci. Our village as a whole was poor. There was no electricity or gas, and there was only one telephone line that served the local police. Policemen were financially a little better off than other villagers, because they did hard work from dawn until late into the night.

But our family was lucky. Dido (Grandpa) Petro had his own loom and made canvas for our family and for profit. Tato learned blacksmithing in the Manor of Nezabitovsky and later opened his own smithy. So our family lived a little better than the other villagers.

But this didn't satisfy Tato. Tato's mind was always set on improving the village as a whole. So he organized the villagers into conscious groups and societies in order to create camaraderie and prestige among the peasants.

More and more farmers brought their requests to Tato's smithy. The smithy caught even the village host's eye, and he brought him jobs too, hearing his work was some of the best.

SEPARATION

When I was fourteen, I also began to help him in the forge and plenty of fascinating stories made their way through.

The men that came in talked of their service in the army, fighting against the Russians and Poles in World War I, competing for Lviv, Kyiv, and Eastern Ukraine from 1914 to 1921. Even older soldiers showed up too, who'd served in the Austrian Army when Galicia was still under her occupation.

They told stories of being taken from their homes to serve in the army and were sent far off to the Italian front, into the Alps, from which many of their comrades did not come back alive. Many young Ukrainian boys perished there, of whom there are still no traces. Children were left orphaned in the village. Many soldiers returned disabled.

The soldiers told one story about Italians rolling large rocks and barrels of combustable petroleum at them down mountain-sides. After surviving that horror, they often asked themselves why they had to go fight for another person's country? For Austria, for Poland, for Russia... why fight for them to improve *their* lives? Why can't we fight to improve our own Ukrainian land?

After hearing this, Tato wanted to know more about the world happenings and subscribed to more newspapers. In the evenings after work, villagers would gather round our house, sit on stools and benches, or even on the ground, and ask Tato to read to them. They were interested in how other farmers maintained their lands, what predictions were being made for the harvest, potential upcoming weather patterns, and who was fighting what war where.

Tato also managed to be the first in our village to buy a

radio, and for better sound quality, he put the antenna high up above on two tall, adjacent ash trees. It was called a "Detector," and it sounded clearly throughout our home. Whole groups of peasants came to our home in the days following. They wanted to listen to the "miracle of a far-away voice coming from the little box." Sitting in prison, thinking of home, I hoped and prayed for a miracle too but what came next was not that.

A nice interruption broke up our locked-up monotony - Zbyshek got a mystery package with sausage, bread, and two dozen raw eggs. Because we shared our weekly roll with him, he broke us off a piece of sausage and bread. We welcomed the goods with gratitude.

"I'm gonna keep the eggs to myself," he said, "because my chest is sick. Doctors prescribed that I drink raw eggs. Funny thing is - I have no idea who could have sent me this package. I have no family in Lviv. Only a few friends know of my illness... and I didn't think anybody knew I was here."

Then Zbyshek started to cry, just like I had when I got the linens from Mama.

He said, "I hope this package isn't a bad sign..."

Prison life had soured his gift. But what marveled us most was that his gut was spot on.

After breakfast, Zbyshek was summoned away for investigation. He'd insisted that he'd only been called once before, but from his stories, it seemed like this was his third. He still hadn't admitted anything about his arrest - for what, where, and when these Germans grabbed him or what they had asked him in questioning either. He always walked about the cell very hidden in himself, disclosing his affairs to no one, perhaps doing so because he didn't have full trust in us Ukrainians.

To Tato and I, it seemed like Zbyshek had been beaten and was afraid of that happening again. He limped the last time we'd left the chamber for fresh air, and when we had first seen him, his eyes were bruised and he had red goose egg on his head. We felt awful for Zbyshek, partly because we were all waiting for our own beatings too.

But with Zbyshek gone, we Ukrainians spoke bravely about the Underground. We didn't worry about talking in front of the Jehovah's Witness, because he wasn't interested in anything but the Bible.

Lunch then came and went. I tried holding onto Zbyshek's portion for him, but the guards didn't let me. They said and most likely lied that they'd bring it when he returns.

Then two hours past lunch, the chamber doors opened and Zbyshek couldn't even make it to his floor spot before immediately collapsing to the floor.

He was badly bruised and completely exhausted.

"How can I help?" I asked.

"... water."

The other prisoners lifted him off the stone floor and onto his coat. We dusted him off too. His grateful eyes, with bruises underneath, shined through us all. Tears rolled down his cheeks. He tried talking, but lacked the words.

Then Michael Wolf, gently at first, began to sing "I Look

to the Sky," Zbyshek's favorite. A verse in, Michael's voice transformed from whisper to a roar that filled the entire chamber!

And as if this wasn't miracle enough, a *female* voice flowed into through our chamber window.

Her incredibly-developed voice took over for Wolf, giving us a version of "I Look to the Sky" like we'd never heard before. *She's right above us!* This woman was a seasoned soloist whose words could be so crisply heard that it sounded like she was right outside our window.

Zbyshek was entranced. We all were. She went on:
A poor man died in a military hospital...
bidding a fervent farewell to a distant girl
desperate for his love...

When she trailed off, Wolf finished the final verses of "I Look to the Sky." Zbyshek drank water and listened attentively. He calmed down and lay in place until dinner. His lunch never came. He probably would have refused it anyway, for he refused dinner.

He then asked me, "Could you take out an egg, poke it twice, and pour it into my mouth?" I did so.

That egg was all he'd eaten that day.

Feeling his pain, I comforted him and he started to open up to me.

"He speaks more freely to you than the others. Sit close with him. Keep him company," Tato advised.

After sitting quietly with him for some time, I again asked him about his family and where it originated. This time he opened up.

"I was born in Warsaw. My family lives there now. I have no relatives here in Lviv," he said. "I'm a member of the Polish Underground, and they sent me to Galicia on organizational matters. The Germans arrested me here in Lviv. Apparently their agents had infiltrated our Underground."

So Zbyshek was fighting for the other side. Well, *another* side. There were so many pieces to this puzzle... but as his walls started to break down before me, I saw we weren't so different.

"I'm also convinced you Ukrainians aren't so bad. You've treated me like one of your own. Being stuck here in this prison with you, I've realized that my Polish leaders may have been wrong about your country. I'm also so fond of good singing, Michael, and your Easter prayer," he said.

I smiled. Our Ukrainian patriotism, friendship, compassion, and belief that we all could coexist together was influencing Zbyshek greatly.

"And how is it that your father comes from a village, but is still so well-read and educated of everything that goes on in the world? ... Speaking of books, have you ever read 'With Fire and Sword?'" he asked.

"No. I haven't seen it in our library," I replied.

"Yes, well, the Polish government banned its use before the war, because it sympathizes with the struggle of Ukrainian Kozaks against the Polish. If you see it, read it."

"I will."

"You Ukrainians once represented a great strength in this world. It's unfortunate that during that time we couldn't understand you, because we could have developed a nice friendship. Maybe we could have avoided all this," said Zbyshek.

I always felt that we Ukrainians were strong, but I never thought that anybody else felt that way. We weren't a world power or a strength or ever really in change of our own land even. But it was nice to hear kind words from Zbyshek, a Pole.

For the next three days, our Michael continued to entertain us with his singing. And every time he sang, the voice of the Polish lady-soloist soon followed. It was as if she spoke to Michael, telling Wolf that she would go on as long as he did too.

We prisoners listened contently, letting their voices cool our bitter, tied up situation.

Four days later, Tato was taken out our cell for another investigation. Up to this moment, I naively thought Tato and I would be released with no more questioning. I felt troubled.

I felt troubled and was scared for Tato. *Would they bring him back in the same state as Zbyshek?* All the other prisoners felt sorry for me and sympathized with me.

The prisoners tried cheering me up, saying that I shouldn't worry, that nothing bad would happen. I watched as the words left their mouths, but I could see that they were almost as worried about Tato as I was. I took no stock in their consolation but at the same time hoped that they were true.

Zbyshek, who still didn't feel any better, called me close to him and said, "Be patient, courageous, and most of all, pray that nothing bad will happen... but rightly be prepared for the worst."

His words brought me no comfort, and I became even more disgusted and sad.

I paced around the chamber and fervently prayed for Tato. And I prayed for myself too, because I was convinced that they'd take me right after him. It felt like hours.

Up until this time, it was easier for me here in prison because they had kept us in the same chamber, but my vivid thoughts of him being beaten burdened my heart. *Maybe it would be better if we didn't see each other after a beating...*

My worry grew stronger. *How long are they keeping you Tato?*

After some time I heard the door open, initially thinking that it was time for lunch. But I looked up and Tato was in the doorway with the guards. He walked in slowly, with no signs of being beaten.

But cutting off a chance at reunion, his escorting officer read my name. Tato quickly tried to tell me something, but the officers yelled at him and pushed him into the chamber.

Tato gave me a querulous look. He was trying to tell me something, but I couldn't deduce a thing and the officers shouted at him angrily and pushed him into the chamber. The guards immediately grabbed me by my hands and ripped me out from the chamber.

Tato, were you beaten?!

Just like the initial investigation, I was taken through iron gates and to another floor.

The guards led me into a room, closed the door, and I was alone. Heavy, iron bars sat in the window, and tram traffic trickled in-between them. In the middle of the room stood a heavy table and two chairs behind it. On the table lay a chain sheathed in some kind of animal hide.

Two doors from this room led to two adjoining rooms. I could hear screams, thrashing, cries, and muffled blows from behind them.

I then realized where I was - the room where they would question me and where they would beat me. Fear poured out of my body.

I tried comforting myself by telling myself that Tato was returned unharmed to the chamber. *Maybe they'll return me just the same...* I silently prayed "Our Father."

Our Father, Who art in Heaven, hallowed be Thy name;
Thy Kingdom come, Thy will be done on earth as it is in Heaven.
Give us this day our daily bread;
and forgive us our trespasses as we forgive those who trespass against us;
and lead us not into temptation, but deliver us from evil. Amen.

Please, God. Help me. Don't let them ask me about the shooting.. I stared at the two doors, wondering which one the investigators would walk through.

As if on cue, one door opened and two young men dressed in military uniforms walked in. I immediately noticed that they weren't the same investigators that had questioned me before. Both looked healthy and tall, like athletes, and they quickly walked over to the table and one guard pulled out an index card and read it silently to himself.

Up until now, I imagined the most brutal interrogations and prisoner abuses being held deep in dark, dreary basements, tunnels, or underground catacombs. *How bad could this get?* And the posture of these investigators didn't remind me of the sadist or alleged torturers like those described in the criminal novels I'd read.

And there's no chair, so you won't keep me long, right? But my reasoning was interrupted by the guard with the index card. He muttered something in German to his partner. Then he carefully laid his index card on the table and sat directly behind it.

The standing interrogator then asked, "Do you speak German?"

I answered "A little," thinking that they might choose a different language.

The guard then picked up that whip and admired it closely, as if he was looking at if for the first time. He walked towards me and in the same accent-broken Ukrainian as the other Germans said "We don't have much time to play with you, so you better tell us the whole truth, and quickly too. Then together we can all make it to lunch. But! If we see that you are lying," he continued, "you'll stay here oh so long that you'll be singing the truth. Now see this whip. Look good."

I looked down at it, the chain intertwined with leather.

"See its strength. And we surely know how to use it." He came even closer and slowly grazed the whip across my hands.

"Ok, good, now that we have that straight, approach the table and answer our questions," he said.

I hadn't even gotten to the questions and I'd already received a good lecture. It looked to me like I'd have to comply with everything they'd pin on me if I wanted to make this simple. Must have been the same with Tato.

The investigator behind the table opened up another notebook and began asking me questions about my life, like my name, birthday and birthplace, school in Lviv, and my arrest with Tato.

Both investigators seemed to have their defined roles. Questioner and enforcer.

The questioner confirmed my answers with the card and very deliberately turned the index card, pushing it to the side of the table. He then put his hands behind his head.

Slowly, he said, "Here it's written... that during the first investigation, you said that you did not know anything about the Ukrainian Underground acronyms. But here, in your notebook, you've written in three large letters, U... P... A... So tell us - what do they mean?"

I didn't consider this question long, carefully repeating the answer I'd given in the first interrogation about the Division Galicia soldiers on the train.

The investigator gave me a stern look and yelled at me, "What WE know is that ALL Ukrainians know the meaning of those acronyms and YOU just happen to be the only one who says something different, saying YOU don't know. So say it! Tell us that you know! Because otherwise, we'll... *enlighten* you with the answer."

I said nothing.

"Come now, come closer. Bend over the table nicely," he said.

I reluctantly crept closer. *If they beat me, at least it'll be in the name of the Underground and not for shooting the Germans.*

The enforcer grabbed my head and pressed my face into the table and started to beat my back with the whip.

At first, I handled it, groaning at each stroke, squirming from side to side.

But he kept going and going and going and would not stop. The pain overtook my mind's ability to cope. *I can't take it anymore!* I cried out in pain and pulled away from his grasp. The investigator leapt in step with me and and sent quick strikes ripping across my back. I could clearly outrun him, but the room was too small. There was nowhere to hide. The intensity of his whipping grew with his anger.

He hit my hands. He hit my back. And then he struck my head and that was the worst and I fell to the floor frightened and exhausted. I couldn't run any more. *Stop! No!*

He struck me twice more and then walked away.

The interrogator at the table said, "Get up. Come back to the table."

Full of fear, I arose. My legs were trembling and the thirst in my mouth was unendurable. *Water...* There was no saliva in my mouth, and I couldn't say a word.

Again, he asked, "What is the UPA?"

But my mouth was too dry to speak.

Seeing as I was deathly frightened, he then said, "These Ukrainian UPA bandits who call themselves the Ukrainian Insurgent Army! *They* attack our German villages, trains... raiding and stealing weapons... but worst of all is that *you* say these fools belong to Division Galicia, *our* army to fight the Muscovites!"

I then realized how silly my story was. They won't believe a word. This was now less of a sell and more of a fight of survival.

"We just heard from your father, that *he* knows what this abbreviation means. He really didn't explain any of this to you?!" he shouted.

I needed to make him think I wasn't interested. "I come from a small village. Only school and science mean anything to me. I study so I can live an easier life than my parents did. I swear to you. I put all my energy into being the best student I can be - I'm not interested in anything else," I somehow got out.

"Oh yes? Not interested in anything else? Then why do you have so many songs recorded in your notebook?" he pushed.

"I was trying to impress girls!" I blurted. "Our girls love the guys who can sing."

He didn't buy it and kept pushing and pushing and pushing. I kept repeating the same answers.

"Who is your OUN village rep? You've got OUN written in your little notebook too. You even said it was part of Division Galicia!"

"That's all I know! I heard it from some guys on the train!" *Believe me!*

"Your father is the leader of the OUN! *That's* why you don't want to admit anything," he kept berating.

"I don't know anything about it. I'm only interested in school," I said. With every push, it became harder and harder to lie. He was right. I thought of Tato and how strong he must have been during his questioning. He didn't look hurt at all. I needed to stay on track. I couldn't break.

"So why did your father talk at the tombs, and no one else?" he asked.

"The priest also spoke. And it was a religious celebration. Tato is a religious man!" I said.

After each subsequent question, I kept the same story and thought that maybe in that way I'd still prevail. But the investigator just got more and more infuriated. His face reddened, and he pulled a wooden table leg out from underneath the table, stormed up to me and maybe for the tenth time asked me what OUN means and who in the village is its guide.

I felt the worst coming. But I couldn't stop now. I held to my story: "I'm only interested in school."

"My patience is exhausted!" he said, "This is the last time I'm going to ask you! Who is your village OUN leader? The UPA leader? Maybe even the Bandera leader?!"

It was Tato. Of course it was Tato. But I answered him just like every other time and braced myself, "I'm not interested and I don't know and..."

Before I could finish, both interrogators lunged at me and attacked. One beat me with the whip. The other beat me with the wooden table leg. I had never been beaten before. I was a 17 year old boy. They were grown men.

I ripped myself away from them and tried to run throughout the room. But again, the room was too small and they cornered me, grabbed my arms, and beat me wherever they wanted. I cried out with whatever little energy I had left.

I was terrified. I weeped.

With my last ounce of strength I managed to get one arm free, and I covered my head and face.

But they kept beating me everywhere else. I had no strength to flee. I couldn't even move. I was a rag doll. I felt myself stop reacting to the strikes. The blows to my legs had sucked me dry. My last ounce of strength let up and my arm protecting my head dropped. As my arm fell from my face to the floor, the interrogator gave my head one final blow with the wooden table leg and I lost consciousness.

I don't know how long I was out.

As I opened my eyes I felt my entire head drenched in sweat. One of the investigators pulled me up and propped me up in a corner of the room that was spinning. My whole body shook. *Is this the end? Are you done with me? Are you going to keep beating me? ... Fine! Do it! It's all the same. Kill me here and now! Because I won't say a word!*

In the distance, the investigators spoke quietly to themselves. Maybe they were writing, arguing. I sat quietly in the corner, my head low, waiting for what they'd do with me next, trying not to move.

After some time they both left the room, leaving me on the floor. Across the room from behind the other door carried screams and sounds of a beating. *Is that what I sounded like?*

Slowly I began searching my body for pain. It wasn't hard to find. I lifted my arms and legs to make sure nothing was broken. Nothing was.

SEPARATION

My whole body was swollen, but the worst pain was in my head. I tried to sit still, because each adjustment was so painful. But no use. If there was any stillness, I couldn't find it.

Two guards who weren't the investigators came into the room and ordered me to stand.

But I couldn't. Every part of my body trembled. One of the guards came over and slowly helped me up. "Look - he's all wet," he said to the other.

They ordered me to follow them but with no urgency. *The investigation must be over. Thank God.* But we took a different path then before. *Where are you taking me? A new chamber? Away from Tato? No, anything but that.* When we stopped, they opened the cell and I saw that it was my old cell. I felt relief and walked in and the guards shut the door.

Tato ran over to me first. He noticed that I was completely soaked and began to grope me, asking me what hurts and whether anything was broken. My face was swollen. My head was covered in calluses. Everywhere Tato touched he found pain.

"Tato - don't worry. I didn't say a thing," I said, and then whispered, "I wasn't asked about the shooting."

"Well maybe our punishment won't be so bad after all," Tato replied.

"Help me," I said, and Tato calmly laid me down. "Tato, don't worry. Everything will be fine."

I didn't complain to him about the beating because he saw how bad it was. "Tato, were you beaten?" I asked.

"No, I was not," he said.

I think that might have been the first time that he'd ever

lied to me. But I didn't ask again and I no longer brought it up, because I saw no signs of him being beaten.

The interrogation had lasted through lunch, and just like Zbyshek, the Germans left me nothing to eat. Tato gave me a piece of bread, but I couldn't eat it and gave it back to him. I had no appetite. I asked Tato to give me water because my mouth was still quite dry.

After I laid for a bit, Zbyshek finally approached me and said, "I have three more raw eggs left and want to give them to you. I'm better now. I don't need them."

He felt terrible for Tato and me, partly because I was the youngest prisoner, but mostly because I got the worst beating of everyone.

I couldn't resist his offer and said, "Leave me just one. That's all I have room for. I'll drink it tomorrow. Finish the rest, Zbyshek. I won't need them."

That night I somehow fell asleep but woke up often and slept very little. Moving my body was so painful, but I had to keep switching sides because whatever side was against the stone floor quickly became unbearable to lay on.

That night, I escaped into thoughts of my carefree days, my family, especially Mama, school, and friends too. *I'll never see them again.* My hope was gone.

Tato didn't sleep much either. He suffered watching me squirm, as if my pain doubled his.

That night I sympathized with others who had been beaten, interrogated, mocked. I admired those who didn't break. But I also realized why some did - they couldn't bear the pain. Their minds wouldn't let them take it any longer.

Some may have been beaten even worse than I was.

I felt how easy it was to get to that point, where you're being tortured, slowly being dismantled without any notice of the end. That night, I realized that if any prisoner signed a confession, I wouldn't have been surprised or judgmental, even if it was a false one.

Mostly, I was just surprised that I *didn't* break. I told myself, *Let them beat me - I'll tell them nothing different.* But then concern flooded in. *Why didn't they force me to sign something? Would they call me again?*

That thought latched onto my mind, keeping me awake that night. I also thought of Zbyshek, who was interrogated three times and beaten at least twice. The anxiety and pain made this was the longest night of my life.

Slowly, the tiny window near our ceiling trickled from dark-blue night to rosy morning to white day. I said a prayer, thanking God for all I still had, most of all for letting me live.

Other prisoners awoke and approached my beat up body. They tried lifting my spirits, telling me that I was young, that I'd survive, that I shouldn't worry, and that we'd all come out of this alive and free.

Our professing roommate came up to me and encouraged me, saying, "God will help you. And I'm praying for you too." My beating seemed to give him strength to preach even more courageously. Then he went on about the end of the world and said we'd all be released from suffering soon.

"I had repeated visions last night. They told me that there

were only two more months of life left on Earth," he said. He so thoroughly spoke of this vision, so wisely too, that it was tough to challenge. None of us had enough religious education to somehow convince him that he was mistaken.

To add to that, this prison, this unknown tomorrow, this war... they were all good grounds to doubt life as it was. *Maybe this really is the end the world.*

I laid on the floor almost that entire day. Prisoners continued to walk in circles around the chamber, but they didn't walk as long and barely spoke to one another. Each one of them lamented their own fate. The three prisoners arrested with us wondered why Tato and I were called twice for interrogations and they hadn't been called once.

"If this 17 year old boy could be beaten like this, what will happen to me?" their faces said.

Michael Wolf didn't sing that day, but he did sit close by me to chat. "I imagine the war ending soon. I picture myself going to Italy. They raise the best of singers there," he said.

I wasn't sure if he was opening up about his true ambitions or if he was just trying to console me. But I liked the attention nonetheless.

That night I fell asleep to images of compassion from the other prisoners.

The next day I already felt much better. To minimize Tato's worry, I got up and slowly walked about the chamber. The prisoners poked fun at my turtle pace.

"We old men can't keep up!"

I smiled and looked to Zbyshek and said, "Thank you for the egg. Apparently it gave me quite the boost."

But with every passing movement, my attention drew a different blow from the interrogation. I could feel where the whip had struck my body and where the table leg struck my head. My head hurt the worst.

But that day we also got clean linens from home, which made me feel a little better. I thought of my family and was glad that none of them besides Tato knew about my beating.

Seeing these linens got me crying again. *At least my family is at home. Mama, my sister, my three brothers. You'll always remember us if something happens.*

Wolf perked up some too and sang "I Look to the Sky." He even won over the soloist upstairs, who sang a couple nice Polish songs as well. However, our weak hope for a quick dismissal departed and dwindled as every moment went by, mainly because fiery rockets again lit up the city sky that night. Anti-aircraft artillery pa-rat-a-tat-tat-ed at the aircrafts above. Guards still ran into their bunkers. We still stayed put.

Tato and I huddled close and tried to change the topic away from the bombs. "If we're called again, just say the same," Tato said. No one heard us talk over the ringing of the iron gates and Jehovah's Witness' belting prayer.

Then a bomb fell close to the prison and shook it to the point where I thought the whole thing would crumble. Tato whispered a prayer. So did the rest of us.

Throughout the night, the bombs fell further and further from the prison, in between them longer and longer waves of calm. The alarm again sounded and Tato and I both slept in our coats in case we'd have to flee. This was our measly, little bit of hope - maybe we'd get lucky and a stray bomb might pop open a wall and set us free.

A few mornings later, our chamber doors opened wide. Jehovah's Witness reported our numbers, as he'd kindly been doing since I was beaten. But this time along with the guards walked in a sergeant who looked around the chamber, pulled out a note and then read Tato's name and my name.

We gave each other surprised looks. *Where will they take us this time?* Other prisoners looked at us with disbelief, and they didn't know whether or not to say goodbye. They'd never called us together.

The sergeant looked suspiciously at me, then at Tato, and then ordered his men to take us both.

Maybe they were taking us in for a joint investigation? The guards told us to take all our things. So we grabbed our coats and we passed by Zbyshek and he whispered, "Germany." *Germany?*

He gave us a Polish "cholem" in parting. I wanted so badly to give meaningful goodbyes to all my friends who remained in the chamber, but the guard drove us out and told us to shut up. I wanted to tell my friends that if they were freed, not to tell my family about the beatings.

To our soloist Michael Wolf, I just waved my hand. It was all the thanks I could give for his singing and consolation.

Following the guards, we walked into a room and met several other prisoners. We were ordered to undress and go into the next room with a shower. Ten other prisoners were inside

This shower room was lit up, and only then did I see that

Tato's body was covered in bruises as well.

Surprised, I turned and said, "Why didn't you tell me that you were beaten? Where else could you have gotten all these?"

"You asked me whether or not the Germans beat me hard. And I answered - 'Not that hard' - remember?" he laughed. "And after I saw your soaked and swollen face I felt so horrible that I'd forgotten my own pain. All I cared about was you. I saw your head and immediately thought that they hit you with that table leg. I was so worried. I thought something really bad had happened to you."

I thought back to Tato's querulous look after his investigation - maybe it was a warning.

"I have the same hard head as you," I joked. "I'll be fine."

Tato rejoiced. Below the neck, he was equally as bruised as I was. We let off some steam by complaining about our beaten bodies and then looked at the others who were a sea of black and blue. None of them spoke to one another like Tato and I did. Maybe they were scared of the guards, who looked on through a glass peek-through in the door.

"You think we're being let go?" I asked Tato. "They told us to take our stuff. And they're making us wash up too."

"That would be nice," Tato said, "but why only the two of us? There must be another reason."

"When we were leaving the chamber, Zbyshek whispered to me 'Germany,'" I said.

Tato thought for a moment and said, "He may have guessed right."

Then I leaned over to Tato and said, "Tato, we're already half freed."

"I'm glad they kept us together. I couldn't do this without you," he said.

The water seized, and we were ordered to shake off and put our clothes back on. They put us into rows, and we were ordered to follow the guards into a bigger room which contained rows of shelving and on each shelf were bags.

Each prisoner was called and given a bag.

Tato and I were called last and the guard gave me a bag and said, "Check whether it's yours."

I opened the bag and saw all my things. *My pictures! And my student ID!*

The notebook wasn't there, but getting the rest of my things back led me to wonder whether or not we were really being transported to Germany or if maybe we were being freed. *Why would we get our things back if we were being taken to Germany? We must be getting released!*

Relief flooded my body.

Tato and I were the last remaining prisoners in the room. The others had been taken away. One guard remained. He told us to follow him. We did and I noticed that we were on the lowest floor of the prison and there was no where else to go but the prison yard.

Freedom! We're coming!

The guard pulled out his key as we approached the door, but then he stopped short and opened the last door right *before* the prison yard.

About twenty prisoners stood inside this room - prisoners just like Tato and me. Assuming nothing bad of it, we calmly walked in, and the guard locked the door behind us. We greeted them with a bow, but to my surprise, the prisoners started asking us questions like the Germans had during interrogation.

Cheekily and forcefully, they asked who we were, what our nationality was, what neighborhoods we hailed from, and why we were arrested. I assumed they were all Polish, because they all spoke it. It didn't seem like there were any Ukrainians among them, and if there were, they weren't speaking up.

Tato and I told them the truth, that we were Ukrainian and that we were arrested in our village because of the shooting of some Germans. They immediately became hostile.

"You bandits!"

"Ukrainian Nationalists!"

"You Bandera following Ukrainian pigs!"

None of them called us patriots, and they all sinisterly laughed at us.

"We'll quickly learn whether you mocked us Poles too. Ever pick a fight with a Pole?" the lead one said.

Another menace spoke up, "You won't survive the night."

The large group started to approach us.

At this moment, I thought of Zbyshek and his four-week stint among Ukrainian people and his regret that he had very little past understanding of us Ukrainians. None of us had threatened him. I even sympathized with him and was disgusted that he fell into the hands of the Germans and was a prisoner like us. *It would be nice to have you around now, Zbyshek.*

Examining these people, I saw that they were well dressed, talked amendable Polish, and seemed to know about all sorts of world affairs. They shouted to each other, something about Ukrainian partisanship killing Poles in Volhynia and in the Carpathian Mountains too.

One them jumped forward, chest to chest with Tato and threatened him: "You! All those Poles will be avenged... avenged upon you!"

Great fear surged through me. *What do we do? Lo and behold, this man is ready to hit Tato! There's way too many of them. Why doesn't anybody stand up for us?*

Tato also realized that this was no joke. He said, "Listen - we were arrested for shooting Germans. My son, who you see here - the Germans beat him well. And now you want to beat us too? Because you can? What kind of gang are you?"

This didn't look like it would end well. Tato was small, of strong structure... but the Pole was healthy and tall and primed to fight. He also had numbers.

Just then the door opened and the Germans added another prisoner. The enraged Poles briefly retreated from us, and when the guard closed and locked the door again, they shifted their attention to the new prisoner.

This man's head swiveled about the chamber as he was berated with questions. He assessed his situation and understood that he was about to be alienated.

He bravely straightened himself up, walked over next to us, and then asked the mob, in Polish, "Why is it necessary for you to know anything about me? Are you striving to help the Germans, those Germans who imprisoned us all? Or is this for your own curiosity? I already said everything that I needed to say to the Germans, and if you're interested in who I am, you can go ahead and ask them. They recorded everything."

I didn't expect such a response or such courage from this man. The Poles didn't either, because they backed off and left him in peace and departed to the side of the chamber to quietly talk amongst themselves.

Tato and I spoke to each other about what the Germans might want to do with us. *Why put us with such awful company?*

The brave man came closer and started talking to us in Ukrainian.

"Before they brought me to this room, the guard told me that everyone in here is bound for Germany. So we're all waiting for the Reich," he said.

The Poles overheard us and one disgustingly yelled, "You won't even make it to Krakow! We'll finish you on the road you Ukrainian bandits!"

I was comforted that we were three instead of two. We're harder to take out now.

And maybe some of you will hold back. Maybe there were a few cowards among you 'brave' men?

But there were just so many. There was no way to know. These prisoners were my first proof that danger didn't just come in the form of Germans. Other prisoners could be just as threatening. Maybe worse. *What happens when we get to Germany? IF we get to Germany... who will govern us there?*

The Ukrainian newcomer went on: "These Germans are seeking out us healthy prisoners, especially those with a profession, bringing us to military factories where we'll be forced to work as slaves under strict military supervision. I heard that these prisoners are being bullied, and that nobody is ever freed. I learned all this from a man who miraculously escaped from a camp... For now, it is our destiny to be deported and we'll see what our future holds. A long and dangerous road I'm sure."

More dangerous than Lontsky?

He paused to think for a moment and said, "It might be better than the Communist transports to Siberia."

I admired his knowledge and courage. This brave man's name was Ivan Soroka. He'd been in Lontsky for three weeks. His presence brought me some calm, however, not for long. Our Polish cell-mate had had enough silence and began to loudly berate us Ukrainians once again, complaining about some controversy in Volhynia where Ukrainians had set houses on fire in the middle of the night. Apparently Poles were disappearing without a trace.

This is when I realized that we weren't just fighting the Germans or fellow prisoners. This was a bigger beast. This wasn't just military force. This wasn't just a bunch of angry prisoners. This was much bigger. Bigger than any of us could understand.

Our Soroka tried explaining to the Poles that they might be disappearing because of Soviet Communists agents. "They're most likely afraid of you and your people, wanting to destroy you. And they don't just kill your Poles, but our Ukrainians too."

But his words didn't penetrate the hot heads of the agitated Polish prisoners. They complained defiantly and cursed the Ukrainian people for this reason and that. They wouldn't let up. Just then the guards opened our chamber door. We all perked up.

"Take all your things and follow us," said the guard from behind the door. The hallway was filled with waiting prisoners and more guards. The main door to the prison yard opened, and we were funneled out. Several tarp-covered trucks already stood waiting.

At that moment I hoped that Zbyshek wasn't right. That Soroka wasn't right. That the front would show. Anything. *Were we really going to Germany?*

The guards divided us prisoners into two groups in the Lontsky prison yard, each group going to a separate truck. We were ordered to sit on the floor. Four guards were posted in our truck, sitting by twos facing each other.

After everyone was loaded, two small cars accompanied us out of the prison yard, one lead and one caboose. The convoy immediately turned left, rode by Yezuyitsky Park, the post office, then made another left onto Smolsky Street, which housed the main office of the German Police Gestapo.

After a short stop at the Gestapo, we rode further down Kazymyrivka Street, driving by the main gate of Prison Brygidky, which I knew well. It's address was 20 Kazymyrivka Street, and my first apartment in Lviv was at 25.

Back when I was free, every day I'd scurry past this scary prison on my way to school. The other people of Lviv did the same, and most everyone walked on the opposite side of the street.

Germans locked up random people there whom they'd

catch getting off at the main railway station or on the Krakow Trading Market. Then they deported them to slave away in Germany. This street was always covered in traffic too, so much so that I couldn't sleep the first few nights after my move to Lviv. Streetcars didn't exist in our quiet village of Uherci.

My apartment was also close to Lviv's main theatre and the Hetman Entrenchment, a square in front of the theatre. It was lined with trees on all sides, with benches among them where the evening entertainment played for the young people of Lviv. I often met up with fellow students here.

The Gestapo mandated a civilian curfew of 11 for all gates and business around this square. Sometimes a friend and I would get caught outside past eleven and have to bother our lazy landlord to let us in to our building. His wife would always give me a crooked eye as I walked in.

I thought back to one particular evening - I was in my apartment doing homework - when I heard gun shots and a loud cry and then fleeing footsteps. Everyone in our building cried out in unison, and none of us wanted to go down to the gate to see what had happened.

Our landlord was also too scared to go down. His wife, full of tears and holding a frightened child, begged him not to go.

And I don't know why, but I said, "I'll go."

I lived with my aunt at the time, and she begged me not to. She didn't like the landlord and probably didn't mind if he was the one who went to check out what happened. I was 15 at the time.

"Well if you go first," the landlord said, "I'll follow you."

So we walked down the stairs into the entranceway of our building and came across a man lying limp in the middle of our cement entranceway. He was well dressed, looked 30 something, and fresh blood flowed down his back.

My God.

People hurried along the street, averting their eyes from what happened.

"Let's not move him. Don't move him," the landlord said, trembling. It was his duty to report any incidents to the local German police. But we didn't have a telephone in our building, so calling the German police was out of the question. He had to walk.

"Let's go together," he said, completely frightened. "I don't want to go alone." The streets were minute by minute becoming more and more deserted. Although I myself was about to sincerely suggest we go together, he was a step ahead, even adding, "Remember that I've often let you in past curfew. I'll gladly keep doing so if you go with me to the police."

So we went. I really, really didn't want to, because earlier that day Germans raided the Krakow market for workers to send off to Germany and I had just barely escaped. Armed guards blocked one entrance, funneling many young people into trucks at the other side. I somehow managed to hide on a side street, and then I climbed over a fence between two buildings and bolted. The captured were taken to Brigidky Prison. Some were released, if their family somehow had guessed that they were arrested.

My anxiety got the landlord and me to the Gestapo Police Station, and once again I don't know why but I did the talking. The landlord was silent. The on-duty policeman calmly listened to my story, and then he consulted his superior over the phone.

"Yes... got it... ok..."

He hung up and said, "What's your street address? And was he dressed in a German uniform?"

We gave him our address and said no, and then he said, "Alright, go back and lock up your building with the man inside. You sure he wasn't a German?"

"Yes," I said.

"We'll send someone to check in the morning," he said.

I was surprised that the German Police didn't care about this man. Must have been because he wasn't German.

"What if he's still alive?" I asked.

"Just don't move him," he said. "If he's still alive, he'll live until morning and then he'll get help." We said nothing.

On our way back, the landlord and I both wondered if we could help the man, but we knew of no nearby doctor.

When we got home, we checked to make sure no one else had gotten into our courtyard then locked the door and walked up to the shot-down man and saw that blood no longer flowed from his body. I put my hand on his neck and felt no beat. The landlord took his hand and listened for a pulse. Nothing. His body would stiffen and grow cold that night.

We went back to our rooms. The next day, a military transport came, and without questioning anybody, they took the body. That was that.

SEPARATION

My mind skipped forward to autumn 1943, when I moved away from the previously mentioned building, because it was too claustrophobic for six of us to live and eat and study all in one tiny apartment. My sister Maria, who started school that year, moved in with me onto Lviv's Children Street.

In front of our new apartment, there lay another square and about one hundred yards further was a former school that was occupied by a German military unit.

One morning, a few months later in February 1944, with Lviv covered in snow, I heard some shouts and clanks and shuffles. I approached our window and saw German guards burying two wooden poles, laying an iron rail across the top, and then hanging four ropes tied in loops.

Why are you up so early? What are you doing? I figured it was an exercise.

Our landlord had already gone to work, and the landlady, hearing all the noise in the yard, got scared and asked us to wait up a bit and not head off immediately to school. She was always so frightened of being home alone.

So my sister and I sat down at the table and studied our lectures, waiting for the hostess to calm down. But I couldn't keep my eyes on the books, and I looked through the window as one of the soldiers pulled a whistle from his pocket. He gave it a good blow to signal that everything was ready. A few other soldiers stood beside him and looked towards the school.

Suddenly, from the mouth of this abandoned school,

guards pushed four men towards what I then realized were gallows. My sister and the hostess caught a glimpse and the hostess immediately panicked and screamed "The Germans! Here in front of our house! They're gonna hang them!"

My sister and the landlady both sprung back out of sight. I kept watching. I'd heard of Germans sending messages like these.

All four prisoners had their hands tied behind their backs and their heads hung low. They looked exhausted and broken. When they got to the gallows, one of the guards tied handkerchiefs around each man's eyes.

Then two guards grabbed the first prisoner by his pits, dragged him to a loop, laid the loop around his neck and pulled it tight. They then stood him up onto a chair and gave the rope a tug. Another guard saw that everything was ready and gave the chair a big blow with his big boot. The prisoner dropped and hung by his neck and jerked about.

I was glad that my sister wasn't watching.

The guards didn't waste much time and nonchalantly hung the remaining three.

Usually, around this time, the streets were busy and filled with residents hurrying off to work and school. But no one dared to go outside, because like me, they were terrified of getting mixed up in this tragedy.

One guard pulled out a poster and nailed it to one of the pillars. Out my window, all I could read was "Achtung" (attention). The rest was too small to read. Our landlady sat and sobbed, and my sister decided to stay home with her that day.

SEPARATION

I felt so much pity for these hanging people.

Who are you? Do your families know? What happened to your relatives? What's that poster say?

But nobody approached the gallows, so I stuffed my curiosity and went out our building's back door and off to school.

At school, I explained why I was late and my friends advised me not to go read the German sign. They heard that the Germans actually lurked and waited for people to walk up and read the sign, because they believed that these were people of interest, maybe just the kind of people they were looking for. The rest of school went by as usual.

When I walked home that day, I made sure to steer clear of the gallows but accidentally maybe out of curiosity peeked up to see if someone familiar hung there. They were all strangers to me, and their faces looked like they'd been dyed with blackish blue ink.

The next day at school, I was still curious about the men, who still hung there, and a friend and I decided to make plans to skip class and take a trip to the poster.

We hesitated at first to tell our religion teacher, but upon hearing our plan, the priest told us to go ahead: "For the Ukrainian people... fight for their independence, defend her, and in desperate times, give up your life for her... but make sure you're careful. Don't draw any unnecessary suspicion to yourselves. If there are any names written, you each remember two of them. Some of our Underground boys might be hanging there. Do come back with their names."

The priest's words were encouraging, and we left school at

lunch, making sure to wear a mix of each other's clothes so that none of the neighbors would recognize us.

Just before we arrived at the gallows, which once again stood along the street named Lviv's Children, we snuck along a side route, pulled out our school books and pretended to passionately discuss them. We got to the square and looked up and saw that the hung men hung no longer. We walked over carefully.

The inscription was in German. We didn't see any names, but it read "Here hang men who plundered weapons, attacked German soldiers, and tried to steal a police car."

We walked back to the other side of the street and continued to "discuss books." Passersby paid us no attention and there were no German guards in sight. We were sad that we got no names and relieved that no one saw us. That evening, the landlady told us that a military truck arrived before dinner and took away the bodies, leaving the gallows as a warning.

Being lost in my flashbacks, I forgot for a moment that I had been arrested, but reality reminded me as we drove through the gate of the terrible Brygidky Prison. Brigidky was named after a saint, mocking our beliefs. I was terrified.

I overheard Tato telling a story to villagers back in Uherci about two Ukrainian boys, Bilas and Danylyshyn, two members of the Organization of Ukrainian Nationalists (OUN), who were ordered to steal money from a Polish bank that was located in the nearby town of Horodok.

This stolen money was supposed to go to Underground work. But they failed, getting caught by the Polish Police and were judged with a hanging, which took place in this very yard of Brygidky Prison.

Is this really where fate has led me?

I examined this yard to see if I'd see a familiar story. Maybe catch a glimpse of a firing squad wall. Or remnants of criminal gallows. But the tarp covering our truck hid most of our view. And I was sure I'd find out soon enough. Tato also tried peering into this monstrous prison, but he couldn't get a good look either.

Three prisoners were added to our truck, and we joined up with another convoy already formed in the yard of Brygidky. Our convoys started moving out.

The prison gate opened back up and we rolled onto Kazymyrivska Street. I crossed myself as we moved through the gate. *Thank God we weren't being investigated here.* I'd heard far worse stories about Brygidky than Lontsky.

But my relief was quickly drowned out, because I realized that we weren't staying in Lviv. Our convoy left the inner city walls and headed for the train station. Only then did I actually believe it:

We were going to Germany.

We drove west on Kazymyrivsky Street and turned down Horodots'ka. We passed St. George's Church, the temple up on the hill, and St. Elizabeth's as well.

As always, these streets were packed, many people hastily

hurrying somewhere for whatever reason. None of them were interested in us. Each had their own troubles, so they steered clear of the Germans as much as they could. I used to be one of those people, dodging Germans. But now I'm in here, ignored like the prisoners I used to ignore.

Our convoy stalled before we got to the station, because the streets were jam packed with people. We were ordered off the trucks and set into rows of three. Luckily, I was shoved into Tato. Trams raced down both sides of the street. Guards and officers shouted, trying to give and receive orders. I certainly couldn't count everyone, but it looked to me like there were about 60 of us.

Behind us the lead Pole who had interrogated and threatened us in the last cell at Lontsky bravely spoke to a guard in Polish. To my surprise, the guard took his name and address and promised him that he'd relay the news of his deportation.

What is going on here? Why are you helping him? And what does this mean for me? How connected is this Pole? I imagined him asking permission to finish us. I couldn't think of a reason why the guard would mind.

He also gave the guard an appointed password so that his family would know it was actually him relaying this message. Finally, he requested that he was transferred to the group with his five comrades who were arrested with him.

The guard calmly listened to every word, repeated it all and promised that he'd still transfer him today. *Are you Polish? Maybe a German born in Poland?*

The next minute I heard another guard speaking Polish to

another prisoner in the same friendly tone. As a Ukrainian, I started to feel very alone. *Are we sitting ducks? Is everyone in on this besides us?* The prisoner gave him some last names and the guard promised that he'd settle it amicably. *What is going on here?*

I overheard them saying that we were being taken to prison in Krakow, Poland, and that we'd continue on to work somewhere in Germany.

Fears, confirmed.

A few guards moved up to the front of our hike and pushed aside the passersby to make way. These guards corralled us into the main train checkpoint, where the chief conductor checked our documents and then passed us on to another set of troops. This checkpoint was quite familiar to me - for the past two years, I passed through it twice a week coming from Lviv to Uherci and back.

Guards pushed away more passengers and led us in rows to the same platform that I'd often waited on for a train home. On the wall, near the clock, I saw it was Friday, which was the same day and perhaps the exact same time that I'd normally stand here, waiting for a train home. That train stood waiting.

And until today, I never closely examined the train. The first car didn't have conventional windows, but tiny ones intertwined with skinny iron rods. One group of prisoners were separated and ordered into that first car, Tato and I among them.

We stepped into the train and walked down the narrow train corridor which was lined with tiny cabins on each side. At the end of the hall was a tall, healthy military officer, and beside him sat a leashed German-Shepherd, who barked and snarled at us, flaring its razor-sharp teeth.

Tato and I were pressed into a cabin, which was more likely built for one. We were forced to stand, leaning on each other and could see very little through the tiny, glassless window.

I stood, my eyes transfixed out the window. *Maybe I'd see my friends? I could tell them that Tato and I are headed to Germany. Then at least Mama would know.* But no such luck. No familiar faces of what little I could actually see.

And passengers weren't really walking by our car anyway. *There must be a guard I couldn't see,* I thought, trying to look down. *Nobody would risk getting close to him or us. Rightly so.* The car was quickly loaded and that other guard passed our room, jerking back his furious dog.

My mind began to panic. *By some small miracle, Mama knew we were in Lontsky. There's no way we'd be that lucky with us going to Germany, right?*

This seemed like the last thread of connection to home, the last link to Ukraine and to family. *What could I do?* Then it hit me.

A message! I could throw something out the window! There was no glass cover. Anyone, some curious person maybe... maybe they'd pick it up!

I furiously searched the documents and photos that the Germans had given back to me. No pencil. Tato didn't have anything either.

What do I do? The train's going to leave soon.

And then I remembered my pin stuck in the collar of my jacket. I grabbed it and told Tato my plan: pierce holes in my student ID and write a message to the family. My picture was on it too. Tato agreed.

As I started to poke out 'Taking us prisoner to Germany,' the train jolted forward. *Oh no!*

I started to panic but Tato calmed me down: "It'll be better to throw it out in Horodok anyway. It's closer to the village. Maybe someone will find it sooner and deliver it straight to Mama."

As the train pushed forward, I noticed that it stopped at the same stations it always stopped at, from the village called Cold Water and among them Mshania, with our fifth stop already being Horodok. I poked and poked and poked. The train delayed at Horodok a bit.

Maybe the Germans will set us free? Maybe they're taking us home! But I quickly shelved my naive thoughts and searched through our tiny window for a familiar soul. But because of the awkward window position and being scrunched up to Tato, I couldn't really see any faces. Our car was the first one linked up after the locomotive, and nobody other than prisoners had a reason to come up this far.

The only thing I could see was the road to the station that sat parallel to the railways. Squinting my eyes, looking at this group, I suddenly saw two girls from our village who also studied in Lviv.

One was our village precentor's daughter Anya Mayher and the other was the principal's daughter Anelya Kroupa, the same principal who'd initially led the Germans to our home. I was close friends with both.

I started shouting and yelling louder and louder, until that

German guard sprung to our cabin door and yelled, "Enough! Enough or my dog will show you what it's really like to squeal," he said.

Terrified of the dog, I stopped. The hissing steam of the locomotive wouldn't let my voice get far anyway. The whistle screamed, and the train slowly began to depart. My silly hope for being dropped off in Horodok evaporated.

But I continued to look for the girls and hoped that they'd walk closer. I wanted to see their faces again. To help us, yes, but to remind me of the village too.

As we rode across the road that led to our village, I threw my student permit out the window, hoping that the girls would find it, recognize me, and quickly inform our family.

I became very sad that I was so close and couldn't get in a word.

How's life at home?
How's our family?
Is Maria in school?

But my questions hovered unanswered. The train jerked forward, made a swooping turn and quickly disappeared into the countryside. We plowed west.

Through the tiny train window, my eyes soaked up the fields, forests, rivers, and parks... *Would it be the last time I see them?* I said my separate goodbyes to each and every one. They had never looked quite so near and dear to me.

Along the way, the train stopped at smaller stations, finally reaching the city of Przemyśl, Poland, which was officially my first time in the city and the furthest west I'd ever been. I wanted to see it so badly, but the tiny window gave me no opportunity to soak any of it in. *Who lives here? What do you look like? Do you live like us?*

We crossed the San River and quickly moved further west. The iron rails underneath the train click-clacked, almost as if they were trying to interrupt our progress. But they didn't. We kept going. *Could anything stop us from heading to Germany?*

CHAPTER SIX

KRAKOW

The sun sat in the afternoon sky as our train arrived at the main station of Krakow, the ancient capital of Noble Poland. Military guards stood on the platform and told us all to get out as they chased aside the sea of the civilian population.

Tato and I wondered why we stopped here in Krakow. *Why weren't we going any further? Maybe more interrogation?* The guards ordered us to stand in rows of three. We were counted, which was starting to become a common theme of our arrest.

After roll call, the guards escorted us to trucks with more armed guards waiting, and I overheard that we were being taken to jail located on Montelupich street. We hopped in, the trucks started moving, and I tried getting a good glimpse of Krakow, but I couldn't, because the trucks were sheltered with tarp, and I was ordered to sit near the driver's cabin. I thought back to the Polish prisoners' threats in Lviv, who told us that they'd finish us here in Krakow.

"How did those prisoners know we'd land in Krakow?" I asked Tato, surprised. He had no answer.

We arrived at the prison, were unloaded into the yard, and

again were put into rows and counted. The tough Ukrainian bull Ivan Soroka approached us and said, "We should try to stay together as long as we can. I ended up forced into a cabin with that Pole from Lviv... he didn't say a word to me," he complained.

Then we noticed the lead angry Pole pointing at us three and half-snarled something to the guard. We three Ukrainians waited to see what would happen. *Maybe he's a Polish leader? How else does everybody know him?*

"Looks like we'll be re-aquatinted with him soon," said Soroka.

Rows of prisoners were corralled into cells, with us three in the last group to be placed. The guard who spoke to the Pole about us walked over and smiled.

In Ukrainian, he asked us, "Why do they want to be holed up with you so badly?" *Ukrainian? A miracle!*

Coming closer to him, Tato replied, "We just met them in Lviv. We were locked up with them this morning and these people... we don't know them... they started harassing us as if we were some kind of Ukrainian mobsters. They told us that we wouldn't reach Germany alive and threatened to finish us here, in Krakow. We didn't even know we'd end up in this city."

The guard smiled at Tato's answer. He saw we were all worried.

"How many of you are there?" he asked.

"Ukrainians - us three," replied Soroka.

The guard then loudly spoke up, asking, "Who of you are Ukrainian?"

Four others walked up, and the guard told us seven to stand aside.

"You won't be dealing with them anymore," he said.

I was dumbfounded. *Why is he helping us? A German guard protecting us from Polish prisoners? Whose war is this?* I began to wonder if there really were any sides to this war or if it was just a farrago of lost souls trying to survive.

"Tomorrow, from Krakow, you'll voyage to Germany in two transports, and then in all sorts of directions. I'll have you seven Ukrainians put in the second transport, away from the Poles. Let's get you to another wing of the prison."

Who was this man? What was his rank?

But we couldn't ask him a thing. He wouldn't let us. This man could have been a Ukrainian-German folksperson... maybe he lived in Ukraine, giving him the lay of the local relationship between nationalities.

"Bring these prisoners to the other end of the prison to chamber number five," he said, passing back into German like he'd never uttered us a word. Tato, Soroka, and I were so happy that we were separated from those vicious prisoners. *Thank you unknown soldier.* I felt such gratitude.

But I still couldn't wrap my head around the fact that we were in jail because of the Germans AND had to protect ourselves against forces other than Germany - other prisoners and their colonial ideals of Ukraine. *And they themselves were arrested by the same Germans!*

We Ukrainians were led by a guard into a tiny chamber with no other prisoners inside.

"Accommodate yourselves on the floor tonight," the guard

said.

There were no beds. Windows neither. Only a toilet and sink. But to us, everything seemed luxurious compared to being holed up with those angry Poles.

We prisoners hadn't even gotten a chance to introduce ourselves before some kitchen workers showed and gave each of us a meager dipper full of porridge.

"Eat quickly. We have a whole prison to feed," one of the servers said.

After they left, no one else came to the chamber that evening.

Our group of prisoners that night felt as normal as we could locked up in this foreign land, with the welcoming news of separation from the angry Poles shifting our minds away from our anxious drive for immediate survival.

Since we Ukrainians were alone, we sincerely opened up about our arrests and about our families that we'd left behind. These prisoners felt most sorry for Tato and me, because we left Mama alone with four small children. It started to seem like everywhere Tato and I went, we had it the worst. At least we had each other. My mind went to the fight for freedom.

What's going on with the Ukrainian Insurgent Army? Are you growing? Still training? How quickly will you find yourselves helmet to helmet with the Red Army? Is there really help coming from the Western world? How long will Germany remain in power?

"The Germans still expect some new weaponry, some new hope for them to win this war," one prisoner said.

"However it turns out, it probably won't be good for our Ukrainian people, already exhausted in wars and foreign exploitation," said another.

"Our best hope is that the West knows Germany's dreams as well as Stalin's ugly theory of World Revolution and Internationalism," said Soroka. He spoke the most.

Soroka argued, "Because of this protracted struggle and this great sacrifice, Ukraine could actually gain its independence this time. But it must be more prepared than ever."

All the prisoners argued that building its own army was a necessity, and that army may well be the UPA.

After hearing everyone's thoughts and opinions, I realized that all of the arrested were part of the Ukrainian Underground. I had listened intently to their conversation and was proud that, even in prison, the Ukrainian people held strongly to their views. Such conscientious and loyal patriots! They may have lamented about their families, but maybe even more-so about the fate of the entire Ukrainian Nation.

Little by little, the chamber conversation quieted down. Then one prisoner added, "Thank you to the guard who put us in this chamber."

The lights in the prison automatically shut off, which sent me into reflection. *How different today was than the others.* We got some air outside, rode on trucks, passed through checkpoints, got packed into a train car with the tiny window, and then saved by a German guard from a potential fight for our lives with the angry Poles. I wondered what the other prisoners were thinking as they all quickly fell asleep.

Tato and I said a short prayer together, thanking God for all he's done for us. My last thought ended up being about the train - something about it had made me sluggish, and I felt a scratch at the back of my throat as it started to pulse. I paid it no real bother and dozed off.

As the eastern sun illuminated the western night, guards ordered us into a larger prison hall. Each of us were handed a small piece of bread and black coffee and then immediately ordered to the yard and counted. We boarded the trucks again, which took us back to the train station.

But when we got there, something was horribly different - the commuter train we arrived on was replaced by a freighter. It looked to be completely empty and there definitely wasn't enough of us to fill the whole thing. *Maybe we're picking up more prisoners?* Armed soldiers were posted up around the train with their angry dogs. Prisoners were separated into groups and each group was confined into their respective car. Exhaustion thickened the prisoners' faces. They were all sorts of ages but none as young as me. I walked into my car.

Four guards were assigned to our car and sat lined up against one wall. The forbade us to speak, probably because they didn't understand our language and feared revolt. Fear seemed to drive these Germans. *What else was this war about but fear?*

After some time, the train was fully loaded. I looked around and saw that some prisoners looked recently shaved and tan, like they'd just been arrested. *Where did they steal you from?* I really wanted to learn about their arrest.

Right before my curiosity peaked enough to open my

mouth, one prisoner start to talk quietly to his neighbor. Two guards immediately pounced on them both without warning, jabbing the blunt ends of their guns into their chests, arms and sides. Tato and I sprang back, trying to get up against the wagon wall, but every prisoner was trying simultaneously to do the same, and we all squished together. As the beating slowed, I suppressed my curiosity to talk to others.

After they were done, one guard returned to his seat but caught his foot on a prisoner sitting beside me. Without looking back, he retaliated by kicking the prisoner and the prisoner cried out. The guard whipped around, mistook me for the prisoner, and cracked my head with the edge of his lantern, slicing me open right above my eye. Pain shot through my head.

My eye immediately swelled, and I was instantly reminded of the table leg to my face in Lonstky. Blood flowed down my face, but I had nothing to stop the bleeding with. Tato pressed my finger on the wound until it stopped bleeding.

It wasn't even me! What do I do? Nothing. I couldn't. But in not retaliating, in *not* sticking up for my life, I was elongating it. I couldn't bring attention to myself. I didn't want to get picked on. So I suppressed some anger as well.

The locks of our wagon clicked shut, trapping us inside. The cars were eerily dark, and the only lights came from the guard's lanterns. The train slowly creeped up the tracks. All prisoners were silent, brooding about their fate.

I tried forgetting about being hit in the head with a lantern by thinking of the previous evening's precious moments, simply listening to our Ukrainian friends. One had mentioned that back home he was a teacher, and he taught the students about the war and about Ukraine's fight with foreign nations - the Russians, Poles, and Germans. He told them that these fights made the Ukrainian people suffer.

But at the end of his lecture, one of his students went to the Germans, reported him for treason, and the Germans swooped in and arrested him. In his interrogations, they forced him to admit his Underground work by beating him.

But the Germans couldn't pull a word out of him, so they punished him with work in Germany. His only true happiness now laid in the fact that he was a single man, independent, and didn't have to worry about family as did other prisoners.

But he couldn't sit still. He had elderly parents, and he was their only son.

"They're really conscious Ukrainians. They sold most of their land so that I could get a high school education. They wanted me to find knowledge, so that maybe my life could be a little better than theirs.

"But then they became weak and sick and the front's heading their way and I'm on my way to Germany. I've tried so hard to think of a plan of escape, maybe from this transport even," he said. But he was kidding himself if he thought he could get away from all these armed Germans and snarling German-Shepherds.

My thoughts were interrupted by a stop at a noisy station. Many people passed, talking loudly to each other in a Polish dialect I wasn't used to hearing from the Poles back home.

Every sentence, even more frequently maybe, these Poles repeated the word "thunder" or "let this thunder crash." In school, we were taught that this saying was used heavily in Śląsk, Poland. But our train cars didn't open here so we couldn't find out if that's where we were.

When the traffic outside ceased, we moved onward. Sometimes we rode fast. Sometimes we stalled. I had no idea why we did that, because all the doors along the wagon walls were locked shut so we couldn't see a thing. I quickly found myself in boredom.

To interrupt the monotony of travel, I began counting each iron rail we'd skip over, up to a few hundred.

Then our train completely stopped. It was eerily quiet outside, with no sounds besides the door locks. Our door slid open, and great plains appeared before us. Besides the guards, there wasn't a living soul.

We were ordered to exit and "purify" ourselves behind some nearby bushes. Tato pointed out the blood stains on my clothes, spit on his finger, and used it to wipe clean the blood caked on my neck. My eye was still swollen, but at least I could see.

Are we on German soil? I surveyed the seeded fields and thought about Spring back in Ukraine. *Was it blossoming? Were the nightingales singing their sweet, sweet song?* Buildings much larger than any I'd seen in Ukraine sat in the distance. *How did they get so big? What are they made of?*

After emptying, the Germans made sure to accurately count us, and we were again back in the same dark cars. As we sat down, I watched the guards slurp up their canned preserves like monsters. In between mouthfuls, they told us to sit quietly on the floor and wait for the train to keep moving. I

SEPARATION

was hungry.

CHAPTER SEVEN

AWFUL BRESLAU

So our train poked out of Krakow, stopping periodically, finally ending up surrounded by the sounds of a bustling city. German language carried in from every direction, and the train doors opened once again.

I read an inscription on a nearby column: The City of Breslau (now called Wroclaw). Armed guards again circled our train, shoving civilians away to make room for us prisoners. They unloaded and separated us into smaller groups. Then we got into trucks, and they drove us through the city. These trucks were tarp-covered, but I could still see people walking amongst buildings not yet damaged by war.

These trucks drove us into a prison yard lined with tall, brick walls, and we flooded out the trucks.

Tato grabbed my hand to make sure we wouldn't get separated amongst the confusion. A guard tried to part us, but he saw us holding hands and dismissed us into the same group. Soroka was left behind. We felt bad for him but figured we could somehow meet back up later. Unfortunately, this was not the case - we'd never see our brave friend again.

SEPARATION

We prisoners led into a larger room, which was filled with the thick smell of potatoes. Guards funneled us into lines and we were each handed one plain, cooked potato. I was starving, so I hoped to catch the biggest one, but my hope quickly died when I ended up with what might have been the smallest. Tato desperately tried switching with me, because his was a bit bigger, but I replied, "No. Not in front of everyone. Next time, I'll get the big one."

They then funneled us down a dark stairwell that led to a long, uneven basement bypass. With each step down, commotion grew up from below. My eyes adjusted, and I saw that *now* we were in a prison like I'd read about in criminal books. The walls and ceiling were dirt, dugout from the Earth and clay and left uncovered. My throat choked on the wet air of human stench. My nose and eyes burned.

And then I saw the prisoners.

They were bald and limply lying practically on top of each other - there couldn't have been room for another. But the guards disregarded that, squeezing in more of us among them. Each prisoner stayed silent, even though they were getting crushed and pressed, because the guard's clubs answered every raised word. Some prisoners from our group settled on the cement floor, but Tato and I were ordered to stay standing.

A door opened in front of us and guards led us remaining prisoners deeper into this prison out of a criminal novel. Dim lights overhead shined just enough to show us how awful this second section of the prison was. There was no cement floor in this chamber, just mucky, dug out shlop. And even at my height of 5'2", I wasn't able to stand upright.

"Sit!" said the guard. "For the night!"

And down here in this cave prison with no blankets or straw to lay on, I saw how quickly prisoners transformed from people to predatory animals. Each of them hoarded their space and more, pushing weaker prisoners away, forcing them into cocoons too tiny for comfort.

They fought as if this was where they'd live out the rest of their lives. *Is there where I'll live out mine?* Tato and I somehow settled against a mud wall in the mud floor of this catacomb-like cellar. *Please God. Please get us out of here soon.*

After some time, all the prisoners settled down, while guards in twos walked along the edge of the prisoners. This walkway had a higher ceiling than the rest of the cellar, allowing the guards the freedom of moving completely upright. The sound of heavy boots carried in from the upper room, which had the luxury of a floor.

There's no way I'm sleeping tonight. Humid, barely breathable, the damp Earth beneath me, the awful smell of rotting people...

Fear and hopelessness flooded through me. Tato prayed and tried lifting up my spirit, like he always did, pleading with me, "Please, don't lose hope. Maybe we can still survive this all."

When bed time came, the guards didn't turn off the dim lights. But they were bright enough so that I could still see people and the dirt walls.

And as I finally curled up into a half-bent seated position, with eyes that wouldn't shut, I felt something climb across my face and immediately smashed it and it squished.

Blood stained my hand.

Another something fell onto my head. I actually *heard* it hit my face. As it slowly crawled up my head, a third and a fourth fell on me too.

What is that?

I looked about, admiring the many prisoners that had actually fallen asleep. *How can you sleep down here?* Their snoring carried throughout the cramped space and guards laughed, one saying, "Quite the symphony!"

Then I heard a prisoner smack himself on the head, and another in Polish grunted, "So many bugs!"

Another bug landed on my head. A few others on my arms and legs. They were like giant lice, but with legs like a centipede, and slimy. They needed warmth, and they burrowed their way into my armpits and between my legs.

In Uherci, I encountered lice and nits and fleas, especially now during times of war with soap being a limited luxury... they burrowed into clothes and couldn't be washed out. But this was different. This was torture.

It looked to me like these bugs were rooted up above us in hundreds of nests. And they kept falling on our bare hands and feet, their reflections glistening as they searched like locusts for comfort.

Tato and I went to war with them all night. Throughout the night, many prisoners sprung up and shouted:

"Something's biting me!"

Some lay exhausted, letting these bugs the freedom to roam to their slimy satisfaction.

It was so uncomfortable that the guards didn't beat anyone for yelling out.

I waited all night with impatience for the first sign of dawn.

"Maybe we'll get taken out of here soon," I said to Tato.

"Maybe the Germans brought us down here to get devoured by these bugs," Tato joked. "Either way, this is no place for us."

I agreed. A few hours went by and they day must have come and pinked over because the guards yelled at us, ripping us out of our places and up from the moist floor. *Movement!* I hadn't slept, so another night of this and I wouldn't have slept for two. *Get us out of here!* I wanted nothing more to do with these bugs.

Walking towards the top level, I glanced at the prisoners who laid on cement the previous night, their eyes piercing mine with depression and desperation. This image of miserable prisoners gave me the shivers.

Or maybe it was a lack of sleep or the stuffy air or fear... either way I felt sick. I started coughing. To add to that, I had been sliced open by a lantern and dragged through an interrogation room, which at this point I couldn't fully remember the happenings of.

From the basement we were brought back into the kitchen, and we were again put into rows and each given a scoop of some hot soup, which we chugged down within a step or two of the kettle. No words could describe how us starving prisoners ravaged these bowls, leaving no trace of food behind.

SEPARATION

After eating, we were shoved out into the prison yard, counted, and ordered into the trucks.

Tato and I held hands the entire time, so that no one could separate us. Although completely spent, we rejoiced that we were being taken out of this prison and thankful that it was just for a night. After the rest of the prisoners were chased into the trucks, we were taken back to the freight trains.

After a short ride, we hopped out the trucks at the station and were organized into rows of five. I stood first in our five, with Tato right behind me. *We'll never get separated. We can do this together. We can survive if we have each other.*

Around this train looked to be the most prisoners I'd seen in one place so far, so many that I couldn't count them all. Hundreds. Guards ran around, trying to keep the civilians at bay, and in this confusion, prisoners hurriedly and courageously got acquainted with each other.

Most complained about the prison we'd just left.

"I heard the guards say we weren't even supposed to stay there last night," one said. "Allied planes bombed our rail line, so the Germans had to fix it."

"I hear we're being taken to a concentration camp called Gross-Rosen," said another.

This was the first time I'd ever heard the name Gross-Rosen. I repeated it to Tato.

"I haven't heard of it either," he said.

We'd learn soon enough.

The freight train moved on. The only thing different with

this train was we were given a collective tin container to wash in if need be. This was a sign that our ride would be longer than the last. This train was also in no hurry. But I wasn't sure how to feel about that. *What was worse? Sitting cramped on a train floor or wherever we were going in Germany?*

Suddenly, the train paused and from outside we heard sirens similar to those I heard when the bombers flew over the city of Lviv.

These sirens wailed in threes. Guards got on high alert and once more we were strictly ordered not to speak to one another. They also forbade any of us to stand or empty ourselves in the container. Guards as scared of the prisoners as a raid.

"Whoever doesn't listen will be shot immediately!"

For whatever reason I wasn't scared. Maybe I was used to bombing because of my time in Lviv. At least now we were a moving target.

But we never heard any planes and the siren wailed once more, letting us know that the danger was gone and we could move on. We poked along but halted again. I heard screams from outside the train.

"Sit still! Don't move!" threatened a guard.

In my head, I started talking to the bombs. *Go ahead, fall. Land on these Germans, and let us go. And if they do fall on me? ... Well actually, it's good that these bombs fall in Germany. Maybe it'll end the war soon. And you know what? Death doesn't seem bad. And it doesn't seem too distant either... but being a cripple with my leg or arm blown off?* I still feared that.

The guards were wide eyed and wary. Time passed and

prisoners raised their hands to go to the can but were strictly forbidden. One of the guards stood up with his whip, walked over to the prisoners, and waited to whip the next person who asked.

The train hadn't moved yet, and the sirens weren't wailing, but the guards were called outside. The breathe of fresh air that swirled into the train behind them was nice but short lived, for they closed the cars right back up.

Only through tiny cracks in the freight's hull could we see small rays of daylight, which helped everyone see each other's sleep-deprived faces. It also helped us see what a sight we were - lying, stacked rather, malnourished, in all sorts of disordered shapes and poses on the floor of this freight car.

From outside, the guards ordered everyone to get to the barrel and empty themselves before the next stop. This was probably why the guards left the cars - the stuffy smell of everyone's shit swelled my nostrils and my eyes.

And each prisoner was frozen scared - either afraid to burst or cut in line or afraid to make the wrong move, holding in whatever horrid things needed to come out. Fear came in many different forms, and in the end, it felt unescapable.

These proud German guards! Apparently too disgusted to look at us doing what every human does. It seemed to me that the guards performed their duties to Germany as a penalty, like prisoners, or through guilt, rather than actually wanting to do any of this. Probably why they took out their frustration on us.

After each prisoner finished his duty, we had a moment alone without the guards. A strange silence settled in the car. Each prisoner tried to get down as he could on the uneven wooden floor of the wagon. Although there was no one to discipline us, for whatever reason, we all stayed silent. We each worried and waited for the next unknown trouble following this most current hell.

A few moments later, the door opened, the guards stepped back in. The steam engine's horn sounded once, twice, thrice, and in short time the train developed such a speed that I thought not even a bomb could stop it.

But after some time, its speed indeed decreased. The space between the clicks and clacks of the wheels on the track increased, like the train was frustrated, yearning to creep forward but lacking the force. One more push and one more click came and then a gradual hiss of the steam engine blew out, followed by a minute of silence.

There was movement outside the train as guards popped free the iron locks. The doors opened and they appeared in the doorway more furious than ever, yelling, "Get out of the car! Get out of the car!"

Here and there I could hear the guards hitting prisoners and the prisoners moaned, especially the elders, who couldn't jump off these high railway carriages without ladders.

Coming out of the stenchy box I saw that we stopped just short of a town. There was a sign next to a road with an arrow and a barely-readable inscription - "Gross-Rosen" - which was the same name I'd heard from the prisoner that morning.

Apparently, my first concentration camp was near.

CHAPTER EIGHT

GROSS-ROSEN :: OUR FIRST CAMP

As the rest of the prisoners flooded out the traincars, the chief German commander stood at the front of the train, ordering us into rows of five. "Prepare to march!" *We must be close.*

I took notice of the civilians. They didn't pay us any attention, as if hoards of prisoners were a daily condition.

Guards with their snarling dogs again checked the trains for stragglers. *Where did all these prisoners come from?* There must have been hundreds.

I had clues of when they were arrested, because some of them were still dressed in their winter coats and warm ramskin hats, others only in a thin shirt and trousers. Some had bundles of things, probably care packages from their families. Some were well dressed, wearing factory made clothes. Others looked like beggars, wearing homemade clothes of all the same dull gray color. What we had in common was a lack of life - this fifth year of war dragged us down.

Talking amongst prisoners was once again prohibited, but those that broke the rule came from all over - I heard Polish,

Czech, Russian, German, Ukrainian, and even some languages I didn't understand.

"March!" the lead officer commanded, and we started moving forward uphill. The secondary officers repeated his command.

Tato and I made sure to stay together, marching in the same five-person row. I was one of the prisoners dressed for winter, with a warm overcoat and long, heavy boots. This had been an incredible advantage in both the prison and on the road, especially during cold nights spent on cold floors. The coat was so thick that it sometimes even softened a forceful blow from a guard.

But today? No such luck. The red hot sun burned mercilessly. No wind blew. Underneath us lay jabby, recently poured white stones, which for some reason made my legs sink heavier, making my malnourished body work even harder. I started sweating. And that cold I got back in prison certainly wasn't helping.

Some of the prisoners tried taking off their coats, but the guards, for whatever reason, banned them from doing so. A few brave prisoners - or perhaps they just didn't understand German - took them off, and they were promptly dragged to the side of the formation and beaten hard.

Tato and I were somewhat in the middle of the formation. "Gently... unhook your coat," he said.

I did, slowly, but it didn't help much. I started coughing. My throat was a desert. I was miserable. So I started cheering myself on. *The camp is close. I'm sure it's close. Just keep moving. Fight, Stephen.*

SEPARATION

I turned to my left and caught sight of a vast valley. It was covered in color. An assortment of flowers, endless fields of grass and tall trees stood serene, complete in their springtime glory.

Even the birds are happy! They swirled about, flying in formations much more natural than ours. All nature rejoiced in its exuberant bloom. I wanted to rid myself of this ball and chain and fly with the birds, to marvel in nature's magic and admire its mysterious ways of developing.

So I guess I did get to see Spring, but it wasn't the same. *What am I doing here with this terrible company, with these overgrown, unclipped, unwashed men who are petrified, unconsciously following the orders of these guards?!*

I looked at Tato. He seemed to me the only exception, walking beside me with a bowed head and a meditative look.

Then, I turned to the right and was stunned. I couldn't believe my eyes. There lay shiny, stony clearings and among them hoards of men in striped garments. They were ants, first bustling in one direction, and then the other.

A poem written by our Ukrainian poet Ivan Franko came to mind.

"The masons beat their rocks,
while transfixed to an iron chain."

And these prisoners before me were transfixed by their German custodians. The Third Reich imprisoned these bones to break stones.

"For a new Europe!" I'm sure they'd say.

But indeed it was just for the good of tyrannical German leadership.

Terrifying thoughts swarmed my mind. *How many convoys like ours passed down this road? How many parents have been ripped away from their now orphaned children? How many people bid farewell to their world only to unwillingly trade it in for this hell?*

I watched as two prisoners carried a big white stone on a stretcher, their rubber knees bowing outwards under the pressure. Behind them, another prisoner walked and supervised.

A prisoner supervising?

Suddenly, the prisoner holding the front of the stretcher fell forward face first on the ground. The stone rolled down onto the fallen man's legs.

The supervising prisoner behind them jumped up and passionately struck the fallen man and yelled at him:

"Get up! Carry it further!"

But the fallen prisoner didn't budge. The supervisor yelled and yelled and then ordered a replacement and told the two to carry the stone further.

I was surprised to see that a prisoner could give orders to another prisoner.

The prisoner crushed by the stone was left lying. The German guards escorting our formation saw all this and ordered, "Look straight ahead! Move faster!"

Such a scene proved to me that locked up life could still get worse.

Step by step, slowly, wearily, we got over the hill and I saw that before us lay maybe the worst site I'd ever seen. Rolls of barbed wire intermixed with other taught wires created a wall about four meters high, which surrounded, without a break, what could only be the concentration camp known as Gross-Rosen.

Armed guards stood perched on elevated platforms, and they kept prisoners from getting near the constructed wire obstacles. All these images made me even weaker.

To add to that, the sun seemed to inch closer to the back of my neck. My hips could barely pull my feet forward, and looking over at Tato, he was in similar shape, shocked and weary.

I couldn't stand the silence. "Tato. This is where we both find our end," I said.

He didn't say a word. He couldn't. He was exhausted, and perhaps he blamed himself for all this: *"Why did I let my son get arrested? Why are we going into this together? This should just be my imminent death. Not ours to share. I want this alone."*

He stared at me and suffered. After a long moment, he said, "Son, I'm praying to Almighty God that you leave this camp alive, because for me? It's all the same. Let God's will happen to me."

The reality of camp had struck us both.

"Do you have enough strength left to walk down this hill?" he asked.

"I must," I replied. "And look, it's not too far."

But he was right to ask. I was shivering, maybe even sparking a fever, and to add to that, my winter coat was an oven. Tato and I walked the rest of the way to the front gate in silence. What else was there to say?

As we walked up to Gross-Rosen, guards at the gates prodded us with sticks, ordering, "Faster! Faster!" We were cattle.

Tato and I somehow luckily dodged these prods and our formation stopped in front of a long wooden barrack. Only now did they let us remove our coats.

I immediately ripped off my jacket and undercoat, which had a waterproof cotton-wool lining, a fabric that kept me in persistent sweat. Tato did the same. He was completely cooked. My clothes were soaked through.

I watched other prisoners ring out their shirts, and I twisted mine out as well. After a good five minutes, I came to and began to feel much better. I pulled my shirt back on, laid out my coat and jacket for the sun to dry them out, and rejoiced. Tato looked happy as well.

"I'm a hundred percent better," he said. His positivity was back. Good sign.

We both took a closer look at this camp. In front of us sat a table with three prisoners dressed in blue and white striped clothing. To my surprise, the German personnel who brought us into this camp immediately walked back outside the barbed gates and away from camp. They explained nothing else. *Where were they going?*

The three prisoners at the table began calling up each prisoner who arrived with us. *They must be re-registering all of us new prisoners.*

The lined poked forward. Because they lined us up right in front of the first barrack, we weren't able to see any other camp buildings just yet.

But we could see a somewhat leveled-out slab of land where four men carried two pots filled with what must be lunch. My stomach grumbled.

Another prisoner propped the lid open with a beautifully-carved wooden and out-of-place-at-a-concentration-camp stick. Steamy vapor plumed out. A sixth prisoner then gave the sign to the others to approach.

Two rows of prisoners ran to the pots and more followed until the clearing was filled with blue and white stripes. Each prisoner had a bowl tied to their belt.

The prisoner with the stick divvied rations, and his assistant separated those who'd received from those who hadn't so that they didn't get seconds. Every prisoner was near bald, and many of them had a two centimeter strip of hair stretching from their foreheads to back of their necks, like the beginning stages of a mohawk.

Each rationed prisoner carefully walked away, as not to spill a drop. *That will soon be me. Standing in line. Begging for food.*

Suddenly a cry erupted from around the kettle and, armed with a wooden stick, the on-duty prisoner began to beat another prisoner, ripping into his shoulders and back, chasing him to the group of prisoners who'd already eaten their portion.

Why would someone be beaten for such a small thing? It's just a scoop of soup. Did this poor man try lining up again for the same meal? How could anybody tell? Everybody looked the same. Or maybe this on-duty prisoner had a grudge to settle against this man?

What an awful scene. *How was is possible for one prisoner to beat another with such malice?* I couldn't comprehend it.

However, this wasn't even close to the ultimate frustration I'd experienced that day. This was the most painful and unforgettable day of my entire life. Its image is so deeply implanted in my memory that I often wake at night and relive the entire thing.

Our rows poked forward. In front of us, the scribes continued developing their registry of prisoners. *How are these scribes not German, but prisoners, like us?* They wore nicer dress than the others, washed clean and made of better material. Coming closer, I heard German, Polish, Russian, Czech... Everyone was being asked their basic info like name, date and origin of birth, occupation, as well as their nationality.

Our turn came, and Tato stepped up first. To this day I cannot forgive myself for not going first. Why didn't I go first?

Tato answered all their questions in his native Ukrainian tongue without obstacle. These scribes understood Ukrainian well. Finally, he was asked his nationality.

Tato answered calmly and quietly, "Ukrainian."

One of the scribes responded in Czech, "There's no such nationality. You're either Polish or Russian. Pick one."

Pick one?

"I've been Ukrainian for forty-two years and today, I don't think that will change," Tato said, still calm.

Two of the three scribes then stood up tall from behind the registering table and one grabbed a rubber tube.

One cried out in Polish, and the other in Russian, "Choose!"

Would these prisoners really beat Tato? What happens when Tato again says that he's Ukrainian? And I knew he would. *How will they react? Maybe they're just scaring him.*

The scribes pressed closer to Tato, again crying out, "Polish!"

"Russian!"

How could he choose? Ukraine's spent centuries enslaved under both!

Tato, now visually agitated, confirmed his prior response. "I was born a Ukrainian... and forever will remain one."

Both these clerks ceased questioning and with such force attacked the heat-exhausted, starved, and weary Tato. They beat him with the rubber whip wherever they could, just steps in front of me, my eyes engulfing it all. I could touch them.

Up until this point in his life, Tato had never admitted to being hit by anyone else. But he couldn't hide this one from me. My heart shattered. My eyes, with every blow, filled with tears. And worst of all? I stood there as if my feet were buried in the ground. All I could do was weep.

Tato was my guide. Tato was my father. He was my friend. What he lacked in height he made up in strength, cheer, humor, and wisdom. He loved our family. He gave us all that he had.

But all I could do was look on terrified, powerless, unable to offer a thing. Under these blows from the rubber whip, Tato bent over, covering himself with his hands, trying to soften this beating in any way he could. *How long could he keep this up? How long would he hold out?*

And just like that, they stopped. *Thank God. It's over.*

The interrogating scribe again asked Tato for his nationality.

Tato, bent over and winded, looked up and said, "I was

born a Ukrainian. I still am a Ukrainian. I cannot tell a lie. I don't know how."

Without any further deliberation, both these same officers attacked the defenseless Tato, and this time, with such speed, such power, such fury, like lightening they tossed Tato to the ground and kicked him with their big boots over and over and over again.

They struck his chest, his belly, and his head so hard that I couldn't hold back any longer and with a cry of despair, covered in tears like a child, I jumped up to these brigands and

all I did was stand. I trembled. I wanted to tell them to stop, but my voice never left my throat. What came out was a vague mumble. *Why can't I speak?! Stop hitting him! Stop!*

The officers saw my frightened look and crying and immediately stopped beating Tato. These investigators looked at me like I was crazy.

They ordered the other prisoner to lift Tato, who at that point was lifeless on the ground, and these prisoners put him back up to the table. None of the other prisoners responded to this beating. Each was stuck in their own selfish thoughts.

Is it over?!

The clerks at the table laughed at him. They each spoke to him in a different language, saying, "And now show us what a great patriot you are. Do you still want to remain a Ukrainian? Or maybe you'd like to be someone else? Don't be bashful."

Tato didn't answer. His lips were swollen like plums, and he trembled from pain and anger. Tato's silence caught the interrogators off guard, and after a short stall, one of them in Czech angrily said, "You Ukrainian dog! We will register you as a Russian, and here they'll quickly teach you who you really are. Remember this too - your camp number is 41379. Sew it into your clothes!"

I was just glad the beating was over.

The other registrant gave Tato two white triangles upon which his camp number was printed and two triangles of red cloth upon which a big letter "R" was sewn on.

Russian.

Another registrant pushed Tato aside with a stick saying, "Go, you bandit." *Couldn't you just have given him the Russian patches? Couldn't you skip the beating? Isn't this bad enough?*

I imagined what a Frenchman would say, or a Pole, if they were forced like this to say they were German. *How would a Jew feel if he had to wear a swastika?*

I walked up to the registration table and it felt much easier being there myself, rather than watching Tato. I wanted his beating to be mine. I wiped tears from my eyes. I was on fire. I was thirsty. Perhaps I was catching a cold, but at this moment, I wasn't scared. Tato's posture gave me strength. I was ready for anything.

I don't want to live in this unrighteous world anyway. Us Ukrainians have somehow become a completely abhorred and persecuted people. We were the only people here who had our nationality taken from us, which was slowly wiping away the traces of our existence. Anybody could spit on us! How is it that we're stuck in this vicious cycle? How is it that much smaller nations have their own state and live by their own laws and we don't?

Until this point, I thought that all people had at least the right to call themselves as their history awarded them. *Why did they take this from Ukrainians? Isn't being in prison bad enough?*

I was more sure at that moment than any: *Ukraine should die fighting for its natural right to be free.* Because whenever our neighbors had a chance to ruin us, to steal away a piece of our fertile land, they did. The Muscovites used and abused us to build their empire, and then cried that we were equal! Ha! The Poles ripped away our Western lands. The Czechs and Hungarians encroached on Ukrainian Transcarpathia, the Romanians on Bessarabia. If Ukraine's history has said anything, it's that we have not ONE neighbor to whom we could trust or lean on for help.

Even though they too were exiled to Germany, I couldn't believe that these prisoner scribes were the same prisoners as Tato and I were. These Poles, Russians, Czechs, or otherwise are being persecuted just like us, but could still shove such hatred on us Ukrainians! You're doing German work! You pitifully and so severely beat Tato, a fellow prisoner! And for who? For the people who put you in this hell!

At least the Jews, who were being so ruthlessly and inhumanely persecuted and destroyed, weren't forbidden to call themselves what they were! Rather, they wore the Star of David!

I looked up at Tato standing in the next line, him looking back at me as well, and at that moment I decided that when they asked me my nationality, I would tell them the same as Tato did. When they frighten me, when they threaten to beat me, I'll loudly cry, so that all present could hear, that I too am Ukrainian!

At that moment, the registrants spoke quietly to one

another. They ordered me closer and looked at me suspiciously. *Maybe I look younger to them than in fact I am. Or maybe just too small.* All the prisoners around me were much older than my seventeen years. Their children were home.

The first question they asked was my age.

I said trembling, "Seventeen." I was anxious about the nationality question. I tried remembering what order the questions came in. *Is it now? Will they ask me now?* But next was my name and date and then place of birth. They whispered amongst themselves after I answered.

One then in Polish asked, "Is he your father?"

"Yes."

Then they wrote something in my registry and said, "Your camp cipher will be 41380."

Did they forget to ask?

They then gave me the same white clothe pieces and two red triangles, with an "R" on each.

I was Russian.

And they spoke to me different than they did to Tato. More reserved. They gave me the sewing instructions and asked me nothing else.

"Now go," one of the registrars said.

But I didn't want to. I hadn't said everything I wanted to say yet. They didn't ask me everything.

So I didn't move.

The second registrar got up and pushed me towards my unfortunate Tato, and they called the next person in line. Tato rejoiced when he saw that they let me by so easily. No beating. How he could be that happy after being beaten so badly was beyond words. I walked up to him suppressed, defeated and bubbling.

"Why didn't I step up first?" I cried. "Half that beating was mine... Next time I'll go first. I promise." I felt awfully responsible. *Was this what our fate was? Being dragged from cage to cage and beaten by "fellow" prisoners? Is this what this war has come to?*

A different on-duty prisoner ordered all of our clothes off in the stark-open air. He ordered us over to rows of prisoner-barbers, where each prisoner was buzzed.

Dropping all of my clothes, I pulled out the picture of Maria, and stashed the little memento in hand. Another on-duty prisoner, who for some reason had a stick, noticed that some people were stashing things and said, "Raise your hands high."

Several notes and pictures fell from people's armpits. "Now open your fists and turn them over," he said.

The photo of my beloved sister hit the ground. Passing by me, the on-duty prisoner struck my bare shoulders with his stick and he hit others two or three times.

Tato and I lined up to get our haircuts. Prisoners departed this station stroking their smooth heads as if they'd never felt it this short. Some prisoners got those short mohawks.

On both sides of me I heard grumbles, quarrels, and curses from the prisoners. "They're not even shearing! They're ripping out my hair!" The clippers were dull, and fresh blood trickled down shaven heads.

Tato came close and grabbed my hand. "It's really hot," he

said. "Do you have a fever?"

"I have something... I'm freezing, but it's probably because we're naked in this wind," I said. I trembled and felt sick and had no idea what was going on with my body, but I didn't want to worry him.

Our turn then came and I stepped up first, learning my lesson at the registration desk, but at the same time a second shaver took Tato.

"What's your nationality?" he asked Tato.

Without hesitation, Tato said, "Ukrainian."

"Don't you get it? There are no Ukrainians. You're either a Pole or a Russian," he said angrily and stormed off, shouting to his superior that he's going to call the scribes. "*They'll* teach you what to call yourself," he yelled back.

The barber who finished my haircut didn't ask my nationality. And for whatever reason, I told him, "This man is my father."

To my surprise, the barber grabbed Tato, quickly shaved him and said, "Get on, quick!" He didn't give us the mohawks reserved for Russians. *So maybe we aren't so fully converted.*

We got out unscathed. *That shaver had a conscience. Maybe he felt bad for Tato's busted face and blackened, swollen body.*

From the registration table, we heard shouts and wrangling, which we later found out was another Ukrainian, like Tato, who didn't want to change his nationality. We didn't stick around to find out if Tato's angry barber made it back.

They led us to the next building, and we were driven into a room which had showers mounted up on walls.

"Wash," another on-duty prisoner ordered. We picked up

the meager pieces of soap and scrubbed ourselves. Tato asked me to wash his shoulders and then he washed mine. This was much needed, for we'd spent several days sleeping shoulder to shoulder on dirty floors, with bugs crawling in every crevice... those trains weren't clean either.

Being outside in the fresh air and taking a hot shower relatively refreshed us, physically making me feel quite better.

From the showers we got our striped prison duds. Tato and I switched pants, because my pants were too big, his too small. None of the prisoners considered whether this garb suited them or not, taking what they were given. "And take a hat from the corner of the room," the on-duty prisoner said.

We walked over, but there weren't enough hats for all of us. I reported this to the on-duty prisoner, and he laughed, replying, "More will be brought to your barracks." *What's so funny?*

Our group was in need of three such hats, including Tato and I. We figured there would be enough for everyone, and even when they were out, we thought that there'd be more. However, as the proverb says, 'For every teaching, one must pay dearly.' And a very dear cost it was.

Leaving the washing station and going outside, we immediately felt the sun beating down on us. My dry throat screamed thirst. To add to that, our heads had been covered by hair and dimly lit prisons for a month. Not anymore.

Our heads were ghostly white, and they were cooking under the sun. At our request, we weren't allowed to take shade.

Our group of about 100 prisoners was taken to an area scattered with those white stones again. We were ordered to sit and wait.

I looked up at the sun, which I had once so much adored, but now saw it as my enemy. My nose quickly burned, as did my skull. My eyes were still swollen from the lantern.

I asked a couple prisoners if they could lend me their hat, but begging brought no success. This introduced me to the camp law that prisoners wouldn't help each other without incentive, so I told prisoners that if they'd simply spare their hat's inner liner, I'd give them my new hat when I got mine from the barracks. I begged dozens until finally an older gentleman agreed to do so.

I tried doing the same for Tato but had no such luck. Every prisoner was rude and cared only for himself. They were alone in their fight and in their fear as well. I could barely get someone to answer, more or less consult me about hat liners. And to add to all of this, I had no idea what language anyone spoke. The most practical starting point was German.

Why won't you help? This stupid liner doesn't help you! Or you! Or you! You'll be no worse! But I didn't let my frustration get to me.

Then I noticed a man squirming about, shifting from one side to the other. His eyes were red, his face was swollen and his nose was crooked. He held a piece of white clothe to his ear which covered a fresh wound. He also seemed to notice Tato - he kept looking over in our direction, probably because Tato was the only one that looked as bad as he did. So I got up slowly and walked over, but when I got to him, he turned away.

"Can I help you with anything?" I asked him in German, and then in Polish. After a moment, Ukrainian words beautifully spilled from his lips: "I don't need any help."

"I'm Ukrainian," I said to him.

He mournfully looked at me and said, "Behold son - look at what these prisoners are doing with us Ukrainians. Look how they beat me - those 'brothers...' 'neighbors...' those fellow Slavs at the registration desk. They tried to make me a Pole or a Russian."

This must be the man we heard from registration after our haircuts.

"Look here, on this red triangle, they wrote a 'P' which defines me as a Pole," he said.

"My father was beaten for the very same reason. He's sitting right over there," I said. *Please help.*

This man looked over and then asked me to sit by him for a minute. He talked and talked and talked, but what I really needed was that hat liner for Tato! Suddenly, before I could get around to asking, a bulletin rushed through the prisoners:

"Here comes Kapo Ivan."

"Kapo Ivan's coming."

"Kapo Ivan..."

"Kapo Ivan..."

"Kapo Ivan..."

Prisoners fled from their little hangouts and one said to us, "Get back to your seats! He'll punish you!" the prisoner said.

Whose Kapo Ivan?

I apologized to the beaten Ukrainian man and ran over to

Tato without a second hat.

Maybe he's military? Or a German officer in charge of camp?

Just then beside Tato and I passed a medium-structured man, dressed in dark green military pants, tall black boots that shined like the bugs in Brigidky, and a white shirt unbuttoned at the chest. His sleeves were rolled up to his elbows.

He strolled, waving his hewn stick backwards and forwards, time to time slapping the flaps of his pants. He stepped boldly, self-assuredly, proudly... somehow this new 'prisoner' paid us no attention at all.

Beside him shimmy-stepped a slender prisoner who also had a stick, and on his other side, walked a dark, stocky rock of a man. Prisoners later told me that this second man was a German Gypsy. The three walked together and said something funny amongst themselves, greedily chuckling at their inside joke.

They walked into barrack number nine. We stood and waited.

I found out later that Germans appointed their cruelest prisoners as Kapos. These jackals of different nationalities spoke German and for all intensive purposes *were* German within the barbed wire. They had full trust of the German guards and for this they received better food, new and clean prison clothes, they didn't slave away, and sometimes under escort were even allowed to go beyond camp walls.

In order to fulfill this roll, one had to be a malicious sadist, an undercover agent, and after passing that test, they got to hold absolute power over all other prisoners.

Under their supervision were Shtubos, who were each

responsible for a barrack. They chose prisoners to work or cook in the kitchen, dished out food rations, assigned barbers and tailors, and assisted the German command. The Kapos, Shtubos, and German command manifested itself in camp two or three times a day to count all prisoners to make sure numbers measured up.

Kapos and their aides mocked each and every prisoner who wasn't like them or who wasn't performing their duty as ordered. Such people were beaten, even killed or tortured, and none of these faux-Germans were punished for it. A Kapo was the right hand of the German command in camp, the one who kept order. So all the Germans had to do was make sure no one escaped.

The slender prisoner then walked back, swinging about his stick and shouted at us, "Get up and get over here! Stand in front of me in rows of five... Quickly! Quickly! We don't have time to play with you!"

We moved over to Barrack #9, and the slender assistant beat the first prisoner who got there. Our sea of prisoners finished the migration, all pushing each other in different directions as if someone wouldn't get a spot. In all the confusion, I couldn't get into a row with Tato. He was in the next one over. Ivan's assistant ran around and beat prisoners who hadn't found a spot yet, and then he beat some who had.

How could one prisoner and one stick control so many people? This terrified me. No one dared to oppose him. We were all so instantly terrified. *We're sheep!* This to me was equally strange and scary. I wondered what went through the other prisoners' heads: *'Maybe if I'm obedient, I'll somehow come out of this alive. Let them hit others, just not me.'* It felt like everyone was thinking for themselves.

When all the prisoners were arranged appropriately, Ivan's assistant shouted in German, "Prisoners! Ready and waiting for you!"

On the doorstep of the barrack, in the cool shade, Ivan and his German Gypsy assistant appeared. And for a reason I really didn't want to know, they each held their own rubber whip. The other, slender assistant joined them in the shade.

Ivan slowly laid his whip on a chair, and from that chair, he raised a cap.

In a rough German accent, he referred to the whip and said, "This is my favorite assistant as well as my favorite translator. All prisoners are well aware of this, and they all respect him," he said smilingly.

"He understand all languages, and when someone doesn't listen to him, this translator sticks it to him well. You will soon see for yourself that I speak truth," Ivan said.

Don't you have anything nice to say? I couldn't believe it. *Why such primitive insults and threats? A fellow prisoner, no less!*

Ivan then started again, this time in mixed German and Russian. "Another important lesson for the day - allow me to demonstrate!" said Kapo Ivan, with the German gypsy translating.

"But I'll only show you once. Never again! And if my aides note that you don't obey, then you'll see just how hard they can beat you for your guilt. You will all soon become my very obedient lambs..."

That already seemed to be happening.

"So why have you ended up here, you wonder? Well because you're all criminals! If you were good people, you wouldn't be here. Then there'd also be no need for me." He cursed at us in Russian.

Then Ivan pointed to the hat in his hands. "You see, this cap should always be on your head. You'll be recognized by every German as a prisoner. All of you must have it. All of you must wear it. This is the law. Now all you take heed! When you pass a uniformed German officer, you must, in his honor, remove your hat and hit it on the right side of your pants. Now, take off your hats and on my command beat your pants!"

Ivan then placed the hat on his own head and gave the command: "Meetzen Avs!" (remove caps). He took off his hat and proudly slapped it on his pantleg. All the prisoners did the same.

"Good, very good. But! Not all prisoners participated," said Ivan. "And this should be done louder! And with greater enthusiasm!"

Ivan once again gave the same order. This time, the prisoners hit their pants louder.

Then Ivan for some reason walked closer to Tato, whose face was red as a tomato. The sun, although on its way down, was roasting our heads, especially Tato because he had no hat. At that moment, I realized why Ivan complained that not all prisoners were complying. And unfortunately for Tato, his fresh wounds didn't stop Ivan from singling him out.

In an elevated voice, Ivan asked Tato, "Why didn't you slap your cap?! Where'd your hat go? Why is it not on your head like all the other good little prisoners? Is this how you plan on carrying yourself here?"

Tato somehow understood that Ivan asked for a hat and replied, "There weren't enough hats for all the prisoners. They said they would deliver us more in the barracks."

Tato's response was in very polite Ukrainian, and Kapo roughly responded back in Russian, "Then you're an idiot for not finding yourself one! Time for your first lesson."

I was stunned. *Is he about to get beaten again?* Thoughts nervously shuffled through my head. According to Ivan's logic, Tato should have fought for a hat, or stolen one. And even if Tato had known that, he wouldn't have. Tato's priorities dove deeper than stealing and thinking only of himself.

Suddenly, without any order from Kapo Ivan, the Gypsy jumped to Tato and struck him across his face with his whip. The second assistant ran over and punched him in the stomach, toppling Tato to the ground.

To keep pace, Ivan also kicked Tato and shouted at him, "Here's to you damn zapadnik!" (derogatory term for a Ukrainian from the Western part of Ukraine). Tato lay on the ground lifeless.

Both aides dragged him by his armpits to the front of our group, scraping his knees against the tiny stones, and then dropping his limp body. The slender one brought a bucket of cold water and dumped it out on Tato's head. Ivan then ordered all prisoners without caps to come forward. Other than Tato, there were nine.

"Face down! On the ground!" Ivan ordered. All these

prisoners laid down obediently. Ivan and his two assistants walked down the line, whacking the prisoners' backs with sticks and kicking some unlucky ones too.

These prisoners, just like Kapo had said, laid like lambs until Kapo and his assistants returned back to their shade. A few moments later, Tato recovered his senses, rose to his feet, and slowly walked back into his row. His head was low and his back bent, like he'd aged decades in days.

He didn't look up at me. Somehow I felt even more awful for Tato than before. *Beaten twice today already? How could he survive this pace? How can, after seeing what goes on here... how can I continue? Will this happen again tomorrow? And the next day? And after that? Where do we gain strength? How do we keep up with these reptiles? How can an honest person last a week?*

With red flushed faces, breathless yet satisfied, Kapo and his assistants peered out at all of us. Kapo Ivan's nostrils flared like an angry bull as he looked at us prisoners with great fury. *Who entrusted us to this man?* Kapo seemed to welcome and revel in his own anger. Our collective fear fed his hungry ego.

He split his feet out wide into a V, gently tapped his stick across his left palm, and hissed through his teeth the following instructions.

"Time for food. Bowls are beside these boilers. You won't need spoons. Now get over here and take a bowl with your grimy hands. In the next line, you'll get blankets which will be quite useful to you at night. Just know that you'll only be detained a few days here. Afterwards, the healthy will be taken further."

I wondered what he meant by "healthy."

"And each of you gets only one bowl. One! If we catch you taking seconds, and we will, then I'll break your head and send you straight to the devil.

"When you've eaten, quickly wash that bowl and return it. If that bowl is dirty, or you keep it to yourself and I catch you? Then I swear to God I'll choke you. Your mothers are whores!"

This man is insane! He's playing God! How could the Germans, people, actual people, appoint such a crazy man to run our lives? I don't get it! How does anybody survive this place?

I thought back to him saying that if we weren't here, then there would be no need for him. So my only hope was that this crazy man's thirst for my subordinate existence was greater than his need to end my life.

The cooks brought us food on a little trolley, and the sun had finally snuck back behind the barracks. We were exhausted after a long day, baked through by the sun, terrified of Ivan, waterless and without food, so we welcomed this first meal in this terrible camp.

I noticed Tato barely moving towards the kettle, other prisoners passing him by. I pushed my way through them, grabbed Tato's hand, and pulled him along. He didn't resist, obediently following my lead.

Tato, you're so strong! But why did they test you?

The on-duty prisoner poured a dipper of soup into each of our bowls, and we walked into Barrack #9. I overheard a few prisoners saying the soup was cooked with turnips. I had never eaten a turnip, but my focus was on Tato.

He ate slowly. It was painful for him to open his mouth. He was swollen through, skin to bone. After we finished, I asked Tato to watch our blankets while I washed out our bowls. I worried about leaving him alone with the blankets - I didn't want to end up without hats *and* without blankets.

But I left, washed the bowls, and came back to the barrack, which was basically four walls surrounding an open toilet and sink covered by a roof. No beds. Just a wooden floor. There was a separate area for Ivan and his assistants.

The prisoners, after eating and washing their bowls, squeezed down together on the floor to find a spot to sleep. This barrack was way too small for all of us. It was shoulder to shoulder again.

The last prisoners who got back to the barrack tried pushing themselves past the prisoners closet to the door, but these lying prisoners wouldn't let them pass. Nobody wanted to be closest to the aisles, which was prime position for whenever Ivan thinks up of another reason to torture us.

All this confusion was noticed by Ivan's assistants and their sticks forced those still standing to collapse where they were. Luckily, Tato and I had found a place near the wall, where hopefully we'd be safer until morning. Those closer to the aisle would have a tough time sleeping soundly tonight, with anxious thoughts of being woken up at any moment by the law of the stick.

Ivan then returned and said, "Get to the toilet. Now. I don't want any of you knocking around at night while I'm asleep. I will not remind you again, as I am not your mother. Understand?"

After a satisfied glance around, he answered himself, "Well then good. Tomorrow morning, you'll rise at five. On my whistle, you'll organize yourself in rows of five before this very barrack. Make sure you nicely, very nicely, fold and stack your blankets before leaving this building. If someone brings up an unmade blanket, then I will *help* him make it. You fools! I'll help you make it with five whacks to your shoulders! Understood?"

No prisoner dared to answer.

"Understood?! I can't hear you," Ivan roared.

We shouted "Understood!" like school children ... among them even me.

Ivan continued: "Tomorrow morning, the German camp commandant will arrive during roll call. All of you must acknowledge him with your hats as he walks by. I have already done a wonderful job teaching you," he said, proud of himself. "And after this, you'll be led to the hospital, where they'll call you by your ciphers. If they call you, and you don't reply... oh the 'praise' you'll get," Ivan said with irony.

"Tato," I whispered, "If we do everything the other prisoners do, then we won't stand out. We can blend in."

Ivan continued: "Now I don't want to hear any questions from you. I have spoken and you better have listened and do what I said. Understand?"

No one answered.

"Understand?!"

Everyone answered. We were all humbled before the wrath of Ivan. At that moment it became clear why dictatorships so easily exist in this beautiful world. *So this is how entire nations can become so obedient.*

Here I saw prisoners, that when their lives became difficult, when the risk of death was so close, something gave birth inside of them, inside of us, a strange hope and hunt for a better tomorrow. We prisoners figured that we could somehow prevail over all this humiliation and injustice, fear and hunger. But the hope was actually fear. We were scared so we stayed obedient today so that maybe real life could reappear tomorrow. *Could this really be the right way to survive? What about living today? What if there is no tomorrow?*

And then Ivan reminded us, "If you don't have a cap, then steal one. If, however, your's is stolen, don't come crying to me, because I'll give you an opinion you don't want. Now get to those toilets."

That ended Ivan's instructions. I was exhausted from listening to him, making sure I had all these rules memorized. I gave my hat liner to Tato and said, "We'll get another." I looked about for someone to ask and saw the badly beaten Ukrainian prisoner to whom I was talking to before Ivan came.

He saw how terribly Tato was beaten... for such a stupid thing! ... And he quickly and happily gave up his liner. I thanked him and went back to Tato. We went to the toilet, and then laid down on the floor together.

Tato took me in his arms and hugged me close. I kissed his forehead, and we laid to rest. Tato sighed heavily and began to pray the same way our Mama used to, and we, aloud, spoke together in turns. "Our Father..."

Thank you God for not letting today's beating break him.

After prayer, Tato realized I was restless, anxious about his beating. He hadn't said anything about it yet, and he knew I wouldn't bring it up.

He finally spoke: "I'm so sorry that you had to watch all that at the hands of those criminals. But don't be so sad. They didn't break me."

Tato re-instilled my faith. I listened intently. He had remained himself. I turned my attention to myself.

My face burned. Sweat that was once hot was now pouring cold from my forehead. I got in touch with my own body after realizing Tato was ok and I noticed I was powerless. I was weak, nervously exhausted. *What did I need?* Probably rest and maybe get some medical care, but I was too afraid to admit it, even to Tato. It was as if saying it out loud would make it real, and I didn't want to worry him.

This tore me up inside, keeping something from Tato. But with every passing moment I realized that survival might override truth. *I can't show weakness now. It's time to be strong.*

Finally, I said to Tato, "Try to sleep. Who knows if Ivan will surprise us tonight."

I took my own advice as well and thoughts of Ivan and his assistants and whips and sticks drifted me into a heavy sleep.

I woke up to rattles and screams. I sprung up and saw the Gypsy barreling his way through prisoners like a gorilla, ripping away blankets and shouting, "Get up! Get up!"

I was soaked through. My head rung. My eyes were crusty. My fever was through the roof. Tato woke up a moment later.

He can't know. I don't want him to panic. But I felt awful! *How could I get through today like this? I barely made it through yesterday!*

Everyone folded their blankets, put them away, and then fought over the sinks, the stronger prisoners pushing and shoving the weaker ones away. This time Tato and I didn't heed to the others. We pushed through and splashed the ice-cold water onto our faces. I felt a moment of refreshment, but then I shivered even more.

The sky had just started to pink as Kapo Ivan ordered us to form rows outside the barracks. The Gypsy rushed us and prodded us out of the narrow door with his stick. Once we were all outside, Ivan and his assistant disappeared somewhere.

Not a cell in my body had defrosted. My clothes were completely soaked. I shook, my teeth rattling like they were being dragged across a railway, and I was impatient. *Please, do something with us. Anything.* It was as if they were intentionally delaying us. Like they knew that I wanted to move, that I was sick. We waited for what felt like hours.

"They're probably off having breakfast. No hurry," said one prisoner. Some prisoners sat down. I did as well and asked Tato to do the same.

But he pridefully didn't... also maybe out of fear that he would be beaten again. "I'll keep watch," said Tato.

"Why did they wake us up so early?" I complained to Tato, knowing he really had no answer. I was cranky and nervous. I felt terrible. *How long could I last?*

And only when the sun rose and the clouds cleared, did a half-asleep Ivan appear and I perked up. "Did you enjoy breakfast?" he asked in his primitive witticism about the breakfast we didn't have.

No prisoners answered.

So he answered himself.

"Ah silence - so that means you're well fed. Since that's so, I'll go eat my own breakfast now," he said. *These are the rules... We live under camp law... But who came up with them? The Germans? Or these camp henchmen?* Ivan disappeared.

I fell back into my sickness. *So what happens if someone actually gets sick here? Whom could he tell? Who would believe him? Who takes care of the sick here? Do they just wilt away? Are they beaten to death, so as not to waste a dipper of turnip soup?*

After he ate, Ivan came back to the stoop of the barrack and started exercising by waving his arms around, twisting his head, and bending over. He then walked over to our rows and ordered us to re-align. His assistant counted us.

"Remember - when an officer walks by you, you must take off your cap and hit the flank of your pants. Now, step forward all of you that did not receive caps yesterday," he said.

Ivan looked about, but no one walked up.

"You have made me quite the surprise! Yesterday, you complained about the lacks of caps. Today? I generously bring them to you, but it seems to me that, well, you don't need them," Ivan said. I noticed that all the cap-less prisoners from yesterday scrounged up some cap liners.

Ivan's assistant then came out of the barrack with arms full of prison caps. My throat closed, like someone was choking me. *WHY? Why was Tato beaten yesterday over these rags?*

Did they have them the entire time?!

And even though these hats looked much better than those sitting on the prisoners' heads, no one dared to step up. Prisoners told me later that the camp command kept hats from prisoners on purpose to show off their power. We were counted again.

Today I stood in the same five-man as Tato. I asked him that he no longer stood in the front row, because it was always closest to the guards, therefore closest to punishment.

"I feel much more secure here in back," he said and also noticed that I wasn't feeling well: "What hurts? You're white as a ghost."

Only then I admitted: "I woke up all wet and I have a terrible headache and I'm freezing. I've got the chills... But maybe it'll pass when this day warms up. The sun will heat me up," I said.

Tato wanted to get some help, but what could he do? We had no idea what was done here with "patients."

At that moment, an unmerciful world swirled around and swallowed me. I became increasingly indifferent and impaired. Thoughts started to slow.

Three actual Germans showed up at the barracks, two with rifles and one with papers. Ivan saluted them and reported our numbers. Upon his greeting, the officer answered him with an easy smile. The German with papers counted us too, with the armed guards flanking his sides. Ivan, like a dog, stood behind them. The officer recorded something on his index card and patted Ivan on the shoulder.

When the Germans passed by Tato and me, I barely had

enough strength to lift my arm up to my hat, and nearly missed my pant leg on the way down. Nobody noticed.

After getting counted, the guards led us to the hospital. And I'm not sure where I got the strength to do so, but I saw those darn hats lying on the bench, and since no instructors were near, I reached out and snagged two of them, one for me and one for Tato. I was beyond tired. I felt distant.

Tato and I immediately put these two caps on top of our liners and everyone was too preoccupied with their own thoughts to notice. Seeing his son do all this, Tato shed a few tears and said nothing more. *Thank God we're going to the hospital. I didn't want to complain to Ivan about my pain. If the sick are so severely abused, at least let it be at the hands of someone else - not Ivan.*

I could barely lift my legs over the doorstop into the hospital. Tato helped me through. I stood up before the doctor and without acknowledging me, he grabbed my hand. His face shot up and he noticed my wet forehead. "You're so pale. And you're shaking. Medic! Take him to isolation."

What's isolation?

I was delirious.

With half-open eyes I looked to the side at my sorrowful Tato, who was being inspected by another doctor. I realized they were separating us. So did he.

My eyes blackened, I coughed my lungs dry and everything started to spin. The assistants grabbed me by my armpits, led me, or carried really, out of the hospital and into a building which was fenced off from all the other blocks with barbed wire. Then I blacked out.

A young man's voice trickled into my mind, a Polish song to the melody of a Ukrainian Christmas Carol, "In Bethlehem:"

Today in London
A happy news:
Thousands of bombers, thousands of bombers
Flying to Berlin.
Some fly in, others fly out
Throwing these bombs, throwing these bombs...

The song kept repeating.

A few rounds later, my eyes crept open and I propped myself up. I was lying on the upper level of a bunk bed. There were prisoners lying in beds all around me and a man dressed in prison garb smiling and listening to the singing boy. *Where am I?*

This man saw me stir and immediately sprung up and in-German said, "I am the doctor. Don't be afraid. I'm here to help you as best as I can. What language do you speak? Because in your fever, you seemed to be quarreling with someone in German, Ukrainian, Polish, and even Russian."

"I am Ukrainian, and I speak it best," I replied.

"Here we speak Polish, because we've got three Poles in here," he said. I politely thanked him and immediately asked for water. After giving me a cup, he said that he was initially very worried about me.

"Your fever was dangerously high and today is already your fourth day here. On day one, you just slept, and then your fever broke and you tried running off to some train." *A train?*

This doctor looked to me quite calm, friendly, and I felt I could immediately trust him. The boy who was singing looked to be my age, and he gleefully started yapping. As he did the doctor left to grab me some food.

Listening to this boy talk and his wonderful attitude, I couldn't believe that I was still in this same dreadful concentration camp. *Four days?* My nerves tensed and attitude turned 180 degrees. *Can I trust you people? Who are you anyway? No, no, I can't trust you.*

But the doctor came back quickly with bread and margarine and a cup of warm water and with no hesitation I dug in.

"Next time don't sleep so long! I would have brought you something sooner," the doctor joked. My trust seeped back in.

After eating, the doc opened up my shirt, tapped my shoulder and chest, listened to my heartbeat, and laughingly said that I would live and on his watch would soon find good health. I thanked him for the good meal. I actually felt alright.

"I need a toilet," I told the doctor, and he helped me down from this second bunk. Somehow, even after not walking for four days, I didn't fall, and he led me to the bathroom.

"Just be careful," he warned, "Don't look around too much, because sometimes at this time of day there's things you don't want to see... Please, trust me, don't look underneath the tarp."

I walked into the stall and tried doing as he said, although I couldn't help but notice someone's shredded leg sticking out from underneath the tarp. My eyes adjusted and more bodies appeared underneath this tarp as well. There were streaks of blood across the cement floor.

Gotta get out!

I was scared and back in the hallway. The doctor stood nearby and waited for me, perhaps anticipating my fearful reaction. "This block is for the sick *and* the dead. In the evening, the dead are taken away on a truck and transported to who knows where," he said.

How close was I to being under a tarp?

"What you saw there - forget it. You're still young and can endure a lot, as long as you keep an eye out. I'll keep you here for another week and you just concentrate on healing yourself and resting. We get a bit more to eat here too," he said. And to my great wonder, these words of hope were in Ukrainian, some dialect unknown to me.

"Might you be Ukrainian?" I dared to ask.

He dodged my question and asked, "Where exactly in Ukraine are you from?"

"Galicia," I said.

He smiled. "Good to hear," he advised. "But the Ukrainians in this camp are prohibited from calling themselves so and are punished harshly if one of them refuses to switch to Polish or Russian. Some of these Ukrainians are beaten so badly that they were brought here and then taken away in the middle of the night, never to be seen again."

I was amazed by the doctor's words. This news made Tato's beating seem easy compared to what could have happened. *No wonder the doctor didn't answer my question about being*

Ukrainian. He doesn't want to get beat.

"And let's change your registration from Russian to Polish. Those wearing P's sometimes get food parcels from the Red Cross brought by Poles across the border. It'll make your stay here a little easier," he said. "And I'll hold onto you for another week."

"Doctor - I can't stay a week. I left my Tato in the ninth block. We were arrested together, and up until I got ill, we were always together," I said. I told the doctor about his beatings. "He might need my help. He doesn't know German," I said.

The doctor's face sunk. "I feel for you. As soon as you're well, I'll release you. You need to stay here and calm down your body... That being said, if your Tato resides in the ninth block, then he might be shipped out soon, because the ninth is Gross-Rosen's transit block," he said.

I can't leave Tato. No way. I'll fight through this. The doctor immediately read my face and said, "Alright, I promise, I'll lead you to the ninth tomorrow morning. I'd strap you down here if I could, but after hearing your story, I don't have the courage to do so. Your Tato is probably depressed, having no idea what happened to you since your separation."

Leaving was my only option.

He continued: "Unfortunately, I don't have any friends in the 9th who could tell me whether he's still there. And I can't go over there myself either. You'll be going in blind," he said.

So it was a longshot. The doctor wants me to stay seven days. I'm staying one. *But what if he's not there? I was just in a four day coma. I should stay... But what if he is there and I miss him?*

I asked myself what Tato would do - which immediately gave me my answer. Our strength together beats anything a doctor could do.

The doctor led me back to the room, and the Polish singing boy got sad after hearing that I'd be gone in the morning and he'd have no one else to talk to. He said that he'd been laying there for three weeks, with no one even close to his age coming in until I was carried in. He broke his foot.

The doctor explained my situation with Tato to the boy, which satisfied him and he calmed down.

The boy said: "My dad went to war in 1939. I have no idea what happened to him. Is he still alive? ... Maybe he's dead."

The doctor left to check on other patients, and the boy continued: "I'm Chester." And because I spoke Polish well, he probably thought I was a Pole. Without my request, he began telling me how he came from Warsaw and that he's connected with the Polish Underground. "We're prepared in Warsaw to revolt against the Germans and to meet up with the Soviet Red Army. We're going to help them drive out the Germans and redeem Warsaw!"

This boy's imagination apparently hadn't been introduced to what it was meant to be "liberated by the Red Army." I, on the other hand, was immediately reminded of such "freedom." But I didn't want to alienate myself against him by telling him about the Soviets ripping families apart, murdering some, sending others away for enslavement.

I paused for a moment.

... but maybe I could get him to critically think a little

differently about another possible partition of Poland.

"Have you ever heard of a village called Katyn?" I asked.

"Nope."

"Well maybe you heard something about Germans excavating graves there? Because they did so and then sent some International Red Cross medical examiners to analyze these graves. They found thousands of people buried in the ground. The medical examiners stated that the men were buried in 1940. They were all shot, many with their hands tied behind their backs. The Germans then opened up this grave site in 1943 and announced to the press and on the radio that there in the forest of Katyn, ten thousand bodies were discovered, all shot and murdered, and all of them Polish officers. The Germans leaked this information to justify to the whole world why they were fighting the Soviet Union. They said, 'Here, look at these innocent victims, these Polish officers that were murdered by the Russian Police - the NKVD - and judge for yourself why we began a war with the Soviet Union."

Chester listened with great interest. He asked me several times: "Did that actually happen?" It amazed him that Russians now get help from England, from America, and he questioned why in Warsaw they were told to greet the Union as their liberators.

After my story, his mind was changed and he said, "The Poles shouldn't welcome the Soviet Army at all. I just wish I could spread this word back home!"

"Well the Germans have done so much harm, each of us forgets just how evil these Russians are. After all, people see them as Slavs, like Poles, and therefore think they can't be so evil," I said.

The doctor walked back in, bringing us dinner, and then tried rousing the two prisoners who'd been asleep since I woke up. He encouraged them to eat, but no reaction came and they laid further without moving.

"Might not last much longer," he said to us. *Did he say that about me?*

Chester then repeated everything to the doctor about what I had told him about Katyn. The doctor said that he heard this too from other prisoners as well as in the papers, before he was arrested. After a little more conversation, we decided it was time to rest, and I went back one more time to the toilet. This time, it was empty, the floor was clean, and there was no trace of dead bodies.

The next day, the doctor transferred my nationality over to Polish and gave me Polish badges.

"Sew these on whenever you get a chance, before you get back to your block if possible," he said.

I said goodbye to Chester and thanked the doctor for his advice: "I'll always remember you. You have a place in my prayers."

The doctor led me to the barbed wire fence that surrounded the isolation unit, handed my documents to the prisoner/doorkeeper, and told him that I needed transport to the ninth barrack. As the doorkeeper led me back, I introduced myself, but he coldly ignored my attempt at cordiality. Neither of us spoke another word until we got to the barrack.

"Where might I find Kapo Ivan? I have a prisoner for him," he asked another prisoner at Barrack #9.

"Kapo's not around, and he won't be for the next three days," he said.

Relief flooded my body. At least I didn't have to deal with Ivan.

The on-duty prisoner handed me some papers and told me to go inside and find one of Kapo's deputies. I walked into the barrack that was filled with prisoners preparing for transport. They all scurried from me when they saw I was carrying papers, probably thinking I was a camp official.

My eyes frantically searched for Tato, but I couldn't find him. *He must be here, somewhere. Tato, where are you?* After not finding him, I walked into the sectioned-off part of the barracks where Ivan and his assistants lived.

I knocked on the door and crept in and saw the Gypsy, prostrated on a bed with his shirt opened down to his chest, like an overgrown monkey. He paid me no attention. I waited in silence, not knowing how to start a conversation with him.

Finally, he sneered, "What do you need here?" He lazily reached out for my papers.

"My father is somewhere in these barracks. I was separated from him four days ago. I would like to know where he is so I can meet up with him," I said.

He got up off the bed like a drunk, peered at me attentively, and asked Tato's name or whether I could recall his camp number. I gave him both. He took out his register, read it over, and said, "Well you shouldn't look for him anymore. He was transported with some others to another camp early this morning."

This morning? No. Can't be.

He reviewed the documents and said, "Everyone else is still in this unit, and now you're among them. You'll continue your journey tonight after dinner. Now get out," he said and laid back down in this lair.

No! That's not right! I lowered my head and silently left the Gypsy. But I refused to believe that Tato wasn't here.

I frantically searched the barracks. *Maybe the Gypsy lied! Or maybe he made a mistake! Tato! Where are you?*

But with every unfamiliar face, I started to realize the truth.

Why didn't I stay longer in the hospital? I could still be healing. Why didn't the doctor release me last night? Tato and I could still be together!

Terror came over me. I was left alone in an ocean of strangers. And in every stranger I saw only the worst things. Their selfishness. Their pain. Their anger.

I felt like an orphan. I was arrested and separated from Uherci... from Mama and my siblings. And then I fell into a coma. *I'm in a foreign country separated from Tato!* I leaned into a corner of the barrack and wept. No other man paid any attention to me. They didn't even look in my direction. Each prisoner had enough of their own problems. They weren't interested in mine.

If you want to cry, Stepan, cry. You're alone. This is what this is now.

SEPARATION

After a tearfully long cry of regret, a realization came to me: *From now on I must only think of myself.* I recalled the words of the doctor - "You are still young - you can overcome anything."

Maybe this will be easier. At least now I won't see Tato's beatings. I won't feel his pain.

At that point I decided that I would do everything very carefully to somehow keep living. *Who knows? Maybe Gross-Rosen is the worst camp? Maybe the others will be easier?*

I no longer wanted to seek conversation with other prisoners. The coma had left me independent, separate, like everyone else.

For lunch they brought us barley soup, and we were ordered into rows. Out of no where I felt a sharp *thwack* on my back. I spun around and the Gypsy shouted at me, "Why haven't you sewn on your cipher?!" He jabbed his stick into my chest, asking, "Where are you triangles, huh? Why aren't they sewn on yet?"

Terrified, I said, "I'm... I... just got assigned to this unit. I haven't had a chance to get a needle and thread. I looked everywhere. I couldn't find any."

He calmed a bit and ordered that I immediately sew them on after lunch. "I've got the needle and thread. Come get them so that nobody else punishes you." I was relieved that he didn't hit me again.

After lunch, I did as he said, carefully sewing all the patches onto my clothing, as Mama once taught me, and then promptly returned the needle and thread. He examined my patches and asked, "Did you do this yourself?"

"Yes," I replied.

"You sew much better than the others," he said.

This praise shocked me.

The Gypsy walked into the prisoners' quarters, summoned everyone with his whistle, and showed them how I had sewed on my camp designations.

"All your patches - they must look like this," he said. He walked amongst the prisoners and starting ripping off their patches and said, "Sew it again! Like his!"

Prisoners gave me hostile looks. What bitter praise! But I quickly squashed my fear and erased my guilt. *Think for yourself, Stepan.* Then some senior prisoners came up to me, and at their request, I sewed their ciphers for them, gaining myself a few friends.

After sewing, I walked over to the barrack window and looked outside. *Where are they taking us tonight? Maybe we'll be reunited, Tato.* I started to wonder where they took him, but Gypsy's whistle woke me out of thinking. He ordered us outside and counted us again. We waited for the German officers.

The Gypsy loudly reminded to us all, "Lest you've forgotten, salute the German officers with your hats to your pants." *For what do you need such respect? Respect because you caught us all and put us in a concentration camp?* At the same time, I knew it was their routine, and if I wanted to live, I had to follow it.

"Oh, and I don't have to worry about you anymore either. After dinner, you'll all be liquidated on the very train that got you here. The difference being? You're going deeper."

And then, walking back, he wickedly added, "You'll be

ever so sorry that you couldn't stay here longer." But his words apparently didn't weigh too heavily on the prisoners, because we were just glad to leave Ivan.

The German officer then appeared and the Gypsy stiffened and reported to him. The German didn't respond and counted us himself.

And to me, for some reason this whole situation became funny. *One man walks by who has power and dozens of men who don't - they slap their pants with their hats.*

The officer's count must have lined up with the Gypsy's, because he walked off without speaking. We stood for the next half hour and then cooks brought us food. We quickly ate and were ordered to the barracks. As we walked in, several armed guards started yelling at us.

"Get to the toilet! A long journey awaits you!" Each prisoner, as if using the toilet was actually a military action, stood pat in turn and dropped off their waste. Among them, nearly last in line, was I.

With the sun drooped down into the west, the Gypsy pulled us out of the barrack, counted us, and ordered us to start moving towards the gates.

We walked beside the isolation hospital where I was for four days and still should be, and I noticed that the doctor to whom I owed my return to health stood behind the wire. Passing by, I waved and whispered goodbye, but he didn't seem to notice.

We were counted again before we left the gates of Gross-Rosen and then loaded onto trucks as dusk settled into evening.

"They must be scared of someone runnin away under twilight," one prisoner said, "because last time we walked to the train."

Another prisoner added, "I heard we're going deep into Germany at night, because the Allies have been bombing the day-traveling trains."

The truck trip was brief, and we stopped near the train awaiting us at the station. *Last time I was here, I was with Tato.*

The train guards looked like senior soldiers, and none of them disturbed us. Gross-Rosen guards and their snarling dogs corralled us. We loaded up and when my turn came, it was almost completely dark. The only lights were the guards' lanterns. I thought back to the rumors I'd heard at the start of the war about trains traveling without lights at night in Germany. This was no rumor.

Finally, our train car was loaded and three armed guards walked in with just one lamp with a faint flame. At the end of the car opposite the guards, there was a barrel to empty in. *Another distant journey?*

Being without Tato, I immediately pushed my way to the wall of the car, so that at least I'd have something to lean on. *Maybe over here I won't be bothered.* The train poked forward, rolled for a bit, and then jumped onto the main rail, speeding off, rushing us into the unknown depths of Germany.

Soon thereafter, the train rocked many of us prisoners to sleep. I was still well rested from the hospital, so I stared awake at the guards, two dozing and one armed with a rifle and ready. I thought back to the deranged prisoners working *for* Germany, specifically Kapo Ivan. *How could he be so cruel?*

How did he get so evil? The extra bread, bigger soup portions, maybe some other privileges... was that why? What's really going on inside the heads of these faithful executors of the Nazi law that put them behind bars in the first place? Power? Maybe Ivan thought that if he tried hard enough, he'd somehow actually become *a German?*

Throughout history, people have wondered how dictators got supporters. Meanwhile, Hitler figured out a way for his enemy to terrorize itself.

And because of Kapo's cooperation, the German camp council could comfortably settle beyond the barbed wire fence, living in absence of any fear of prisoners. The camp ran itself.

An image of an exhausted and beat up Tato appeared before me. *Could you endure any more violence?* I hoped that maybe we'd both seen the end of it.

I looked around at the other prisoners, and the fear in their faces had disappeared. It seemed to be replaced by complacency. *Are you already adjusted? Have you accepted your fate?*

Then for whatever reason I started to repeat a mantra over and over in my head:

I will stay alive.
I will find freedom.
There's nothing out there I can't handle.
I will stay alive.
I will find freedom.
There's nothing out there I can't handle.

My hope of a quick resolution to this war grew. *I wish I could share this hope with you, Tato! Where are you? These guards aren't so bad!* The work they performed was not so much personal desire, but more because they were military men and it was their duty. During these visions, the rocking of the train put me to sleep.

In my sleep I heard bits and pieces of the guards conversations... "... German capital..." "... Berlin..."

I woke up with a start. A prisoner had jumped up and ran to the other side of the train car, stomping down on other prisoners with the wooden soles of his shoes. Prisoners yelped. A guard must have stepped on him. Everyone sprung up.

A fight broke out. Guards shouted and beat prisoners with the butts of their rifles, which dropped all us prisoners into an obedient sit and stare. The guards poised their rifles on us, waiting for another to act up. I was happy to be against the wall, away from the action.

Just as the guards were about to sit back down, the train froze and the wheels sent a grinding screech throughout the cabin. This sent the standing guards sprawling across their bench. I laughed inside. They cursed the conductor.

I heard voices and clicking locks from outside our train car. Our door opened up to two of the meanest looking men I'd ever seen. They were dressed in jet black military gear, such that I'd never seen before.

At this point I realized that things could get worse. Much worse. Fear rushed back in.

CHAPTER NINE

SACHSENHAUSEN

"Alles heraus!" one of the officers in black shouted. (Everyone out!) We jumped out onto the road leading to a place called "Sachsenhausen."

They ordered us to line up in fives again, and to my amazement, the two guards in black uniforms spoke to each other in Polish. Two more of these guards joined them and all four began to speak... *Ukrainian?*

What happened to taking away our right to be Ukrainian? Can I come talk to you? But I hesitated. *How would they react? Maybe they were brutal guards, like those that made us wear our coats while walking that sun-scorched path to Gross-Rosen.* Two more showed up and they spoke now in German and then walked off down the road to Sachsenhausen.

We were counted again, numbers agreed, and we followed the guards in black. A few minutes later we arrived at a camp with a gate made of iron pipes and wire. Tall walls of barbed wire lined with spiny skeins stood high on both sides of this gate and surrounded the entire camp, just as in Gross-Rosen. It looked as though prisoners couldn't even *get* to the electrically-charged barbed wire. Guards sat perched up in towers, peering down at us. There was no way out.

But the guards here seemed different. Almost calm. They didn't prod and push or beat anyone, like in Gross-Rosen. No one was yelling. *Why?*

Beyond the gate, we moved into a large field, where local prisoners prepared for an exercise. Several fire-hoses attached to machines plus a set of ladders laid at the edge of this field.

What's going on?

But the guards led us further to a long, wooden barrack, which was separately entangled in its own barbed wire, a bit shorter than the main walls of the camp. Others were surrounded in wire too.

Interested prisoners from other barracks walked up to their wires and asked us where we'd come from, how long the war would last, who's winning, and if we have any hope of getting out alive.

Most of us held back answering, probably because we still imagined Kapo Ivan of Gross-Rosen popping up around a corner with his whip. But these inquisitively brave prisoners said that we had nothing to fear today, for today is a special day.

"The German government is allowing the International Red Cross to conduct a humanitarian review," one said.

A humanitarian review? For a concentration camp?

"They want to show the world that prisoner life in their concentration camps is not as tough or cruel as the media has painted it overseas. They want to show off their medical care, sanitation and cleanliness, and also that prisoner food is sufficient. So you won't see as many guards here today. They're all hiding out and will be back tomorrow," the prisoner said.

One of the prisoners behind barbed wire continued: "Yesterday, we were all ordered to wash our rooms... windows, floors, and everything outside the barracks too. Some of us even planted flowers. Many of us got new clothes. The last two days? We were fed like never before. Thick pasta with red meat. Some prisoners said it was horse meat - we enjoyed it."

My empty belly growled in hope for this thick, meaty pasta.

I noticed that there were no guards in this barrack either. Just wire. *So are we... alone?* As alone as we could have been, which was a nice change. Each prisoner was free to move about, sit quietly on the toilet, or simply take a drink of water without being pestered.

But I was more interested in whatever preparations were going on in the square. Suddenly, the main gate opened and several open-top personal vehicles drove in. Nicely dressed civilians in white shirts and perfectly tied ties sat inside, peering at the camp. *Must be the Red Cross.*

These cars halted in front of the square, and then I heard the shrill of a whistle. A group of prisoners dressed in clean prison clothes then built a tower out of the ladders. Then they deftly sprung up these ladders like monkeys, and at the top, they simulated a burning house or factory. Other prisoners drove out the firefighter "wagons," and they started pumping water on the people who were fire.

They're distracting them! No!

They were distracting us too. Prisoners from every building came out and watched in amusement.

Then one of the nicely dressed Red Cross members got out from his car and photographed the scene. German authorities followed him around, pointing out what he could and couldn't take pictures of. The other members sat in the comfort of their cars, further examining the exercises.

We were a zoo.

After the show, a few prisoners walked over and spoke with the Red Cross as their car slowly moved about the entire prison yard, following the supervising German staff car. The commission was allowed out of their cars to observe the barracks, but they couldn't go inside. The photographer followed separately and took pictures of each barrack and the prisoners which stood beside them.

Why aren't you going inside? Look inside! It's awful in here.

But none of them did.

We're in a camp! Under rule of other people! What part of this isn't humane?

None of them spoke to any of us and after some time the entire convoy of cars disappeared behind some long wooden barracks.

What could they learn from this fake tour? They didn't have a clue as to what was really going on. The Germans allowed this inspection for international propaganda, showing the world how "humane" they are. *"This is what our camps look like. See! It's not so bad!"* And if this is what the world saw, was anybody coming for us?

So we sat. Hungry and depleted and dumfounded.

At the complaint of a hungry prisoner beside me, I quoted Ivan of Gross Rosen: "Why should they feed us? We still haven't done anything today." Unfortunately, this joke didn't seize the march playing in my stomach or his.

Prisoners and a rough looking German command then spilled out from another barrack that I thought was empty.

These prisoners wore the same stripes we did, but they had black X's painted on their faces, one on each cheek and one on their forehead as well. *Paint maybe? But they're so dark! Tattoos?*

When the German command left their barracks, we tried asking these prisoners about their markings, but the block official caught us and forbade further communication. Prisoners from another nearby barrack filled in the blanks. Apparently, they were the most dangerous prisoners in the entire camp. Many of them had tried fleeing several times and were therefore marked with black X's, so that if they did get beyond the walls, they could easily be found.

"What about that building over there?" I asked, pointing to another barrack that was wound up with double the barbed wire as the others.

"Political activist prisoners from all over Europe, even Germany, all who opposed Hitler. That's why they're surrounded by that extra layer of wire," he said. I learned later that Yakov Dzhugashvili, Stalin's son and a former Russian artillery officer was held there. There was a rumor that Hitler wanted to exchange him for a German General Field Marshal who was caught at Stalingrad. But Stalin turned him down, saying, "I will not trade a marshal for a lieutenant."

At the end of that day, the German command arrived at our barrack. We were organized and counted and sent off for lice disinfection. They ordered off our clothes, threw them all in a pile, and we stepped into the shower. *I just got these clothes a week ago. They're still clean.*

Prisoners started to panic:

"Maybe we're getting gassed?"

"Why'd we pile up our clothes?"

"Why aren't we getting back our clothes?"

Some even asked the on-duty prisoners if they'd keep their camp ciphers and triangles from Gross-Rosen. Why they'd want them, I'm not sure.

I looked around the bathroom, but all I saw were water taps. Nothing else. No razors. No shears. Thoughts of getting gassed started to invade my mind too, but then the cold water spurted from the taps telling me otherwise. It was ice. Prisoners jumped out of the frigid water and tried hiding amongst each other, but it was no use. The cold water sprayed everywhere.

After that torture, we were ordered out and given prison clothes without ciphers, a pair of wood-soled shoes, and a hat. This time, there were enough hats for everyone.

The shtubo (or barrack prisoner/officer) met us back at our barrack and gave us dinner instructions. "After dinner, find a spot inside. There are beds for everyone. You'll be detained here for a night and then transferred to a sub-camp."

Dinner that night was as described too - thick noodles and red chunks of meat. We each got a scoop, but I could have chugged down a dozen. That macaroni and meat was so delicious. Each prisoner licked their dinner so clean that washing the bowls out wasn't even necessary.

After dinner, I went back outside and observed the block with the X-faced prisoners. *How could someone escape? And where would they go? Could they make it home?* But they were inside the barrack.

I turned around to look at the political prisoner block. *Maybe I'll see someone familiar. Maybe Stephen Bandera and Yaroslav Stetsko?*

But no one was being let out of that barrack either. I went back into my barrack and that night I felt calm and quickly fell asleep.

A cold fog hovered in the fields as the guards pulled us out of the barracks. After counting, we remained standing until the rest of the camp was counted. Breakfast was hot coffee and a bread roll.

"Hurry up and use the toilets. Come right back, too. You've got a tough day today, and you'll get nothing else to eat," said a guard.

That's it? All the food I'd get is already in my belly? This food scarcity dragged me down.

The guards then ordered us to organize into alphabetical order. I stood with the F's, and then they walked us over to the building next to yesterday's fire show. Big circles in the sides of the building opened into windows, revealing on duty prisoners. We lined up in front of the windows and one by one got a new patch of white cloth with a completely different cipher.

But I noticed that people seemed to linger longer in front of these registrars than back in Gross-Rosen. Almost as if these on-duty prisoners were *listening.* And no one seemed to be punished for their nationality, so as my turn came, I stepped up bravely and was ready to answer any questions.

One clerk sat at the window and another watched over us. He asked my name, Gross-Rosen number, and then the prisoner behind him handed forward my registration.

He then repeated my name and I was surprised at his demeanor. In German he asked, "Do you want to continue as a Pole?"

I felt a chill. *He knew I wasn't?* I calmly erupted.

"I am Ukrainian and I was forced in Gross-Rosen to be recorded as a Russian and then a Pole! They claimed there was no Ukrainian nationality! And anyone who didn't accept it was severely punished!"

Then to my great wonder, the clerk spoke to me in Ukrainian. "Well here you're allowed to call yourself Ukrainian. So on that red triangle, you can be marked with a 'U.' There are so many Ukrainian prisoners here - don't be afraid to call yourself so."

I couldn't believe it.

"But I warn you - look out for yourself and avoid the camp instructors. They can be brutal. You're still young, and you gotta live through all of this to tell others about us," he said. He said it cause I was younger than the others.

"Find a way to survive. Leave these camps. Now go. We're

backed up," he said, with a supervisor-prisoner looking over his shoulder.

I left the registration window and went to the bench, feeling uplifted. *I don't have to be a villain anymore, wearing some foreign nationality on my chest!*

I quickly stitched on my new identification and walked over to other prisoners who were sewing. One of them stopped me and asked, "What nationality is that? Hungarian? The Germans call you Ungarns, no?"

"No," I answered. "I am a Ukrainian."

This amazed some prisoners. I had worn a P up until now.

Since no guards were around, I helped some others with their sewing. Prisoners came up to me and kept asking me, "Who let you wear a U?"

I kept pointing out the one clerk, "He's Ukrainian. Talk to him. He said that all Ukrainians have the right to call themselves so here."

No one had told them. I just got lucky, because my registrar recognized my Ukrainian name. Those Ukrainian prisoners weren't allowed back in the registration line, but they did rip off their triangles and replace them with "U" patches they'd found on the benches. It was nice to see Ukrainians sneaking a bit of pride into this dreadful situation.

Officers hurried through registration as a few trucks arrived, two of them mounted with machine guns. The lead officer drew our attention saying, "Our convoy is well armed, so if any of you try to flee, our orders are to shoot you on the spot. *If,* on the road, some airplanes do fly over us, you do not have permission to leave the trucks unless given so by the guards. Under my command, nobody's escaped. But there were those who tried, and today they are not of this world... We are taking you to work in the aircraft factory, a sub-camp called Heinkel, near Oranienburg, close to Berlin." It was actually nice to get some bearings.

We were loaded 30 to a truck, and we left this great camp Sachsenhausen, onward to its sub-camp Heinkel. I couldn't see the road or the neighborhoods we passed, for our vehicles were covered. We wouldn't know the route.

CHAPTER TEN

SUB-CAMP HEINKEL

Our ride ended and before us appeared a beautiful, tall, rarified pine forest. Quite the change from cold and lifeless prison barracks. The guards ordered us out of the trucks for more counting. The sun stood high in the sky. We marched on.

A magic hung in the air. My body felt better. And although it was already summertime, an icy wind blew through the needles, swirling and whirling about our heads.

"W h o   a r e   y o u ?   W h e r e   a r e   y o u   g o i n g?" this wind asked.

Long buildings appeared one by one before us in these curious woods, and once again, a corral of barbed wire circled them, with a second lining of some *other* kind of wire just in case. Above the wires, Germans were perched in their towers, just as in Gross-Rosen and Sachsenhausen.

They moved us through the camp gates, we were counted again and then brought to an open clearing in the middle of the buildings. Again, we hungrily watched prisoners eat.

After their lunch, a group of German civilian masters

walked up. They each held a sheet of paper.

One guard spoke up: "Listen up. These masters have your ciphers and last names. When one calls out your number, go to him and wait there until everyone is called. He'll introduce you to your work."

Masters started calling names, and when the fourth one read a number with no corresponding answer, a fuss spread throughout the guards. They searched us for this prisoner. The number was repeated.

Suddenly, a frightened prisoner ran out after someone told him that it was his number. *He must not know German. And he certainly didn't know his cipher.*

The nearest German guard jumped to him and struck his shoulder with a rifle butt so hard that he immediately collapsed to the ground. These guards were serious.

This fourth master also called my number, and I ran hastily to him. I was the last one to his group, but for some reason we didn't move on. Instead, the master walked up to me and asked, "How do you say your name?"

I wonder why he asked. My name was on his sheet.

"My name is Stepan Fedenko," I said.

He then repeated my name clearly, began to smile and then looked quite suspiciously at me.

What did I do?

He noticed my agitation and said, "No, no. It's not bad. I don't want to scare you. It's just that I already have a Fedenko working in my group and am very happy that I now have a second."

My mind spun and the world flooded in. *Tato! I'm reuniting with Tato! How could this master remember him so well? Who cares! Tato!* My chest released. I could breathe again.

Our master was about 60 years old and in no hurry to get back. *Let's move! Could it really be? Could it be Tato?*

We slowly passed several large factory buildings, prisoners filing in and out of each one. But our master led us further, through the windy forest which never ceased to whisper. After a little hill, more factories appeared.

I looked closer and major chunks of these buildings were in ruins. One of them looked like a skeleton, with its glass windows all blown out, and its frame mangled like the barbed wire fence. The front awning had completely collapsed, and on the inside, instead of a floor, there was a huge pit, probably dug out by some powerful explosion. *There must have been some kind of accident.*

A prisoner asked the master what had happened, and he said, "Two weeks ago, in the middle of the night, enemy aircrafts did a little damage. But don't worry, our anti-artillery, one of the best in the region, drove them off and even took down one of their aircrafts," he boasted.

That hole was from a bomb?

"We aren't too far from Berlin," he continued, "so aircrafts fly over our heads, but Germany is still very strong and will surely win this war."

He said that last part for himself. Because none of the prisoners asked.

"Funny too, because these bombs have done more harm to prisoners than to the factory itself," he said. "This is why you've been sent here today - to replace them."

He said this quite nonchalantly. *Who replaces those people at home? Who cares for their families?*

I noticed that not too far from us another bomb had dropped and completely annihilated a prisoner barrack.

Just take me to Tato already.

The master then led us into a large, open factory building, which was still intact, no damage to be seen. Part of it was built entirely of steel frames and some kind of transparent material acting as its roof. I had never seen such a thing.

Hm. No need for electric light.

This was the last building before the end of camp that was guarded by barbed wire. Beyond this wire, a group of German soldiers walked by a large, duel-engine transport aircraft. *They must be building them in the factory and putting the finished ones outside camp for protection. But aircrafts built by... prisoners? What were these Germans thinking? Who here from us prisoners... the arrested, the ones ripped from family, those beaten and kept hungry... who of us wants to sincerely work for Germany? And what German pilot feels safe in a plane built by a malnourished prisoner? It must take amazing concentration to build a plane! These Germans must be in a critical spot, putting their lives in the hands of such unreliable workers. And what of sabotage? What a speedy destruction this could be!* I decided then and there that these Germans wouldn't find much benefit from having me here.

We walked into the factory - it was never-ending. *Hundreds of prisoners must be working on these aircrafts!*

Next to these workers was a lengthy corridor lined with a long table. On the table lay a great storm of all sorts of electrical wires - a rainbow of colors and different sizes. I'd never seen so many wires in my life! *Do they all fit into these planes?*

As the workers dismantled and cut and pinned and designated, my head spun about, looking for Tato. No sign so far.

The master stopped us and said, "You see these next four aircrafts? I am responsible for finishing them. You'll work for me here. When the buzzer sounds at 6am, we work. The others go off at 12 for lunch, at 1 after lunch, and then again at 6pm when we're done."

He pointed out our barracks too, which were right beside the factory.

"But you, Fedenko, are assigned to a special building, home to those under 18. You'll be joining up with them later over there," he said, pointing to a nearby gate.

Walking further through the plant, I saw groups of prisoners up on wooden platforms working on planes. When we approached nearer, they boldly asked us from where we were brought from, without even asking the master!

We answered and as I took a look at all of the identically dressed and shaved prisoners, our master shouted, "Fedenko! Come down and get acquainted with my other Fedenko!"

The master called me over and my spirits soared. *Where is he?!* As I searched, a man of about 30 walked out, and he walked over to us. *Is this the one? Is this Fedenko?*

The master turned to him and asked, "This one's also a Fedenko. Are you relatives?"

The young man then reached out his right hand and said, "Be well. My name is Grisha Fidyenko."

I barely extended out my hand, like I was frozen in a nightmare. I was not a FIDYenko. I was a FEDenko.

I drowned in disappointment.

He immediately noticed my embarrassment, shook my hand with vigor, and said, "Don't be afraid of anything here. The work is light. I'll help you, kid."

Tato... we aren't so close as I expected... A tragedy. *I'm among strangers. I'll open myself up to no one. No one else.* I shut myself in.

The master walked on, leading the other prisoners through the worksite. He left me behind and said that I should work with Fidyenko.

I started bawling and somewhat cordially said, "I'll stay here with you. I'll work. But I'm devastated because I thought that you'd would be my father. I was arrested with him and about a week ago was separated from him in Gross-Rosen."

"I'm so sorry," he said, then looked over to the others and said, "Hey comrades! This Western Ukrainian has a surname just like mine!" They came over and we shook hands and talked some in Russian, some in Ukrainian. My attention drew to their red triangles, each of them donning the U.

They joked and listened to my story and asked me questions about the second coming of the Soviet front and why I was arrested.

They gladly and intently listened to me and compared their accents to mine. Some of these Ukrainians laughed at my Ukrainian words, because they'd never had the chance to learn the language. That was commonplace in Eastern Ukraine because of the Russian occupancy.

They all understood me well enough, but then one

commented on our languages, "Everything is all the same. We all eat the same soup." I noted that but wasn't in the mood to argue.

After several minutes, we went back to work. Grisha's task was inserting electrical wires into a machine gun, which was located on the top of the aircraft. The awning over the machine gun turret was made of a transparent plastic. I marveled at its properties. So shiny. So clear.

Grisha said, "If a German comes by, get in there and pretend you're fixing something."

Another one of Grisha's tasks was to install a control unit, which was transportable from one plane to another. It was so heavy that two prisoners had to carry it. This unit made sure all the lights and electrical wires communicated properly.

"Camp work is dragging," Grisha said. "After the last air-raid, everything slowed down. Most of the supervisors and masters let up and became more gentle... I think they're starting to fear us. Looking for our friendship even. But I suggest not to test this - keep a piece of wire in your hand at all times to fool these guards into thinking you're working. Our master himself is pretty good to us. You don't have to fear him. He even tells me to take my time."

This all slightly eased my realization that Fedenko was indeed Fidyenko. As Grisha started to instruct me about the wire and light unit, an air-raid siren went off.

I nervously perked up.

Grisha noticed my unease and said, "Don't worry. They go off several times a day. You'll get used to them. They're coming from Berlin, which is only about 30 km away. On a sunny day, you can actually see the aircrafts over the city."

We prisoners piled out of the factory and into the designated safe-zones among the pine trees to wait for a raid or a call-off. Grisha and I joined his comrades and took a seat in a small, nice, sun-heated meadow. No clouds were in sight.

Along the horizon over Berlin, the Allied aircrafts appeared. There were four-engine bombers, flying row by row, and among them in all directions darted smaller and much faster airplanes.

"The smaller ones protect the bombers," one comrade said. "Otherwise, Germany would run them out with their Messerschmitts, which create air havoc for the much slower Allied extermination aircrafts. But I've never seen this many planes in broad daylight. They only run this heavy at night."

The prisoners among the pines clapped at such a sight. It was like a play we'd put on in the village, with an audience clapping for the hero.

Suddenly, the sky was covered in what looked like a swarms of bees, dense bursts of shells from the German anti-aircraft artillery.

Frequent and almost-deafening explosions rattled. The number of aircrafts further intensified. There were dozens. Firing and bombs and firing and bombs. All of this must have lasted an hour.

And then what felt like maybe the greatest misfortune I'd ever seen, one of those Allied planes was shot down by German anti-aircraft artillery. *No!* The German guards watching this air-raid became ecstatic. They shouted and loudly whistled.

During the raid, I took a look around and got a better feel for camp, watching the clusters of prisoners, seeing their faces, hearing their language, and observing their behavior. There were hundreds.

The biggest surprise was their triangles. Every fifth prisoner wore a U! *Were there really this many Ukrainians? Was it like that at Gross-Rosen too?*

Most of them said that they served in the army when they were snagged by the Germans.

"We were starved. Some were shot. The healthy and able were taken deep into Germany to work. So why were you arrested so young?" one said.

For whatever reason, without thinking, I replied, "My Tato is connected with the UPA, and when the Germans found out about it, they arrested us together."

"What's this Underground? Whose your leader? Who supports it?" he asked.

"The Underground fights for Ukraine's return to independence. Its members are Ukrainian patriots who are willing to fight and give their lives to improve the fate of its people," I said.

"So what do they think about the return of the Soviet Army to Ukraine?" he asked. "Are you still scared of Stalin? When will this war be over?"

It wasn't easy for me to answer all his questions at first - I had no idea who he was, I might of said too much already, and honestly, I didn't know some of these answers.

Then he told me his story. "I come from Vinnytsia." Midwest Ukraine. "I worked as a schoolteacher there. But then one beautiful day, our healthy and capable working men were deported by force to Germany. I was put to work on a farm, and honestly, it wasn't bad. There was plenty of food. But then the farmer's daughter, well, she tried tricking me into sleeping with her, but I knew it was completely forbidden for foreigners to have sex with Germans. I stopped her, and then she went off and lied to her father, saying that I chased her after she wouldn't sleep with me. The enraged farmer complained to the police, and they arrested me. I've been stuck in here for two years now. Injustice rules within these walls, but injustice rules back in Ukraine the same. So I ask you - what do we do if the war ends and we're left alive?"

His question shifted my perspective. *What do we do if this war ends?* I noticed my fear had been hopping around. First I hoped I wouldn't die. Then I hoped I wouldn't be taken from Tato. Then I hoped I wouldn't be crippled. But this man's question sparked a new question - *What if I live? What happens then?*

"I don't know whether I'd dare to go back to Ukraine," he confided in me. "Stalin's threatened that those who fell into German hands will be considered traitors," he said.

He paused, as if letting that sit with me, and then said, "I remember the great famine in Ukraine. As a young boy I survived because I had family in the city who helped out... just remember to be careful about who you talk to about all this - there are lots of younger people who don't understand politics or know of the famine. They might see *you* as the traitor."

He went on to say that many Russians try to blame Germany's rise on Ukraine, the main reason being that

Ukrainians didn't want to join up with the Soviets to fend off Germany. But what Ukrainian in his right mind would help a country who'd just force-fed us a famine driven by ethnic cleansing?

"And I feel comfortable talking to you about this, because you're from Galician Ukraine, as opposed to being born in the East," he added.

"A lot in Ukraine has changed," I told him. "The consciousness of Ukrainian independence from Russia has increased, and these two halves of Ukraine are much more in line."

I wanted to talk more, but the air raid ended and the howling sirens brought us back to work. We got nothing done there, but Grisha offered to show me to the gate where I'd meet the youth unit. Just before six, we walked over to the factory gate, where the guard halted us.

"This one's new today," said Grisha. "He's staying with the minors and wants me to show him the way. He doesn't know where their barracks are."

A prisoner can talk so openly to a guard?

"Normally, I wouldn't until the horn goes off," said the guard, "but go ahead, just this time." Interesting.

A few minutes after the 6PM horn went off, a group of young men lined up in threes marched along the main road through camp.

They each wore the same striped prison garb as the adults, but on their heads were green military caps. A middle aged man led them, chanting counts to which all these young men marched to.

I joined in, last in line, mimicking their steps. We marched back towards the main gate and arrived at a barrack which was sunk 3/4 of its height into the ground. Behind it was a small area for assembly and a volleyball net.

The man's command stopped us in front of this building. "Prepare for dinner," and to me he said, "And you, follow me." I did. All the other boys gayly ran into the building as if they weren't in German captivity.

This leader of our group wore cleanly washed prison clothes. A "P" perched on his shoulder. He looked cheerful and friendly and I slowly treaded behind him into his room.

To my marvel, he actually shook my hand and then told me to sit down. "My name is Stefan," he said in German. "Please, do call me that. What's your name and cipher?" This was no Kapo.

I replied and he said that he heard about me. Apparently I was the only underage prisoner off of today's transport. He asked me if I understood Polish or Russian, because those were easiest for him. I told him I understood both.

In Polish, he began to explain the rules exclusive to this unit. "This block is organized to raise morale among the other prisoners. The Germans are humane, which is shown through their treatment of underage prisoners. They'll treat you with respect, if we conscientiously work. They made me the mentor, because I know a few languages, and back home I was a teacher, so I understand youth well. Additionally, I can teach others how to sing. Tomorrow morning, when I take all of you to work, you'll march and sing German marching songs. By doing so, you'll get more food."

Sing German marching songs? I didn't want to sing those.

"So today after dinner, we'll have rehearsal. You must learn these songs quickly and by heart, he said.

He handed me the lyrics to the songs and told me to learn them quickly. "Can you read German or do you want someone to read the songs to you?"

"I read and write in German," I said.

"Oh good!" he said. "Once a month, prisoners are allowed to write a letter home and I usually have to write everyone's letter because these boys can't write in German." *Write home? Really?*

The block leader Stefan seemed friendly enough. He led me into the barrack so I could find a bed and then warned me, "Sometimes, at night, there are air-raid alarms, and maybe even actual raids. If they go off, we'll all rush out into the grove next to the factory buildings and wait in the trenches, which can partially hide us in case of danger."

I then grabbed a bed and he gave me a tin bowl that I had to hold on to and wash and answer for. "Now get outside and grab dinner before you miss it. And go find some friends. You shouldn't fear anything here," he said.

I left Shtubo (blockleader) Stefan in good spirits. *Maybe this place won't be so bad.* I walked into the end of the line with my bowl. Four boys stood ahead of me. As I peeked over the rim of the kettle, I saw thick pasta, with pieces of meat!

Thank you God! Good food, nice Shtubo, beds... not so bad.

The on-duty prisoner handing out scoops noticed my awe and realized that I was new here and that this was my first time getting food. After the first scoop, he asked, "Maybe you'd want a little more?"

"Yes," I said immediately.

He gave me another full scoop, which threatened to spill over the brim of my bowl. Behind me, boys lined up for seconds.

"Hey! Why does he get a second scoop already? He didn't even finish his first!" complained the boy right behind me. "Svinya," (you pig) he muttered in Polish under his breathe. "I'll reckon with you later."

But I didn't care about the boy. I paid him almost no attention - the food was too good! I stepped over to the side so that I wouldn't disrupt anyone and enjoyed every bite. It was the best meal I'd eaten since being arrested.

Is the food always this good? Or is it just for us youth? Maybe if I fit in with these boys, I'll keep getting good food and gain some much needed strength.

After supper, Stefan called us to study the German marching songs. He sung first. We repeated. And it looked to me like all these boys had already memorized the words.

I didn't like these songs that praised how wonderful Germany was, and I decided that I wouldn't put any energy into them. *Why should I glorify Germany? Russia already forced us to do this, to sing about the "happy" life in the Soviet Union, which was actually the opposite - it was a slave life.* The other boys weren't excited about these songs either. Many mumbled through it.

Stefan rebutted, "Hey! You're not doing this for me. You can refuse to sing if you'd like, but how will the camp administration react? Will they keep giving us the best food? Will they still keep us separate from other prisoners? Think about it. I want to help you. I am the same as you, a prisoner, and I'm only doing this because of obligation - *not* for any personal satisfaction. So please, sing as you know how. The Germans need to see our appreciation."

After hearing Stefan's words, the other boys sang with a bit more enthusiasm. I did not.

In the Camp of Heinkel, hoi ra ra
Hoi ra ra, hoi ra ra

And another:

Zovi zovi ee ha ha ha
Zovi zovi ee ha ha ha

After the boys got a hang of the songs, we started marching on Stefan's command, with a right foot stomp, then a left. He had a good grasp on the youth, and the sung pretty well.

After practice, Stefan said, "Get to bed soon. There could be an airstrike tonight, and you need your sleep. I want you all to be well-rested so that tomorrow you'll sing as beautifully as you have today." We were dismissed.

I washed up with soap and enough hot water and laid down in my own bed that night. Thoughts circled about - this new location, the fascinating factory, the airstrike on Berlin, being treated better as a youth, more freedom, more food, and finally, a friendly Grisha Fidyenko - all these images rocked me to a hard night's rest.

I awoke the next morning to Stefan's whistle. Us youth ran half-asleep to the toilet and then quickly assembled outside.

Stefan organized us into rows of five and he happily counted us, joking with some of the boys.

Am I still in camp?

Three military officers walked into camp Heinkel through the main gate, confirming that I was. But their stop at our barracks was quick, as they trusted Stefan's number and didn't double-check his count.

It was a weird sight.

After breakfast, we assembled again and were commanded to put on our berets. "Everyone who doesn't have theirs, get back to the barracks and get them." In his hand was one such green beret. He called me over and gave it to me.

After the youth came back with their hats, and the German command finished counting the prisoners, Stefan ordered us to march in place, and then onward. This morning was clear and calm.

Marching towards the factory, I saw other blocks getting roll called, with block leaders and prisoners hurrying to separate factories. This was the first time I saw how many prisoners were here - it must have been thousands.

Stefan gave the command "Ain Leed!" and in step, all the boys started loudly singing:

"In lager Heinkel..."

"Louder!" he said, as we passed the German administration building. As we marched along, I suddenly felt someone step on my heel.

At first I thought someone misstepped, but when I turned around, I saw it was the boy who had called me a svinya (pig) the night before. He laughed wickedly.

Again with this? A bully? I had grown Poles threaten to kill me and now I've got a little bully on my tail?

I turned back around, trying to ignore him, but then he stepped so hard on my heel that my wood-soled boot jumped off my foot and I had to scramble out of line to grab it and put it back on. As I bent down to look at my foot, I saw that he'd ripped my skin open and it oozed blood and it started to sting. I wondered what could make this boy so brash.

Block leader Stefan noticed that I'd left the line to fix my shoe. He slightly paused and looked back but didn't mention anything.

We marched up to the factory I worked at, and I parted ways with the boys. I stopped to look down at my heel. It wasn't too bad, but that didn't stop my anger. *I haven't done anything to you! Why cling to me? I'm gonna tell Stefan! ... No... The other boys would laugh at me. 'You just got here and you're already a burden! Svinya!'* I held it in.

I looked up and saw prisoners walking into the factory in no hurry, their German civilian masters unsuccessfully ordering them to hurry their pace. But nobody listened. Masters shook their heads.

I met Grisha over by the plane which was closest to completion. He greeted me with a smile and asked, "How do you like living in the youth barracks?"

"So far so good. I like Stefan. But singing those German songs gets to me. What do the other prisoners think about our singing?" I asked.

"Don't be so concerned about what others think," he said. "The Germans are giving you more to eat *and* better treatment. Many of us would love to trade places with you, but we're too old already."

"Well the singing isn't good for my soul, so I'll keep opening my mouth, but I won't make a sound," I said. Then I showed him my stripped heel and he poured iodine on it, which prisoners used frequently in the factory.

"People bang their elbows and knees on the sharp corners and ends of these planes, so I keep this around just in case. Today I'll introduce you to the device that controls all the electrical connections in the aircrafts," he said.

It wasn't school, but at least I was learning.

Since the master was right next to the plane, we immediately pretended to work. Grisha began explaining all the various inscriptions of this apparatus. He read them out loud. I repeated. The master was satisfied and moved on.

"So what did you do before you were arrested? How's life in Ukraine? How do the Germans treat the people? Will the Soviet Army hit Berlin?" he asked, among other things. I liked that he immediately put his trust in me.

I told him about Galicia and my family and school, and then he began to complain about Communism. "It's tough for me to understand why life in the Soviet Union is so severe." And he spoke to me in Ukrainian, although he spoke with his other comrades in Russian. I made a mental note to ask him why later.

"The Germans, as they're built now, will lose this war," I said. "The main reason is that they're too proud and cocky, so much so that they don't think they need anyone else's help. Instead of equip the Soviet POWs, who would do anything to be freed from Communism... instead of actually helping them flee from a Satanic system to establish their own republics... instead of offering help... they did the exact same thing as the Russians. They confined us to camps, starved us cold, mocked us, forced us to work for no wages, planted us in these disgusting camps, and in a short time they've proven that they were the same goons and cutthroats or worse even, than the Communists."

Grisha listened on.

"Sometimes individuals or groups, who were lucky enough to escape from the Germans and actually return to the Union, were used as agitators in the army and amongst the people. They passionately cried, whining of their horrible experiences under the Germans. This was probably a big reason why the Soviet soldiers changed their neutral attitude towards the Germans. They shouted that the Nazi-occupiers were deporting whole villages from Ukraine to work in Germany. And that these Germans would send trains-full of arms to the Eastern Front, and then transport those trains back to Germany filled to the brims with Ukraine's fertile black soil."

Grisha was intrigued.

I continued, "So Ukraine created the Ukrainian Insurgent Army (UPA), which set itself one goal - to free Ukraine's forced dependency on other nations. So Ukraine is now fighting against both Russian Communism and German fascism, which is no small feat, so we're waiting for help from the West. We'll surely find our independence then."

Grisha thought for a moment, then said, "I served in this Soviet Army. I was surrounded by Germans and captured too.

We couldn't fend them off - their arms outnumbered and out-classed ours. When I was captured, I immediately thought that German captivity couldn't be worse than life in the Soviet Union, but I soon found out that these Germans were no better than the Communists."

He added, "But I do request that you don't mention any of what we said to any of my friends. Many of them have forgotten their pre-war conditions and how they fell into German captivity. They long for family and think that as soon as they get home, all will be better. They praise the Union now, so if you say anything against it, they'll harass you with all their fury."

After lunch, we aimlessly wound up electrical wires pretending to work and kept talking.

Grisha said, "Prisoners around here are messing with the planes, even sabotaging them, which is a danger to everyone involved. The Germans know about it too and are trying to catch them. I thought about cutting the wires to machines guns, but it was just too obvious. My electrical work is the last thing in the assembly line, so after me the master himself checks the entire plane to the smallest detail. After him, the German garrison comes and takes the plane outside the camp gates."

"But," Grisha promised, "I will do something else, something even the master won't find."

"Careful," I said, "Don't fall into the hands of these Germans, because nobody knows how much longer this war will last, and it would be a shame if the Germans ruined you right before it ended."

"I already thought of that, but trust me, no one will know who did it," he said. "One thing that does worry me is that this factory can be so quickly demolished. The Allies know about it. They've bombed her once and have flown over again, spying and firing shots. Plenty of us could lose our lives this way, or worse, get crippled."

"No worries here," I said, "I'm glad that this war has finally fallen into German territory. The German people have begun to feel the horrors of war that they've inflicted on others' underserved lands."

"So you're not scared of being struck?" he asked.

"Not really," I said, "I left my fear in Ukraine when the bombers flew over Lviv."

He laughed at my courage, especially after I told him that I don't worry at night at all. The better I should sleep. But even though I wasn't worried about myself, I *was* worried about Tato, and Mama and my siblings.

The next few days passed like that, with Grisha pretending to show me things, me pretending to work, and the master pretending to care. At nights, after lip syncing German songs, I kept to myself, not wanting another run in with a bully.

In the youth barracks, one boy with a "U" on his chest kept approaching me, but I shied away time and time again because of my bloody heel. I didn't want to make this situation more complicated. I wasn't in the mood to meet people.

But then one evening I got curious and decided to go out

into the yard to see what the other boys were up to. The boy with the "U" came up to me and in broken German asked me where I came from. I immediately replied Western Ukraine and he gave me his hand, saying he was from Galicia and that his name was Vasil. We were both pleased with the acquaintance.

"I've been in this youth barrack the last three months, and I was here when the Allies air-raided the factory! When planes come in the middle of the night, we'll run together into the forest," he said.

I joked with him and said, "I won't be doing that, because I'm sure nothing will happen to me in the barrack, and I'll probably just sleep through it all. Who knows where these bombs might fall anyway?"

He tried to argue with me, but when I told him about the strikes in Lviv, he calmed down and began telling me about the other boys. "There are others from Ukraine, but they hold tight with the Russians. They don't like me."

"I'm not scared - it was the Germans who arrested me," I said. "Just ignore them."

Vasili went on: "I've had some trouble with a specific boy here. He's always clinging to me, wanting to fight. Watch out - he always picks on the new guy."

I described him the boy who called me a pig and how he stripped the skin off my heel and how angry I was at him. We were confident it was the same boy.

Vasili said, "Don't fear him. No one here likes him. But I gotta go - it's my turn to wash dishes. Let's talk again soon. And remember, this Saturday we write letters home."

Really? "Have you written your family yet?"

"Yes. Already got news back too! We'll talk more later," he said and ran off.

I stood there pleased. *I could let Mama and the family know I was alive! But what if it doesn't get to them? Did the Soviets get to them?*

A few young men then came outside and tossed me a ball. I gladly tossed it right back.

"Wanna play volleyball?"

I accepted and joined the side with less players. Instead of a net, there hung a thick web of wires probably brought in from a neighboring factory.

After a few points, I felt someone push me from behind. I looked back and saw the same boy that called me a pig.

But I didn't budge and continued to play. But on the next point, he jumped in front of me and began screaming: "Svinya! Get away from my spot! I want to play here."

I politely responded. "Maybe someone else would move for you."

He challenged me further, jumping closer to me, shouting, and then he poked my chest. "Move svinya!" The other guys broke the game and started laughing at us.

One egged us on: "Who wins this one?!"

More boys spilled out of the building and surrounded us on all sides and started egging us on to fight. The boy kept poking and prodding me. I didn't react.

I started to leave, but he hit me even harder in the chest. Without another thought, I launched my fist through his face. He hit the groundhard. It all happened so fast. Blood spurted from his nose and he cried loudly. I didn't move. *Will you rise?*

Will you fight?

At that moment Blockleader Stefan ran over and indignantly demanded that someone tell him how it happened: "Who did this to him?!" No one said a word.

Then he walked around asking the boys one by one until he got to me. I was scared. But Stefan would find out at some point.

"I hit him," I said.

"Go wash yourself," he told the boy.

"You, get in my office," he said to me.

I did and Stefan slammed the door and began to berate me.

"What you thinking? Why'd you fight him? Don't you know that I can banish you for this? You just got here, and you're already starting fights? And what if a German officer would have walked by? He would have given you a *real* lesson on the spot. He'd show you how to fight alright. What do you think he'd say?"

Are you kicking me out?

"What kind of discipline do you think I run here? One that allows you the right to fight? I won't tolerate this any longer. You're going to the adult barracks. Got it? You've already been a nuisance to me anyway - when we were on our way to work, remember? You probably didn't tie up your shoes, and of course they flew off your feet during our march. You know well that the Germans watch us - how we march, how we sing. I'll give you one more chance - you get no more warnings!"

I didn't expect that.

"If I see you do anything else to disrupt this barrack, you're gone."

I listened carefully, bowing my head down to his threats, grateful about a second chance. Then finally, after this long lecture, he softly said, "Come now, tell me how it all happened. Why'd you fight?"

I told him everything from "svinya!" to the heel stomp to the fight on the volleyball court.

"I didn't want to say anything!" I said, showing him the scab on my heel. "Now I regret not speaking up to you. I thought he might just leave me in peace. Maybe not touch me anymore. I didn't want to get laughed at by the others for being an informer. He pushed me during the volleyball game, and without thinking I punched him once in the face and he fell down and all that blood spurted out of his nose. He started crying. I regret hitting him. I promise, I won't do it again."

The blockleader listened carefully. He told me that the boy's name was Yurek, and he's had disputes with others too. Stefan spoke with him before and Yurek promised that he wouldn't touch anybody else. "I'm giving him one more chance after this, telling him exactly what I told you. He will either fix himself or find himself in another block."

He gets another chance? It felt unfair. But I didn't say a word. I was in the clear. I again repeated that I wouldn't fight with anyone else, bowed to Stefan, and went and laid on my top-bunk bed.

The next day was a Saturday. We were only held at work for six hours and then let go for the rest of the day. Stefan handed us specially printed postcards covered with codes and ciphers, which would serve as return addresses. I was excited to write home.

I got a card and then Vasili walked up to me and said, "I heard about your fight and being locked up in the office."

I explained what happened.

"He should have learned his lesson long ago," said Vasili, with a postcard in his hand.

The cards had very little space to write and Stefan explained, "You can only write that you're healthy, that you're working, that you live well, that you'll all still meet, and that you love your family and send them kisses. If you still have room, tell them that the weather here is very good."

At least they'll know I'm alive.

A line of boys who couldn't write in German filed in front of Stefan, and he started writing cards.

I grabbed one of the pencils on his desk and sat down to write but no words came out. *Where do I start?* My hands trembled as I wrote, "Dear Mama, sister and my brothers." Tears fell from my eyes.

Vasili encouraged me, saying, "Don't cry. You'll still see them," as if he knew what I was thinking. "Write that you love them."

I tried, but I couldn't. I was sad and I couldn't write a word, so I wrote Vasili's first. Writing his calmed me down a bit, so then I went back to mine, but it was agony writing those first words, "Mama, I love you..." I had to get up and pace about the barracks before I could actually finish the letter.

Vasili took his over to Stefan where he collected those who finished. Seeing Vasili's letter, Stefan asked, "Who wrote this for you?"

Vasili pointed to me, as I was finishing up my own.

Stefan told the others: "Head over to Stepan if you'd like him to write your letter - he can write them as good as I can."

Hearing such admiration for me, I gladly perked up and the boys came over and I wrote some letters. One of Stefan's friends then unexpectedly came up to him and pulled him away from writing letters. The boys in his line all came into mine. None of them wanted to wait for him to return.

The line grew long, but I was glad that I could serve in some way. Every letter was pretty much identical besides the family names and a few phrases.

At that time I noticed that *none* of the other boys could write their own letters. Writing lifted my spirits. In the end I saw that the line was empty, and I had written everyone's letter. Stefan still wasn't back.

As I started to get up from the table, Yurek walked up to me with his postcard. He still had a black eye, and his face was swollen. I couldn't believe that I'd hit him that hard. He looked awful.

Looking back on it, I must have unloaded all my anger out on him from my arrest until now. I felt bad, but as soon as he walked up, I relaxed. I smiled and took the postcard from him and asked him who he wanted to write to.

"My mama," said Yurek. "She's alone at home. My father

was shot by the Germans. This is my first postcard home. I want to let her know I'm still alive."

He thanked me when I was done and just then I saw that in a strange way I'd found myself another friend, this Yurek from Katowice, Poland.

Vasili sat beside me the entire time. After Yurek left, he said, "If it's possible, I want to switch my bed next to yours."

"I'd like that. One thing though - at night, when the alarms sound, don't wake me up," I said.

Stefan came back and asked "Who's left? Who else needs a letter?" Nobody answered.

"Did you write them all?" he asked.

"I did," I said.

He smiled with pleasure and said, "From now on, you'll be my secretary."

"Can I move my bed next to Stepan?" Vasili asked Stefan.

"As long as there's a free one," he said.

Vasili did so that night, and I sternly repeated myself, "If there's a raid, do not wake me. I'll wake up if I want to get up."

That night, alarms blared, but I didn't hear them. The next morning, Vasili told me that throughout the entire night planes flew over Berlin as well as our camp. He barely slept and told me that next time he'd do exactly as I did. Things were starting to look up.

The next morning, Stefan called us out of the barrack, lined us up in fives, and counted us. But he made a mistake and started over. His second count didn't line up either.

He counted us twice more, even realigning us, but something didn't add up.

"Is anybody missing?" he asked.

I looked about and didn't notice anyone I knew. He sent a boy to the barracks to check if maybe someone had overslept, but the boy came back empty-handed.

Stefan got shifty and said, "Take a good look. Who's missing?"

No one answered.

He counted again, and the numbers still didn't add up. Then the main gate opened and the German officer accompanied by two soldiers walked up to our block.

"We lack one," Stefan said, twitching nervously.

The lead officer then went before us and told us to straighten up our rows, and he counted us himself. He was off by one as well. He ordered Stefan to go and check the entire barrack. Stefan came back empty-handed.

The officer then ordered us to take one step left and he re-counted us. Same result. He then commanded Stefan and a soldier to go to the air-raid trenches to see if anyone had fallen asleep there last night. The officer left with his other soldier to count the rest of the camp. Stefan ordered us to stay in place until he got back. We stood.

After they all left, Vasili said to me quietly, "I know who's missing, but I was too afraid to admit it. I didn't want the Germans to interrogate me."

"Wisely thought," I said.

"Some have already tried to flee from camp," he said, "but

the German Garrison and their dogs caught them. They were beaten in front of each and every barrack, completely humiliated. After the beatings, they were never seen again. How could anyone see this and still risk escaping?"

He continued: "But the boy whose missing always hung out by himself. He was no friend to anyone. If anybody tried talking to him, he'd walk away. So I left him alone. But here in camp, when someone goes missing, the law says the whole camp must stand in rows until the Germans say otherwise."

After waiting for an hour, we saw the officer with the other soldier turn back behind the wire gate and into the administrative building. Stefan and his accompanying soldier reappeared from the trenches. The solider went through the gate and Stefan silently walked over to us. He could barely speak.

"Wait for the command's orders," he said.

After some time, two soldiers came out of the German post, with two dogs sniffing. Behind them walked two more soldiers and the head of the camp himself.

This man walked to Stefan and asked, "Which boy is missing?"

"I don't know," said Stefan.

The Commander scolded him. "Bring out the prisoner list and read off their numbers! Quickly! Quickly!" he shouted at Stefan and Stefan ran off.

He returned nervous and started shouting the numbers. No one responded to the fifth, and Stefan realized who the boy was.

"I don't see him," said Stefan.

"Well what bed does he sleep in?" the Commandant asked, impatiently.

"Yes, I'll show you right away."

He led the Commandant and the soldiers and the dogs into the barrack, letting the dogs examine the bed to familiarize with the boy's smell.

He rudely scolded Stefan again in front of us saying, "You taught these boys nothing. I never expected any of these kids to escape!" He then shook his fist and threatened us, saying that he'll recount us all soon.

He ordered Stefan to keep us in rows and sent his assistant soldier off towards the other blocks of prisoners still standing.

In a short time, we watched them all break off for breakfast and then work. The cooks never came our way.

What now? Some complained about the missing kid, Stefan ordered them quiet, and our feet ached as we stood until lunch. Then the 12pm bells went off, and the Commandant stormed out of his bunker with a few more soldiers.

"Step aside!" he ordered Stefan. He commanded us to continue standing and get ready to march. He continued screaming, making us the scapegoat for the missing boy.

"I gave you better food, easier work, guard against the fraud of those older prisoners, and you repay me with an escape from camp?! What will higher command say to me? They'll say it's *my* fault. That *I* was too good to you. So today? You'll get nothing to eat. You're too strong. You want to flee? I'll show you who I should be to you."

He was fuming. I didn't know what he was capable of.

He turned back, giving his soldiers instructions, then

turned to us and said, "March!" Then with an even greater cry, he said, "Run! As you're assembled!"

So we started running down the main road of the camp.

The Commandant shouted, "Run, one, two, three... one, two, three, run!"

He ran with us for a bit. I myself hadn't ran in over a month. And I hadn't eaten since yesterday. I was woozy.

Then the Commandant got tired and ordered the guards to continue our run. So without interruption, we ran, from one gate of the camp to the other, back and forth, back and forth.

The sun burned and air was still, with no wind to cool us off. Although we were still young, our muscles stiffened and it was harder to move and it became more and more difficult to run in the shoes with the rigid wooden soles. They had no give, and I felt my feet blister up.

Meanwhile, the Commandant lounged back as his sentries took turns running with us. He sat boastfully, proud of his punishment, watching us carry it out in misery. Even the well-fed guards who were taking turns got weary, shoulders slouched.

Some boys started to lag behind and were hounded by the Commandant: "Chase them with the stick!"

So the guards did. I grew powerless and started to pace. *Strike Berlin. Now.* But we weren't granted that happiness.

And no breaks came. We had no way of knowing when this would end. We couldn't keep up with the Commandant's count anymore. Each young man ran as he could.

Our running continued through the lunch bell, so I knew

we'd been going at it for an hour. The workers returned to their factories. We went on.

Finally, the Commandant joined back in. He kept counting but then ordered us to turn right onto a recently bombed path, which was covered with deep pits, some head-to-toe deeper than I was. He drove us right through one of the craters, then through another, and a third. He easily danced little steps above us.

At least there were only three pits...

But my relief did not last long. The Commandant called his guards over, and they ran us right back through these bombed-out wells. Some boys dragged their dead legs. The Commandant beat several young men who could barely move. I somehow kept up.

"More sticks!" he ordered the guards. Some boys got hit and couldn't even change stride. They were too tired to react. Some fell down, losing one or both their shoes. Mine somehow stayed on, but they sure did hurt.

And these pits weren't dirt but covered in sharp stones and cement. Barefoot boys bloodied their soles. I tried to not get too close to the guards. I didn't know where I accumulated enough power to out run the others.

I was breathless, sweaty, starved... I could barely lift my legs, but those things didn't scare me, because I outran the others. The guards kept replacing each other. Boys were beaten, those on the ground even. But they didn't move.

And then my eyes started to darken and I felt myself stumble and just then the Commandant ordered us all to line up. I stopped running. Some young men who lay in these bomb pits slowly pushed themselves up and re-attached to the rows.

But some didn't move and had to be assisted by the guards. They straightened us out, and then one of the guards... I don't know why, counted us again.

The Commander got his calculation and smiled. "This is not the end of your punishment - today, no food, and these barracks you've lived in will now be closed. I'm scattering you throughout the other prisoners. Maybe once you're there you'll wise up and no longer want to run away."

He ordered the guards to lead us back to the youth barrack to await instructions.

We trudged back drained and collapsed broken into our beds. We didn't see Blockleader Stefan. No one else was there to tell us what would happen next.

Each of us boys laid back and wondered how long we'd remain in this unit and when the Commander would go through with his threats.

But then came a small spark of hope. The camp cooks brought us dinner, albeit the dinner that the rest of camp received. The on-duty prisoners from the kitchen felt awfully sorry for us. They told us that the whole camp watched us suffer during lunch.

Each of the boys grabbed their rations and complained. It wasn't the delicious leftovers from the German garrison, but the usual camp gruel.

But that didn't stop us from eating any of it. *So we got dinner, when the Commander said we wouldn't. Maybe he'll change his mind and let us stay in this block.* I didn't want to get thrown back with the older prisoners. The worst thing that happened in this barrack was a bully. Out there might be worse

That night, there was no Blockleader, so we went to sleep when we wanted. Vasili and I complained to each other but then soon went to bed so we could be ready for whatever they'd throw as us tomorrow.

The next morning, I woke up to Stefan's familiar whistle, giving me a quick sense of relief. He told us to line up but angrily drove away anyone who approached him, not wanting to talk to any of us.

Our numbers lined up, one still missing, and he didn't count us again. We stood in silence until the German guard showed. They ignored Stefan and counted us themselves and then went off to other blocks.

After a modest breakfast, Stefan summoned us to what I thought would be work. But when I looked up, a German Garrison came our way from the main gate. A few prisoners dressed in clean prisoner clothes joined up with them. *Must be the other blockleaders.*

A German officer began reading off our names, shooing us to respective blockleaders. And apparently standing next to Vasili didn't help, because he was called off to the first group and I was not. I simply waved my hand to him and he to me, an understanding that we'd still find each other later.

For some reason, I along with only two others fell to the last group. Each previous group had ten. These two boys were French and inseparable. Vasili mentioned that they were the last ones to come into the youth unit before me.

Our new blockleader led us in a completely different direction than all the others to a building that sat at the end of camp. I felt uneasy.

The building was really long and different from all the others. It had several large, wide-open sliding doors. Plenty of prisoners lied on three storied beds inside. They seemed angry and looked at us like we were animals, not people. Additionally, this building was cordoned off for some reason by an extra set of barbed wire, like the black-X isolation block in Gross-Rosen.

Our attendant led us through the gates, told us to wait here, and then closed the gate behind us and he went on further.

Both French prisoners said something to each other that I didn't understand, but they were definitely as surprised as I was to find themselves here. *Why this barrack? Maybe they brought us here to die.*

The blockleader approached us with his secretary and told us we have no right to leave this barrack.

"You'll be classified into whatever work group you're able and taken off to other camps in Germany," he said. "After classification, you'll be assigned a bed that you can't leave, because trucks could arrive at any moment to take you away."

What a pity. I'd just found a good friend, a decent camp, and once again, I'm being driven into the unknown. Don't look for me, Vasili. I won't be around. And Petro Fidyenko, my friendly mentor - did you see me as we were forced through the pits of broken cement? Did you see us get punished for the escape of that young man? You probably didn't expect

SEPARATION

I'd leave you so soon.

We still had so much to say to each other. He wanted to know more about what was happening at home - the current life in Ukraine under the Germans and more about the people's movement to freedom. I regretted our parting. I wanted to tell him more.

In turns, we youth were taken into a small office and asked what we could do and what we've learned. I told them that I'd attended two years of technical school in the electrical department.

"What else did you do at home?"

I told them Tato was a blacksmith and that I helped him in the smithy. I also helped him make our farmland more arable. One of the officers then showed me to my bed. The French boys were assigned to a different group and taken to the other end of the building. I climbed up onto the third bunk and looked around to see if anyone looked familiar, but none of the prisoners even acknowledged my presence.

They were all weathered and occupied by their thoughts. I sought out some U's on red triangles but even they wouldn't talk to me.

Lying face up on the bed, I tried rationalizing why so many prisoners were designated for export from this camp. *Why bring me here just to send me out? So much for German manners, but maybe these Germans know something. Maybe they know that this camp is going to get hit again. They must be taking me to a factory the Allies don't know about yet.*

My thoughts were interrupted by a neighbor climbing onto the top bunk right next to mine. He had a U. I politely asked him if he knew where we were being taken. I spoke Ukrainian and he answered in Russian: "I don't know."

"Where are you from?" I asked.

"Don't bother me," he said and waved his arm at me and turned over.

My separation to this new barrack depressed me even more. I hadn't even warmed up my spot here and off I go. I thought of home.

After a small dinner, we were told we'd stay here another night. I went back to my bed and did just as the other prisoners did - stared at the ceiling. But a funny little satisfaction came over me - the day before I had somehow survived that run and dodged a beating from the guards! And I came out the other side with just blisters! They still burned, but it could have been so much worse. My exhaustion and pride put me to bed quite quickly, but it didn't last for long.

I woke up feeling something crawl on my arm. I took a closer look and saw the same creature that I'd seen in the cavern prison of Breslaw. I looked down at my blanket, and it was covered. They slithered out from underneath the blanket and then back in again.

I got out of bed and shook my blanket and went back up to my bunk.

"You're working too hard," one prisoner said. I looked up.

"Those bugs multiply so fast that you'll do nothing but waste time trying to shake them off," he added. I got back into bed and the bugs came back as promised. Somehow I fell asleep amongst the slithering.

To my wonder, we woke the next morning to no counting.

SEPARATION

But that made sense - we were completely surrounded by barbed wire and an on-duty German guard as well. I looked through that barbed wire and saw the German garrison hurriedly transporting finished planes away from camp.

We got breakfast and trucks arrived at our barrack. German guards started howling off numbers, immediately loading prisoners into the trucks, many with breakfast still in hand. I was called. I was loaded. I sat on the floor.

CHAPTER ELEVEN

ON THE MOVE

Nobody told us where we were going. We sat obediently on the floor. The guards dozed on their benches. A few hours later we arrived.

The guards opened the hatch and a similar sight appeared - the "Sachsenhausen" sign. They organized us into fives and counted us and took us to registration. There were no ladders or faux firefighters or fake fires this time. They took us to the same barracks we stayed in last time. Two blockleaders sat outside this barrack and one said, "Go inside. Do what you like. You'll be held here until another train comes to take you away to another camp."

I thought it was funny that he said we could do what we like.

I tried laying down like the older prisoners, but that got boring so I went back outside for some fresh air and a look at the neighboring barracks. I thought maybe I'd catch a glance of the prisoners with black X tattoos on their faces.

But no luck. I was alone. I looked to the sky and my thoughts soared again to my family. *Where's Tato? How bored I am without you! But a barbed wire stands between us. Who invented such a thing? Whoever did must have known what it was going to be used for. Surely they know that the wire would be used for criminal hedges.*

My thoughts were interrupted by a voice from the black X barracks. A prisoner was hiding, pressed up against the barrack, and in broken German whispered, "Where you bring from? Another camp? You just arrested? Will war end soon?"

He spoke quickly and, it was impossible for me to answer all his questions at once.

"We were turned back here from a nearby camp called Heinkel. It was just recently bombed and the guards are starting to export workers from there to other camps," I said.

He interrupted my answers, asking, "When arrested? Where?"

"Not even two months ago, in Ukraine," I said.

Then in a clear, soft Ukrainian tongue, he said, "I'm a Ukrainian from the city of Zhytomyr. Who's winning between the Soviets and Germans? How far east is the front?"

I told him that at the end of May the Soviets were near the town of Brody, which is about 70 kilometers east of Lviv. He was surprised that the Soviets had moved so far west.

But I was more interested in his personal fate. I asked him about his arrest, and he said that he served in the Soviet Army and was captured as a prisoner of war.

"I tried escaping twice. They caught me twice. The second time I was sent here and straight into this awful block."

"What's on your face?" I asked.

But I got no answer, because from inside his barrack belted an angry voice that commanded him to immediately

274

get inside. He ran off and like that he was gone. I stood for some time observing the building. From inside I heard heated shouts and clamorous abuse.

They must be forbidden to leave the barrack or talk to others.

I walked back into my barrack and ran into the on-duty officer's announcement - tonight we stay here and we'll be sent off in the morning. At the time, most prisoners were lying on their beds. I did the same, staring idly at the ceiling until dinner, which was one dipper of potato soup. I had been hoping for the pasta and meat we ate when the Red Cross was here.

Eating left me no satisfaction, as if it didn't even happen. We didn't get seconds.

After dinner, we talked through our wire to some prisoners of all nationalities in the other barracks. A good number of them were Ukrainian. Many were military prisoners, arrested for the most minute reasons, but before we could get any more out of them, a camp officer walked up to our barracks and ordered us inside.

I went in and looked out the window and saw the black-marked X prisoners being let out of their barrack. Other prisoners watched over my back. The X prisoners strolled about for a bit and were driven back into the barrack less than half an hour later.

I went to bed that night glad at the lack of today's incidents, but hunger quickly took over. *How long could we survive like this? Months? Weeks?*

These thoughts somehow led me to slumber.

We awoke the next morning to a chippy Blockleader, who

hurriedly rushed us out of bed, sped us through a breakfast of coffee and slice of bread, and then drove us out to the field in the middle of camp. Some prisoners didn't even get their bread.

Our trains waited and choo-ed impatiently. I looked back and was sad for the older prisoners slowly trudging, who got their backs lashed by the guards' sticks. After being counted, guards led us to the train, with Germans and snarling German-Shepherds lining the route. *There's no way to escape. They have every gap covered. How could someone even think of getting out?*

Once again, an ugly freight train stood before us, part of which was already loaded with prisoners. We were led into a car with two armed guards already inside.

They ordered us to sit on the floor in rows. I somehow got a wall spot again, smack dab in between the guards and the toilet tub.

The loading was done, and the openings slid closed and we drove further into the unknown.

"On the road, we might have to slow down or stop. In those cases, not one of you dare to get up. If any of you need the tub, you raise your hand. And only two at a time. There's no other reason to get up. And if you do, you'll be beaten right where you are. We're going on a long journey, so I don't want any trouble," the lead guard said.

The train got hot quickly. A small hole sat in the top corner of this wagon for sunlight and ventilation. It gave us very little of both. The train then picked up from trot to full speed and off we went into the depths of Germany.

But its speed wasn't uniform. Sometimes it plowed, sometimes it was stagnant. At one point, its breaks screeched and we halted. Both guards tumbled across the wagon and sneered at the train's driver. The train sat in silence.

Then the plaintive howling of sirens carried our way, signaling nearby aircrafts.

The guard ordered us quiet: "Bombs may fall on our train. Your orders are to sit. Don't even *think* about running. The doors are closed from the outside anyway," he said. Then he grabbed his rifle and said, "Let there be peace. Otherwise, I'll shoot you without warning."

The sirens stalled, the train moved forward but then stopped. We heard the howling of the sirens again, this time in threes. A strike was coming. For some reason I felt calm, even rejoiced a little bit. *Bombing the Germans leads to a quicker end to this war. We'll have a better chance surviving out in this open field anyway!*

Guards again ordered us to stay put and pointed their rifles at us. We could hear from afar the sounds of explosions. These sounds crept closer until I could feel them start to rock the train. The guards grew tense. Hopefully a bomb wouldn't slip a trigger finger.

Explosions got nearer and nearer and most prisoners, who sat motionless on the floor, silently prayed and whispered and waited for whatever would happen next.

The next bomb rattled our train car and then we heard the clatter pit-tat-tat of the anti-aircraft artillery. It was just like Lontsky. Sitting ducks. We couldn't even see what was happening outside.

Pit-tat-tat-a-rat-tat-tat-tat-tat!

But the artillery noise quickly died down and the hum of the aircrafts fizzled out. The all clear sirens went off and several prisoners quickly lifted up their hands, begging for the tub. The guards allowed them up in twos. After some more idling, the locks from outside the train opened and cooks appeared. We each were given a slice of bread and a bit of liquid. Both guards were ordered off the wagon and joined the general prison staff outside the train.

I overheard two soldiers saying that here, in a nearby town, American planes had flown over and bombed it twice. "They were flying so low that we could have hit them with our rifles."

The other asked, "What about the anti-aircraft artillery?"

He replied, "The town didn't have any but it was bombed anyway... We're gonna be delayed a bit, because the tracks got hit during the last raid."

After several hours of sitting, our wagon was assigned two new armed guards. They peeked inside and said that we'd be going further when it got dark. After their smoke break, they jumped back inside and the train got moving again, meaning the tracks must have been back on line.

The guards assigned to our wagon spoke freely amongst themselves and were both quite young. They complained that their training wasn't fully completed but they'd been ordered onto convoys to transport prisoners anyway. They praised local girls, how there were plenty to choose from, with whom they had various adventures. But those plans changed with today's air raid.

They spoke candidly about German trains being attacked by Allied bombs, almost as if we weren't around. I then realized that these young guards weren't so afraid of us, so I figured they wouldn't be so quick to abuse us like the older guards. I decided to lay near them and listen in. Their stories about girls carried me deep into a firm sleep.

I awoke in the morning to prisoners saying the train had stopped and started and gone backwards and forwards all night. They were so amazed that I could sleep through it all. I noticed a prisoner get up to the tub without permission. One guard was passed out and the other looked like he was about to be.

We stopped at the next town, our car doors opened and two civilian workers traded out our full toilet barrel for an empty toilet barrel. Cooks brought us dippers of some kind of grout soup. We ate and the train cars closed and we moved on, driving fast then slow then fast then slow. The whole day, fast then slow then fast then slow.

Night came and older guards replaced the younger ones and we got a small piece of bread and went on. That night, the train traveled very slowly, sometimes being held up for several hours.

The next morning we came upon a stop littered with voices. I'd officially spent two full nights on this train.

"We're here," said a guard. It was the only words the guards said all night, even to each other. "Get ready to disembark." *Where were we?*

CHAPTER TWELVE

Dachau

I jumped down off the train car with stiff legs and saw a white board with large black letters: "Dachau." At that moment, the name meant nothing to me, so I paid it no attention. It was my legs that needed attention, which had fallen numb from three days of sitting on that freight floor. I saw an older prisoner walk like he was relearning how. He wasn't the only one.

Officers roared like lions: "Get into fives!"

They chased us with clubs, bigger than the sticks at Sachsenhausen.

"I heard about this camp," a nearby prisoner said. "It's one of the oldest Nazi concentration camps. Hitler sent anyone here who got in the way of his rise to power. They have crematoriums here, where they burn bodies and make soap from their fat. They've got gas chambers too, where prisoners choke to death on poison."

This was the first I'd heard of such wild and brutal inventions. *Am I still in the same world I was born into?*

The guards and German-Shepherds led us to the main

gate of camp. We stalled out front, so I got a good look at the place. Because Dachau lay on a plain, I could somewhat gauge its enormity, which was about a square kilometer. And just as in previous camps, it was completely surrounded by a barbed wire fence, with electrical wires entwined. Big buildings towered over us.

Around the camp, hugging the barbed wire fence, was a deep ditch filled with water. There were elevated platforms round the camp too, which housed military guards and machine guns to keep eyes watching.

In front of us stood a wide iron gate with the inscription "Arbeit Macht Frei" (Work Liberates). *Hm.* I carefully re-read it, making sure I'd read it right. *What does that mean? If someone works faster, better, or more, would he be freed? Or was this a lie? Is it giving prisoners false hope, only to snatch it away with Germany ending up the sole benefactor?*

Peering deeper through the gate, an open area led to a road lined with wooden barracks. *And who decided to plant poplars along this road?* In any other instance, I'd see this as a nice avenue, but this wasn't pleasing at all. Their height and slender immediately reminded me of the proud German mentality and their brutal attitude towards other nations. I felt like these poplars were guards, not trees, who worked with the German garrison to control all its prisoners.

And then I heard a terrible scream and a whistle from the prisoners.

What was that? My head spun. *A beating, already?* All the prisoners looked left and I did the same, only to see a vegetable garden. *Did a hungry prisoner jump into the garden?* But I didn't see any prisoners in the garden. *The guards must have chased them back.*

Then a prisoner moved over and two beautiful, young German women appeared before me. They were working the garden. Prisoners were hooting and hollering. But I was confused. *What good does yelling at these women do? Who benefits?*

One prisoner cried beside me: "For the past three years, I'd forgotten what women looked like. Give me just a moment with one. I'd be happy just hearing her gentle voice!"

Another answered, "I want to be alone with a woman. Just once! Then, I could die without regret."

Because I was so young, their pleas looked quite strange. These people were starving. Tomorrow, they could be killed. But they were desperate for women.

I didn't holler and stayed focused - *How do I make it out alive? How do I find freedom?*

To my wonder, even the German guards didn't calm them down. They watched and laughed. Many of these prisoners must have left wives at home. That yearning was undeniable. A minute before, the prisoners were exhausted, terrified, but then such a strong desire for women sparked within them, so much so that they became alive and young again!

Another said, "I want a pile of bread. Never ending. I'd eat so much that I couldn't eat another piece. And I'd like to sleep with my wife, just once more. That's it. That's all I want from this world!"

I stared mournfully at them. *What has this war done?*

The guards whistled and ordered the prisoners shut up. The gate which held the words "Work Liberates" opened, and the guards ordered us into camp.

We were counted again and then once more handed off from the Germans to the on-duty prisoners. The on-duty registered us and then gave us new camp ciphers. Mine was 80320. The sewing instructions were the same.

The on-duty prisoner then looked at my registry and said, "This letter 'U' that you've been wearing - such a nationality is not permitted here in camp Dachau. There are no Ukrainians here. You're either a Russian or Pole, and since you were a Pole upon your release from Gross-Rosen, I'll write the same here."

I rebuked: "You're wrong! I won't agree to be Polish. In Sachsenhausen, I was marked as a Ukrainian! Please record me as a Ukrainian."

"I will not do that. And if you don't like it, then you yourself can go protest to the blockleader or the Kapo... Or maybe you could even talk to the camp Commandant? He'll convince you of who you are now. There are others before you that have tried to be Ukrainian here and shortly ceased to do so."

He called up the next prisoner and began to examine his registration. But I was angry and wasn't ready to leave the registration and the on-duty prisoner, who had, just like me, been arrested by these Germans. But the prisoner behind me pushed me aside and I walked into the next building.

There I undressed and walked into the showers. Entering the bathroom, I carefully considered the shower head openings, wondering whether these were the gas chambers that I had heard about. This room started to crowd with prisoners. The showers didn't turn on. Prisoners grew restless.

But I couldn't take my mind off the registration table, and I became melancholy. *Is this what the world is like now? Dirty and unpleasant and unfair? A place where I can't call myself what I am?*

All sorts of old, weathered and naked prisoners shook with uncertainty in this shower room without water. But I became so frustrated and indifferent that I had nothing against us all being gassed. *Go ahead. Do it.*

More prisoners were brought in. The room was full.

Just then icy cold water spurted out of the showers. Prisoners fought it off by pushing each other into the water, trying to crowd together to stay warm. Many yelled until the water became a little warmer.

There was barely any soap. And it was black and rough, like it'd been mixed with sand. This potentially human fat soap wouldn't break into foam, so I just rubbed the coarse chunks on my feet.

We dried off in the next room with tiny pieces of clothe. Each prisoner shook like a dog and quickly rushed and ran to the next room where they gave us striped clothing that smelled like disinfectant chemicals. We got another pair of wood-soled shoes and a shirt, pants, jacket, and hat. The clothes were still eerily warm from the de-licing. Somehow I got the proper size with no rips, and this pair of prison garb felt much cleaner than the ones I had before.

After getting dressed in our "new" clothes and shoes, they put us back into ranks. Our numbers were called and we were divided into several groups, mine being about 50 prisoners. The guards ordered us to march down the main road, which was located between two long rows of wooden barracks, of which I counted seventeen on each side, all-together thirty four.

Our group was assigned the last block on the right. On its wall hung the number seventeen. And for whatever reason, unlike the others, it was surrounded by a barbed wire fence. *Another isolation block?* It was long and had four openings and a fence that separated it in half. We were led to the front square of this isolated unit, assigned to the fourth quadrant, and the gates were locked behind us. Guards said that the other three were filled. There must have been hundreds of prisoners in barrack 17 alone.

We walked in, saw the same three story bunks, rested a bit, and then the Blockleader introduced himself and told us that any orders that come into this barrack will come from him. He called out ciphers, and we grabbed our patches.

"If you can sew it yourself, good, do so. If not, there are assistants to help you," he said.

After his introduction, I felt that he was not as cruel as Kapo Ivan of Gross-Rosen. This was a relief. He called my cipher and gave me a Polish triangle and cipher patch, and I quickly sewed on my patches and went outside.

Seeing us newcomers, the old prisoners ran up to us immediately and hurriedly rattled off all the usual questions:

"What's going on in the world?"

"Who's winning the war?"

These prisoners came from different countries, spoke different languages, and searched for fellow countrymen. We had no newspapers. No phones. The only source of news here were other prisoners, who hopefully hadn't been caged for too long and potentially had recent news. Not knowing what was going on made many think the worst, too.

The most important requests were about the war and whether the Germans were still in their respective lands: Holland, Belgium, France, Italy, Greece, Yugoslavia, Romania, Russia, Poland, and there may have even been others. Germans weren't just arresting Jews. They weren't just arresting Ukrainians. They were arresting everyone they could.

I was approached mostly by Poles because of my 'P.' They were most interested in what kind of progress the Soviets were making:

"Has the front hit Poland?"

"How do the Soviets treat the locals?"

"What of the German folkspeople? And the Dutch? Are they being taken to Siberia?"

"Do the Soviets have concentration camps like Germany?"

"Are the Germans destroying cities in their retreat?"

... and many more. I couldn't answer them all, but I did say that Germany retreated from the Soviet Union, Africa, and the Balkans.

"The main point is this - Germany is losing on all fronts. They're retreating. They're being cornered into their own territory," I said.

The joy on their faces was great. This news raised hope that they'd stop suffering and that they could soon return home.

As the prisoners explained the sleeping situation that left many prisoners sleeping on the floor, the blockleader came by again and said, "Breakfast is only given to those prisoners who work. Those who remain unemployed are only served brewed water tinted with burnt grain."

The local prisoners told us that the healthiest prisoners are often snagged up for dangerous work. Some even volunteer.

These ever-willing prisoners are taken by the command and taught how to disassemble undetonated bombs. After some quick training, they're taken to sites where these bombs fell, and the prisoners attempt to disarm them. Often times, not all prisoners who left come back, because the bombs explode mid-job. This is also why these bombs aren't being disarmed by the Germans themselves.

So over the next few days, the German command came and picked willing prisoners. Some left, less came back. I was pleased that the number willing were always more than the Germans needed. *I'll never volunteer. I don't care how hungry I get.*

But one day the Germans picked prisoners to work on farms instead of bombs. I jumped at the opportunity, but to my misfortune, probably because I was short and skinny, they didn't pick me. Seeing these prisoners return with turnips and potatoes put a hole in my stomach. To add to that, they beamed with pride at how well they ate on the farm too. No one shared their achievements.

I sat and watched with envy. *Maybe they'll take me next time.*

But they didn't. And although many of us didn't have to work, they still woke us up at five sharp, organized us into rows, and forced us to stand for hours until the other workers were taken off to work. They repeated such a ceremony three times daily, day after day after day.

This inactivity had an awfully negative impact on me. I guessed it was July, and the long summer days of standing and not eating and stagnancy dragged down my spirit. Neither day differed from another. There was no Sunday. There was no weekday. We didn't know *what* day it was. Boundaries dissolved into grayness.

Are we even needed anymore? Why'd they bring us here? How long will this drag on? I soon began to think that boredom might be the worst killer of all.

But then finally, two weeks of this life later, my original group of fifty prisoners was ordered to stay in formation after roll call, and the on-duty sent the rest off to the barracks. They started to move us towards the gate, but at the complaints of some of the older prisoners, we were allowed back to empty ourselves and return quickly. *Time to work?* I ran back before the others so that I could be selected for the farm. The blockleader counted us again, pleased that the numbers held.

"The German garrison is on its way," said his assistant.

While we waited, the blockleader kept re-aligning us to present himself well. A few moments later, the gate opened for three military officers and a sergeant who coldly greeted the blockleader and made him read off ciphers from a registration sheet. Mine was called almost immediately, and those of us who were called were put into separate rows of fives by the German guards.

Forty five were read off and the rest were sent back to the

barracks. Peering over the chosen, we all looked a bit younger and healthier than the others. *Oh no. Please no. We've been picked. The bomb team... But why didn't they ask for volunteers?* Something wasn't right. My stomach roared in hunger too.

The senior officer counted us again and ordered us down the main road of camp. I again looked up at the tall, slender pairs of poplars planted in front of each barrack. Prisoners looked at us with curiosity.

But what most bothered me was hunger. *I'll do anything. Any work. Just give me food. Please.* Some prisoners told me earlier that workers sometimes got additional coupons to buy German cigarettes, some grouts, and sometimes even a piece of bread.

I wanted that. *Let me work for food. Please. I'm so hungry!*

CHAPTER THIRTEEN

Baumenheim Factory

Armed Germans perched on three transports trucks and two smaller cars sat waiting for us as we walked up Dachau's main gate. The guards loaded us onto these trucks, fifteen prisoners each. As the trucks left camp, I was somewhat pleased, because this time we weren't covered by a tarp - I had a good view of our journey.

I looked back at the dug-out ditch overflowing with water and the gate with the inscription: "Work liberates." I looked at the walls of barbed wire surrounding the camp, the guards who looked down on us from high towers, the long rectangle barracks, and finally, at the poplars.

"The best protection from escape," a soldier explained as we drove away, "is the electrification of that entire fence. The interruption of the current immediately gives guards notice that a prisoner is trying to escape."

So escape was impossible.

"Several have attempted," he said. "And all were caught." He was giving us a guided tour of our own locked-up life. *Thank God we're moving on.*

Our convoy moved slowly through small villages and towns and then we found ourselves on the open road surrounded by farmers' fields. I marveled at their beauty, all planted and sowed and carefully trimmed. Nothing lay uncultivated. These fields were ripe for the harvest - orchards full of fruits and vegetables and trees in full bloom. Birds whirled above and gayly sang. If all I knew of Germany were these fields, I'd have no idea that it was in its fifth year of war.

But then I looked a bit closer and saw that women, not men, worked these fields - a sign up their departed loved ones.

Everywhere we looked, old housewives and old men worked on those bavor lands (bavors are male German farmers). Women and girls and their small children too. No young men or boys. They were off fighting somewhere, if not dead.

After several calm hours of silence, our progress slowed into a German village by the name of Baumenheim. *We must be here to work on these farms,* I thought, looking about the village for a bavor.

But I was quickly shown otherwise. Although we did arrive in a village, through the tall trees and greenery I noticed a few large factory buildings. Around them stood completed agricultural harvesting machines wearing clean, yellow coats of paint. On the flanks of these machines were black letters: "Dechenreiter." They were threshing machines.

They brought us here to build combines for Germans?

To the left of these factory buildings sat a gray and gloomy, recently-built two-story building. The ground floor had no windows. The second floor had just one, and it was covered in thick, iron bars. The German guards ordered us to gather in front of the gate, which was made of more iron pipes, with barbed wire lining the top. A small yard lay in front of the building, also surrounded by the wire. A few steps from that gate stood a tall tower, with a ladder attached to the front that led up to a platform. An armed German guard stood up there.

Our corralling guards organized us into rows of five and counted us and then told us to wait.

A German officer walked out of a small house that stood next to the gray building. The soldiers saluted him. He spoke a little with the leading transport officer and then again counted all of us. His numbers lined up with the registrar, and then he gave the order to open the gate and lead us into the yard.

We walked in and a huge factory I somehow hadn't noticed before appeared from behind a curtain of trees. Barbed wire encircled the factory and the gray house. German guards stood perched in towers at the four corners of this factory. In front of the factory fence lay an extra roll of barbed wire, like those I'd seen in other camps. From the yard of the gray building to the plant was a large garage door, and beside it smaller ones for people.

As I stood in this yard, I realized my reality. *I can forget working alongside bavors in those fields. Forget the plants, the fresh air, the cultivated soil beneath my feet. The factory was my workplace.*

A tall, lean prisoner then walked out of the factory. He approached the other German and handed him an index card. Later I learned that the German was the Commandant of the camp. After their conversation, the Commandant went beyond the fence.

The lean prisoner walked up to us with a folder in his hands and said, "My name is Chokolyada. I am the Kapo here. Shtubowy(blockleader) Rudyj will be helping me out," he said.

Just then a prisoner of the same skinny build, but more average height, came out of the building with a smiling face. This was Rudyj.

Two other prisoner-mentors walked out and were introduced. One of them was Max, a man of about 50 years, dark skin, strong structure and a serious look. The second was Vili, who was about 40, somewhat paunchy, red in the face, clamorous, and grinning.

The only things I knew about Kapos was what I learned from Ivan. I thought back to Tato missing his hat and being beaten for it. I was not happy about meeting another Kapo.

Shtubowy Rudyj then spoke up, "I'm responsible for all of you and what happens to you in this building. I report directly to Chokolyada. When it comes to day to day, you'll be dealing with these two," he said, pointing to Max and Vili. "They'll wake you up every morning, tell you what you should be doing, oversee the distribution of meals, guide you to work, and then put you to bed at the end of the day. They'll follow you everywhere. And they'll punish you if you transgress in any way. Listen to them, listen to me and most importantly you must listen to Kapo Chokolyada. Memorize your cipher, because that's what you'll be known by and called by here and if you don't respond to it in time, you will be beaten - twice if the Commandant is around."

More rules.

"Another warning for you - remember that when you pass in front of a German officer, you must take off your hat and slap it against the side of your pants as a sign of honor."

Rudyj was done and Max and Vili read off our ciphers and led us into the gray, gloomy building to show us our beds.

The first floor contained a common washing basin, toilet, hospital, office, and kitchen. Vili walked us up a set of narrow wooden stairs that led to the second floor, which was divided into two large rooms, or "shtubas" (blocks). There were no doors to these rooms, just two big openings. Between the shtubas was a smaller room built for Kapo Chokolyada.

We were introduced to shtuba #2, which was filled with three levels of bunks. The passage in-between them was narrow, barely enough for one man. Every bed was made. New straw mattresses lay dressed in canvas. A blanket laid on each one. It looked like we were the first to arrive.

Max, who walked behind us, said that we could pick whichever bed we'd like.

"The remaining beds will be dealt to subsequent transports. Every morning, Make sure to cover your beds carefully with your blankets and keep this space clean. Now you're free and can walk about and get acquainted with the facilities. You're also free to go out into the yard - just don't touch the barbed wire or the fence beyond it," he said.

Prisoners rushed to claim their beds and wash up. I usually grabbed the top bunk but decided on a lower one this time to change things up. I could always switch later. But instead of running to the bathroom like the others, I went outside. I saw no Kapo. I saw none of his henchmen either.

The yard was about twelve by forty meters, surrounded by the wire. I walked back and forth several times, finally stopping near one end of the wire. From there I could clearly see each guard's face that peered down at me from up in their towers. They looked older, weary, and showed no signs of emotion. I had an inkling that this yard is where I'd be spending much of my spare time.

I stared up at the beautiful blue sky, simply and presently soaking it in and would have stared for hours if it wasn't for the shrill of a whistle that came from the factory across the way. The doors to this factory opened, and a hoard of girls and women poured out.

I walked up to the gate and they walked right by me and I saw a white strip with the word "Ost" (East) written across their chests. Most passed me without saying a word, simply looking timidly in my direction. *Ukrainians?*

A group of girls then approached me and one of them courageously asked me in Ukrainian, "Who are you?"

But before I could answer, the guard in the tower overheard her, couldn't understand her Ukrainian language, and shouted and condemned her and pointed his rifle at me.

"Get inside!"

I ran back in, hoping that guard wouldn't shoot or tell Kapo or any of the other on-duty prisoners. I walked straight into the shower and washed myself well. Most of the other prisoners had already washed up.

And even though I was a bit jarred, I was more-so glad

that I got to see so many beautiful girls. But I felt bad for them too. *How was it that these women, just like us prisoners, couldn't call themselves Ukrainian? Just "Ost?" And how come so many of them were taken from Ukraine? Why have they been marked like us prisoners? Are the Germans afraid that they'll somehow escape?* I wanted to learn more about them.

After washing up, I climbed the stairs and peeked into shtuba #1 where I saw loaves of bread and pieces of shiny white margarine on a table. Vili sliced the bread into pieces while Max stood by counting. I couldn't look away.

"Supper," someone whispered from behind me. We were entranced.

Suddenly Rudyj saw us and shouted, "Get out!"

He probably thought I was going to steal a piece. Other prisoners had apparently gathered behind me too with their cunning eyes and hungry stomachs.

"All of you! Scram! Otherwise you'll get nothing!"

The prisoners pushed slightly back into shtuba #2, but just barely, holding at the edge of the doorway. Everyone wanted their portion first. I spent some time with them but after a moment decided to get back to my bed and lay down and just wait. As I laid back, I thought about this new camp. *This isn't so bad. And as time passes, maybe the end of the war will soon pass too. And we've got decent soap too so I might even be able to keep the lice off me.*

From my waistband, I pulled a piece of soap I snagged from the bathroom and hid it in my straw mattress. Then for whatever reason Mama popped into my head. *What's it like back in the village, Mama? Do you know that I'm still alive? Did you get my letter? Are you reading it right now?*

Shtubowy Rudyj's whistle interrupted my dreams. He ordered us out the building, with Max and Vili at the entrance urging us and shouting at us.

"Move!"

Rudyj counted us and then Kapo Chokolyada appeared and did the same.

Kapo walked calmly and joked with Rudyj, who gave a signal for the other on-duty prisoners to join us. A doctor, a counselor clerk, three chefs and three others walked out, who I later learned were the barber, cobbler, and tailor. They all served the German camp guards. Kapo organized these on-duty into a separate group, leaving us with a good view of the entire internal camp administration. From their triangles, I deduced their nationalities:

Kapo Chokolyada bore the letters "Ch," which denoted Czech nationality. Rudyj and the barber wore the same. The cobbler and tailor both wore "P" for Polish. The doctor and scribe each wore an "H," for Holland. The three chefs were a swarthy folk, wearing black triangles. I found out later that they were German gypsies. Rudy's helpers Max and Vili both wore red triangles without a denoted nationality - Germans. Vili's triangle was upside down. He must have made a mistake.

Suddenly the Commandant and two of his guards appeared. They opened the padlocks and marched up to us. I noticed that the Commandant was elderly and somewhat bowed over. He carried the SS insignia, a skull that I later learned was a Totenkopf. All the guards wore the same.

SEPARATION

Kapo Chokolyada met the Commandant, saluted him and said that the prisoners were ready for counting. The Commandant didn't pay any attention to Choko's report and he himself turned to us and began slowly strolling through our rows, carefully counting us himself. Each prisoner he walked by took off their hat and hit it on the side of their pants. The Commandant counted the on-duty prisoners as his officers recorded his findings and without a word he left the camp, his guards clamping shut the padlocks behind him.

"Dinner time," said Kapo Chokolyada. "And after our signal, get to bed. In the morning, we'll wake you up and again you'll be counted out here. This will happen three times daily: in the morning, at lunch, and in the evening."

The on-duty prisoners went back inside, and Rudyj dismissed us. After Rudyj walked in, the prisoners no longer heeded his orders and all pushed each other aside to get to the front, scared to death that being last meant no bread.

And although hunger hallowed out my gut, I didn't compete. *Look at how small a group we are. Each prisoner will get their portion.* I also thought that maybe I could stretch out dinner a bit longer. *Maybe I wouldn't get hungry again as early.* I knew that I needed food, but I didn't want to obsess over it if I didn't have to.

The food line grew smaller, and I was just about the last one. Max gave me a piece of bread with a little piece of margarine lying on top. Vili handed me a cup of "German" coffee.

After the last prisoner got his food, I stared at the leftover pieces of bread and margarine on the table. Max and Vili took them into the Shtubowy's room. We stared mournfully. I probably could have eaten nine of those servings and maybe on the tenth felt a little full.

Slowly prisoners trickled back into shtuba #2. After getting away from Dachau with a somewhat better dinner here and a decent shower, many prisoners felt it was time to lay down, even without the command of the mentors. But I stayed in the first shtuba for some time, curiously listening in on the mentors behind their locked doors.

"Look at how well we cut this up!"

"More for us!"

"Ah, so skilled."

"We'll never go hungry."

These were fellow prisoners.

So here's how justice is introduced on this first day of Baumenheim. This camp surely lacks no thieves.

I finally had enough of their derision and mockery and was the last to head out of shtuba #!. Most prisoners were in bed. I followed suit.

A fog of the conversation from next door carried into our room, but I gladly couldn't make out the words. As the eleventh hour approached, Vili walked in and gave a whistle to signal lights out.

I dozed and thankfully slept as well as I'd slept since the youth barrack at Camp Heinkel.

I woke up to a whistle and ran outside. Vili and Max yelled us out the door.

"We aren't gonna wait for you!" Vili yelled.

Kapo Chokolyada met us at the front door, urging us out into rows. Everything about the counting was the same as all the other counts, except that this time the Commandant announced that another transport would be arriving today. It was sunny and a light rain fell.

Shtubowy Rudyj picked two of the stronger prisoners to get to the kitchen and help the cooks carry the food. The prisoners rejoiced - eating *before* work?! The food came and everyone waited their turn, no longer pushing each other aside like last night, convinced that this time there would be enough. Once again, Max and Vili served and our meal was a cup of coffee and a piece of bread.

"Food will always be dealt in the first shtub or outside if the weather's good," said Rudyj. "But I warn you all - if we catch you creeping back into line... take a look over there by the door - see the stick? It's *always* there. You'll get that stick *at least* five times. Understood?"

After their decrees and a light breakfast, each prisoner returned to bed, because it was the only place we could sit in peace and not disturb anyone. Prisoners gladly stayed out of shtub #1 because at least one mentor was always spinning about in there and they didn't need a reason to punish us. The only exception was if Rudyj asked us to sweep and wash the floor, which got us an extra slice of bread or serving of soup.

So camp seemed simple enough, but I found myself deeply entrenched in loneliness. Even after the first transport came that day, I tried talking to these new prisoners, but most were French, Belgian, or Dutch. Our language didn't overlap, and they minded their own business, sticking with their own people. I tried talking to Poles and Russians too but didn't have any luck with them either. Nobody seemed to trust anybody and most people just held to themselves. I also couldn't find any Ukrainians, probably because they were all marked as Polish or Russian. It wasn't the type of scene where you could just yell out for familiar friend. Yelling could get me whacked.

At noon the sirens buzzed for the neighboring factory to break, which meant it was our turn to eat too. The mentors called us out to get counted, and then they sent us back in to the first shtub. Max was waiting there already, pouring each prisoner a scoop of noodle soup. Vili stood next to him distributing bowls.

After handing out bowls to a couple of prisoners, for whatever reason Vili got beet red and struck a prisoner hard with a closed fist and banished him to the end of the line. He carefully observed every prisoner and then he stopped and stared at me longer than the others.

Are you looking at me? This is my first time in line! But he just stared and smiled and filled my bowl, and I ate without disturbance.

After we all ate, some prisoners got back up, hoping for seconds. But no such luck. Max and Vili filled their bowls with this dense soup and took it back into their room. They ordered two prisoners to carry the kettle back to the kitchen, and although there was nothing left in the bottom of the kettle, a few prisoners fought for and scraped burnt macaronis off the side of the kettle and were excited about the slaughter of big prey.

The anger and greed in their eyes scared me. I didn't want to give in to those feelings myself.

After lunch, I went to my bed. I noticed that Vili for some reason didn't seclude himself in the first shtub, but lingered in ours. *Must be his duty.*

He closely peered at each prisoner, hanging around my bed the most. He stared at me and smiled. But I was afraid of him. I saw him strike that man.

Vili returned to the first shtub, with Kapo Chokolyada following. I heard a muffled conversation from them and then they called all the prisoners to the first shtub and announced that they needed six people to work. Vili picked these prisoners himself, me among them.

"We'll be going beyond the wires of the camp. But take heed! Two armed soldiers are going to watch over you," Vili said. I was not happy about being chosen. Rain fell, and I didn't want to get my clothes wet. They were my only pair, and the idea of sleeping in a wet bed later annoyed me.

"Now run!" Vili said and ran behind us down the stairs. The camp gates opened and the two German guards escorted us out. *Maybe we'll be introduced to the factory with the girls.* But we walked right by, and Vili led us to a small shed where we grabbed six shovels.

Next to this shed, by the barbed wire fence, sat a pile of sand as tall as me. "Shovel the sand and hide it under the garret so the rain doesn't wash it away," Vili said.

We started, but the sand was wet and heavy and the going was rough. Each shovelful was dead weight. I tried keeping up with the other prisoners, but they were older and bigger and I struggled.

Vili then came up behind me and said "Lyangzam" (slower). *Why just me?* I didn't like being singled out.

The rain fell harder, and Vili commanded the other prisoners to hurry up and finish.

"The quicker you're done, the faster I take you back. You," he said, pointing to me, "hide under the garret."

I reluctantly walked underneath the dry shed, really wanting nothing to do with this extra attention. I didn't want to look weak around the other prisoners.

The soldiers guarding us stood under that same tarp too. One of them came closer to Vili and said, "This work should be finished today," nodding to me.

Vili immediately replied, "I placed him here because he is a minor."

The guard didn't protest, but instead leaned back with a strange smile on his face.

After their conversation, I felt a little better. *An understandable German wants to show me compassion? Great!* After work, I thanked Vili for his attention and for taking me out of the rain. He smiled with pleasure.

Returning back to the prison building, one of the prisoners spoke up as we were out of earshot of Vili and the guards.

"We had to work more. In the rain. Why'd they even choose you to work? He saw that you're young. Why not just pick someone else?" one complained. The others were annoyed as well.

"I don't know why. I'd feel much better if he didn't pick me. I didn't ask him to do what he did. I also couldn't argue with him. We're all doing what we're ordered to do," I said.

After I cleaned and washed up, I laid dissatisfied on my bed. *Even when I get help here it makes things worse. I don't want to stand out. I want to blend in.*

I looked up and Vili strolled into our shtub. At first, he walked about like he was on duty, but then he came closer to me and stood by my bed.

"You must be very hungry," he said.

"Thank you. I'm not," I lied. "But when dinner comes, I'm sure I will be."

I didn't want any more special treatment. Vili stood for a bit against the empty bed next to mine and then sat down on it.

"Where were you born?"

"Uherci, near Horodok."

"Did you go to school?"

"Yes, in Lviv."

"What camp did you come from?"

"Dachau."

He spoke with a compassionate tone. It felt genuine. For the first time during this war it seemed like someone was asking me about my life without wanting something in return.

When he asked me about my parents and family I start to cry. He laid his hand on my shoulder as if he was my dear Tato and said, "Don't cry. I'll always be here for you in camp."

I cried harder.

"You're the youngest prisoner here. You require more care," he said and then got up out of bed and left me alone to bawl. My heart warmed up at that moment - *Such a good person, so deep into Germany! Not all these Germans are so evil, like Hitler, like his aides from the SS. I wasn't alone here - I had someone - I had Vili!* I started to feel myself open up again. I felt like maybe I could trust another person again.

Even at dinner that night, Vili skipped the smaller piece of bread that fell to me and picked out a bigger one. *So giving!* But the prisoner behind me got this smaller piece and complained in French for a while and shook his hand at me. I still ate the bread.

Over the next few days, more and more prisoners arrived. They filled out the remaining beds and when all the lower ones got plugged up, I hopped up to a top bunk. I figured that these new prisoners may have lice, so the higher up I was, the longer I might stay lice-free.

One day Vili strolled in and saw that another prisoner was lying in my old bed.

"Find another bed!" he shouted at him.

The prisoner jumped up frightened and moved to another empty bed in the first shtub. I came back down to that bed and Vili asked me, "Why is someone else lying on your bed?"

"I moved to a higher one," I replied, "so I could stay clean."

"No. I don't want to hear it. Get back into this one," he said. "If you do as I say, you'll have an easier time here in camp. I'll always help you," he said.

It was strange, but I didn't argue.

"Now look. They need another clean prisoner to work in the kitchen. I can get you in. You can eat whatever you want. I even told the cook already - he said tomorrow you'll be peeling potatoes," Vili said.

Of course! I was starving.

"They only cook in there for the guards. What do you think?" he asked.

"Yes! Thank you Vili!" I said. Most prisoners would never see an opportunity like this one.

"You'll never be hungry again," he said.

From then on, I decided that I would do everything in my power not to offend Vili. He looked to me often. When we got soup, he poured me a bigger scoop. From time to time, he laid down in the empty bed next to me. But every time he came over and showed his compassion, I began to think about my family and bawl and this would annoy him and he'd leave. I just couldn't help it.

The next day a kitchen worker woke me early to get to work. At that moment I realized that Vili was telling me the truth about this kitchen duty. This was no dream.

At work I got introduced to the three kitchen gypsies, who all looked quite young and very clean. They greeted me politely and kindly and showed me my job. A fourth gypsy was their mentor. He was somewhat older, short, and fat. He paid no attention to me, but scolded the others:

"No good!"

"More salt!"

"Too thick!"

"Where's the taste?!"

"What will the garrison think of us? 'What kind of cooks are they!' they'll say."

He wouldn't stop.

"If we keep this up, they'll kick us out of here and give this work to someone who deserves it!"

He shouted and shouted and then sat down at his table, trying to concoct new flavor combinations. He was planning new meals to submit to the Commandant for his approval.

As ordered, I peeled potatoes, and the gypsies immediately noticed my work.

"How'd you learn so fast? Have you done this before?" they asked.

"No," I said.

This new kitchen duty was boosting my confidence too.

We got a break in the middle of the day, because we rose so early. How lucky I was! And the food! I relished in eating as much potato soup as I could. This was the happiest I'd been in camp. Other prisoners were jealous. It was a dream job, and every prisoner hoped to be chosen for it.

The gypsies kept praising me and said that they'll need even more help when the camp completely filled up with prisoners. *If so, my job must already be assured.*

In the evening, after I washed the dishes, Vili visited my bed and listened as I excitedly told him about my day. After I told my story I thanked him, so grateful that he recommended me for this dream work.

He looked at me with pleasure, but kept repeating, "You

have to listen and do what I say."

In the back of my mind, I wondered what that could be, but I never asked him and figured not to mess with something good. But there were some weird things about Vili too.

Over the next few days, consecutive conversations left him jokingly speaking with Shtubowy, then the shoemaker, and then to the barber too, all while standing together in shtub #2 and staring at me. *Are you talking about me?* During these conversations, he'd wave his hand and smile at me.

Then one evening I looked up and Vili entered our shtub, this time with the tailor. I immediately realized that they were both looking at me and talking about me.

The tailor, however, didn't laugh or agree with what Vili said like the others. They began to yell and argue and I could clearly hear the tailor say, "I'll report you to Chokolyada, and if that doesn't help, I'm going to the Commandant!"

I laid low on my bed, thinking something was wrong. I wanted to believe that they weren't talking about me, but how could they not be? *Why would he denounce Vili?* I'd never talked to the tailor and had no idea who he was. But I respected Vili. *Such a great friend. What are you doing, tailor?!*

That night Vili didn't come by my bed. He just walked hurriedly through our shtub, checking to make sure prisoners were in bed, and then walked off to his room. *What happened? What did I do?*

I waited until noon the next day to be called for work, but then the thick kitchen gypsy, who was good friends with Vili, told me not to come in.

"We'll call you when you're needed," he said.

Later that night, I stood with the other prisoners for dinner. When my turn came, Vili, who was scooping soup for prisoners, didn't pay me any special attention. He gave me the same size scoop as the others, but to me it seemed like even less.

After dinner I sadly went outside to my barbed wire fence. I felt so sorry for myself. I had doubts about Vili and was ready to burst into tears. *Why was he so good to me, but then suddenly changed? What did I do? Why did I get taken out of the kitchen? The gypsies praised me and nobody ever told me I did anything wrong. Am I off kitchen duty for good? Or maybe they made a mistake?* I also worried that instead of finding a good friend, I found in Vili an unnecessary enemy.

I stood there for some time, mournfully gazing at the fence, which kept me bound to this awful place. Then I looked towards the sky and over to the guard. I waited for him to order me back into the building, but he didn't talk to me either. My head drooped, and I walked back inside, washed up, and went to bed.

Turning over slowly in bed, I noticed that a few beds away lay that same cordial Vili that once lay beside me. But he laid next to another prisoner, who was a bit older than me. I was envious. *Why didn't Vili tell me what I did to offend him? Did I lose the only friend I had here?* I wanted to approach him and ask him what happened, but he caught sight of me looking at him and simply turned over. *Maybe it would be better to talk to him alone. Maybe I'll still be called into work tomorrow.*

But the next day came, and I didn't get called. I also noticed that the man that lay next to Vili the night before wasn't at lunch with us. I hadn't seen him anywhere. *He probably took my place in the kitchen on Vili's recommendation.* This depressed me, and my start in a new camp was a sign of nothing good.

I tried finding some comfort in other prisoners, because many a new arrived, but they were mostly French, some Poles, Russians, Dutch, a handful of Germans and even two Italians. I wanted to meet a Ukrainian so badly, but we weren't allowed to be marked with a 'U' here. This forced me to walk bed to bed and start conversations with each prisoner who had a Polish or Russian designation to find out their actual nationality. This approach failed miserably, as many prisoners weren't interested in talking to a stranger. Of those that answered, they coldly replied, "Don't you see my triangle? What are you asking for?"

As I was about to give up, the sudden plaintive howling of sirens startled me, announcing the possibility of an air raid. I've heard these sirens now over and over and over, and at every camp I went to they sounded more like a mournful cry than whistle.

Vili and Max appeared outside the shtubas, followed by Kapo Chokolyada. One in front of the other they shouted, especially Vili, yelling at prisoners to get out into the yard. Like a bandit, Vili passionately beat and shoved prisoners down the narrow stairs. Some fell, clogged our route and we ran them over with our wooden soles. I somehow escaped Vili's swing and ran out into the yard. The armed soldiers and the Commandant himself were already outside waiting.

The Commandant hoarsely yelled, "Schnell! Schnell! Heraus! Heraus!" (Faster! Faster! Away! Out!).

The guards and on-duty prisoners counted us quickly and the working prisoners joined us too. *Where are we going?*

Civilian workers from neighboring buildings fled. Up until now, we weren't allowed to even *be* outside when they were let out. And from both those factories, which were allegedly making rustic threshers, hundreds of girls with the "Ost" written on their chests poured out. *So many Ukrainian girls!*

Finally, the guards opened our gates and we were led down the rural road the opposite way the girls went. Local villagers stood beside their houses, curiously examining us. They clearly heard the guards hounding us, screaming at older prisoners so they moved faster. Some of these bavors hid down in their own shelters and some even fled to the fields in the opposite direction we were headed. I wondered if they hoped that these foreign planes would pass over their village and bomb the factory.

This village seemed more wealthy than ours back home, and I also wondered if any of these bavors could spare a loaf of bread.

Even during this emergency, my stomach's opinion did not depart. To my head came the proverb, "Hungry godmother always has bread on her mind." The older villagers of Uherci used to say this during dire times.

After we ran through the village, I noticed the tailor was running with his sewing machine in my five man group. I got angry. *Because of you I'm out of the kitchen! I'm back to eating prisoner food!* But it was hard to stay mad at him because he looked terrible. He was frightened, covered in sweat, wide-eyed and nervous. He was shifting his sewing machine from one arm to the other. I dropped my hate and curiously kept looking over at him.

"Can I help you?" I asked, not really sure why I did.

"No thanks," he said, without looking over.

He had a P on his chest and looked about forty. He was puny and had a large head. When we got to the end of the village, this tailor barely moved and snorted like a blacksmith.

That silly machine pulled him down so low that he could have dropped it at any moment.

So I jumped over to him, grabbed it and in Polish said, "I feel strong. Let me help you."

He finally loosened his grasp, and we ran along further. We ended up at a zig-zagging dugout about a meter deep and 3/4 of a meter wide.

One of the prisoners in our five-man quietly said, "Every day they've got me digging this trench. I had no idea why we were digging it. If I knew that this was where I'd be hiding during a raid, I would have done a much better job."

A tall iron fence separated us prisoners from the village and at both ends of the trench sat soldiers manning machine guns ready for use. We plopped down into the trenches and waited for further instruction. The tailor somewhat calmed down and started speaking in broken Polish.

"Air raid first here since factory get military clearance," he said.

Trying to soothe him, I replied, "It's only an alarm. Who

knows whether the planes will even fly over us. Maybe they're just flying in our direction."

"Why I'm so frightened of these sirens. Sorry - this is first time happened to me," he said. "Alarms same in last camp, but I no fear. And running to hiding with sewing machine? Never so weak. Thank you for help. Good to know you."

I still wondered why he got me out of the kitchen.

After a while, he asked, "How you learn speak Polish well? I read last name in registry, I think you from east Ukraine. Name like yours? Known good to us in Ukraine."

When I heard the tailor say 'to us in Ukraine,' I replied, "I'm not Polish - I'm Ukrainian. And not from eastern Ukraine, but western, from Galicia."

And then with a smooth Ukrainian tongue he said, "I'm also Ukrainian. They call me Osip Karas. I was born in the village of Dyniv, the county of Bereziv, which belongs to the Peremyshil Diocese."

"I was born in Uherci," I answered, excited to find another Ukrainian. "It's in the east, but it also belongs to that same diocese."

"I've been sitting in camps for two years already, and because I'm a tailor by trade, they hold me for tailor's work - I stitch up or sew new clothes for the camp guards. I get to live a little better than the others. I even get to stay with Shtubowy Rudyj in a private room," he said.

"Why were you arrested?" I asked.

"Same as the others - for my Ukrainian heritage. I belong to the People's Self-Defense and someone ratted me out. The Germans arrested me, interrogated me, and now I'm here," he said.

I sat back and started to feel a little better sitting out here in the trenches. It was a gorgeously warm day, and the air outside the village was much better than the air we constantly sucked while caged by closed windows in the gloomy building. I didn't mind the alarm as long as the aircrafts weren't visible.

After some time I dared to ask, "Why, Osip, a few days ago... it looked like you quarreled with Vili. Were you talking about me? Or was I just seeing things? Really, I'm sorry if I caused any strife, but since then he hasn't talked to me. I thought I had found a friendly German, a good friend here in camp. But then I so quickly lost him..."

His mouth curled into a smile: "Do you know why Vili's triangle is upside down?"

"No. I noticed, but I thought he just made a mistake."

"Nope," he said, "not a mistake. Have you ever heard the word 'homosexual?'"

"I have, but I don't know what it means and never asked."

"In this world, there are some such men that are not interested in women. They love men, not women."

What? At that moment, I was very naive and couldn't comprehend how a man could love another man. *What do they... How do they... together... what's good about that?*

Seeing my confusion, he said to me, "Men like Vili are looking at the backside of another, especially younger boys. They use them instead of women."

I was so ashamed. *This actually happens? How did I not know about this? How could I let Vili lay so near my bed, and not know his intentions? What did the other prisoners think of me? How did I miss that he wasn't looking to be my friend, but just waiting for me to stop crying at the mention of my Tato and family? What if the tailor hadn't said anything? What would have happened next?*

I blushed with embarrassment. These freaks taking advantage of young boys was not yet known or widespread in Ukraine. To me it looked so perverted and made me sick just thinking about it.

Osip went on: "I heard that those in Germany who are caught with minors, girls or boys, are strictly punished. So that's why I'm not afraid to quarrel with Vili. He bragged, just as he did with the others... he was preparing you to be his lover. I look at the prisoner records often, and from the records, I try to deduce who is Ukrainian. When I read yours, I hoped you were Ukrainian. But I still wasn't sure, so I didn't rush to approach you. But then when Vili began to brag that he'd soon love another, I asked him who he was talking about. He pointed you out. Knowing that you were still underage, I threatened to denounce him," he said.

I had no idea.

"And at that point, I didn't care what side of Ukraine you were from. I had to stand up for you. And I wasn't afraid because all of us in the private room have the same rights as he does," Osip said.

"Thank you for your courage," I said, "I trusted Vili. I cried with him, missing my family. And he was so happy when he told me that he found me work in the kitchen. And all he wanted was to trick me!"

Karas laughed: "He lied about that too. He didn't recommend you for kitchen duty, and he didn't take you out of the kitchen either. You were taken out of the kitchen because they re-checked your documentation and found out you were a minor. Germans don't let minors work in the kitchen. And you definitely weren't in there on the merit of Vili. That was Shtubowy Rudyj's doing. Vili lied to get to you. Strive next time to discern who wants to help you in this camp... Sometimes for good tailoring, I get an extra piece of bread when they have too much. Better soup too. I'll try to get you something too," he said.

"I promise that I'll watch over you during the alarms," I said.

He promised the same. Maybe I had made a true friend in camp after all.

No planes ended up flying over our camp. The howling of sirens stopped, and the guards ordered us into fives. Chokolyada counted us first. Then the Commandant. Their numbers agreed, and we returned to camp. As we walked back, I peered further into the bavor's houses, barns, and granaries. I compared them to the poor peasant homes in our abandoned, alien-invaded Ukraine. Seeing these wealthy German Bavors concerned me, because it highlighted the poverty of our peasants. *Ukraine is fertile, but her people don't own it. Colonial exploiters hoard it all. How long would it take before we could compare our Ukrainian landlords with these German bavors?*

First thing's first - we needed our independence. And we couldn't bend our backs neither to Poland nor Russia. Millions of innocent people died at their hands.

I carried the sewing machine all the way back to camp, and the tailor grabbed it from me at the entrance and joyfully returned to his hedge.

We skipped lunch because of the raid, which made me exceptionally unhappy, but then dinner came around and we got a piece of bread *and* a dipper of pea soup. I took my dinner over to the first shtub to hang with the tailor.

"I watched to make sure Vili didn't give you less food than the others," he said.

"Vili will quickly forget about me, because he's already concerned with another," I said. I had lost one friendship but ended up finding a better one.

About a week after that first alarm, the last group of prisoners arrived. More machines were added to the factory and that evening camp command announced plans for work. After breakfast the next day, they called us out to the yard, organized us, but this time there was no counting.

Kapo Chokolyada appeared with a registry and asked, "Who of you has ever worked on machines? Raise your hands... Alright, now step out and get organized over by Max. Who of you has welding experience? Raise your hands... Step out and get organized over by Vili."

Civilian master workers arrived at camp and took off with their respective groups. The remaining prisoners made a third group, which I had by elimination fallen to. We were taken to the gloomy building and told we'd work the next day after the first two groups got acclimated.

We woke up the next morning at five and the on-duty prisoners hurried us even harder than before.

"Wash up!"

"Make your bed!"

"Eat!"

"Get outside!"

"We're at work by six!"

But things didn't go as smoothly as the mentors imagined. We were in no hurry. Our lack of ambition and food the last week really didn't bode well for early morning effort. The toilets were clogged with prisoners, shoving each other to get empty. Breakfast was given out sporadically, plenty of prisoners getting none. Many didn't get a chance to wash. Others didn't make their beds.

But nonetheless, we were all driven into the field by Max and Vili's cries and beatings. Kapo and then the Commandant counted us. He ordered Kapo to take us to the plant, and when we got there, I saw the clock - five 'til six. Prisoner-mechanics went to their places. Iron welding prisoners went to theirs. Then a group of civilian masters came and took the rest of us to tables covered in wires, hammers, iron brushes, tongs, pliers, and other tools.

This first day working in the factory was filled with shouting and disturbances. The masters, through this thunderous noise, relentlessly tried to show us what to do. Two young, armed German guards walked along a corridor in the middle of the factory, keeping watchful eye on the chaos. Each master was swamped with prisoners, unable to properly explain anything. Many prisoners didn't understand German and many more didn't know the German words for factory parts and pieces. In the end, many prisoners just stared off into the distance, not listening. The toilets got clogged with traffic too, mostly because prisoners used them to hide from work. Guards had to shoo them out.

After taking a good look around, I realized that these parts were not going to threshers - these were military parts. *So those threshers are a cover up.* As I walked over to the bathroom, I peeked my head curiously into a partially closed room. There were heaters lamps and tubes of various paints. Next to them were barrels of all sorts of chemical liquids. I remember one of them - acetone.

Over time, the hum of running machines drowned out the voices flooding the factory. Motors loudly hummed from all sides. Hammers knocked about the benches. Acetone torches shot off frequent explosions. Prisoners tried learning how to use them but were too green to understand how to properly mix the oxygen and acetone.

The smell of this ugly acetone filled up the factory. It was sharp, pungent and minty, burning my eyes, nose, and lungs.

While lazily stretching out my duty of carrying iron back and forth, I saw my master yelling at his 'student,' who had initially said that he had experience with an acetone burner. But this prisoner couldn't get a handle on it, even after seeing the master do it. He'd unscrew the acetone, light the torch, and poof, long strands of black soot would shoot out. When he added the oxygen, a loud explosion and a chink happened. The frustrated master showed him again how to do it correctly. He explained it exactly and showed him exactly. The prisoners tried again, but the outcome was the same. Scraps of unburned acetone flew about, and when he added the oxygen, BANG. The master snapped. He couldn't bare to watch it anymore and grabbed him by the collar, ripped him out of his chair and yelled, "No more! And don't volunteer here again!"

A few hours later I found this same prisoner and he confessed to me that he had volunteered himself for the job with no concept of what it was. He himself was healthy, tall, and gentle, and his name was Boylek. He told me that he was afraid of fire and when he gets close to it, his hands begin to shake and he gets very nervous.

"Why are you so scared?" I asked.

"I was in a house once that caught on fire. I saw people burned alive. I still hear their screams. Especially the children," he replied.

"Since then," he said, "I sweat and unconsciously tremble whenever I'm near fire."

Seeing the letter P on my triangle, he stopped speaking German and started speaking Polish. He sat down beside me on the bench and told me that he comes from the noble Polish city of Gdansk.

"My whole family was arrested by the Germans on suspicion that we were helping the Polish Underground. I'm alone here. They Germans arrested the rest of my family. I don't know where they are, and I have no idea if any of them are still alive."

Then he asked where I was from and I told him I was born in Galicia. He corrected me and said, "You mean Malopolska."

I immediately objected: "Galicia is not Poland. This is

Ukrainian land, which was *occupied* by Poland and it's a mistake to call her Malopolska."

To my surprise, he didn't argue.

"I'd like to learn more from you," he said, "My fellow countrymen in this camp are envious of me. I come from Polish gentry, and they heckle me for it."

"Yes, let's talk more," I said.

He gave me his hand, and I gave him mine.

"I'm Ukrainian," I added. "The Germans don't let us call ourselves so."

He gave me a sympathetic look, and I didn't sense any hostile attitude. He then walked off as the master walked up.

The master explained to me more about my job, which was to carry and organize metal and tools for the welders.

"These parts should be well made," he said, "because they're going to our best combat aircrafts - the Messerschmitts." My thoughts were confirmed - this was no thresher factory. The master walked on, and I wondered how much time it would take Allied intelligence to find out about this factory and bomb it.

The factory horn went off for lunch. Chokolyada and Rudyj met us out in the prison yard and told us lunch was now 45 minutes, instead of an hour. After lunch, we headed back to work and found no masters. Apparently they still had an hour.

After they got back, we started to work again. Prisoners picked up a piece of iron, examined it, and then put it back down. I did the same, focused on being useless. Hours went by like this. I looked up at the giant clock up on the wall and stared at its slow moving hands. After that got boring, I rearranged the order of the already organized weaponry and pretended working some more. The master looked at me from time to time but didn't mention anything - my lazy work ethic lay unnoticed. I doubted they could squeeze out any productivity from the prisoners. Throughout the day I spent lots of time in the bathroom, as did other prisoners. Ugly machines idled over, roaring empty.

Even the guards seemed completely oblivious to us as long as we *looked* like we were doing something. *Did they know what we were supposed to be doing?* I don't think anyone really did. I quickly assessed that the mighty German government wasn't going to squeeze their desired productivity from these forced and disgruntled employees.

At six, the dinner bell rang, telling us that we were done working. The guards led us outside, and after being counted, the Commandant gave Chokolyada some instructions and then disappeared behind the gate.

Choko announced: "Starting tomorrow, all prisoners will wake up at 4:30am. Work starts at 6:00am, lunch is from 12:15 to 12:45, and work ends at 6:00pm. That goes for every day but Saturday, when you'll work up until lunch and then shake out your blankets, clean camp, and those of you with hair over a centimeter long must cut it. Beards - cut those too."

So we had more time in the factory that we didn't do anything in.

"We'll need barbers too, and if there are none, we'll quickly make them of you. We'll be giving out a second portion tonight to those of you who identify yourselves as barbers," he said. "So raise your hand if you were once a barber."

To my wonder, about a third of the prisoners raised their hands. Kapo laughed to himself. Apparently he didn't buy that the Germans had arrested a full union of barbers. "Whoever is truly a barber - that will be determined by Shtubowy. Volunteer to him after dinner, and he'll find out if you're truly a barber or not."

After dinner, prisoners actually warmed up to one another and searched for fellow countrymen. Some even exchanged beds to be closer to their brothers. Osip Karas came by my bed when his sewing was done, and he told me names of potential Ukrainians. I approached those prisoners and tried starting conversations with them. I discovered ten Ukrainians from Galicia, and among them even more from Eastern Ukraine.

So began our scheduled life in Baumenheim. Prisoners got used to the frequent brute behavior of Max and Vili, especially Vili, and they got used to "working" as well. Kapo Chokolyada played the good cop and was a bit more tolerant, never really swearing or hitting anybody.

But Chokolyada's promise of half-day Saturday then became every other Saturday. Daily work was then split into a day and a night shift. *Is this for economic reasons?* We weren't even working. *What's the point of splitting us up?* Materials were always lacking too. Maybe these shifts looked better to the Germans outside the camp, who really had no idea what was going on inside. I was just pleased that I was assigned to the day shift.

The distrust among prisoners seemed to slowly melt away as well. More and more prisoners were uniting with their own - French with French, Poles and Poles, Russians with Russians, Belgians and Dutch, gypsies with gypsies, as well as Ukrainians with Ukrainians. It felt much better to share this fate of being caged than to suffer alone.

The French, Poles, Belgians, and Dutch even got Red Cross packages. Us Ukrainians and Russians did not. I often looked on with envy, waiting and hoping that maybe one of them would toss me a little piece of a cracker. But that never happened, and I simply spun with hunger. Our meals in camp were tiny and poor, especially compared to my feasting as a kitchen worker.

One day I saw a prisoner get a package, then bow down, turn away and try to shield everybody else from his treasure. But none of us hungry prisoners were deceived.

Maybe I should learn French. Maybe they'll spare some food! At first, the French were so excited about my passion to learn their language. They were happy to teach me. So I learned a few sentences and greeted them in their language with a smile. *On my way!*

However, they quickly learned that I was Ukrainian and stopped communicating with me. At the time, they considered the Russians their allies, respecting them and believing that Russian Communist life was a thriving life.

"The Russians will soon beat down Germany," one said, "and France will once again gain independence."

They occasionally shared morsels with the Russians.

Ironically, sometimes packages were stolen. The French would try to drag on the life of their packages through multiple days, but more often than not, they fell asleep and woke up with nothing. In the morning, the French would find their big boxes completely empty, unwillingly shared with another prisoner.

One day, a few more prisoners arrived. I immediately ran out to take a look, thinking maybe Tato was among them. He wasn't, but I did spot a young boy. He wore a P.

We made eye contact, probably thinking the same thing: *Another youth!* His bed was assigned to the second shtub as well, and I immediately walked over to meet him, but two Poles kept him busy and I couldn't find him for a few days after.

Then one night Shtubowy Rudyj came to my bed and ordered me to take my blanket and follow him. *Who did I offend this time? Where are you taking me?*

"Wait here," he said, as we walked into the corridor. I watched him grab the young newcomer, and he and his blanket came my way.

"What did you do?" another prisoner asked me.

"I don't know. I don't understand," I said. I was just getting used to sleeping near a few other Ukrainians - we had decided to look out for each other.

Rudyj came back and ordered us to follow him to the first shtub, where he led us not to where the other prisoners slept, but to Max and Vili's beds.

"Tonight, you sleep up on the third bunks. You, sleep

above Vili," he said to me and ordered the other boy to sleep above Max. I didn't like this situation because I was afraid of Vili and had been trying to avoid him.

"You're the only camp minors, so you'll sleep here until you're eighteen. Then we'll move you back. No one can visit you here, and you can't go into the main shtubs. If someone tries to pull you out of here, you shout or tell me about it as soon as possible. Otherwise, if you don't, you'll be punished. Kapo Chokolyada ordered this and Vili and Max both know about it too," he said.

Rudyj left and I quickly gave my hand to this boy, telling him my name and asking him which bed he'd rather have.

"My name is Yusef. I'm taking the bed over Max, like the Shtubowy said."

I wasn't happy with his selection, because it brought me back into my unfortunate adventure with Vili. We spoke a bit more later that night:

He said that the American Army had landed on the shores of France and that the Germans were on the run from their conquered lands and that the Soviet Army entered Polish territory and was approaching Warsaw.

I wanted to tell Karas about my transfer, but I didn't see him that night. Yusef couldn't tell his friends either, and we both laid down before Max and Vili showed, minimizing the potential for their complaints.

But I was scared. And I felt the same from Yusef. We didn't know how these mentors would react to us being in their territory.

The cooks walked in and were glad to see us youth in the

cleaner part of the grey house. They quickly laid to sleep, because they had to get up early.

After some time Max and Vili walked in.

"How do you like your new company?" one of the cooks joked to Max.

"I like it but they better keep things clean," said Max.

Vili didn't say a word, put out the lights and whistled to the other prisoners, signaling that it time to sleep. When he returned, I was thankfully half-asleep. He laid down in his place and nobody said another word.

I woke up and realized that I hadn't heard Max or Vili or the cooks get up. I must have slept well. And after making it through the night, I felt better now that we were separated from the other prisoners. It was quieter, cleaner, and I could hide things in the mattress. None of the other prisoners were allowed in our area, and Max and Vili already had more access to goods than anything I could stash away, so I needn't worry about them.

I met with Karas on the next free Saturday and told him about my move. Osip was very happy, because it was he who suggested it to Kapo, and Kapo listened, even though he usually wasn't open to advice. He said the barber backed him up too.

"But listen to this - I have more good news," he said. His eyes sparkled.

Osip - are they going to free you?!

He said, "For my good work, and the barber's, the

German command spoke to the people in charge of the woman's camp, and in a few days we're meeting with them!"

It wasn't freedom, but this news was enough to make him ecstatic.

"This is my first time meeting with anyone other than a prisoner or a German. I'm going beyond camp walls! And with girls! Ukrainians girls!"

They'd get two hours. The Camp Commandant himself allowed it, because Osip had just tailored him a new uniform.

"I'm jealous but happy for you too. Bring me back a good story," I said. "How close are you with the barber? Can you trust him? Is he friendly?"

"Sometimes I can't really understand him. Or trust him. But the Germans seem pretty fond of him. He's beyond the camp gates daily to shave the Commandant. He even plays cards with him. Chokolyada's not a big fan of that. Either way, I'll make sure to split up from him when I visit the girls, because he understands Ukrainian, and I'd like to speak freely," he said.

A few weeks passed. I worked but didn't every day. We had our break every other Saturday. And from time to time we were driven out to the trenches outside the village because of nearby Allied aircrafts. But I got so used to these alarms that sometimes at work I started welcoming the howls, hoping for the sirens to ring and get us an early chance at dinner. As long as bombs weren't falling, I was fine.

One Saturday, Osip came back from the girls' barracks, and luckily I had time off to chat. I was excited to hear his stories. He said that the guards dropped him and the barber off at the gate and they were allowed to go wherever they'd like. He and the barber were both immediately surrounded by girls, split up and invited into their barracks.

"They were so amusing! They asked me why I'm in camp, where I came from, whether I was married, how long I've been in here, if I could come see them more often, how many Ukrainians are in camp and whether we could get more of us over there," he said excitedly. "They asked me so many questions and at such a clip, that I could barely answer or ask anything back."

Then to my surprise, Karas said, "Every one of those girls came from Eastern Ukraine. Entire villages have been sieged by the Germans. Everyone was taken. They deported the young who could work, separating tearful families into groups of men and women and transporting them off to Germany. One of the girls started crying, saying she ended up here alone - her family was taken elsewhere and she has no idea where to look for them. She compared these deportations to the Soviets ones in Ukraine in 1939. She kept crying and repeating 'What will they do with them?'"

I thought of my family. *Is our village okay?*

Osip continued: "Another said, 'We're forced to work and we're terribly underfed and no one cares if we're ill. They don't listen. And they sewed this disgusting *"east"* on our clothes, saying we had to wear it. But we are not east! We are Ukrainian! But they threatened to punish us if we didn't listen - taking our food away or even threatening imprisonment. If anyone tries to escape, they'll start taking lives.'

"Oh these girls! So beautiful and wonderful and kind to

me - I immediately felt awful for each and every one. They wept and complained and grieved for their families. When I got a chance to speak, I told them I was Ukrainian, and they, in awe, got closer, huddled around me and asked me about home. I told them about the ten or so Ukrainians from Galicia and the more-so even from eastern Ukraine. I promised to get them specifics when I came back. Then one girl came up to me and asked, 'Why would a Ukrainian wear a P?' I explained how, just as they had to wear 'east' instead of 'Ukrainian,' they've done the same with us concentration camp prisoners... worse even because we had to wear a nation on our sleeve that ruled us. I told them about the beatings that Ukrainians got for refusing to change their nationality. They wept some more, but on the other hand, they were happy that I was Ukrainian. They told me to come back as soon as I could, and if the war ends, they want us to come get them," he said.

"But it went by so fast. I was so excited and tried to stay with them as long as possible. These girls were ecstatic - they snuggled against me and told me to stay even longer next time. Then each of them came up to me and kissed me goodbye! They joked around, saying next time I'd get an even better kiss. Stepan, I fell in love with each and every one. They were all so beautiful, intelligent, friendly. I left with regret... then met the barber out front. He was beaming too. All the girls were waving and smiling and bidding us farewell. The guards met us at the gate, and even they were envious!"

Osip wanted to tell me even more, but Max came out to announce that we needed to shake out our blankets. We dispersed.

Walking back to the barracks, I thought about how we were being treated here in Baumenheim. Initially, I figured that because it was small and that we were responsible for such intense military production as building planes, that maybe we might get a break and some good treatment. But this was not the case.

Our blankets were stiff and dirty and in need of washing. We had been sitting in the same shirts, jackets, and pants for months. I tried washing my one shirt every three weeks, but it began to fall apart at the seams. It didn't help that someone else had worn it out it first. We slept in these clothes as well, minus our shoes and jackets.

To add to that, we always sweat through our clothes during our runs to the trenches. Soap was available at first, but with time it became more sparse, and then there was barely any. Several prisoners foresaw this and hid a lump in their mattresses. A prisoner was caught doing this and Rudyj beat him well in front of all of us. This happened more than once - the desperation to be clean was worth the risk for some. After seeing these beatings, I put my soap back.

The only thing I had going for me was that Max and Vili ignored Yusef and me.

As we took our blankets outside, a new problem sprung up - the prison yard was too small for all of us to shake our blankets out. Seeing this, Rudyj ordered the prisoners to lay all our blankets in one pile. He picked twenty of the stronger prisoners to shake them out.

I hated the idea. All the blankets were mixed up and I didn't get my same blanket back. And most of the older prisoners had completely stopped washing themselves. They just couldn't get moving fast enough in the mornings, so they dropped general hygiene. These older prisoners got the most beatings and ended up in the dirt. Then their dirtier blankets made their rounds to the cleaner prisoners.

When it got colder outside, these older prisoners took cardboard out of the factory, cut it and shaped it into waistcoats, and wore these pseudo-coat liners under their jackets, hoping to block out some of the wind. I wasn't sure if this actually worked - they looked quite strange and most prisoners got a good laugh out of it. I always felt sorry for them.

The French were also getting desperate. They were plucking milkweed and dandelions and eating them. I thought it was weird at first, but apparently these flowers were used for salads and wines back in France.

Our days went on.

I silently gazed as a smiling Vili sincerely poured each prisoner a full dipper. My turn came at the end of the line. I got my scoop and gladly and carefully weaved through

Sometime during the end of September, we got soup for dinner that was not our usual soup. Up until now, soups were cooked with potatoes or peas, most often with turnips. But this time it was some kind of grain and much thicker than before.

I silently gazed as a smiling Vili sincerely poured each prisoner a full dipper. My turn came at the end of the line. I got my scoop and gladly and carefully weaved through prisoners so as not to spill. When I took a better look at it, I saw not only barley, but also a scattering of small white and yellow worms with black heads.

So that's why Vili was so liberal with his scoops! At first, I didn't know what to do with it. *Can I eat it?* I looked around at the others. Some who didn't notice scarfed it up at their heart's content. Others noticed like I did. They looked into their bowls and couldn't believe they contained so many tiny worms.

But as they say, "hunger is not my aunt." Some slowly started giving it a try. Many with their eyes closed. I dared a try. *What happens to them, happens to me.* And I must confess - I ate the whole thing.

Some prisoners even praised it. We were fed the worm soup for the next week. Who knows where they found these worms, but I guess feeding it to the prisoners instead of throwing it out meant the camp counselors could eat the other food. And to my surprise, nobody got sick.

And speaking of food, living together with so many prisoners brought many last wishes to my ears, but none as repeated as to have so much food to eat that they'd refuse another bite. Rumors started circulating that Germans would have to give us more to eat. So it went.

One day after work, Kapo Chokolyada himself informed us that there was a whole loaf of bread waiting for each prisoner.

Our rumors were answered! And prayers too. Some figured this out earlier in the day - we hadn't gotten breakfast. *Maybe they were making up for something?* Joyous noise carried throughout the rows of prisoners.

After this proclamation, Chokolyada, along with his assistants and the Shtubowy, roared with laughter:

"Listen carefully! The bread that you get today - you have to make it last a week."

Our collective rejoicing vanished into distrust. *How were we supposed to look after a loaf of bread for seven days?* Whispers went through the crowd:

"Where are we supposed to hide it?"

"What if it gets stolen?"

"How do we cut it? No one's even allowed a knife!"

Each prisoner looked at one another, as if thinking, *What will come of this?* Some planned how they'd break it up. Others still rejoiced.

The bread wasn't delivered to the first shtuba as usual but was set in a pile at the entrance to the building. As each prisoner walked through the doorway, he received a full loaf of uncut bread and carried it like a golden treasure to his bed. I did the same. Yusef hadn't got back yet. So I was alone with my bread.

Where could I put you? ... Thank God I was moved to this part of the building where everyone else is properly fed. No one in here is interested in stealing my bread. That brought me relief but then I peered a little closer at the bread, and green mold ran up its sides.

No, no, no. I gently tried breaking off a little piece, and it immediately crumbled away crust-fallen. The inside was also tainted green.

I just then realized why they gave us an entire loaf of bread. It was already molded through, and if they cut it, it would have crumbled.

So what do I do with you? Can I eat you? Will I get sick? I looked at the other prisoners. They all seemed content.

Calm down, Stepan. Calm down. Maybe its just your bread. I decided to wait for Yusef. He came a few moments later glowing and joking: "Let's make a bet of who can hold onto his bread the longest?"

"I definitely won't rush," I said, wondering about his bread. "It's a long seven days, and we have a good chance of keeping it safe in here."

"I wonder how much I should eat tonight?" he asked himself. "This is amazing! My master really likes me too - he said that he's already trying to get me released from camp. He even gives me little pieces of bread here and there and maybe he'll give me more. So I'm gonna eat a big chunk tonight!"

I was jealous. My master didn't give me bread. Just work.

"Take a good look at your bread, Yusef," I said, "and see whether or not you'd like to exchange yours with mine."

He looked down at his bread and asked, "Does yours have green spots too?"

I showed him that mine did as well.

Yusef ran out to his Polish friends, asking if their bread had grown moldy. Same answer.

One of the prisoners asked Shtubowy, "Why did you give us spoiled bread?"

He replied simply: "If you don't like it, bring it back to me, and I'll give it to another prisoner."

The hungry prisoner corrected himself: "Oh, no, it's good bread."

At that point, some prisoners couldn't hold out any longer and began to eat that night's portion. They carried the rest as if it were gold. To the bathroom, under their arms. In bed, they clutched it to their chests. Most loaves didn't last the week. My bread quickly crumbled, and I finished it in five days. Yusef in four. But to my surprise, no prisoner gave up his bread or got ill.

After some time in camp, another problem crawled in - lice. And they did what they do best - multiply. The consistent lack of soap and wearing the same clothes over and over gave them the environment to multiply. The exchange of blankets we kept doing at the shake-outs spread them faster. Vili one day asked Yusef and I whether we had lice yet. He was afraid of our lice crawling down and becoming his.

"We don't," Yusef replied, "but if we keep shaking out blankets and exchanging them with other prisoners, then we'll get them soon as well."

Nice work Yusef! He understood that since Vili and Max's blanket were also taken off to be dusted, they were exchanged too.

Vili said, "From Saturday on, us four are shaking ours out separately."

Seeing what Yusef did, I asked, "If you can, could you get us a little more soap, so we could try to wash our shirts?"

Vili agreed and walked off. After he left, Yusef said to me, "I'm full of lice."

"Me too," I replied.

We promised to each other that neither of us would say a word.

On the next free Saturday, Shtubowy Rudyj announced that we were all being disinfected. At first, I pictured that they'd do it like previous camps - hot steam. But this went a little differently.

We were ordered to take our clothes off and stand naked in rows, and one by one we were pumped with disinfectant liquid by a selected prisoner. Max and Vili both stood and watched.

The prisoner prisoner with the disinfectant ordered the first prisoner to put his arms up to the sky, and then he splashed this liquid under both armpits. Then he told him to spread his legs and he splashed there. Then he told him to turn around and bend over. He splashed there too.

Yusef was right in front of me in line, and when his turn came up, Vili went over to the on-duty prisoner, took the pump, and ordered, "Put your arms up."

Vili drenched Yusef from head to toe. Much more than any of the other prisoners. I didn't like the looks of this.

"Bend over," said Vili.

Yusef did so. Vili disinfected him and rinsed him slowly.

Then Vili stood up in all his great height and like a hungry dog started suckling his lips. Other prisoners laughed. Yusef moved on.

When I took my turn, the prisoners in line and those already disinfected started to hoot and holler. Vili mutter something to himself and the prisoners hollered even harder.

"Arms up," commanded Vili.

I lifted my arms up in the air, and he poured the liquid all over me.

I was ashamed.

When he told me to turn around and bend over, I couldn't bear it. I hesitated. The prisoners continued their roar.

Suddenly, Kapo Chokolyada wandered in and wondered what all the noise was about. Vili saw Kapo, tossed the hose to another prisoner, and he skidded off to the side.

The selected prisoner finished my disinfection and the rest of the prisoners followed without problem. Choko realized what had happened and called Vili to his office and scolded him well.

Over the next few weeks, disinfection changed. They put a tub filled with the same liquid in the bathroom and hung a few rags up for us to dip into it and clean off between our legs, armpits, and backsides. Only Max watched this time. But the liquid was stronger than before, and it immediately began to burn my skin, like someone was cauterizing me. I ran to the shower and tried scrubbing it off, but it got even worse with the rubbing.

I later learned that this was acetone, which was used in the factory for painting. I decided not to rub so hard next time, but either way, this method of burning out the lice failed. They kept on multiplying in our dirty shirts and blankets.

The camp counsel tried electric lamps too. We held up our seams to these steamy hot lights, but that didn't work either. Seeing scenes of prisoners spending their free Saturdays squishing lice and sitting naked in front of electric lamps depressed me.

To try to get this off my mind, I went out to the yard and again stood behind the barbed wire fence. My dreams of seeing my home and my family soared into the sky, while I stood here, enclosed. I opened my eyes wide, trying to see as far as I could, through the fence and trees and beyond. *How many times have I done this already? Why has the war brought me here? Why am I not free, like the birds, flying over my head, not constrained by these spiny fences?*

I looked up at the guards in the two towers. I had grown accustomed to their presence, and they knew me well - I'd been coming to this fence almost every evening. Unless a prisoner attempted to flee, they didn't interfere with camp life.

One night, another prisoner joined me for my walks. He was once a prominent German politician.

"I opposed Hitler, was arrested, and after some time I was taken here. But for some reason, they've left me alone. They haven't killed me off, but they haven't taken me to work either," he said.

I never saw a camp mentor speak with him, or he with them. He'd simply put his arms behind his back and walk for hours in the yard.

I asked Karas why he walks so much and he said, "So he doesn't go crazy."

After all his walking, he'd go back to his bunk and read books. He was the only prisoner in camp entitled to receive and read them.

When we walked, it was usually just me and him and two

guards above. He'd often look in my direction, briefly pause as if he wanted to say sometime to me, but then continue walking.

He remained in my memory for a long time. I found out later that the Germans holed up their opposing prominent leaders in hopes that they would then "see the light" and line right back up into Nazi formation.

On the other side of the fence, I'd observe the "ost" girls go about their day. I'd also watch the so-called German Business Support transport farm machines back and forth. They were occasionally repainted, but I never saw any new ones.

Mentioning this later to Karas, he explained that the Germans were moving the same machines back and forth to confuse the Allies, showing them that this camp was solely for agricultural use and not worth their time. This was of course, not true. Even those girls found themselves making tank parts and other military machines.

As Autumn turned to winter, the air got colder and colder, and the clouds alternated pouring rain and sleet. This didn't stop us from still running to the trenches, even more-so, because the alarms were more frequent.

We'd shiver our way out of the building in our thinning prison rags, get counted, and then run down the road which was covered in sludge and mud. The bottoms of our pants stayed permanently caked with cold, wet mud.

The trenches were even worse. We'd crawl down into these swamps and some would even lose their shoes. Many prisoner complained that they'd rather sit in camp, living by the mantra 'What may happen to me, will happen where I may be.'

Even the German villagers started getting used to the frequency of these airstrikes. Some of them didn't come out of their homes, not even bothering to hide down in their shelters. Others came out and just stared at us.

One time, a prisoner motioned to the bavors that he was hungry. Others started screaming of hunger too: "Throw us bread!"

These prisoners were quite deceptive in their howls. The guards couldn't figure out who it was or sometimes couldn't even hear them. The meals in camp were just so meager - prisoners got stealthily desperate for a piece of bread. Sometimes we wouldn't even eat, because the cooks who were supposed to prepare the food were sitting right there with us in the trenches.

After the camp counsel caught on to prisoners trying to get food from the Bavors, the Commandant threatened that if someone was caught speaking to a Bavor, they'd go multiple days without food. This shut prisoners up.

One day, we were called out of work two hours before dinner. Usually sirens took us out of work for a raid, but this wasn't the case. The night shift was already standing in rows in the yard. The prisoners were amazed. *What was happening?*

"Get in line with the night shift," ordered Kapo. An angry Commandant and two guards holding leashed dogs hurried through the gate into camp. They stormed into our grey building and then into the factory. Kapo Chokolyada paced nervously in front of us.

"Stay quiet. Don't say a word," he ordered.

My curiosity didn't fester. *It's the middle of the day - what's the commotion?* I looked up at the guards in the towers, still watching over camp.

From afar, I saw the tailor Osip standing in the front row and looking very troubled. He occasionally looked in my direction and gave me some hand signals, but I didn't understand him.

I watched as the Commandant and his helpers leave the factory, linger for some time around the grey building, spoke something to one another, and then storm into grey building again, this time staying longer. When they walked out and beyond the gate again, they left us standing, saying nothing even to Kapo. He didn't know what to do with us.

A sharp, cold rain with no end in sight started to pour - thick, black clouds advanced closer and closer. Our rags quickly got soaked through.

After some time, the soldiers came back out and, as if they were searching for something, maneuvered around the factory and its structures. We had been standing there for hours. The end of our shift passed. After talking to the guards, Kapo ordered the night shift to head straight to work, drenched and shivering wet. The rest of us were let go.

What was that all about?

I walked up closer to the camp gate that led to the Command's quarters thinking I might decipher something, and not a moment later, Karas walked out. Seeing me near the gate, he hurried over, completely nerve-wrecked, his eyes bulging.

"Remember the barber?" he said, "The one that went with me to the girls camp? They can't find him."

"I fear he's escaped," he said. I was surprised because up until that point, I didn't think it was possible to get out of here considering the guards, the risk, and the wire.

"Fortunately, they still haven't called me or asked me anything about it. I hope they don't think I'll do the same," he lamented. "Camp mentors think he's hiding somewhere close. They said that they'll still find him, and they aren't saying much else. Chokolyada told me all this. He asked me if I knew his intentions. I said I didn't and I don't. Please don't tell anyone - nobody else knows."

"What happened?" I asked.

"Apparently the barber went into the military barrack early this morning and was supposed to cut and shave two soldiers. He finished with the first, while the other still laid in bed. That second soldier ended up falling asleep.

"The first one went off to take a shower, get dressed, and went to his shift, not knowing the other had fallen asleep. The second woke up later, and, figuring that the barber didn't want to wake him, he shaved himself and decided he'd find the barber for a haircut another time.

"A few hours later, after lunch, both of these soldiers met up again. The clipped one asked the unclipped one why he didn't get a haircut, and he replied that he overslept and shaved himself, figuring the barber didn't want to wake him. They immediately got suspicious, because none of the on-guard soldiers had let the barber back into camp. One of them ran off to the other soldiers to ask if they'd seen the barber, but they hadn't since the morning. The second soldier ran off to find Choko and told him to immediately deliver the barber to the gate. Chokolyada came back and said that the barber hadn't returned from the military barracks yet.

"Completely frightened, both guards burst into the Commandant's quarters, told the Commandant everything, and he became so furious with the soldier who overslept that he hit him in the face and screamed, 'I'll shoot you! I'll kill you!'

"He immediately reported the barber's escape to Dachau. Dachau sent two soldiers with trained dogs here, and the search started while you were working. It just so happened that earlier today a couple heavy trucks arrived at the girls' factory. The Commandant thinks that the barber quietly climbed up into one and then ran off somewhere."

CHAPTER FOURTEEN

A NEW COMMAND

The next morning we were assembled and counted and they didn't take the day shift or the night shift to work. A few personal cars arrived at the gate, and officers dressed in black leather coats stepped out and walked into our field. The Commandant joined them and greeted them with a salute and waited for their orders.

The visiting chief petty officer from Dachau ordered the entire camp, servants and all, to meet in front of our building. He ordered one of his subordinate officers to count us and his number suited his documents.

The officer then walked proudly before us and said, "Yesterday, one of the prisoners, entrusted by *this* command, fled the camp. It's the barber, and we will catch him. And because of this oversight, the current camp Commandant will be removed. He is dismissed from his position and has been replaced."

e showed us the new Commandant, who didn't seem much different, just slightly younger.

"This Commandant will now show you what discipline

should look like here in camp," the officer said.

"And Kapo Chokolyada was too good to you too, so we're taking him away as well. In his place, we brought Kapo Hugo.'

"We'll still catch this barber," he repeated. "And here, on this very field, you will watch him hang and he will then realize what it means to flee."

He then called over Kapo Hugo and ordered him to get busy.

Hugo himself was dressed in the same striped prison dress as all the others. But it was newly sewn and made of thicker, winter material. His feet were wrapped in tall and shiny leather boots, similar to those worn by Kapo Ivan in Gross-Rosen.

His face was dark red and he was average height. He had a tough, strong structure, and was the only one in camp who wore long hair, dark and combed back behind him. He wore a red triangle without inscription, which meant he was a German. His look alone seemed to scare the prisoners.

Hugo immediately summoned Shtubowy and the two mentors Max and Vili, gave them orders, and then sent them away.

Then, with Shtubowy, he walked very slowly through us prisoners to see what he had to work with. Walking back and forth at a slow stroll, he closely observed each prisoner and then ordered one of them out of the ranks and told him to stay put.

Standing amongst us all, Hugo puffed out his chest and said, "Here in camp, there must be a discipline. Everything shall happen on time. None of you will ever be late. I was also told that there is a hospital here. Not anymore, I don't want to see it. I do not recognize hospitals, unless someone is dying. So if any of you get sick, you must first come to me, and I will soon cure you. You dogs are here to work and not mess around."

Then he pulled out a leather whip and tossed it from one hand to the other.

He lifted it over his head and said, "Oh and look at this! The doctor for all your diseases! Now get to work, and I will get to know this situation in which you live."

Kapo Hugo immediately reminded me of Ivan from Gross-Rosen. *He can't be as terrible as Ivan, can he? Maybe it's just the first day and he'll soften later.*

I looked closely at the prisoner he chose and recognized that it was a Ukrainian from Lviv. He was medium height, clean and handsome. But I never did trust him. He always talked a lot, praised himself, and half his words were lies. Because he came from the city and the rest of us Ukrainians came from the villages, he considered himself better than us. I told him that I too knew a little about Lviv after spending two years in school there.

He was maybe 25 years old and was over-flattering to the camp mentors. Karas, like the other Ukrainian prisoners, was very careful with him. *What did Hugo want with him?*

After dinner, I looked and saw that this boy's bed lay empty, and in the corridor before Hugo's door, the boy stood and cleaned his boots. I found out his name was Yuri, and I wanted to speak to him, but as I walked up, he turned away, pretending not to see me. I didn't approach any closer, because he was near Kapo's room, and I definitely didn't want to stumble unnecessarily into trouble.

At work the next day, the lathe where Yuri had been working was empty, and from that time on he no longer worked in the factory. Prisoners of other nationalities suspected that Hugo, at first glance, had fallen in love with Yuri. Nichola, one of the oldest among us Ukrainian prisoners, advised us that we ignore Yuri and see what he'll do. So we did.

After a few days, this Yuri couldn't keep away from us. One day he brought Nichola some cut-up pieces of bread and told him to divvy it among all of us Ukrainians. We rejoiced and gladly shared this bread. There was more to Yuri than I thought.

After the barber's escape, this new Commandant scared us more and more. He learned to swear in Polish, used this skill liberally, and on his newly sewn uniform was a clearly seen skull insignia of the SS.

Every time he passed through and counted prisoners, he found someone to hit. He'd count and count and in the middle of it all would raise his hand up high to the sky, hold it there for a second, making the targeted prisoner wait, then strike him in the stomach with all his might. Hugo shadowed him, copycatting with strikes as well. I made sure to always avoid the first row; they seemed to get the brunt of the beating.

Osip the tailor and the shoemaker didn't bode well with this new command either. They were forbidden to go beyond camp gates and were cramped to sew and make shoes in their own rooms. They were given whatever material they needed and nobody gave Osip any extra bread or soup anymore. Karas complained of being hungry again, and for whatever reason, maybe pity, told me that he'd no longer have me carry his tools when the air raids came.

"Do you know what happened to the hospital?" I asked him.

"Sorry! I forgot to tell you - on his first day, Hugo went into the building and straight to the hospital. Three patients, all older Frenchmen, lay inside. Hugo berated them and waved his club, screamed at the doctor and scared all of the prisoners back to their shtubas. Since then, the hospital has been empty, and the lonely doctor has had nothing to do. Kapo told him, 'You shouldn't be so idle. Scrub this room daily and keep it in exemplary order.'"

To my surprise, just before Christmas, each prisoner was dealt some cigarettes. The prisoners rejoiced at this tiny gesture.

Up until now, a group of heavy smokers would stand underneath the guard towers, waiting for the guards to toss down even the tiniest butt, which they called a "tsyuk." They'd pounce on it like dogs and rip these tsyuks off the ground and take the last dirty drag.

I hid my cigarette ration in my mattress and gave some out

to my friends. Yusef tried persuading me to trade a cigarette for a slice of bread. The heavy smokers were desperate enough to do it. I saw this awfully unfair, taking advantage of an addiction, but hunger was the lien of all my decisions and I confess that I did it, but never with any of my friends. I felt terrible doing so but was convinced that the heaviest smokers were so addicted that had they not traded with me, someone else would have gotten that bread.

Over time, factory work dwindled. Masters stopped supervising us and instead gathered with each other and talked for hours.

One day, as I was staring at all the materials, I noticed some brass and copper and an idea popped into my head. I knew that brass handled easily, and it resembled a golden hue. *What if I made a ring? I won't tell anyone.* I was famished, but for some reason the threats of the mentors, "For such work you'd be strictly punished!" weren't holding me back. The factory was dreadfully monotonous. I needed something to do.

So the next day I walked amongst the parts and masters and guards and blatantly searched for sharp files and materials. I set myself a few welded pieces, as if I was correcting them with a saw, making it look like I was actually working. I figured it would look worse if I tried to be sneaky.

So I took Tato's smithy lessons in hand and cut myself two pieces of brass, drilled a hole in each and began to carve their form. While I was focusing on this work, I realized that I could probably make these rings pretty quickly, do a good job and then trade them for bread with the gypsy cooks. They were very fond of anything that *looked* like gold. One of them already had a ring that he constantly showed off to the kitchen staff.

Two weeks of focused work later, the rings were finished and polished. They looked to me the nicest rings I'd ever seen. Even nicer than the chef's! Bringing it up to him was a risk, but he slept close to my bed and treated me quite well, so I figured to trust him.

The next day I asked the gypsy where he got his ring.

"When I was arrested, they took everything from me. But I slipped it off my finger and into my mouth," he said.

"Do you want another?" I asked.

His eyes lit up. "You've got a ring? Did you hide it in your mouth too? Why don't you wear it? Show it to me. Show me the ring," he pushed.

I panicked. "I'm joking!" I said. "How could I get a ring into camp?"

"Really? I was about to offer you half a loaf of bread for it. My friends in the kitchen would do just the same," he said.

"Well even if I did have a ring, I wouldn't show it to anybody, because I'd probably just get reported to Kapo or even the Camp Board." I was testing the waters.

"I can't believe I was arrested in the first place. I hate the command and the Kapo. All of us in the kitchen are true friends and we carry secrets and we definitely keep them, especially from the Germans and camp counsel. If you traded with me, I wouldn't tell a soul," he said.

He and his gypsy friends were such a tight knit group. I

felt I could trust them.

"I'll show you the ring in a couple days, because I hid it in the factory and have to clean it up," I said.

The gypsy was so impressed by this ring, even though he'd never seen it, that that same day he brought me the bread.

That evening I told Karas.

"That's exceptional! I would have never imagined you pulling off such a stunt. Just be careful - that's dangerous work. If the camp board finds out, they'd make an example of you and punish you in who knows what way, but it would definitely be in front of everyone," he said.

"Nobody's seen the ring just yet, and I already got the bread for it," I said.

"From who?" Karas asked.

"The gypsy," I said.

"Oh! The gypsy! I know him well. Yes, you can definitely trust him," he said.

My fear subsided. I shared the bread with Karas, but he only broke himself off a little piece and told me to hide it for another day.

A few days later, I showed both finished rings to the gypsy. He lit up like a kid. "How did you... Where did you... Look at that shine! They glisten like gold!"

"This is all I've got. I snuck it in from Sachsenhausen," I lied. "Again, don't tell anybody who you got it from."

"They're so beautiful! I'll give you two halves for the second one," he said.

And he kept his promise. Within two weeks he got me the bread, and he even added a bowl of soup. I shared the bread with Osip the tailor, as always, and gave some small pieces to my other friends as well. They asked me where I got them from, but I didn't say. They assumed I got them from Karas.

Encouraged by my first real achievement in the camps, I thought I should keep this up. Maybe even try my hand at something different.

Aluminum was everywhere to carve out all sorts of things, and within a few days I found some leftover toothbrushes in the bathrooms. French prisoners got them in care packages. I grabbed two of them and hid them in my bed. With an aluminum piece, I carved a fish head into one with a wide open mouth and into the other, a dog's head, mouth open just as wide.

From the brass, I made tiny, thin wheels and connected them with a little wire of brass. I used the bristles to make teeth inside the animals' mouths.

Upon telling all this to Karas, he loved it and assured me that he could exchange them with the guards, who were friendly to him.

A few days later, I brought him two wonderful animal-cigarette-holders made of toothbrushes that were so nice I could barely part with them. When Karas saw them, he felt sorry that I had to give them up. But my empty stomach was in first place. Karas bargained for each one, getting one of his guard friends to give up a loaf of bread for each.

The guard liked them so much, that the next day he brought a loaf and promised to bring the second one sometime next week. I was so excited! Karas gave him both at once, but a week passed and we never saw the bread or the guard again. Osip later learned from the other soldiers that the guard was transferred to another camp and didn't tell him. My heart hit the floor.

I was so hurt that I decided not to make anything else for anyone - I didn't want to waste any energy on fruitless labor, no matter how hungry I was. Osip was also distressed by all this and lost his confidence in the guards.

It took a few days to calm me down, but time did the trick and I thought: *To remember all this, I should make myself a stainless steel ring.* It took longer than the others, because the iron was more difficult to form and carve. But I didn't care. This was for me.

After I finished it, I told myself that I would place it on my finger only when I was free. I didn't even mention it to the tailor and kept it under my mattress, only occasionally looking at it.

Boylek started approaching me in the factory. He was actually the prisoner that would visit me the most. Sometimes he'd make me laugh, sometimes he'd annoy me. Almost every other day, before the end of the work day, he'd call me Stevie and ask whether I might know what would be served for dinner that day.

"I already told you. You yourself know what it could be," I said. And again, I repeated, "There's little else but soup, a biscuit with margarine or jam, and maybe a cup of coffee."

"I know, I know. But when I ask you, it just makes things easier. It makes me think of home, when the footman would announce that dinner was ready. I often sit and wait, hoping that just one more time that footman would call us for dinner," he said.

"Well when he does, don't forget to invite me," I joked.

Time was swimming by very slowly in camp. One day, Max showed up and picked three prisoners, I among them. A bread truck had arrived that day and needed to be unloaded. Max gave me a sheet of paper and pencil and told me to manage the unloading of the truck. It was filled with bread.

"Be very careful. Make no mistakes, otherwise you'll find yourself in trouble," Max said to me, and yelled over to the other two, "And careful unloading! Otherwise you'll no longer be picked for this job."

One prisoner was appointed to the truck and the other to the cart which the bread was to be loaded into. Simple enough.

The prisoner up on the truck started grabbing two loaves at a time and throwing them to the prisoner near the cart. Max stood nearby with a military guard, talking and watching our movements.

Then suddenly, the prisoner on the truck noticed Max and the guard both bend over and he swiftly threw a loaf into an empty sack on the ground next to the cart and innocently continued dumping loaves by two to the prisoner on the ground.

I got confused. *Do I count it?* The command reminded us time and time again that stealing bread brought the death penalty. I didn't want to be part of that. Every prisoner here wanted more bread, but most of us weren't ready to die for such a small reward either.

After unloading, I wrote down the number of bread loaves that ended up in the cart, minus the one in the pack. Then I gave the paper to Max. He looked at the note and shoved it away with no indication of a mistake. I sighed relief.

Later that night when darkness had taken over the field, I stood outside by the barbed wire and the prisoner who threw the bread into the sack came outside and walked a few laps. He then dropped his jacket nonchalantly on the sack with the bread loaf and began to do exercises, diverting any suspicion from the guard, who stood in the tower observing all movement about the camp. Once the prisoner felt secure, he got up and picked up his jacket with the bread loaf in it and carried it inside naturally enough so that none were the wiser.

Later, at his bed, he divided the bread in half. He took one half, divided the second half into two and gave one piece to me and the other piece to the prisoner who stood by the cart.

We both gave him a puzzled look, and he said, "I divvied it right, because if we were caught by the command, I alone would be punished by death. You two could have justified yourselves, saying you didn't see it. But since you haven't betrayed me, I'm giving you each a quarter."

Fair enough. As thieves, we returned back to our beds. At that moment, Nicholka, followed by Basil and another Ukrainian named Roman, came by my bed. I told them about stealing the bread and shared my portion with all of them equally.

"Really?" Roman rejoiced. "How did you manage to deceive Max and the guards? I've done that job a few times and never got a chance to steal a loaf."

He made it sound so noble.

"I don't want to do that again. I'd rather live hungry than die in sacrifice," I said.

Snow began falling in camp and winter had brought us the cold. The frequency of air raids dropped significantly, and we were very rarely taken out past the village into the trenches. This was a great relief to us shivering prisoners. We weren't given any winter clothes and those that we had become grated, pitted and ripped as well. Many prisoners walked around coughing but were too scared to tell anyone about their sickness. They didn't want Kapo Hugo to find out.

One day, the camp board surprised us by announcing that it was the day before Christmas, 1944, and we'd have a half day the next day. *Yay!* Joy overcame me. Me nor any of the prisoners knew what day it had been, let alone that the Christmas holidays were here.

In Ukraine we celebrated Christmas on January 7th, but in camp I didn't care what day we celebrated it. I was glad that the camp board at least gave us time off. Why they were sending us to work at all was a mystery to me - the masters wouldn't be coming in.

That night, I sought my refuge - the barbed wire fence. I looked up into heaven, seeing stars that proclaimed the birth of God's son. My thoughts spilled over into my native land, Ukraine.

SEPARATION

I was overcome by loneliness. *My first Christmas alone! Alone in this alien land!* I so badly wanted to call out to my family: *Mama! Christ is born! Mama! Will I someday see you again? Tato! Where are you today? Brothers! Sisters! Did you save a place at the table for us?*

Tears fell from my eyes, and I wiped them away with my frigid sleeve. The old German sentry in the nearby tower saw all this. *Do you have a son? Maybe he's also somewhere in danger today.*

He quietly and very politely motioned me back into the building, because the courtyard got even colder. I waved to him and went to my bed.

As I walked in, most prisoners sat kneeling at their beds in prayer, probably thinking of years when they'd spent holidays at home. I joined in, realizing that they all had to endure the same difficulty as me, sitting without family during this celebratory time in a foreign country, surrounded by people they didn't know.

Yusef and I reminisced about the first star of the night, which always signaled that it was time for dinner. We talked about caroling and how we missed it dearly. We both then calmly said goodnight, prayed, and bowed into our memories, slowly drifting into sleep.

After work and lunch the next day, Rudyj ordered us to take care of minor chores. When we finished, prisoners met up in groups by nationality. The French prisoners began to sing carols around one bed. A group of Poles had also consorted together, among them Yusef, and they too began to sing carols around another.

"Srud notsney trsishy..."

Then the Germans and Dutch gather and began to sing too. In their corner they sang "Shtille Nacht..." (Silent Night).

And then to my bed came my countryman from Horodok, Roman, and he asked me, "What? We don't know any carols? Why don't we sing too? There are plenty Ukrainians here. What are we scared of?"

His suggestion made me smile, because so far it seemed that Roman wasn't very proud of his Ukrainian heritage, but here he was, banding us together.

We both went to the second shtub and gathered ten willing carolers around Roman's bed. Karas showed up too. Our group had somehow grown bigger than any of the others.

We wished each other a happy holidays, and the oldest among us, Nicholas, started us off: "We've joined here together as a new Ukrainian family. So let's sing"

We started with the carol, "God Eternal."

God Eternal
Born to us on Earth
Heavens gift
From above
Born to save us with His Love
Jesus Christ is born!

Several Eastern Ukrainians then joined in too. They didn't quite remember the words at first, because of their Russian oppression, but then dug back into their minds and remembered how their grandmothers once caroled. They said that during the communist regime, carols were banned. But they really liked our singing and were happy to somehow remember the words. We then proceeded to sing every hymn and carol we could think of.

The other nationalities quickly finished their carols, but we continued and kept adding new and joyful melodies to ours. They slowly approached us and listened intently.

Among us there were a few skilled singers, so we divided ourselves into two parts and created the feel of a small choir. This camp had never heard of such melodies! Prisoners of all nationalities then gathered from both shtubas, surrounding us and praising us too.

To my surprise, the camp instructors listened in as well. This evening they behaved much more calmly and understandably, and at the end of our singing, in a peaceful manner, they suggested that we go to sleep and put out the light.

But the Christmas peace didn't quite last as long as we wanted. It was the coldest night we'd had in camp. Several prisoner awoke at night and complained that someone had stolen their blanket. It was freezing, and they had nothing else to wrap themselves up with. Vili and Max shouted at them and told them to get back to sleep, threatening them that if they didn't calm down, they'd be driven down to the washroom and ordered to sit there until morning.

The next day, Vili ordered every prisoner to bring his blanket to breakfast, otherwise he'd be punished without food. After hearing his threat, random blankets appeared underneath beds of prisoners who were missing theirs. The stolen blankets had been returned.

The next day, an older man came up to me and introduced himself as a Russian professor of mathematics. He liked our caroling from the night before.

"I wanted to talk with the tailor, but he's always busy, so I thought I'd talk to you," he said. "You two are always meeting, so I figure I might be able to learn something from you. You're young, yes, but these Ukrainians, they look up to you... so I wanted to know, in Western Ukraine, how do you celebrate Christmas? Did the Polish occupation allow you to have your church services? Did the Poles force you to follow Latin customs?"

"In Galicia, our Western Ukraine, there are two churches: the Catholic, which has more members than the other, Orthodox," I said.

"Really? I was told in the Soviet Union that all the Ukrainians in Galicia were baptized into Latin customs and then after that, you were called Poles," he said.

"The Poles wanted to do so, but it wasn't so easy. In Galicia and in Volhynia, there were too many Ukrainian patriots that fought against the conversion. These Ukrainian kept themselves organize through creating organizations that built cooperatives and unions around butter factories. Conscious Ukrainians worked and therefore didn't have to fall into Polish labor or get Latinized in order to keep their family fed. Surely there were those who just cared for their own survival and didn't care whether they were Ukrainians or not - their main goal was putting food on the table. But for my family, the largest center of preservation from Polandization was the Ukrainian Greek-Catholic Church. We are Catholics, not Roman but Greek, and our ancient, Ukrainian church was left alone, allowing us to stay publicly awake Ukrainians. Here, now take a look at me, do I look like a Pole? I am Ukrainian and my eyes are turned to Kiev, and I fight and wait for the time that Ukraine becomes an independent state."

He then changed the subject, wondering how our school system worked, and I took advantage of this situation by asking him if he tutor me in math.

"Gladly. But I haven't been able to get any paper or pencils," he complained.

"I'll figure that out... I really like algebra. It's my favorite subject," I said.

"We'll start with that," he said.

I told all of this to the tailor the next day. Karas promised me that he'd try to get two pencils and a notebook, but after a few days, he came up empty.

So then I reluctantly appealed to Kapo's "assistant," Yuri. He was still for the most part avoiding us, but I asked him anyway if he could get me paper and pencil. After all, he was, whether he liked it or not, close to Kapo Hugo.

"Why do you need them? Letters are prohibited. They're not coming in or going out," said Yuri, curiously.

When I explained why, he immediately promised me he'd try.

A few days later I got two pencils, a notebook, and several sheets of clean paper. The other prisoners were amazed. In the past, if anybody wanted to write a letter, the pencil and paper came straight from Rudyj and had to go straight back, including the letter.

"Nobody else can use the pencil or paper besides you and the professor. And keep your notes in your bed. Hugo himself knows about all this, so don't push these boundaries," Yuri said.

I was humbled by Yuri's generosity. He could have ignored me. He didn't have to trouble Hugo. Thus, my schooling continued within the walls of a German concentration camp.

The professor was very happy that he could actually share his knowledge with someone else. I was too. *I'm learning again! I'd never thought this day would come!*

Our lessons were not complete without him asking about Ukrainian history, too. His wonder and my experience meshed well.

One day, he asked, "Why do you Ukrainians distinguish yourselves from the Russians? We come from the same state of Kiev, no?"

I answered his question with a questions of my own:

"If we are so the same, why were millions of Ukrainians exported to Siberia? Why was an artificial famine induced in Ukraine in 1933, which killed more than five million Ukrainians? Why did the Russian prince Dolgoruky and his son Bogolyubsky destroy the capital of Ukraine, our Kiev, which you happen to call the mother of all Russian cities? Why were all Kiev's treasures ripped away and taken up north? Why didn't Moscow help Ukraine fight off the Polish captivity? Or protect us from the Tatar attacks? Why did the Russians destroy the beautiful Zaporizhian Sich, while forcing Ukrainian Cossacks to build, on marshes no less, your capital city of St. Petersburg? Tens of thousands died there! And when the last Ukrainian Cossack leader-ottoman Kalnyshevsky, who when Moscow's troops were advancing on the island of Khortytsia, told his men, 'Do not fire upon them, they are our brothers!' - why were they taken from Ukraine to Solovki in Siberia and buried in a monastic cell, never to be heard of ever again? Why do your Kings burn Ukrainian books, saying that the Ukrainian language never was? Can you tell me now that we're the same people?"

"I read plenty of books about all this, but Soviet history mentioned the answers to these questions," the professor said.

I then reminded him of the Ukrainian poet Taras Shevchenko, who said, "Embrace yourselves my black-browed, but not with the Muscovites, because the Muscovites are strangers..."

After hearing me out, the professor replied, "We need to forget about all this now, because we're neighbors, and we have to work together and guard against enemy nations, namely these Germans."

I agreed with him. "I'm glad you see us as neighbors. We must work together, but on the basis of equality, not oppression. And finally, Russia itself must say that the 50 million Ukrainian people cannot be without their own state."

These conversations were frequent, but always quiet, with due respect and understanding. He also kept teaching me math - equations with one unknown, then with two and then squares. We planned on moving to physics soon too, which was *his* favorite subject.

However, my hope for further education was interrupted. This, perhaps, because of human weakness, which is so beautifully described in our proverb, "I alone, will not eat, but I also won't let you eat either."

During one of our physics lessons, he complained that his countrymen, who refused to learn from him, told him not to have any students, emphasizing that none of us knew if we'd even get out of camp alive.

"Maybe they're envious," he said, "because they've seen me eat the bread you've given me... I'm not sure, but unfortunately, this is our last lecture."

I wasn't surprised: "Thank you. I'll always remember you as a good teacher, one who even in German concentration camps hadn't forgotten his profession and still fueled his desire to teach," I said.

He gave me the pencil and paper and said, "I'll remember our conversations forever."

I stuck these items in my notebook and hid them in my bed. I overheard a dispute between the professor and his countrymen afterwards. I couldn't hear everything, but I was sure it was about me.

That same night I told Roman that I wasn't getting lessons from the professor anymore.

He laughed at me and said, "Why do you need math here in camp anyway? You can't even buy even a single slice of bread with it!"

I then went to Yuri and told him the story, asking him if I could hold on to the pencil and paper.

He replied, "Yes, that's fine. I'll take care of it."

SEPARATION

Sometime in February 1945, more rags that were clothes were delivered to the camp. It was already quite late into winter - we definitely could have used them earlier. They were shirts and sweaters, and they were apparently taken from other prisoners. I was pleased, because I desperately needed and got a winter shift. Although this new shirt was slightly too big, at that moment, it was perfect.

As more sweaters were handed out, I noticed one woven with threads of yellow and blue, just like the Ukrainian flag, and I instantly regretted that it hadn't fallen to me. We were still being called either Russian or Polish here in camp. I would have loved to wear it with pride.

At that moment, a fellow Ukrainian Basil approached me and said, "I *need* that sweater."

"Well look, you're still standing in line, so then just go get it," I said.

"Whether it falls to me or not, I'm still getting it," he said, desperately.

Wow. You'll probably trade it for a meager meal. You'll go even more hungry.

"You don't need it," I tried convincing him. "Your health is more important than a sweater."

But he ignored my pleas, and I watched on as he approached the table. He was one turn away.

Oh good. He's going to get it.

But the prisoner in from of Basil got the sweater. Basil was pissed.

He received a sweater that was in even better condition than the blue and yellow one, but he didn't care and immediately walked over to the prisoner and tried to exchange it. This prisoner saw how badly Basil wanted the sweater and knew that he could get something out of him. They bargained for a bit, and then Basil came back smilingly with the blue and yellow sweater.

"How did you manage to get it from him?" I asked.

"I bargained for it," he said proudly. "That prisoner wanted five pieces of bread from me, but in the end we agreed on one piece and a serving of soup."

I looked on with compassion, but didn't reply. You don't give away food when you're starving, but I wasn't in the business of belittling his joy either. That evening he showed it off to the other prisoners, proclaiming his nationality as not Polish, but Ukrainian.

And although he did give up some food, this act served as a good example of how a simple Ukrainian cherished his Ukrainian origins.

As winter slowly trudged out of Baumenheim, airstrikes became more frequent.

One night, the alarm went off and the nightshift was taken out of work and all the lights in the building and factory and guard towers were extinguished. The guards came down from their perches to make sure that none of us would escape under the cover of night.

Osip Karas, like he always did, ran over to my bed and shook with fear.

I told him again and again, "What happens to you,

happens to us all. So why is it that just you that worries so much? You're a natural coward, afraid of your own shadow."

This worked a couple times, and he tried to justify himself, poking back at me and giggling, telling me how badly *I* was shaking:

One night, after a raid call and listening to his anxieties, they woke us up again and told us to leave the building for counting. No alarm. This time, Kapo Hugo ordered the whole camp council to join us, including the cooks. None of us wanted to get up again, especially in the cold rain.

We got outside and Hugo yelled at us. His face looked like it was inflated. He smacked several prisoners in the stomach, and for those who bent over in pain, he chopped a second blow to the back of their neck. He kicked prisoners' legs and threw obscenities in all directions.

Suddenly, the tower lights illuminated the entire field and every prisoner appeared with their eyes squinting. Kapo counted us himself and then told his aides Max and Rudyj to count us too. *What happened?*

After counting, Kapo ordered his aides to search the factory and the building, maybe to find someone taking a nap or maybe something worse, like someone got sick or broke their leg.

At that moment, the camp Commandant stormed in and called the Kapo over. Kapo, as always, threw off his cap and smacked it against his boots, saluting him with honor.

But the Commandant ignored the salute, heard that something was wrong, and yelled at all of us as he stomped over to count us himself. He counted, screwed up, cursed, and counted us again. He smacked the last prisoner in line who tried to salute him.

But his count didn't line up. Hugo followed closely and listened intently. The Commandant and Hugo quickly agreed on something.

Hugo ordered us to "Take a good look and guess which one of your friends is missing."

I knew that no one would say a word. Nobody wanted to be associated with an escapee.

Since no one answered, the furious Commandant ordered the prisoner registry to be read off. Shtubowy Rudyj got the list and read. Max and Vili put those read in a separate group. Rudyj read slowly and the tired prisoners answered flatly. When a prisoner was slow to answer, Hugo sent him into the other like by hitting him with his whip. My cipher was called near the end and when there were only a few prisoners left, one cipher went unanswered. Hugo ran about shouting the number and ordered Vili to check the last few prisoners against this cipher. They'd found their missing man.

"Who knows this prisoner?!" asked Hugo. "Who can show me where he sleeps?"

No one answered.

Hugo raged. He knew someone knew, but that someone was too afraid, or too smart, to speak up.

The Commandant stormed over from the factory and called Hugo over. The Commandant pointed towards the factory and made an angry fist. Hugo showed him the registry and told him who was missing. They scurried about.

After making us wait in puddles, Vili returned from the

Commandant's building and said, "The night shift is done - get in the building. Day shift - get breakfast and get to work."

We had been standing there for almost a third of the night, and we went to work half-soaked. *Why haven't they informed Dachau yet like they did with the escape of the barber?*

Some prisoners explained that the end of the war was near and there was all sorts of disorder among the local command. Maybe the crafty Commandant and Kapo Hugo didn't want to admit that a prisoner escaped under their supervision.

After breakfast, we got to work. German masters had long been waiting and stood in groups talking amongst themselves. Roman was one of the first of us to get to the toilet and he came back and said, "The prisoner must got out through the window, because part of it was busted out. He's probably well stocked up with tools."

Another guard told a prisoner that the escapee had carefully re-laid this sheet back into the window, so it took the Commandant some time to figure out how he got out. Apparently the Commandant was quite sure that the prisoner couldn't have gotten far, and that he'd quickly be caught and brought back. Then, one of the masters who was late for work opened his wardrobe locker and immediately informed the guards that someone stole his work clothes and left their prison clothes.

I was glad that he was lucky enough to escape and smart enough to change out of his prison clothes.

After work I learned that he was a Russian who had been driven to work in Germany. His friends said that he'd been yearning to bolt, but they didn't believe he could actually pull it off.

But this Russian knew the German language well. Before the war, he was taken from his German work and thrown into camps because he'd fallen in love with a German girl and she got pregnant. This was illegal for a non-German to do. He longed for her in camps and told the other prisoners how much she loved him and how she tried to keep them from being ripped apart. But the local authorities wouldn't have it and threw him into camp anyway. *Maybe he'll get some help from the outside...*

Kapo Hugo found a new level of cruelty that night. He stormed through the building and scolded all of his assistants. He yelled and dared other prisoners to try escaping. Yusef and I got a short end of the stick too - Max approached us and told us that from this night on we'd be back in with the general prisoners.

"Get back to your old shtub and find a free bed," he said.

I wasn't surprised - we'd both recently turned eighteen and were considered adults. But I didn't want to leave this bed or this area either. It was cleaner and nobody could search my mattress. Nonetheless, I pulled out my ring and a tiny piece of soap and moved back to the second shtub.

I found a top bunk above our blue and yellow Basil, and I was surrounded by other Ukrainians as well. Yusef found a bed in the corner amongst the Poles.

That night I met up with Karas, and he said that I was moved back to this shtub, because of the shoemaker, who'd for whatever reason kept complaining about us staying with the leadership of the camp.

The next day at work, my master was acting peculiar. He walked to a corner of the factory and waved his hand to call me over. He was peeking around to see if any guards were coming as I walked up.

When I got to him, he gave me a small piece of bread.

"Put it in your pocket. Quickly. Don't let anybody see you and don't you dare tell anyone else," he ordered.

I smiled with gratitude and said, "No one will know."

I was glad that he acknowledged how hungry I was and I walked into the bathroom and quickly ate the bread.

But when I returned to work, he acted funny. He immediately turned away from me when I walked up, and when I asked him a question about work, he quickly answered and then immediately withdrew from me.

The next day he acted funny again. He didn't watch over me like usual to see if I did good work.

Why has he been so unfriendly to me after he gave me that paltry piece of bread?

I watched him closely but couldn't figure him out.

Did I offend you? Maybe his conscience was pestering him. Maybe he's torn between being a proud German and a compassionate man helping hungry prisoners get back to their homeland.

One day, he didn't show up to work and another master took his place. This new master treated me much better and even tried to speak in a language other than German. He said the other master was sent to another factory. That was that.

Very strange.

March 1945 arrived. The air raids were more frequent. We often sat in the trenches for hours.

One day we were plopped down in those trenches and a group of Allied planes flew over our heads. Together they approached the neighboring town of Donauworth, about 15 kilometers outside of our camp Baumenheim. Black strands of gunfire spurted from these planes.

The guards warned us, "Stay. If someone runs, we'll shoot without warning."

But we weren't scared and were glad that the planes were so close and coming so often. It felt like the end of the war drew near. But for whatever reason, our Karas still trembled from some subconscious fear. His mind couldn't find a safe place to sit and he repeatedly kept asking himself, "Will they bomb us?"

After some time, the not-so-distant roar of falling bombs started shaking our trenches. Donauworth exalted up in black smoke and red flames. After the first pass and a quick break, the planes on cross route soared above the city and bombed it again. More big explosions followed. Fires spread and black smoke slowly engulfed the entire city.

I tried persuading Karas not to be frightened, because these bombs weren't falling on us. The city was a bigger target. He reluctantly agreed, but then said, "But what do we do if they fly over our factory?"

"Don't worry," I told him. "This is why they dug our

trenches way out here, where we are. When bombs fall upon our factory, let them fall. They'll most likely crush our building, and then we'll get put in a different one."

"And what happens if the bombs drop at night?" he asked.

"Then we'll all perish and finally have some peace," I joked. "What are you so worried about? After all, you yourself know that these bombs don't always fall onto their deliberate target, let alone at night. I'm sure if they dropped on us at night, they wouldn't even shake the factory. Chances are, they'll hit us during the day anyway."

After our discussion, the tailor calmed down a bit.

Fire roared, smoke plumed above the town, and a siren yelped telling us the raid was over.

The aircrafts returned to their countries.

Our guards ordered us out of the trenches. They counted us, brought us back to camp, and ordered us to continue working. Civilian masters stood in small groups, anxiously talking amongst themselves. Some didn't return to work - they rode out to Donauworth. Many had family there.

Over the next couple days, all the prisoners could talk about were raids. Some suggested that the next raid would probably be directed at our factory. But they were just predictions.

One day, we again found ourselves in the trenches during another nearby air raid, and two British aircrafts flew over our heads, so low that I could see the planes' insignias and even the pilots! They swooped down several times over our neighboring bavor village and fired at our factory.

Pit-a-rat-tat-tat-tat-tat-tat!

It was over pretty quickly. The all-clear alarm sounded, and the guards took us back to camp where our building and our factory was shot up, bullet holes lining the walls and windows. Some workers were sent back to work, and others remained to clean up the broken glass and debris. Karas and I were assigned to cleaning.

Inside, we found glass scattered on the floor and all over his bed.

At least I can help him clean.

He was solemnly glad that I could be with him at that time, but he paced back and forth amongst the two shtubas, like he was looking for something he'd lost, incessantly talking about the bombing.

After a few passes, we both slowly picked up all the glass from his bed and mattress and then shook his blanket free of glass outside. After some time, he somehow calmed down and ceased to speak about the bombing.

CHAPTER FIFTEEN

March 19, 1945

And finally, March 19, 1945 arrived, a day that would forever imprint itself in my memory.

It started as usual, with our lunch horn going off at noon in the factory. All us prisoners left our places and hurried to the prison yard for counting. Each tried jumping out in front of the other in order to get lunch sooner.

Vili and Kapo Hugo both counted all the prisoners as the Commandant, just like every day, nervy, breathless, and quite angry, appeared with his guards. Hugo gave him our count.

The Commandant re-counted everyone and then prodded practically every prisoner in the stomach, saying, "Why didn't you take your cap off before me? Why didn't you beat your cap as loudly as you should have?"

He then ordered not the first, but the last row to get food. Some prisoners grumbled in frustration, saying that the food belonged to *them* first.

Fortunately for those grumblers, the Commandant didn't hear their quarrels. We figured his hearing wasn't very good anyway, because whenever he *did* hear something, he would retaliate. He swiftly left the registration area and went back to his house.

After about a third of the prisoners received their portion, the air raid siren went off. Unfortunately for me, I was still two prisoners away from my afternoon potato and a scoop of soup. The prisoners called these un-peeled potatoes "potatoes in military court."

Maybe I could still snag one?

I inched closer to the kettle, but Max struck me with his stick and pushed me back into my row, saying, "What? You can't hear? There's an alarm!"

At that moment, our escorting guards arrived, and we jogged out to the trenches beyond the village.

But I didn't care about the alarm. *I was so close to that potato. And what happens when we get back? What if the prisoners who already ate get back in line? No one's keeping track. Will the last prisoners in line get food? Or will we stay hungry?*

I stared at the bavors in the village, hoping that someone might toss us a slice of bread, or maybe even something more. But none of these Germans thought to do that. Most of them were hidden down in their vaults.

After running through the frigid air, we arrived at the trenches. Snow fell, and these trenches filled with puddles and quickly turned into soupy mud gorges. We sat there for about half an hour, and then heard the brief double beep, declaring the danger was gone. A few minutes later, we heard the siren wail the all clear, advising us that the aircrafts had flown to another location.

We half-ran down the cold, marshy road to camp. Hugo

and the Commandant were angry about the raid and the frigid air and took it out on us by blindly beating and scolding prisoners.

The Commandant then went off to his apartment and Hugo ordered those that had already eaten to retreat to one side, away from those who hadn't. No one moved. On his second, more strict appeal, a small group of punishment-fearing prisoners walked aside. Later, one prisoner admitted to me that he hadn't eaten, but Kapo peered at him so suspiciously that he decided to go to the side of people who already ate. He'd already been severely beaten beforehand at the hands of Hugo's most insane outburst. Hugo had lost his head and mercilessly beat him with his fists, boots, and only stopped when the prisoner lay lifeless on the ground not moving. I didn't blame this man for switching lines.

Even though those who admitted eating were unmistakably less than those who actually got food, Hugo distributed potatoes anyway. I was somewhere in the middle of the line. *Please let there be a potato left for me.*

I inched closer and closer and finally my turn came, but the sirens again wailed. Vili immediately stopped issuing potatoes, pulled the boiler off to the side, and used his stick to corral us prisoners immediately into rows.

The guards ran in from behind the gates and hastily led us all out. We weren't even counted. The sirens sounded like they were mourning more than ever before.

Running through the village, I noticed that some civilian workers and bavors didn't rush into their cellars. Maybe, like me, they thought this was a false alarm.

Osip Karas then ran up next to me and complained, "I didn't grab all my sewing gear, because I'm convinced this is it. We're gonna get struck."

He had been sewing a jacket for the Commandant and was caught off guard by this alarm and ran out without the machine.

"Calm down, Karas. We're running too quickly. If we keep up this pace, we'll end up ahead of the all the prisoners and with the guards. And those angry guards are way more dangerous than any air raid," I said.

Karas pretended he was calm, trying to smile, but it was all artificial, like a machine.

Elderly prisoners, especially the French, who had stopped getting food parcels recently, couldn't keep up. The guards impelled them the butts of their rifles.

The Commandant glanced at his watch and shouted, "No one remains behind!"

And then something happened - the bavors standing by their houses began yelling at the guards. "Why are you mocking them?!"

Even tiny bavor children were screaming at the guards, "You shouldn't beat *any*body!"

"The war will soon end, Karas. Even German civilians are threatening to defend us," I said.

We were crammed into the soupy trenches and ordered to wait. But once again, after 20 minutes or so, no raid happened and the two short blasts let us know that the planes flew off in another direction and the long whooooo of the siren cried, letting us know we were in the clear.

I then boldly said to Karas, "See. I felt this would happen. And you were so nervous."

At that moment, the sun appeared, and my soul gayly lifted. I said to Karas, "Only one problem now. This running and sharp air has ruined my belly. I'm starving, and I didn't get anything to eat."

"I didn't get anything either," said Karas.

Walking back to the building, the guards let up on their prodding. Maybe the guards' hate was disarmed by these civilians. To me these guards were more enjoyable than at the beginning of my imprisonment.

We once again entered the camp yard. *Where are the boilers?*

The Commandant went straight back to his quarters, not bothering to count us.

Hugo ordered the prisoners to separate into "eaten" and "not eaten" and even less went over to the eaten side than before. The guards brought out two boilers, and they took their helpings first.

I jokingly said to tailor: "I hope I get something this time, because if I don't, I'll die sooner of starvation than of bombardment."

"I'll get you something tonight from Max. I'm sewing him new pants," he promised.

But he sounded sad. Unconvinced. Like it wouldn't happen. But I was glad to hear him say it.

"Lord, please let the rest of this day be peaceful. And let us get some sleep tonight too," he said.

Kara's turn came up, and he let no time pass between Vili giving him the potato and him scarfing it down.

I got closer and closer to the boiler. There were only five prisoners ahead of me. Then four... three... Vili started to dig deep into the boiler, scraping the remains at the bottom.

And then the siren went off again, the third time today, which hadn't happened in camp before. But the hungry prisoners had enough of these sirens and attacked the potato boiler, toppling it over and clawing for these tiny potatoes. They paid no attention to the camp command. I didn't move.

Then somehow one of these tiny potatoes rolled out from underneath the scrum and I quickly snatched up this great treasure and ran back into rows where we were lining up to run back out to the trenches. Max, Vili, and behind them Kapo, all unmercifully beat each and every prisoner who scrapped for a potato of gold. I ate mine.

Amongst that potato chaos, there were no friends anymore. Just the struggle for survival. I stood and watched this terrible scene, and then stared at the building door for tailor who I was sure would be terrified.

I dodged the guards who tried beating me for waiting on him, and then suddenly the tailor sprinted out of the house and I waved my hand.

"Where are your tools?!" I asked as we ran towards the trenches.

"I'll never drag those things out here ever again! If a bomb falls on us, what use will that silly machine be? It won't help *me*, that's for sure," he said, then paused and said, "This third raid of the day doesn't promise us anything good."

"Karas - this is a small factory. Compare it to all the others! If it was so dangerous, the English would have destroyed it long ago," I said.

He ignored my comment and said, "For one day, this is still too many alarms."

I jokingly said, "Maybe you should file a complaint with the Western Allies. Then maybe they would listen and only bother us once a day."

He seriously replied, "Yes, but we also want the war to end sooner. Let them bomb the factory - just not us."

"Well I too would love to make a complaint," I said.

Tailor knew what I was getting at. "You didn't get anything to eat again?"

"No I did. I'm just trying to lighten the mood. One fell to me and somewhat calmed my stomach."

But for whatever reason he didn't believe me, locked up in his own mind with anxiety. "Don't worry. I promise I'll get you a piece of bread tonight."

Running by the bavors, we saw that they didn't rush into their shelters. Many stood and looked at us with compassion, shaking their heads.

The older prisoners were in awful shape. What a sight for those bavors - some barely dragged their feet.

The swamp of a road sucked at our heels and sent splashes of wet mud in every direction, drenching and caking everybody. Some prisoners who didn't get anything to eat were getting more aggressive.

A prisoner yelled out to a farmer, "Esen! Esen!" (Food! Food!)

"Is bin hungrik!" (I'm hungry!)

Then to my disbelief, several others chimed in. "Esen!

Esen!"

In response, an older German woman threw a few slices of bread in our direction, but they all fell into the mud. But that didn't restrain the prisoners.

Dozens of them pounced and tore the bread to shreds. The Commandant saw this and shouted, "Fall in line or I'll shoot!"

And to the woman: "And you! What are you doing?! I'll call the police on you!"

I didn't hear the rest, because I kept on running amongst the guards. Several prisoners laid back. They just couldn't move. They were drained.

We dove down into the muddy trenches and half-swam through the frozen waters. The only reason we could stand it was the little bit of sun that had graced our day.

Roman and Yuri jumped in next to me. Over the past few weeks, we'd started to really stick together.

So it was Roman, Yuri, Osip, and me scrunched together in this trench, shooting guesses at which direction these planes might come from.

I wanted to joke to Yuri, *"Hey, maybe you should stand near Hugo! It might be safer there!"* but the thought quickly disappeared from my mind.

Roman then boasted, "I got three potatoes today! I deceived all the mentors with my stealth!"

"You probably ate mine," I joked. "Did you enjoy it?"

Suddenly, our conversation was interrupted by the rumble of aircraft fighters, just like those who'd flown over a few days before and shot up the village and factory. Again, they flew so low we could see every detail on the plane.

I looked over at the guards curiously. *Why aren't you shooting? You must have orders not to.* Maybe they didn't want to draw attention.

But this time, these low flying planes didn't fire at the factory or at the village, but simply slowed down to get a good look at both. Then they flew off.

After a few minutes of silence, the heavy rumble of planes approached again. Roman pointed out a squadron flying in from one side of the village and a minute behind, one swooped in from the other.

Yuri couldn't resist: "This is when they hit the factory."

"Don't scare us, Yuri," I said. "They're on their way to bigger and more important targets."

At that moment, I saw Osip the tailor's skin turn ghost white. He started to shake and ducked down deeper into the frozen waters. But I still refused to believe there was an alarm.

Then from the horizon above the tree-line, four motor aircrafts flew over and dropped shiny brilliant belts that looked like fiery tin, right above us and the village.

"They're distracting the anti-aircrafts! There are more planes higher up! They're protecting..." I heard a prisoner call out and got cut off by the noise.

"Get low!" yelled a German guard. "Nobody runs! We're ready to shoot you if you do!"

And that's when I realized that this was a raid.

We laid low, waiting for further developments. A few moments later, a piercing whistle flew over our heads. I ducked down as low as I could into the icy waters and quietly prayed.

The screams grew louder.

I clenched my eyes tighter and kept praying feverishly.

Suddenly, I felt my shoulder tense. I opened my eyes and it was Roman grabbing me and yelling, "Get up! Now! Everything is burning! Look! Osip already ran out and said nothing to us! Look! The prisoners are escaping! Nobody is shooting at them!"

I popped my head up to see if this was true. Strips of fire lit up the entire trench and field in front of us, like someone was lighting the forest on fire.

Desperate cries, wails, and groans of the prisoners came from all directions. Many of them managed to stumble out of the trenches and scatter, attempting to dodge these snags of fire. I looked to the machine guns. No Germans.

Then a phosphorus bomb feel a few steps away from us. It cratered about half a meter deep into the soft ground and caught fire to everything it touched. *Where's Yuri?* But I still wasn't moving.

Roman wasn't gonna wait for me anymore and ripped me out of the trench. We ran through the forest, holding each other and trying to get to the open field. I was so frightened that alone I probably wouldn't have moved. Thank God for Roman. But it's also possible that my own delay changed our fate.

I looked up and saw the entire field adjacent the village covered in hundreds of fleeing prisoners. They scattered in panic, phosphorus bombs falling among them. Many were hit by the fire snags. It was a sight like I couldn't ever have imagined.

Running further into this field, we ran by people burnt and motionless. Roman gripped my hand even tighter. Then from out of nowhere Yuri found our flank and shouted, "Karas is running up ahead like a mad man! He's going so fast his hat flew right off his head!"

We looked up and saw him about 40 meters ahead of us. Suddenly, an explosion went off in front of us and I was punched with a parachute of air. Roman hit the deck and ripped me down with him. Yuri fell too and all three of us buried our faces into the dirt. Debris scattered and sprinkled on the back of my neck and body.

That bomb zapped my strength.

But we somehow got up anyway and kept running and got to the gigantic crater, which could have probably fit a few cars. An Allied bomb had blown a hole in the field and I saw my best friend Osip Karas lying face down on the edge of the pit. More than half his body was buried in fresh black earth. His head was split open. The shirt on his back was torn to shreds. Blood spilled from his head and back.

We stopped, but none of us knew what to do.

I leaned over Osip as Roman took his hand and said, "He's dead."

Yuri then brushed the dirt off his face and felt for breathing. Nothing. Then we started running. There was no choice. He was gone. We fled to the nearby forest.

The entire field was porous with bombs and burning with phosphorus. *Why did these bombs fall on us? It's a clear day - why did the Allies bomb an open field? No one was shooting! You had so much time to line up your target.*

Running further, the explosions of bombs roared behind us. A second round of aircrafts was probably finishing whatever job the original flyby started.

"C'mon! We'll be safer in the woods!" Roman said. I wasn't so sure but we had no idea what to do so we ran.

Is it done? Where's the command? We hadn't seen them since the raid began. Thankfully they didn't shoot us. *Were they dead? Did they get away?*

We got some 200 meters from the village and close to the nearby forest and saw four older male bavors standing before us with pitchforks and guns. They yelled at us.

"Don't come any closer!"

"We'll shoot!"

But we didn't stop. All we wanted to do was get away from the bombs. They didn't scare us at all and we ran up to them and all started yelling at once.

"We haven't eaten all day!"

"We're hungry!"

"Give us something to eat and we'll go back to camp!"

"We don't want anything else!"

We figured the Germans would probably send out a team for runaway prisoners. We'd probably just get re-arrested. *How could we escape anyway? We were so far into Germany. We had nowhere to hide. Winter was still biting. What would we eat?* We had no choice. We had to stick around.

The bavors let their guard down surprisingly quick. They

quickly led us to one of their homes and inside the house were what looked like a daughter and two granddaughters. The kids sat not too far from us, leaning on their mother and asking:

"Why are they so hungry?"

"Why are they wearing stripes?"

"Why is their hair cut so short?"

"Why were they bombed?"

"What was made in their factory?"

But we weren't interested in explaining anything. We wanted to eat and then hurry back to camp. *Will we get punished for being this far beyond the gates?*

We were given potatoes and before we could even finish them, the bavor who brought us to his house had shown back up with two armed policemen who ordered us out. The bavor's wife still gave us each a piece of bread. We thanked her for her hospitality and walked back off in the direction of the trenches where we were just bombarded. The armed civilian policemen followed us. The bombing had stopped.

We tried explaining to them on the road that we weren't going to flee.

"We'd get caught and get the death sentence," Roman told them.

"We don't believe you. Keep walking," one said.

We pointed out other prisoners walking in the same direction.

"See?" Yuri said.

A few minutes later, they stopped following us. We looked back and they stood pat, waiting to make sure we'd actually return to camp.

As we got closer to the trenches, we saw prisoners carrying loads into a truck. A few Germans supervised.

As we walked up, finally the sirens gave us a long wail, announcing that the raid was done. As we got closer, the Commandant saw us and started chasing us around with his stick and shouted and cursed and said, "Get into the trenches and move those burned prisoners!"

I hopped quickly down into the trench and Roman did so just a second too late and the Commandant thwacked him with his stick. Yuri managed to dodge the blow and ended up with us in the trench.

Roman ran over to me and we soon found ourselves next to a scorched prisoner. Roman got near the head and I by both legs and we figured to carry him out of the trench this way. The prisoner wasn't moving, all black, burnt to an unrecognizable crisp. Near him was a pit of scorched gray Earth leftover by a phosphorus bomb.

But before I could figure out how to lift the his legs, Roman raised this man's head, immediately went pale and laid him quickly back down to the Earth. I looked over and under the corpse's shoulder was an unburnt piece of blue and yellow sweater that could only mean one thing.

It's Basil. It's our Ukrainian. We would have had no idea it was him besides that piece of fabric. He was otherwise unrecognizable. We pulled him out of the trench and put him in the truck with several other burned prisoners.

"Just a few days ago he said that once the war was over, he'd immediately return home, back to his wife and two children," said Roman.

This was not your fate, Basil. And with our quick silent prayer, we sent him to eternal rest.

When we placed Basil's body in the truck, I found myself terrified, because I realized that I could expect the same death. That this death actually waited for me under one of these bombs.

Thank you God for letting me live. Thank you Roman for carrying me out of the trenches. We later found out that the largest number of deaths came in precisely these very trenches. Roman, Yuri and I all then ran over to where we'd last seen Karas. However, all that was left of him were traces of blood and burnt flesh. Someone must have already carried him off.

I watched prisoners in the open field slowly trudge back. Instead of praising them for returning, the Commandant ran at them, waving his stick.

"Get back to camp!" he yelled, and we all quickly organized into rows.

"The wounded will be taken to Donauworth. The dead - go get them!" the Commandant said.

We carried the wounded and the dead and then afterwards we were put back in our collection of rows and ordered to wait. Two guards searched the field one last time, the same empty field that the Allies had wasted their bombs on. But this inspection didn't welcome any more victims, and we were led back to camp.

On the way back to camp, I was surprised to see that the village hadn't really been damaged. Only three houses on the outskirts of the village had caught any fire at all. But they were extinguished by the fire guard and the helpful bavor neighbors.

And then we got back to camp and I couldn't believe it, but the whole factory was still there, motionless, without a trace of damage. *Those phosphorus bombs were supposed to light up the village and give those bombers a target. But instead they fell on us, and in a field?*

The same had happened with the bigger bombs. They were meant for the factory. But they got us instead. They hit the trenches where the prisoners hid. They hit not far from where the "East" girls were.

The only satisfied people from this air raid looked to be the bavors. Their village, which was supposed to be annihilated by phosphorus bombs, stood still, barely damaged. Bavors gathered in groups, apparently surprised that all this destruction could happen while their homes stood pat. And those who were especially happy? The bavors who, during this third siren, decided that it was a false alarm and didn't get down into their shelters, but still survived.

The guards on the other hand were pissed. They loudly cursed and complained that their fellow guards were killed and wounded. This was why none of them fired upon us while we ran out of the trenches - they were running and being bombed as well.

We were led inside the gates and into our yard in front of the building where the rest of the survivors were. To my surprise, there looked to be about 20 prisoners left standing from the original two or three hundred. So at most, ten percent of us survived.

After the prisoners were assembled and counted, the Commandant shouted and cursed and threatened us.

"Some are still missing!" he yelled. "Those who escaped - we will quickly catch them - our dogs are already on their tails!" he said.

But the Commandant's words didn't sound terrifying or convincing. We prisoners had just experienced a tragic raid and that's what we were scared of.

And I thought that the Commandant was saying these words for his own satisfaction, rather than for us to fear.

Why didn't you shoot when the raid took place? Where were you when the bombs fell? Was your head buried in the trench and were you petrified, just like us prisoners? Where were you then?

Therefore, I, with some irony, watched him closely and didn't believe a word he said. I again thought about the bombs.

How did this evil not hit the factory? How did these bombs not fall on the village? Why did they fall on the heads of innocent prisoners? And for me personally, the most painful loss was that of Osip and Basil.

After his threats, the Commandant and the guards walked out through the camp gate and to their apartment.

Kapo Hugo said, "The night shift isn't going to work. And there won't be any dinner either - Commandant's orders. The machines that were delivering food to camp were turned back because of the bombing."

And the cooks were with us being bombed.

"Food will be delivered at night, and the day shift should prepare to go to work as usual tomorrow," Hugo said.

Some prisoners didn't even get anything to eat today.

Hugo dismissed us and Roman and I rejoiced a little. We appreciated the food and hospitality of the German farmer bavors. That night we ate pieces of bread that they'd given us for the road. Yuri was busy for the rest of the day in Kapo's room and we no longer saw him.

Sitting on my bed with Roman, we tried figuring out how many of us Ukrainians were missing. We came up with six. Two dead, Osip and Basil, plus fours others unaccounted for.

"Maybe they're still out there," said Roman. "Maybe they've found themselves among the wounded or those that never returned back to camp."

We hoped.

I asked Max to tell me when he finds out later what happened to Karas and what of the other wounded prisoners. Later that day, Max confirmed that Osip was killed by the bomb. He'd been taken to the hospital in Donauworth. The doctors confirmed that he'd been killed on impact.

"There's also a young prisoner in the hospital named Nicholas, who repeatedly asks for you," said Max.

"What's his last name?" I asked.

"I don't know his name or cipher," said Max. "And then the other young boy who slept above me..."

"Yusef," I said.

"He was also wounded and sent to the hospital in the city of Augsburg. When I know more, I'll tell you," he said.

"What happened to the bodies of the dead prisoners?" I asked.

Max didn't answer. I tried asking Shtubowy Rudyj, a good

friend of Karas, but he said nothing more to me either. I wondered if the dead were buried in some common grave or if they were burned so that the camp council could keep their deaths silent.

I asked Max a couple more questions about this boy Nicholas, but he had no other information for me. The fourth Nicholas I'd heard of or known here at camp, who was a very nice guy and especially attentive to Osip and I, came up to me and rejoiced that I was alive. But then he became sad when we told him that Karas was no longer be among us.

A tear dropped down his cheek, and he said, "I always thought that Osip was our power. He held us together."

He also grieved about Basil, who burned to death, still so young.

That night I couldn't sleep. Before my eyes was the image of my best friend Osip. I remembered how severely he suffered. I pictured him trembling, scared about the incoming raid siren. *What a deathly premonition you had, Osip! Did you predict your own imminent death?* I couldn't explain it to myself. *Is it possible for someone to foresee his fate so clearly?*

I thought back to my anxiety and anticipation before my arrest. I also remembered a strange feeling prompting me to act, telling me that something bad was coming. *That same feeling - maybe Karas felt that same feeling.* I was so sorry that I'd laughed at him, when he told me repeatedly that he knew he wouldn't get out of camp alive. I tried to comfort Osip, but really, that anxiety was in me as well.

But I never mentioned my fear to him, so that maybe he'd no longer be afraid. *So how come my feelings were fulfilled with my arrest, as were Osip's for his death?* I felt heavy regret. *Osip! You died in exile! Would your family know?* Could his mother feel him die?

Tears streamed down my face as I looked to God. *Thank you for sending me such a great friend, patriot, and conscious Ukrainian. Please, let him into the Kingdom of Heaven. And Basil too! Please give them eternal peace. Please allow them both into your Kingdom!* I then wondered if that might be the only prayer said for the death of these two men. No one else knew but us.

The work whistle woke me up the next morning. Max was already standing at the entrance to our shtub.

But this morning wasn't the same as the others. No one was beaten at assembly. The prisoners did everything not to be dragged down by guilt. The Commandant appeared quite calm. Besides counting us, he wasn't interested in anything else.

The command announced that there would be no more night shift, and after breakfast, we were all led to work together. The civilian masters didn't show. The guards ordered us to sit down near a couple benches and await further orders. But this didn't stop us from roaming free amongst ourselves, sharing experiences of what had happened just one day before. Boylek approached me, and we discussed our childhoods. This carried us through the day.

The next day, they again took us to work This time we met up with our masters. We each tried to explain to them what it was like to get hit in phosphorus bombs and fiery foil, as well as what it was like to be shaken by the big ones. We talked about those that died, those that were wounded, and those that potentially escaped.

My master, the Croatian, confided in me privately and said, "We won't be kept here much longer. Since the building you live in and the factory weren't hit, the Allies will probably be back to finish the job.

"Other masters are talking about it too. No one wants to come back here. Don't finish any of your preliminary work - just organize and pack everything back up and store the tools on their shelves," he said.

We were called to lunch as usual with a factory whistle and an assembly in the prison yard. But something was noticeably different - two vertical iron pillars stood dug into the ground, joined together at the top by an iron pipe. The structure wasn't much taller than we were. Max ordered us to wait in our assembly for the Camp Commandant.

But before the Commandant came out, the guards walked in through the gates with three of our fellow prisoners, all whom were nowhere to be seen after the strike. I knew they were escapees. All three of them had their hands chained behind their backs. Among them was a Ukrainian, Nicholas. *Oh Nicholas!* I felt so sorry for him. *Why did you run? How could you even think of escaping? You were the most awkward, clumsy, hunched-over prisoner in camp! You couldn't escape the mentors' beatings! How could you escape Germany?*

The two other prisoners walked bravely. Our Nicholas kept his head low, as I'd always seen him. He barely dragged his feet. One of the guards shoved him so he would keep in step. His face looked swollen, probably from being beaten.

When all three were near the gallows, one guard hung three iron hooks across the iron bar. But the bar wasn't high enough for a hanging. *What are they doing?*

The other guard moved a chair underneath one of the hooks and said to the first prisoner, "Get up." When he did so, guards bent him forward and hung his bound wrists on the hook behind his back, above his hips.

The two guards then ripped the chair out from underneath the prisoner and he he dropped.

The same was done to the other two. They were hung by their wrists and the chair was kicked out. They groaned and their shoulders tore under the burden of their body weight.

I was shocked.

As our poor Nicholas rounded out the last hanging, the Commandant said, "They hang until they die."

Then he walked by the three prisoners and gave them all whacks across their backs with his stick.

Then he loudly told us, "From this camp, no man has escaped! And those who tried - they've found themselves in the next world!"

He had forgotten that just a few weeks ago a prisoner escaped wearing one of his master's clothing. The Commandant never brought him back.

"No one dare approach these prisoners. For such a disobedience, you'll be strictly punished!" he said, and then he ordered the guards to watch "these scum" as he went back beyond the gate of the camp.

I felt awful for Nicholas and the others. He looked unhappy to me even before the bombing and now he was hanging. One soldier stood guard near the gallows. The other went back beyond the gate.

After this display, they ordered us to eat and then moved us back to the factory for work. After work, we were counted in front of the hanging men. Their faces were completely blue and there was no movement from their bowed bodies. To add to that, a cold rain had been falling on and off all day.

After the counting, the Commandant ordered, "None of you leave the building tonight. And don't even think about talking to these scum."

The next morning, empty gallows stood. I don't know what happened to their bodies.

After all this turmoil, camp life changed. Although the Commandant and guards showed us just how truly cruel they could be, Hugo, Max, and Vili all became more humane. They didn't beat us out of the shtubs with sticks to get us to work quicker. Maybe it was because there were less prisoners, less of a crowd, or it might have been something else. They often joined up with Rudyj and the shoemaker to chat, looking quite nervous at that.

Among the prisoners, a rumor circulated that our camp would soon be moved elsewhere. Because of the this, the camp council might be worried that they'll lose whatever power or privileges they had here in camp. Some said we'd be turned back to Dachau.

Still others thought the end of the war approached and that was why the camp guard acted more humane to the prisoners. Under the chance of us being set free, they didn't want us to retaliate against them. Whatever it was, on the surface I was happy about the improvement of our quality of life, and most importantly, glad that rumblings of the end of the war grew louder.

But in spite of all this, every day my heart grew heavier, darker. I couldn't accept the fact that the war's end was so close while knowing that the worrisome Karas, our Ukrainian Basil, the hanging Nicholas, as well as the others who died during the bombing wouldn't be able to see peace.

The good that came out of this was that Roman replaced for me the company of Osip. From that point forward, we promised each other to walk together at the sound of any other airstrike sirens.

CHAPTER SIXTEEN

LANDSBERG

At work the next week, the command ordered us to put all the tools away. The cranes were loaded into trucks and taken away. The rest of the parts in the factory were loaded up and taken away too, whether they were finished or not.

A few mornings later, a few heavy-duty trucks arrived at camp. The two German guards standing atop each one unloaded a few chests filled with new pairs of wood soled shoes. Kapo Hugo ordered us to each grab a pair.

As Roman and I switched shoes with each other to better suit our feet, I heard one prisoner say, "New shoes, huh? Looks like we'll be walking."

Another protested, saying, "No way! Why would these trucks be here?"

Either way, I was glad. *If they've giving us new shoes, they must still need us, and we aren't being killed off just yet.* As each prisoner got his shoes, we were loaded up onto the trucks and put on the floor so that the guards could see us well. *I wish I could get back to my bed.* I still had a piece of bread leftover from Yuri the night before. And my ring was in there too. Apparently I wouldn't be putting it on, whether I was freed or not. But I was glad that the trucks had no covers - at least we'd get a view of the road.

The camp board and all the cooks were loaded up too. All the guards climbed down from their towers and joined our convoy as well. No one stayed behind. The guards locked up the camp gates behind us. The Commandant and his fellow guards observed the entire evacuation and then hopped into the lead personal car. Every other machine followed him and at the caboose trailed a single car with a machine gun mounted on top of it, with two soldiers at its service. Our time in Baumenheim was over.

This drive out of Baumenheim fell at the beginning of April 1945. Early Spring had begun to show its face. Fields started to green, trees were budding, and I was happy that we were being taken away from another potential bombing, as predicted by our civilian masters. I found out later that the Allies showed up to Baumenheim on foot a few days after our departure.

Riding along in open machines, the wind whisked through the rags that barely covered our backs. But I somehow felt like I'd come back to life. New energy flowed through me. Our convoy moved through the German countryside and sunlight danced along tiny villages, which looked quite clean and developed. The buildings were constructed with large stone, with beautiful windows and shutters under which often hung boxes cradling flowers. There was no sign of any war here, until a large military transports appeared ahead.

Groups of armed soldiers huddled inside, who just as us,

were driving somewhere. As we passed each other, their faces looked to me still quite young. Perhaps my age. Perhaps younger. And on those faces I saw none of that joy, that enthusiasm that once distinguished the German soldiers when they first broke the Soviet border in 1941. Back then, they were proud and arrogant, rolling up their sleeves and shouting with power and confidence as they plowed further East. I was 14, and I thought they were unstoppable. But now, I wanted to talk to these soldiers and hear what they thought about the war now.

As we passed the convoy, I overheard a guard say that we were approaching the city of Augsburg. They said that we were being deliberately driven through fields, so that we wouldn't be seen driving through towns, potential bomb targets. *Maybe you don't want us to see your damaged country.*

The sun slowly rose on our left - we were moving south. And after several hours of careful riding and crossing through small villages and beautiful landscapes, we arrived at a dense forest.

Driving through, here and there wooden barracks popped up and prisoners moved about wearing striped dress, just like ours. These groups were being led around by other prisoners, all of them donning white bands on their sleeves. Getting closer, we saw hexagonal stars painted on these bands. They also all had red triangles sewn on their chests, and above each of them was another star with yellow numbers.

Just then I realized that these prisoners were Jews.

Why are we being moved into the forest? And in every other camp, the command kept us separate from the Jews. By mixing us together, we'd sharing same fate at the end of this war.

Our convoy drove another kilometer into the thick of the forest and stopped. Overhearing the guards, I learned that we were near a town called Landsberg, and a concentration camp shared the same name.

After the Commandant checked the premises, he ordered us to hop out of the trucks. After this check, they moved us through the gates of the camp.

A barbed wire gate slinked its way through the trees, surrounding the camp along with another rollout of wire just in case one failed to operate. A bit further down guards perched in their towers. *But where are the buildings? The prisoner barracks?* All we saw was a tiny house sitting next to the gate which probably served as a single room for camp administrators, but not us prisoners.

I turned to Roman and asked, "Do you see any barracks?"

"Nope," he said.

But looking closer, I noticed some dugouts, shaped like tents, covered in green grassy moss. There were no walls; the triangular roof reached the ground. There were five such dugouts. I didn't want to believe that they were our shelter.

The guards divided us into groups of 50. Roman and I were assigned to the first group. Rudyj motioned us to the first hut and commanded, "From now on, this is where you'll sleep."

Roman and I stepped up to these dugouts and behind us

walked the other forty eight. I peered in first through the tiny and painted-green entrance. From above they probably blended quite well into the forest greenery. *How will we be rescued now?*

I stepped down into the dugout. Inside, two electric bulbs shone dimly, barely enough light for us to see. The dugout was about 2/3 of a meter below dirt level. There was no floor. Just raw soil. And even at my short height, I could only stand up tall in the middle, at the apex of the triangle. But most everyone else was taller than me and couldn't walk in without hunching. To my surprise, only three tiny pillars held up the entire thing. Nothing else.

There was no table, no benches, and no oven to heat us. In the middle miserably sat a pile of long, gray paper bags. The re-oriented prisoners each quickly grabbed themselves one of these bags, which they spread out on the soil for the night. *It was still winter! How could they do this to us? How much worse could this get? These conditions were awful! We were practically sleeping outside!*

At that moment, Vili walked in.

He was immediately hounded by prisoners who berated him with questions of what brought us here.

"Where are out barracks?"

"Why these crude dugouts?"

"How long do we have to live here?"

"Where's the factory?"

"When do we get blankets?"

Vili was stunned at such a sight. He quickly left the dugout and went straight back to the office building without checking out another dugout. Even *he* couldn't handle it.

Roman and I both took sacks for ourselves and placed them in the middle of the dugout.

"We might be warmer tonight here in the middle," I whispered. He nodded in agreement.

"Maybe they'll still get us blankets to put over our bags," he said.

These dugouts seemed new, as if nobody had ever lived in them. There was also no other leadership here besides our camp counselors, who at that moment, called us out to lunch. Kapo Hugo counted us and said, "From this day forward, these dugouts will be your rooms.

"Tomorrow, you'll be woken up early, just like in Baumenheim, and then the guards will lead you to work. You won't get blankets tonight. They're off at disinfection," said Hugo.

That night, Landsberg frosted over and there wasn't a single prisoner who didn't complain. Instead of finding ourselves in better quarters, we found ourselves incomparably worse off than before. The camp leadership and guards didn't worry of course - they were housed in two separate buildings outside the wire fence.

Roman and I decided to sleep up against each other for warmth. We crawled into our thin, gray paper bags fully dressed as we were that day, with shoes even. After some time I heard rumblings from a prisoner saying he couldn't sleep because his teeth were chattering. Some climbed out of their bags and exercised to get warm. I followed suit and jumped around. Getting back into the bag, I was definitely much warmer. Some prisoners even got up and left the hut to walk and get their blood moving.

As the night grew older and colder, somehow the prisoners all fell asleep, I among them.

The next day, when a sliver of dawn appeared, the camp council woke us up and called us out for roll. They sent to the kitchen, which stood under some tall trees, and we were given a hot cup of coffee and a little slice of bread.

The coffee was a remedy. Prisoners shivered from the cold and lack of sleep and clung to their cups as long as they could for a little bit of extra heat. There was not a prisoner among us who dared to get under the water taps to get washed up.

After breakfast, military guards appeared and led us onto the forest road. *They must have added even more guards to corral us - I haven't seen this many soldiers since before Baumenheim. Maybe that's because of the forest cover. A few less guards and one of us might be able to run off.*

After some time the forest road ended and we found ourselves in a clearing. Another group of prisoners emerged from the woods and headed in the same direction as we were. These prisoners had white bands on their sleeves and were also accompanied by armed guards.

This slow, half hour trudge brought us to a highland. A passageway appeared in front of us, with its mouth covered by tall pines mixed with other leafy trees and short shrubs.

Stepping down into this passageway, a gigantic gorge appeared deep down into the mountains and a big three story concrete structure appeared before us. It's walls were still unfinished and open, and huge cranes leveled out the ground and reinforced the walls. It was then that I realized that here under this forest cover, in a mountainside, the Germans were building a monstrous three story factory. I couldn't believe it.

Large camouflaged trucks waited on adjacent forest roads. Prisoners loaded them up with all sorts of metal tools. These machines drove up in turns to the open walls and unloaded their equipment on all three floors. This factory and it's location fascinated me. *How can these Germans build such a gigantic factory when their war already looked so hopeless? Do they still think that in some strange way you have a chance to win this war?*

Rumors had indeed been spreading. Apparently these Germans had a weapon that could immediately end the war. But none of us prisoners believed it. We didn't want to believe it. But after seeing this factory, I didn't know what to believe. *Could it be true? A weapon that could end this war in an instant? Wouldn't they have used it already?*

Hundreds of prisoners already worked on these factory floors. Some were Aryans, others Jews. The Jews worked on plant construction and part installation. Others mounted machines and added finishing touches. *What are you building here?* A third group of prisoners waited to be assigned. We were pushed into this group.

"Today," a mentor said, "all you need to do is acclimate yourself to the factory, and in case of an emergency, help out immediately. Machines are being installed and within the next few days, they'll be ready for you."

This mentor's task was to acquaint us with the

construction of the factory and what we had to do in case of an airstrike.

"This factory is located in the middle of the mountains and is built of iron and a sturdy concrete. On both sides of the factory lay long concrete tunnels which serve as a repository for workers in case of a strike. There are only a few openings to these tunnels from the plant, so take a good look at how to get into them so that these doors can get closed in time during an emergency. Don't waste our time. The first prisoners in must walk all the way back to leave room for the rest."

My head swiveled around, looking at this underground factory, masked in this mountainside. I couldn't believe this mass of iron and concrete. *How many factories like this are there? What's the purpose of such a thing?* The one thing it did tell me - Germany held power and hope here that it could still win this war.

My hope and probably the hope of the other prisoners of a quick end to this war was being challenged. And to add to that? The primitive life in those dugouts was not what we expected. *When would this war end? Surely not soon... Is it possible for us to survive and stay alive?* I began to doubt it.

After our mentor finished his instructions, he led us through heavy iron doors into the bomb-shelter tunnel. I walked in astonished - it was a long concrete rectangular box that could hold hundreds. The tapping of our wooden soles got so loud that it was impossible to hear anyone speak, almost as if a huge train was passing through. After everyone was funneled in, the iron doors shut, and the mentor ordered us all to sit down.

"Your lowest whisper is increased tenfold in this bunker. So listen to me well. If an airstrike hits us, the tunnel will probably save us all. But we could also go deaf, because the sound of the explosions will be magnified. So hold your hands up tight against your ears and open your mouth. If you don't, you'll probably lose your hearing. Or worse. If you want to stay healthy, do as I say," said the mentor.

"You could have a nervous breakdown," one prisoner whispered.

"You might bleed from your nose, mouth or ears," said another.

The mentor took us back out the tunnel and walked us up all three floors to get acquainted with the structure. There must have been hundreds of metal-processing machines. Many of them were already up and running, and the prisoners who worked them looked down on us like we were trespassing.

One machine made a particularly bad impression on me. Four workers held a thick, iron plate and pushed it between two blades that vibrated so quickly back and forth that it cut the slab in two. The prisoners who held this plate shook with the blade. It looked like awful work. *How do I avoid that job?*

The factory also employed plenty of civilian masters and on each floor there were more guards than in all of Baumenheim.

After our tour, we were ordered to sit among the nearby trees and wait for dinner. More German disorganization. *Why are we here? This place isn't close to being ready for us.*

SEPARATION

Not far from us in a wide open field sat temporary toilets. A narrow trench was dug out in the ground, surrounded by a couple of pillars that were joined by two wooden rails, one for your back, and one for your butt. These toilets were just as much of a hang out than a place to empty. Prisoners seemed to take their time doing their business.

One of our prisoners came back from the toilets and said that he'd met an American pilot. *An American? What does an American look like? Could I meet him? Talk to him?* I had never med an American before.

Another prisoner came back and pointed him out to me. After lunch, I waited until the American finished his and I walked over. He was sitting alone on carved-out log. It looked to me like he was no older than thirty.

I came closer and greeted him. He calmly and slowly greeted me back.

"American?" I asked.

"Yes," he said.

"How long have you been a prisoner?" I asked, in German.

He answered, but I couldn't understand a word.

I didn't know English. He obviously didn't really know German either. We stared at each other for a second, but the language barrier ended our ability to connect. At that moment, for me, meeting an American was an incredible sensation. I had a great respect for America. I thought that it could bring freedom to the entire world of oppressed people.

After everyone finished lunch, we prisoners gathered near the trees again and waited but nothing happened. We sat the rest of the day without responsibility. Mentors called us back to the dugouts.

That night, after getting counted again, we were all distributed a blanket. Each of us gladly picked one up and hoped that maybe we wouldn't freeze like the night before.

After waiting around for days, prisoners started to get Stir crazy. Sitting around made us antsy and gave us too much time to think about the war. But we were never called to work.

We even saw machines get rolled in that looked familiar from Baumenheim. Some of the stronger prisoners were called up to help unload trucks or clean the factory. I was not one of them.

So since we didn't work, the toilets became our center of attention. It also became our #1 news source. Prisoners of all sorts of nationalities and groups gathered to tell each other what they'd learned about the outside world. Progress of the war, news from other countries, etc. The Jews usually got the best news - they had Jewish mentors working for the Germans.

One Frenchman told me, "I heard from the Jews that the western war front is on its way here. The Americans liberated all of France, and they're deep into Germany." This was a big surprise for us prisoner. The last thing we'd heard was that the Allies had just landed somewhere on the banks of France, but how far they'd actually gotten, we did not know.

Over the next few days, as I was finding some solace in resting amongst the trees, our group was sent to the night shift, work that started at 6pm and ended at 6am. At first, I was not happy about this. But after a few days, it turned out to be a better situation. We walked to work during the end of the day and walked back with morning sunshine too. It was nice to sleep during the day too, because days were warmer and we didn't freeze so much.

The work at night was not at all organized of course. Civilian masters barely showed, and when they did, they stood around and talked more than managed. Our task was to distribute various parts to working machines. We put completed parts up on shelves. We cleaned up metal shavings and took them to the materials section. And every so often we were pushed back into the air raid tunnels and told again how to hide from bombs.

These night shifts changed my view of this grand, imposing plant. I just couldn't find any practical value in it. The discipline and supervision was nearly, if not entirely, nonexistent. Masters and prisoners simply *looked* busy. Even the guards walked about indifferently, not caring if any of us actually worked. It was a waste.

After a few days we started to hear distant explosions, especially at night.

Boom!

Boom!

Boom!

And every night, these explosions got closer and closer. The horizon reddened with flames. The front was coming!

One night, for whatever reason, they didn't take us to work. Vili approached me.

"In the administrative building, there's a small hospital. Your friend Nicholas lies there," Vili said. "He was wounded in the bombing of Baumenheim and asked me to take you to him. He can't walk."

I still couldn't guess which Nicholas this may be. *Could he be the one who was caught and hung by the wrists? Could he still be alive? No... Could it be the 25 year old Nicholas? Or the Nikolai from Eastern Ukraine, a young man I worked next to on that bench every day in Baumenheim?* I hadn't seen either of them after the bombing. After dinner that night, I followed Vili to meet this Nicholas.

For whatever reason, I was impatient. *Doctors wouldn't let him out of the hospital? What kind of awful disease does he have?* I thought back to Kapo Hugo: "No patients in my hospital! I treat all sicknesses myself."

The hospital itself was very small, with room for only four beds. On one of them lay my friend Nicholas of Galicia, so happy to see me. He extended his left hand to me and immediately began to cry. Vili left us in the room with two other prisoners lying in their beds.

Nicholas pulled his sheet up and showed me his right side. It was bandaged up and badly wounded.

"How did this happen?" I asked.

With tears still streaming down his face, he said, "I fell unconscious during the bombing and woke up in Donauworth. I have no right arm, Stepan! I got blood poisoning and the doctors thought I wouldn't survive. But then I did and now I don't even know if that's a good thing.

Maybe it would be better for me if I had died. I don't have a right hand today! Who could benefit from such a man?"

I felt pity and looked at him with great compassion, but I saw that this didn't help. So I stood strong.

"In this world, Nicholas, people live in much worse situations and somehow find their place. You're still young! And handsome too! You'll find all sorts of opportunities to set up a good way of life."

Then, to distract him, I said, "I thought that you had escaped during the bombing and maybe even returned home."

He smiled and said, "I'd really like that."

And I began again, "Look - at night we can already see the Allies lighting up the sky. The sounds of explosions and guns are getting closer and closer and soon we'll be set free."

Nicholas, somewhat re-assured, asked, "Could you visit me more often?"

"Yes. I promise. I've got plenty of time, because they stopped taking us to work," I said.

His doctor then walked in and greeted me. "I'm glad you came to visit Nicholas. I tried comforting him, saying that he'll still be healthy and have a good life. But he didn't want to believe me."

He paused and then said, "I should change his dressing."

I understood that I should leave the room.

"I'll come every day I can, Nicholas."

"You can come again tomorrow," the doctor said.

And just before I left, Nicholas said, "I have something very important to tell you, but I'll say it next time. Oh, and

Stepan - in Donauworth, I wound up in the hospital with Osip Karas, but he was already dead."

CHAPTER SEVENTEEN

IN APRIL WE MARCH

On the morning of April 25, 1945, the camp council rushed us out of our dugouts to assembly.

Following our count, they said that after breakfast all prisoners must leave camp in order to be transferred to another location. The cannon blasts were becoming louder and more frequent.

For breakfast, we were given a ladle of coffee and a slice of bread. I huddled around the coffee cup and started to eat but then looked up from my food and couldn't believe my eyes. Before me was our working mentor, our fellow prisoner... Vili, and he was dressed head-to-toe in a brand new German officer uniform.

I couldn't believe my eyes.

Up to this moment, we had only seen him in prison apparel. We were horrified, stunned, and refused to believe that it was actually him. The prisoners couldn't stand it and started groveling and yelling. But as if we were praising him and not heckling, he just stood there, confident and smiling. After several shouts from the prisoners, Max came from the administration building, also in full officer uniform.

Only then, at that moment, did we finally realize who ruled us in these aircraft factories. Kapo Hugo was nowhere in sight.

I looked up at the hospital and saw the wounded being moved into a tarp-covered truck, among them our Nicholas.

What were you going to tell me, Nicholas? What was so important?

They were all quickly loaded onto the machine and taken out of camp. I never saw Nicholas again.

Vili said, "Make sure you cherish this slice of bread, because we're about to take a long journey, and we don't know when you'll get anything else to eat." He then walked amongst us and said, "Now straighten up!"

He counted out 100 prisoners, including Roman and I, and commanded us to separate from the others. "This hundred will go first."

I was glad I was with Roman. At least we'd be together.

And then, at the last moment, Yuri popped into our group. "My work with Hugo is done. I'm with you now."

I kept looking for freight trucks, the kind that always took us from one place to another. But they were nowhere to be seen.

The explosions and firing kept getting louder and louder. They were non-stop now.

Our hundred were led to the gates. The kitchen staff was added, as well as eight armed guards and their commanding German officer Vili Meiler.

The second group would follow us an hour later, followed by the next and next and so on. They told us that we would all take separate roads but end up together, wherever that may be.

The weather that morning was sunny and warm and we started walking. After trudging through the woods, we got to a highway and walked east. Yuri jumped into our five by persuading another prisoner to switch.

Moving along side of us, or perhaps retreating rather, were officers on trucks, horseback, and on foot. When I first met German soldiers at the start of the war, I saw them as the hostile German army that kept us behind the wire. But they looked different now. They looked scared.

At the end of the line, a young, handsome, well-dressed German officer rode and a small group of soldiers in uniform rode behind him. The insignia "ROA" sat on their military caps. Our prisoners of Russian nationality immediately recognized them as part of the Russkaya Osvoboditel'naya Armiya, or the Russian Liberation Army.

One Russian prisoner said, "These soldiers belonged to an army commandeered by General Vlasov, who was captured by the Germans near Moscow in 1942. Instead of being imprisoned, he agreed to cooperate with the Germans to overthrow the communist system in Russia."

Suddenly, a young Russian prisoner couldn't resist and and shouted at the officer, "Look at him! What a pretty Russian corruptible sellout!"

The officer on horseback heard these words and immediately challenged him. He fumed and charged towards us on his horse and in a full rampage attacked a group of frightened prisoners. Vili and another of our guards fired their revolvers into the air to stop the outburst. The shooting shooed off the angry officer of General Vlasov's army.

"Oh I'll still get you," he said and added some obscenities as well.

Fortunately, none of the prisoners were hurt. The only one who got dinged up was a prisoner with a nosebleed.

"Nobody touch any of those soldiers, because if you do, we'll make sure something worse happens to you," said our mentors.

The day ran its course with us still walking in the same direction without break, hugging the left side of the road. On the horizon behind us, firmament flashed red with loud explosions. Night came and they flashed even redder. They looked so close!

But we walked away from them.

Only once that night did we stop walking - a plane roared above our heads and we were all ordered to hit the ground and stay still. Some prisoners complained about why we had to trudge next to the road through uneven holes and grasses when it was still dark, instead of just walking down the road.

Others explained that the Americans have invented such tools that could see really well at night. I wondered how that could be possible.

The guards kept a close watch. Vili, though somehow still fat, ran up the group and once back too, making sure that none of the prisoners tried to flee. Orders were to immediately gun down any such prisoner who would try.

SEPARATION

After the plane flew off, we were organized into rows and counted again. After that, the night was quite calm and not too cold. We kept walking, keeping ourselves warm with movement.

As night turned to morning, a large truck stopped us. Six rested soldiers popped out the back, among them our former prisoner Max.

By this time our energy was spent. We'd been walking all day and night, starved too, but the guards paid no attention to our state and kept on pushing us.

We slowly dragged on. The guards urged us to keep going, trudging through ditches and forests and around villages throughout the entire day. The elevation was rising. We were being lead into the Bavarian Alps.

As day turned back into night, and a light Spring rain began to sprinkle.

The same truck that we saw in the morning stopped us again, and it replaced the guards again as well as brought back Vili. The trucks wore tarp covers and didn't care that rain fell on us without interruption. We kept walking.

Some prisoners asked Vili when we'd get something to eat. We were starving.

"Where are we going?"

"When's our next meal?"

But he ignored them. Others asked how far we were going to go. But he said nothing and walked on. To every question, a guard would pounce on the prisoner and strike them with the butt of his rifle, ordering them to keep silent. But they couldn't help it.

Night came and we walked through that too. We'd been walking for two straight days now without break and we kept walking.

Day three of this march arrived and there was still no break in stride or known destination.

The guards were again switched out and Max was back. Several older and weaker prisoners collapsed upon the guards arrival. They couldn't do it anymore. The night shift guards took the fallen prisoners into the truck and we no longer saw them.

Most of us were on the brink of collapsing. We were weak, exhausted, with no strength to move on. But these fresh officers didn't care. They shouted at and beat us prisoners, threatening, "We'll shoot you down on this very road if you fall behind!"

Rain continued to fall. An older Frenchman dragged his feet next to mine. Up until now he had stayed ahead of the pack. But he slowly and continually fell further and further behind and with each prisoner that passed, he begged for help.

But no one responded to his plea. Other Frenchmen even, like every other prisoner, ignored his pleas. They were hungry, wet, and terrified of being shot. They thought for themselves and had no power left for another. It was one thing to share bread, and another to give up the last light of their life.

Finally, it was my turn to pass this old Frenchman and he looked at me with a look more imploring than any I'd ever seen. So I took his hand and pulled him along. He reminded me of Tato. *Maybe someone's helping him right now...*

So I helped him along, and we slowly advanced towards the front of the march. It was laborious and we planted our feet one by one but we were moving enough.

But then evening came, and after hours and hours of helping this old man along, he couldn't keep hold of me any longer.

He fell once, and I picked him up.

He fell again, and I picked him up with all the strength I had left. It was excruciating. We moved a little further.

A German officer noticed our pokey progress. He kept looking over at us. But I only thought about the old man.

And then the old man fell a third time, and I had no power to raise him up. He was limp. Rain fell even harder and his clothes and arms were so wet and slippery that I just couldn't pick him up again. The officer who watched over us stormed over and kicked the old man's side and shouted, "Get up!"

But this poor man couldn't move.

Without hesitation, the officer pulled out his revolver and shot him in the back, right there in the middle of the road. The old man was dead.

"Pick him up!" he yelled to the other prisoners. "Move him over there... to that ditch."

Seeing this tragedy, the other prisoners gathered up their last bit of strength and pushed on, so that they too would not get shot in the back. At that moment, I realized that those prisoners who were put on the truck were dead too, Nicholas among them.

This third day was the worst.

How long could I survive? Who still has any use for us? Is this how you plan to destroy us?

Every moment that went by made it harder for me to go on. I was exhausted, sleep deprived, and hungry. I felt desolate. Yuri and Roman lagged behind me.

Day died and the night came and the guards changed out and the rain fell even harder, so hard so that I could barely see the person in front of me. It was not just Germany rebelling against us - nature fought against us too. Nonetheless, the guards still scolded and shouted and yelled at us.

"Keep together!"

"Follow the road!"

To terrorize us even more, the guards killed off the weak.

Then a car drove up to drop off another set of guards, but only Max and Vili piled out. No more guards. I overheard them say to the guards remaining that this time there would be no one to replace them. They gave them more instructions, but I couldn't hear a thing. The rain was deafening. *The front is right there! Where are you taking us? We're dying of hunger!*

I kept complaining to myself like this. *How far do we still have to go? Maybe it would be better if I somehow ran away? Could I run?*

I looked around. It seemed that most of the prisoners that left with us from Landsberg were gone. I saw no kitchen chefs. And many of the German prisoners disappeared too. After the second day, they stopped counting us completely. *Could they have ran? Or could they really all have died?*

Either way, I wasn't going to leave my fate in the hands of these Germans anymore. It was time for me to make a move. It was time for me to run. I couldn't march any longer. So I hung back to find Roman and to ask him what he thought about an escape.

But as soon as I got back to him, Vili stopped us and announced that we were close to a building and we would stay the night until the rain stopped.

This announcement gave me a glimmer of hope. I was so happy. *Rest! Maybe they'd even bring us something to eat!* I knew I couldn't run anyway. My legs were dead. So this was welcomed, but my optimistic thoughts were quickly drowned out by the heavy rain, which mercilessly continued to pour.

From the fog out in front of me, I heard Max's voice. After walking a bit further, he and a large building appeared behind the wall of rain, and he motioned us inside. The rain was so heavy and my body so fatigued that all I could see was a dark hole. No lights. Each prisoner in front of me fell into the building and blindly felt around for a place to settle.

The guards tried prodding and hurrying us further into the building, but it wasn't easy. Some of the prisoners who walked in first immediately fell to the floor and didn't budge. Others trampled them with their wooden soles in the pitch dark. Others got tripped up on what must have been benches and fell over too. The floor creaked and we moaned and quarreled, blaming each other though there really was no one to blame.

The pitch black.

The hunger.

The hard road.

This led these people to despair.

Roman, Yuri and I were one of the last to enter. We couldn't see a thing and immediately fell to the floor semi-conscious. None of us said a word. Things started falling from the ceiling and made a lot of noise and prisoners started to yelp. Might have been tools.

In the distance I heard Vili tell everyone to shut up and sleep.

We had probably walked 20 miles, partly through the Bavarian Alps.

I heard the door shut and the clank of door locks. Outside, the rain kept pounding the roof. I could finally rest. My mind went blank and my body shut down.

CHAPTER EIGHTEEN

FREEDOM?

I opened my eyes. We were in a large sawmill.

I lifted my head and saw that I was the first one to wake up. All the others prisoners looked ready for their graves. Drenched and laying in all sorts of contortions, it was as if someone had scattered a bunch of corpses on the floor.

I looked out the windows and saw that the rain had stopped and white light shone through. There were no guards at the doors, and Roman and Yuri still laid on the floor as if dead. I didn't want to wake them, but I was curious about not seeing any guards.

I tried to lay back down and wait for the others, but I couldn't sit another still moment in my drenched clothes. I got up and scattered around the sawmill for a blanket or an old coat to coddle my shivers. But I found nothing useful.

I looked in wonder at all the prisoners so firmly implanted in sleep. *Did the guards just leave us here?*

Without thinking, in full voice, as the German camp instructors had done every single day of this war, I yelled "Aufstehen! Schnell! Schnell! Aufstehen!" (Get up now! Now, get up!)

A few brave prisoners raised their heads.

"What happened?"

"Where are the guards?"

I stood tall among the prisoners and said, "Look! Outside! The sun is shining! And there are no guards in sight!"

I didn't have to say another word. Roman immediately jumped to his feet and ran to the doors, but they wouldn't open. They were locked from the outside.

He beat them with his hands, but no one responded. Another prisoner ran to a side door, but it was closed too. After their heaves and failed attempts, other prisoners began to recover their senses, and, still lit with fear and uncertainty, gathered around Roman.

Two prisoners emerged with an ax and a hammer and they chopped and knocked and chopped and knocked and the main door broke open and we spilled outside. Guards were nowhere to be seen. A little house stood by the sawmill and a couple prisoners dared to search it. No guards.

Did they really leave? This was foreign to us. I'd been imprisoned and under close watch for a year. Many prisoners even longer than that.

Some prisoners pleaded to wait and that the guards were probably still asleep and would soon return. Others said that they must have brought us here to work.

But those feelings quickly melted away. Spirits rose. We all collectively forgot about hunger. We forgot that our clothes were soaked. We forgot that we had spent last night on the floor of a sawmill after three days of marching.

Suddenly, spontaneously, with one voice in all sorts of languages we all exploded:

"We're free!"

"We're alive!"

"We're free!"

"We're alive!"

Prisoners hugged each other regardless of nationality, whether we had tolerated each other before this moment or not.

No one could have ripped apart Roman, Yuri, and me. The prisoners hopped around in epidemic glee, whistling and leaping up to the mountain tops.

"We're free!"

"We're free!"

"We're free!"

Some screamed. Some galloped about. Others embraced and many cried. Others started talking about the train ride home.

But then we all heard the war. Shots and explosions bellowed from every direction. Fear trickled in. I'd been led by this fear for the last year. Others even longer.

"The guards will come back!"

"They'll be back with guns!"

"No way! They left because they were afraid we'd retaliate!"

"Let's go hunt them down!"

Others simply sat in puddles of tears and continued to sob.

"What do we do now?"

"Where do we go?"

"Let's get to the nearest house to get something to eat."

Everything was mixed up: the freedom, joy, fear, hunger, drenched clothes and hair... Sooner or later, every prisoner appeared with tears in their eyes. It was a feeling I couldn't describe in words.

None of us up to this moment put any thought into what we'd do with freedom. We didn't think about what we'd actually do outside the barbed wire. *Did any of us actually predict that these arrogant Germans would leave us in the middle of the night and escape from us?*

Just the night before, all I could think about was if we'd survive and whether we'd ever taste freedom.

I thought of Osip.

Osip where are you? How I'd love for you to be here! I'd pull you close and at the top of my lungs yell "We're free! We're alive!"

But Osip was not there. I got angry.

Why did you go first Osip?! Why didn't you wait for us in the trenches? We talked about this!

But it was useless. He wasn't coming back.

Yuri and Roman then asked why I was grieving. I told them Karas' unexpected end invaded my mind.

But I changed the subject and pointed out a few older prisoner who'd sat down on the floor, having no idea what to do. They were the most starved in camp, and now three days without food left them completely languished.

"Look - see how hard it is to reconcile in their joy? They're exhausted," I said.

At that moment, the one prisoner in camp who'd always

remembered what day it was announced our date of freedom:

"It's April 28, 1945."

I was sure at that moment that each of us would remember that date forever.

But now it was time to act. Roman, Yuri, and I watched the others prisoners, wondering what they'd do next. Nobody dared leave the sawmill. Our conversation was full of disputes too.

"Where should we go?"

"What direction?"

Each of us thought something different.

Boldly, Roman, Yuri and I were the first ones to leave. We were too hungry not to.

The sky had clouded over, but no more rain fell. From the sawmill, we could see a few farm houses scattered about. We pointed out to the rest of the prisoners which house we were heading to and advised them not to follow. We didn't want to overwhelm anyone anymore than we already would and came up with a simple system to warn the others.

One hand waving - all clear.

Two hands waving - problems.

They wished us well and we said goodbye and were off.

A few armed German soldiers passed by in the distance. We kept our eye out but paid them little attention. They were too far away from us to get worried, and we didn't want them to see our fear. We arrived at the first farmer's house.

But to our surprise, from out of the house several German soldiers appeared. We froze.

What do we do? Run?

These soldiers, however, showed no interest in us and quietly moved on. They also looked exhausted and miserably drenched from the rain.

We turned back to the sawmill and each waved one hand, motioning an "all clear" to the others.

We knocked on the door of the house and an older woman opened it and found us in alien form - skin and bones, wet, unshaven, donning striped prison garb, dirty... She froze. *Will you let us in, please? Or will you close your door on us?* She probably had never seen such withered people, dressed in striped, wet rags. And there was still war, so finding herself among uninvited guests was startling.

She looked at us as if to say, *"Why have you disturbed us at this hour? And what will you do with us?"*

Through the open door of the house we saw two others - a frightened, older man and a younger woman. Two little girls pressed closely behind the woman.

Roman quickly noticed their unsettled faces and introduced himself: "Grüß gott!"

The younger woman came to the door and politely and courageously asked, "What do you need?"

Yuri slowly said to her, "Please do not fear us. We have come to ask you for something to eat. We're very hungry. We haven't eaten in three days. We'll immediately leave whether you feed us or not."

Fear hit me. *Are there still soldiers in here? Maybe we came too soon? What if we run into guards? These people might have lodged someone here last night...*

But no one appeared and the presence of these tiny,

wondrous children soon took our attention. It was nice to see children.

The younger woman, even with her own two children hidden scared behind her, invited us in and said, "Mother - please bring them some bread and butter."

The older woman then asked us to sit at the table and went off to go heat up some milk.

"Yes, please sit," the older man said, as both little girls, not quite boldly, but curiously, looked at us and from time to time flashed little smiles.

The older man asked, "Have you heard anything about the end of the war?"

We didn't.

"Hm. Why are you in this area? And are there more like you?" he asked.

We asked him for water first because our throats were dried out. Both girls immediately ran to the kitchen and brought us some.

After guzzling down the water, we immediately took the bread and butter and began to eat greedily. The little girls watched us with fascination. They'd probably never seen such hungry people. Their mother poured us each a cup of milk. How good of a meal was this, you may be asking? The best. We couldn't peel ourselves away.

Little by little we grew accustomed to the moment and began to eat without haste and gave the older man the story of how we got to his home. The rest of the family left us with him.

"Yesterday, just like you today, a prisoner came to our

village to get something to eat," he said. "When he was close to one of our homes, a car filled with several military officers rode up. They stopped and called him over, saying they had to ask him something. He walked over and one of the guards pulled out a revolver and shot him dead without hesitation. They drove off, leaving the body lifeless by the roadside. A few local men took his body and placed it near the church. I haven't told this to my family, but I figured to warn you. I don't want them to fret, so please don't mention it."

After we gained some strength, the rest of the family walked back in and we told them how we got to the sawmill and how our guards locked the doors and apparently fled. The farm family listened to our stories about life in concentration camps with regret, but with compassion as well. They treated us with respect. The old farmer cautioned us to beware of soldiers and not to travel by road:

"If you run into a passing army, who knows what they'll do with you. I suggest you get to the nearby forest and wait until the front passes. I heard from the neighbors that the Americans are close. This war should be done soon."

This old farmer then let Roman and Yuri shave and I cleaned myself up too.

"Take off your blouses and shirts," said the young woman. She hung them up by the stove and ironed them dry.

After a pleasant and useful meeting, filling our stomachs and drying our clothes, we thanked the old farmer's family and knew it was time to move on.

With regret, the young woman who dried our shirts said, "My husband is in the army. He fought on the Russian front, and I haven't heard from him in quite some time."

We looked at her solemnly. What could we say?

So we walked on, towards the forest, diving down into ditches every time we saw approaching cars. Once we got to the tree line, we felt a little regret about not grabbing a blanket or two from the bavor.

How far are these Americans? How long do we still have to wait? To add to my anxiety, our joyous meal made us forget about the now-present future - we should have asked for a couple rolls for the road, but we were so blind with hunger! We sat down to recuperate.

Our mutual joy, gladness, and realization that we'd come out alive at the other end of these camps was now pushed up amongst the fear of the moving front. So we searched for a safer place to hide.

Here and there we saw small groups of German soldiers heading away from the front. Some of them were in full gear, weapons and anti-gas masks too. Others were already stripped naked of arms. We made sure to steer clear.

Looking back at the direction of the sawmill, we saw no movement. Everyone must have cleared out, but there were no other prisoners in sight, so they must have gone in another direction. *Did we go the wrong way?*

Without dwelling any longer, we entered the woods. Trees were sparsely planted and there were no bushes in sight, so we went in a little further to get some good cover. As we walked, above the treetops, what seems like cannon balls flew and exploded in the near distance. We had found ourselves in the middle of the fight! Without a word, we doubled our step towards the thickets ahead.

A few moments later we stopped and I looked down and between two bushes I saw two bare feet sticking out, heels up, and what looked like a military uniform.

I pointed this out to Roman and Yuri and shouted, "Look! A dead man!"

A young girl appeared underneath the body.

When she heard me yell out, she leapt up and the dead man was a young soldier who bounced up as well, and they both fled like the wind to the nearest home.

"What? You didn't know what two young people were capable of?" Roman mocked. Yuri laughed too.

Embarrassed, I tried excusing myself: "It's good that this happened! What if we *did* come across a dead soldier?"

Roman, once married himself, laughed hard and said, "You, in that life of yours, have yet many things to learn."

But I stubbornly refused to listen to any more to their banter. I continued looking about for a place to hide from the approaching front, and when I looked at the spot where the couple had been, there remained a barely-used military blanket.

"Oh, Look! A bounty! Good that that they ran off so fast - they left us a big blanket! All three of us can lay on it while we wait for safety," I said.

We picked up the blanket, and a short time later we were in thicker woods. We found a fat tree trunk to lay under for protection, and then we gathered leaves for pillows, laid down the blanket and had nice bed in no time.

We all laid down to rest, spending the rest of the day as

well as the night recovering from our march, which I had later found out was about 30 miles.

Throughout the night, we the sound of gun fire getting nearer and nearer.

But when day finally dawned, the shots were less frequent. And they started moving further and further away. And although the proximity of war was alarming, it was our hunger that we worried about most. We had eaten well the day before, but that didn't make up for three days without food. We decided to go back to the farmers.

We shook out and folded our new blanket and walked to the edge of the forest and noticed two soldiers carrying two wooden chests. They didn't see us, but stalled to argue, and then for whatever reason, they threw these chests into some bushes and hurried off. They also just happened to take the same path we were about to take towards the farm village. *What could be in these boxes?*

"Must be weapons. Grenades maybe," said Yuri.

"Germans are dropping everything and running!" said Roman, smiling.

We waited some time to make sure they didn't come back and our curiosity, as it often happens with youth, pulled us toward the boxes.

As soon as we got to them, we understood why the Germans had dropped them - they were made of a dense wood. Each box had an inscription.

One read: German beer.

The other: German cheese.

"I don't believe it!" said Yuri.

"Not possible," said Roman.

Without another thought, we picked up these heavy boxes and brought them back to the place we'd slept the night before and carefully unraveled our prey.

First up - the cheese. We opened the box and were overcome with joy - it really was cheese! It was packed methodically and divided into sections. The sharp smell smacked our faces and immediately suggested a taste test.

We took a couple bites and agreed that it was good. True and hearty German cheese.

We propped open the box of German beer and marveled at the carefully packed glass bottles, housed in a way which avoided any breaks when the soldiers threw the box. We each popped a bottle and took a long whiff of the hops and then drank some with our cheese.

When we finished feasting, we took a little rest and then headed off towards the clicks and clacks of machine gun fire.

After we praised ourselves for this bounty, we packed up our booty. Time to keep moving.

CHAPTER NINETEEN

THE VILLAGE OF OLCHING

Roman, Yuri and I kept walking with our boxes of beer and cheese. Time was moving quickly for a change.

We talked amongst ourselves about how we should greet the American soldiers and what they'd think of us in our striped concentration camp garments. We had no clue what their uniforms looked like, what their weapons looked like or what their language sounded like.

We kept on moving in the direction that we thought the U.S. Troops would appear, and we no longer saw German soldiers. They seemed to have fully retreated and that meant Americans would be right around the corner! This boosted our confidence and we courageously sped our pace and nearing the edge of the forest, we came upon another German village and checked it out. We saw no Germans.

Convinced that the German front had passed and danger was low, we walked along the railroad and into the village station. A sign hung reading:

Village of Olching

We walked about the station for a bit, trying to decide where to go next, and just across the road sat a two story house, ensconced by a short wooden fence. It looked to me like a tiny hotel.

"Let's go there first," I said.

As we walked up, a few people walked out, and to our wonder, they spoke Ukrainian! A tall, good looking fellow of about forty turned to us and in German asked, "Who are you looking for?"

All three of us at once started explaining how we were prisoners of a German concentration camp and unexpectedly found ourselves free and we didn't know where we were going.

He quickly replied, "Ahh, so you're not German." He then smiled and said, "What language do you speak?"

We all proclaimed, "We're Ukrainian!"

He was surprised that we were all Ukrainian but then said, "I'm also Ukrainian, a native of Kiev. Come on in. Enjoy the yard. We have space for you here - you can take the last room on the left. We saw you through the window and we walked outside to check you out and your funny clothes too."

Every inhabitant of the house then slowly came out and greeted us like we were their brothers. Among them were women and girls that were so happy that we walked free among the living. Along with Ukrainians, there were Belorussians and Russians, and each treated us without judgement. They spoke to us in their native languages, asking us where in Ukraine we were from, what did the Germans arrest us for, which camps we were in, whether we were beaten, hungry... there was no end to their questioning. Everyone wanted to hear our story.

We asked them theirs.

"The Germans forced us to relocate and work in Germany," one said. "But these past few days, no one has called us to work, so we've found ourselves in a good situation - watching the German army flee and waiting for the Americans."

They invited us into their kitchen where a hot feast was already waiting. But all I ate was soup - I was stuffed from all that cheese.

Our new housemates explained how the German police had been on their cases for a while now, but just two hours ago, they had fled.

"They stayed until the last minute, so that we didn't retaliate against their fellow troops. They also let us know that across the street there was a camp full of military prisoners. I'm sure they'd rejoice mightily seeing you free from camp. They're still locked up."

Children were captivated by our stories as well. They'd listen to a couple and then run off to make sure that the American soldiers hadn't yet broken the horizon. Some of the older men offered us their clothes and told us to wear them just in case the Germans returned. We didn't want to be recognized as concentration camp prisoners.

Then we heard some loud shouts coming from the street. Interested inhabitants ran to the windows to see if this time the Americans were here. But they turned out to be the military prisoners. The guards had finally abandoned them and they broke through the gate and came to the village.

"We are free!"

"Germany's lost the war!"

These military prisoners quickly learned about us concentration camp prisoners and whole groups gathered around us asking about the life in those camps. There was no end to the yelling and joy in the front yard of this building.

And then, from who knows where, an accordion player appeared and started playing music. No one waited any longer for the arrival of the liberators!

Then a creaky old Belarusian man with a hoary Lenin-like beard dove in first, dancing alone, squatting like a Cossack and encouraging each and every girl to dance with him. The young boys joined in and the prisoners of this war formed a dancing circle.

They kicked their legs and waved their arms and then from who knows where more people sprung up and began to sing all sorts of Russian, Ukrainian, and Belarusian songs. Then a full bottle of booze appeared, followed by a second and third and a real ball had begun!

The old Belarusian drank the first glass and cheerily invited the others to join him. He gave a glass to the musician who tried just a little and then continued to play as the old man danced on. He stuck out his goat-beard, bent forward, put one hand behind his back and with this comical dance he overjoyed everyone. Some young girls then asked us to dance. Yuri felt right at home and didn't need to be persuaded. Roman initially just clapped his hands, but after his second glass, he danced with every girl he could catch.

SEPARATION

It seemed that I was the only one with something wrong. I started to feel heavy, as if the ground beneath me was sinking. An awful chill came over my body, and I began to shake.

"You're white as a wall," the man next to me said. The dancing stopped being so interesting to me. One boy tried treating me with vodka, but another stopped him.

"Look," he said, "There's something wrong with him. He's gotta get to a doctor."

My vision darkened and my head ached and I couldn't stand under my own strength anymore. Sweat poured down my head and I was slowly losing consciousness. Two men took me by my armpits and put me on a wide, wooden bench in the kitchen.

Someone put something under my head and I heard "Leave him in peace... concentration camp... needs rest..." and I faded into half-sleep. How long I was there, I do not know.

Then, as if I was dreaming, I heard music and dancing and people crying out: "Americans are coming! They've come on their tanks and trucks! And look - even some black Americans! Look - the girls are running up to them and hugging them and waving their arms..."

But I was alone, no Roman and Yuri even. They must have been fascinated by the Americans, especially the blacks, because we'd never met one before.

Then I suddenly passed out.

I awoke to a nurse and doctor standing over to me. I

startled up and asked them what happened.

The doctor said, "You were brought unconscious here last night, had a high fever, but everything seems back to normal. You'll be just fine."

"But what happened to me?" I further insisted.

"Your friends told me that you went without food and sleep for three days, and before that you were barely fed. They also told me how you found boxes of cheese and beer, which you probably ate too much too quickly. Your stomach was irritated because of all that heavy movement in your digestive system. There was a rapid reaction with the cheese and beer. But it'll pass. You're still young. Just try to eat less but more often and everything will be fine."

"Thank you doctor. Can I go back to my friends?" I asked.

"Up to you. It'd be better if you stayed here for another day, but it depends on how you feel," he said.

I felt good and decided to return to my friends. I didn't want to wait like I did for Tato.

That day after dinner, I went back again to the building near the railway station and into our room. There I found my both of my friends talking to two other concentration campers, who that night were also left by guards and by chance they found this building. They were Russians. Roman and Yuri had accepted them both into our room.

"We didn't expect you so soon!" said Roman.

"The doctor said I'm fine. It was the cheese and beer," I said.

I noticed several packs of sugar piled up under one of the beds.

"Where'd you get all that? And what are you going to do with it?" I asked.

"There's a grocery warehouse with a bunch of goods in it," said Yuri.

"The prisoners opened it and everyone's taking what they want. It's good your back. Stay here and watch the room. We're gonna go back and see if we can find anything else," said Roman.

"Who knows how long we'll be here," said Yuri. "Where else are we going to find food?"

Later that day, they came back with bag full of cereal, oatmeal, flour, salt, and more sugar. Afterwards, they went off to a shop with clothes and boots and told me to hang tight so they could bring back something better for us to wear. They brought back three pairs of shoes for me to try, but no clothes. The shop was apparently filled with military clothing, but nothing that fit us. Of the three pairs of shoes, one fit, and I quickly replaced my old wood-soled pair.

One of the Belarusian guys brought me a sort of windbreaker.

"It's too small for me," he said.

I rejoiced - it suited me just fine. And yet another man gave me a shirt, which helped me transition back into looking somewhat like a civilian.

Then a thought came to mind - "We ought to find a photographer and get a remembrance of what happened."

So we did and luckily he took these shots for free. My photo ended up being the cover of this book. After taking the photo, we immediately burned our concentration camp clothes to get rid of the lice.

So far I hadn't met any American troops. But I was told that some of them were living close to us and our housekeeper invited them over to dance. A group of the troops gladly accepted. I was very curious to see them, especially the colored ones. I'd never seen a colored man before.

In the common kitchen that night, during dinner, the family in charge of cooking announced that they were also free and no longer going to cook everyone meals. Because nobody else wanted to replace them, each resident had to fend for themselves. So along with no money, now we had no cooks.

"It's good we got so many things from the store," said Roman.

That evening, in the yard, the accordion player appeared and cheered us all up again with his music. The older Belarusian with the goat beard again was the first to start dancing. He found lady partner after lady partner and it looked to me that he could dance forever.

A few hours of that went by, and then the Americans showed. I was initially disappointed, because none of them were black. Language wise, a few knew German and some spoke a little Polish. Others had no common language with us and simply and easily entertained themselves.

And speaking of entertainment, they sure did know how to drink. After my episode with the cheese and beer, I was cautious of eating and I avoided taking alcohol. I poured a glass for myself to fit in with the others, but pretended to drink instead.

I delighted in the Americans' military uniforms. They looked quite comfortable. I marveled at their awards and boots and admired their sincerity, joy, and simplicity of relationship between ordinary soldiers and their officers. No one formally saluted anyone. They just laughed and joked and slapped each other on their shoulders, egging each other on to be the first to join the dance.

Initially, they circled around and enthusiastically watched the Cossack squats and clapped their hands in rhythmic celebration. But after the alcohol lit them up a bit, they attempted some Cossack squats too.

Success did not follow. They fell over and over and tried again and again and maybe got one or two. But their lack of repeated success bothered no one. What a nice first impression they made on me.

After playing the national anthem of each represented nation, the musician began to play Ukrainian kolomiykas and each drunken soldier took a woman to dance. They had no idea what a true kolomiyka was, which was a dance circle where Ukrainian solos were done surrounded by people clapping, so they followed their own drum beat and danced about as long as the music played. They were in no hurry to get away and probably would have danced all night if the accordion player didn't cease to play.

Once he retired the keys, a group of us singers gathered and sang 'til the end the night. I looked at the table and noticed that the once full bottles were now empty.

Slowly the yard cleared. The POWs went to their quarters, followed by us to our building and then the Americans left too.

"Goodbye!" said one American.

"We'll be back!" said another.

What a nice way to get introduced to America.

And we didn't have to wait long for our next American military encounter either.

The next night, two soldiers came back to our mini-hotel. They shouted something that at the time I did not understand: "Whiskey! Whiskey!"

They staggered about to the bottom floor of our building, making hand signals indicating that they wanted booze.

Roman and I yelled from the stairs in German "No schnapps!" but they still didn't understand or didn't want to and then waved their arms, as if they wanted a fight. We saw that they weren't armed and Roman opened the door to a storage closet by the entrance of our house.

One of the Americans grabbed a broom, tried to hit Roman, but we managed to stuff him and his drunk accomplice into the closet. They both fell to the ground and we ran out the door into the yard and yelled to everyone else in the house to lock their doors.

These were not the same sincere Americans from last night.

At that moment, a small military car appeared before us and two soldiers with helmets labeled "MP" (military police) stepped out. In German, they asked us whether we'd seen two drunk soldiers. We showed them the storage room, and they apologized for their behavior and dragged them out. This was my second interaction with the Americans... comical and definitely happy that none of us got hurt.

A merry life in this hostel continued. Almost every evening, we danced and sang and drank. It lifted everyone's spirits. But from underneath this new flavor of life, a question arose inside me:

What now?

With Germany losing the war, many institutions collapsed. Supplies stalled. Olching had no store or distribution center. A neighboring town, where we were issued registration cards, allowed us to get supplies there twice a week. But this wasn't really that beneficial, because the city was too far for us to visit regularly.

The POWs resented this system too, also complaining about the lack of transportation. This situation riled up even more frustration against the German system, again reminding prisoners that the awful command of Hitler's nation not only put us here in the first place but was *still* determining our quality of life.

This led to former prisoners acting on the injustices of war, death, and suffering by deciding to take whatever they needed from local Germans. One day, a groups of prisoners walked into a restaurant located near our building. It was the only one in the village.

This restaurant seemed to me quite poor. Sometimes I

went to grab a hot soup there for lunch, or fried eggs for breakfast, and occasionally a beer. It was owned by a single family, who served everyone and was always quite polite.

But the cocky and entitled prisoners sat down at the restaurant's tables and ordered the owner to serve them everything he had. The owner said that he didn't have enough food and that the restaurant was closed that day.

"And we say," said one of the prisoners, "that it's open and you're going to bring us all you've got in the cellar or we'll go down and look for ourselves."

"Please leave," said the owner. "I've done nothing wrong to you."

They answered, "*You* may have not. But others have. Now give us something to eat."

A few prisoners then broke into the cellar. They brought back sausages, salami, bread, canned food, and full bottles of beer. All of them ate and drank as they pleased.

So the prisoners stuffed themselves and complained that the owner lied to them.

"But we thought you didn't have anything? Where's your hospitality?" one said.

The owner and his family were scared out of their store and they quickly disappeared. Fortunately, this restaurant sold only beer and not hard alcohol. It could only escalate so much.

Then, as Roman and I were watching all this, one prisoner who was relishing a salami saw us through a window and cried out to us to come closer. I initially held Roman back. They were hostile and I didn't want to fight.

But then that prisoner ran out to us and gave us a piece of salami and a piece of bread and further prodded us to go inside. We couldn't turn down the food. We were so hungry.

So we took the bread and shared the salami and followed him in. As we walked in, prisoners were already drunk and ready to throw bottles on the ground. I wanted to do something.

"Enough!" I said. "If everything is demolished, where will we go tomorrow?"

The lead prisoner looked up and said, "He's right! He says it well. Let's eat up and drink up and leave and go play," said the prisoner who brought us in.

His other comrades followed. They finished their feast and went back to the building, where the accordion player was already warming up.

Thinking back on what just happened, I figured it wouldn't be long before the local Germans would rat out the prisoners to the Americans and people would be punished.

But this situation passed without recourse, probably because the German locals were still too scared to approach the American authorities.

So this first week of my release wasn't quite the happiness I expected. I kept falling into unneeded adventure.

Yuri, on the other hand, was forthright about seeking adventure. He quickly got acquainted with the local Germans and met the major of the village, who happened to have a very beautiful daughter.

Yuri was also quite handsome and she apparently enjoyed his looks immensely. And I hadn't met any young men in this village so far, because they were probably all called off to war, so it was easy to see how Yuri immediately stole the heart of a young German girl. After seeing Yuri meet up with this family, a few days went by before we saw him again.

But then one day, Yuri drove up in a brand new motorcycle and boasted to all of us, "Yup, it's mine."

None of us believed him.

"So who did you steal it from?" asked a prisoner.

"Got one for me?" said another.

They kept mocking him until he finally admitted, "Okay, okay. The bike belongs to the major of the village. He taught me how to ride it and said I could go wherever I'd like," said Yuri.

Then to Roman and me, he said, "The Major persuaded me to stay at their house. He needs me, because I know German, Polish, Russian, and Ukrainian. He wants me to serve as a translator and help him fix the ugly relations between his village and the former prisoners."

"You shouldn't be so kind to the Germans," said one prisoner.

"Yeah, they drove you into camp and now you're helping them and willing to marry a German girl?" another said.

Yuri was somewhat a taken back by this greeting, but shook it off.

"Hey Stepan, want to take a ride? I want to show you something," Yuri said.

For whatever reason, I hopped on the back of the bike

without hesitation.

Yuri keyed the motor and suddenly, as if with indignation, or more-so a lack of practice, he slammed on the gas and we careened down the road scattered with tiny stones. The motorcycle jumped forward and Yuri hit a hard left and the bike flew out from underneath us and we hit the ground and slid a few feet. All I was wearing at the time was a thin shirt and pants. Roman and the other prisoners immediately ran over.

Roman said, "Your whole right side is torn up and covered in sand. Your shirt and pants are all ripped up too, red with blood."

Then I looked up and saw Yuri, not moving and white as a canvas.

Several men ran over and picked us up in their arms and brought us to the nearby house where the village doctor lived.

The doctor answered and said, "Lay them both on the floor."

He tore off our clothes and cleaned out our wounds with alcohol.

In pain, I angrily hissed at myself, "Am I really that stupid? Why did I get on that bike?"

I was too afraid to look at my wounds. *How could I survive such horrific concentration camps, come out alive, and here voluntarily and so easily do away with my life?* I was angry at Yuri, but much more so at myself for this foolishness. Fortunately, neither of us broke anything, although I thought we both deserved to. The city mayor and his daughter came to Yuri's side and took him to their house.

"Stepan! I'm sorry I was so stupid! I'm sorry that I've done you so much trouble!" said Yuri as he left.

I spent the next few days at home to let my wounds heal.

After a few days of healing, I walked outside and noticed several new bikes. One of the neighbors, a former prisoner, asked me if I knew how to ride.

"Yes," I answered.

"Then why don't you have one?" he asked.

"I can't buy one. I have no money."

The next day he presented me with his bike. He himself got an even better one.

"Thank you," I said. "How did you find one so soon?"

"It's not just any trick to pull it off... I went with my friend to a neighboring village and we hid underneath a bridge. When a German on a bike appears, we both jump out from underneath the bridge, scare him and he runs, leaving the bike, no hassle. Then we run off with the bike. The startled German then goes home, grateful that something worse didn't happen to him. The Germans around here are scared of everything! I have no clue how they found the strength to fight the whole world," said this prisoner.

Then his friend joined us and said, "German girls are coming to our camp, many from other villages. They're ready to go on *adventures* with all willing men. I admire their lack of embarrassment and courage. They don't fear getting tied up. They don't fear illness. 'Our girls aren't capable of this,' they say," he said.

But I wasn't interested and went off to the beautiful Amper River that flowed through Olching. The water was quite clean and warm and swimming around left me feeling rejuvenated. Near the river sat a building where a few American military men resided.

On the edge of the river, two German girls had appeared and tried calling me over. Two soldiers walked out too, because they noticed two German girls trying to coax me.

I left the girls alone and swam further out. I wasn't interested in any of these woman adventures. But the guards walked over and it only took a couple minutes before all four of them returned back to their military residence. I swam around a bit more and headed back to my room.

The American soldiers stopped coming by our parties as well, even though we kept dancing and playing games. They weren't satisfied with just dancing.

But when the Germans began to organize parties, all the soldiers immediately joined, because all sorts of lady adventures awaited them. These American soldiers didn't have to resort to raping women, as it often happened during times of war, because plenty of pretty German women were open to satisfying them.

Food was becoming sparse. We'd traded as much of our sugar for food as the bavors would take, but demand quickly died. So we decided to get over to the next village, because maybe it would be easier to find a trade partner. I had a bike now too, so travel was easy.

One day, right before lunch, Roman and I, along with a former prisoner named Peter, left the village to exchange our sugar for eggs. The first village we came upon looked deserted. We figured they were all in the the fields working.

After visiting several bavor houses and finding nobody, Peter dismounted his bike and, unannounced, walked into a nearby rooster house. The hens were troubled by his presence and bwaaaacked.

But Peter didn't care and he grabbed a fat chicken and snapped her neck. Roman noticed an empty bag lying near the coop and brought it to Peter, who by that time had killed six chickens.

Just then, an old bavor pulled his car up into the yard and I warned Peter and Roman just in time, so they both had time to jump out of his yard.

I ran over to the bavor, showed him a pack of sugar, but he saw Roman and Peter in his yard.

"What do you need here?" he asked with skepticism.

"We want to exchange sugar for eggs and so we came to pay you a visit," I said.

"Oh good," he said, "because I just ran out of sugar."

After some delay, he came back with a basket full of eggs. We traded and as we went off, the bavor said, "Auf wiedersehen!" (Goodbye!), not suspecting that we had just liberated six chickens from his coop as well. We were satisfied with this bountiful trade and quickly departed back to our building.

CHAPTER TWENTY

CAMP GERLINGEN

Several weeks after the U.S. Authorities landed in Olching, the village council-people met to organize the chaos. German policemen were ordered to make rounds, often hanging by our house a bit longer, but never entering our yard. Against our building and the next stood rows of bikes. The police certainly weren't stupid and knew how they got there.

One day, two American officers, two German policemen, and one civilian officer came into our yard.

"We want everyone out of the building. We have an announcement."

After we all gathered, one of the officers, in German, said, "Pack up whatever you own, because tomorrow morning trucks are coming to take you to a camp from which you will all be transported home. No one will be allowed to stay here, because this building is being turned into a school."

Some prisoners asked questions, but no answers were given. The officials swiftly walked across the street to spread the word to the other building. Those prisoners were even more aggressive in their questioning.

"Why aren't we going straight home from here?"

"Why do we have to move again?"

"We're so close to the train - just take us to the motherland!"

The chief officer spoke up.

"There are people of many different nationalities left all over Germany because of this war. And they're causing all sorts of damage to the local population. They're attacking people, robbing and scaring them at night. They're stealing goods and destroying households. We've received plenty of complaints, and I have orders from a higher authority to get you out and into a camp which is located close by in the next village called Gerlingen," he said, quite politely.

He continued: "Everything will be better there. You'll have a joint kitchen. There are plenty of bathrooms and life will be altogether more convenient."

The next morning, heavy trucks arrived to take us to Gerlingen. There was no counting. Everyone gathered their things, which wasn't much. Some had stolen bikes, which they were allowed to keep. We still had a little sugar left and ten packs of millet for gruel. Peter and his friend took five packs, while Roman and I took the rest. The move to Gerlingen didn't take long.

When we arrived, we were assigned to two long three-story buildings that had bunks like those in the concentration camps. Roman and I found beds near each other in the first building, which housed mostly Belarusians and Ukrainians. Peter, though until now he kept a close friendship with me, went into the second building, which housed mainly Russians.

SEPARATION

Everyone spread out as they wanted and wherever they liked, which led us to separate by nationality again. For single women and families, they blocked off part of the barracks with a wooden wall and the family units separated themselves off by hanging blankets.

We walked out into camp and met many others, like us, who'd been transported here from other villages. They were mostly laborers, who were driven deep into Germany to work as unpaid laborers. Among them were a large number of Ukrainians, Belarusians, Russians, Poles, and perhaps even others.

And as far as camp services, the kitchen was open and served breakfast and dinner. We were told to figure out lunch ourselves. Those who worked in the kitchen got paid in German money, which helped them when they went to town, especially those families with more children.

We quickly acquainted ourselves with Gerlingen camp life. Everyone looked about for people from their region. I wandered about, searching for Ukrainians, and moment by moment that same question kept popping up in my head: What do we do now?

I ran into a couple who was from Galicia as well, and after a short conversation, I really took a liking to them. Their names were Basil and Mila Komar, and they immediately confided in me that they were scared to go back to Ukraine.

Basil said, "At home, I was part of patriotic organizations, and I'm afraid that if I go back, the Communists would arrest me immediately."

I was scared of this too.

They asked me to eat with them, and we chatted some more about life in German concentration camps and about my parents and our arrest.

"I dream of us going to England," he said.

Not even a week passed by in our new camp and Russian advocates arrived, none of whom us residents had ever seen before. They spread rumors that we'd soon be moved back to "the motherland," and because of this, we should prepare properly. They brought us pieces of red cloth to hang as flags in our camp, but no one did it. Many remembered getting these red fabrics during the famine and having to paint Russian praise all about:

"Praise the Red Army! Praise Soviet Union! And praise Stalin!"

But instead of liberation, we got slavery.

These Russian advocates who came to Gerlingen spread rumors that a delegation from "the motherland" would be arriving soon, and they would inform us of preparations for our return and grand welcome. "Come lead a happy life after the war!"

Former Soviet Union citizens, longing for their native homes, intensified these rumors, spreading them with blind joy. They were sick of Germany and didn't consider whether or not their life back home might actually be no better or maybe even worse than Nazi Germany. Most prisoners got more and more homesick as the days went on and that reinforced their longing and solidified their hope to return to so-called "Soviet paradise."

Trains started moving through our camp filled with former prisoners returning to "the motherland." Our camp, it seemed, was somewhere in that same queue.

As my deep longings for security brewed, careless life in camp lived on. Musicians appeared. Dancing ensued. Singing continued too. One night, I noticed a slightly older American officer standing against a wall, listening to our language and our singing, which deeply resonated throughout camp. After some inner deliberation, I gained some confidence and walked up to him. I spoke to him in German. He answered in Russian. I switched over to Russian.

"How do you know Russian so well? Is your family from there?" I asked.

"No, but I've been given a gift for learning languages. I graduated from military school in America and there I learned Russian. Two years later, they sent me to work on ships to aid Russia in this war against Germany. I was an intermediary between the Americans and Russians. I loved every day of it. I got to use Russian all the time and carry around a gigantic dictionary too, just in case I didn't understand something. These ships carried tanks, mortars, machine guns, rockets, missiles... all types of weaponry as well as clothes and food. I was also getting letters from the Department written in English, which I translated into Russian."

And then for whatever reason, he immediately told me, "But such a help to the Soviet Union to me seemed quite suspicious."

Why are you being so frank with me? You don't even know how I feel.

He continued: "It was hard for me to understand, because after translating, I wasn't entitled to see where the messages went, if they were in good condition, or if they may have needed some corrections. No one seemed to trust me. In two years actually, nobody ever gave me a chance. I never spoke once to an ordinary soldier. Just officers. But these officers always suspected me of something. They treated me with great distrust. I sincerely gave them my support, but they thought I was a spy. I was forbidden to re-enter any ship I'd done a transfer to... Anyways, how about you? Are you a Russian? And are you Orthodox? Muslim maybe?"

I replied: "I am Ukrainian."

"Ah, it's all the same, you Russki," he said.

I took the whole night to explain to him that Ukraine was a different nation that had its own language, culture, and nearly three hundred years ago, Russia seized and occupied Ukraine and up to this day we're still slaves. He accepted this information with interest.

"Thank you for explaining all that," he said. "And thank you for showing me that the USSR is not one nation, and that each of these Soviet republics was conquered by force, using terror to keep them latched together. Sorry. They don't teach this in American military school. And after hearing what you've said, I don't think I'm going back to Russia, even if I'm told to do so."

"I'm afraid to go back," I said, opening up to him as he did to me. "I'm sure that if the Soviet government knew why my

Tato and I were arrested by the Germans, they would surely replant us in prison or into their Siberian camps."

"Get to America," he said. "I can't help you get there, but go anyway."

A few days later, he brought me a present. It was the great English-Russian and Russian-English dictionary.

"I don't need this anymore. I won't be going to Russia," he said. "Tomorrow, they're moving me, and I won't be able to come see you anymore."

Along with the dictionary, he handed me a giant chocolate bar and several packets of chewing gum. Then he gave me his hand and I gave him mine, saying farewell for good.

Camp entertainment became more and more enthusiastic. Everyone drank as much as they wanted. Why? Because prisoners were scouting out stores during the day and then stealing from them at night. The Germans were too frightened to do anything about it.

There was no policing. U.S. Authorities weren't established yet, and the Germans didn't trust them anyway. No robberies were reported, for the Germans feared revenge from the prisoners. No reports, no punishments. The chaotic free for all continued.

One day, so much chicken appeared in camp that we couldn't eat it all. Another day, an entire slaughtered calf appeared. Then a whole pig. And fresh fruits and vegetables were everywhere... all stolen at night from neighboring bavors. But no Germans came by to investigate. And instead of throwing the meat remains in the garbage, prisoners just ripped up barrack floor boards and tossed the bones and waste inside. They were sprinkled with stolen salt so they didn't stink up the place. And no one cared about cleanliness anyway. Everyone thought that we'd be leaving camp soon, so prisoners saw no point in keeping this camp clean.

One day, as Peter complained to me about his Russian countrymen, I asked him about what he thought about a return to the Union.

"Stalin ordered that all of us German military prisoners were considered traitors to 'the motherland.' But he said it *during* the war, and now that we won the war, he probably changed his mind. So I'd like to go back as soon as possible," he said.

I had much less trust in Stalin and leaned in the other direction.

But to avoid any suspicion, I said, "Me too. I want to see my Mama and the rest of my family."

Thoughts of repatriation kept me up up night. Rumors kept coming in of a quick departure with each passing day. Trains with dozens of red flags waving rushed by, littered with slogans praising the Soviet Union. They were fully loaded with people who shouted and sang all sorts of happy Soviet songs, among those shouts also threats to the German population. My fears to return to Ukraine increased daily.

And a dark jealousy grew in me as well. We Ukrainians were just as deserving of a home as prisoners of other nationalities, and they got to merrily travel home. I imagined them being welcomed by their families, their country, their neighbors, and their closest friends. Tears streamed down my cheeks with great envy.

Why was I not born a Frenchman? Or some other nationality whose country's doors were open to them... where along with their families, a whole country would open their arms up to greet them, helping them out of poverty and giving them post-camp medical care. The war was over, but I was still a prisoner. And why? Because I'm Ukrainian. Because I love my people. And because I'm a patriot. I'm useless and completely unneeded by those in charge of my country - those who oppress Ukraine and further her enslavement.

I so badly wanted to rejoice with the other prisoners who were liberated from this awful system. The hope passed down to me from other Underground members was completely invalid. They said that the Germans would lose the war and the Western Allies would disarm the likes of the Soviet Union. These Western States had captured a victory over Germany, and they were so elated by their achievements that their eyes were closed to the crimes that continued in the Soviet Union.

After hearing about the joint conferences in Tehran, Yalta, and Potsdam, where the criminal systems were supposed to be destroyed or modified even but weren't. I didn't understand. *Why would the Western Allies pay so dearly for the destruction of Nazism, but then be ok with a similar criminal dictatorial system, this Soviet Communism?!*

I heard no Allies speak or mention that the communist system should be rejected, that it's ambitious mastery of the world should be denounced.

This Soviet Army was so strongly armed by Western powers, mostly by Americans, that they quickly grew even more powerful when they captured the German capital, Berlin. And these Stalin-whipped Soviets were even dictating to the Western Alliances how the world should be built after this war.

But that was reality. So I was split. *Should I return to my dear home Ukraine to potential slavery? Or take a shot in the West and look for new opportunities in an alien and still yet unknown world to me?*

Sometime in the month of July, I got an idea:
I wonder what Dachau looks like now. Maybe I should go?

"What do you think?" I asked Roman.

"I've been thinking that too, but I really don't want to remind myself of those times," he said.

But my curiosity didn't fester. After that talk, I went to the local railway station to figure out how to get there. I found out that anybody could ride the train for free, which was good, because I had no money anyway. *That's why these trains are always so full!* Some were filled soldiers, others with war captives from various nations, some with tradesmen and money movers, and these trains were always filled to the brim. At the Gerlingen railway station, I learned that Dachau sat near Munich. The station officers told me to get to Munich first and find out the way to Dachau from there.

The next day, Roman and I took that journey. It was bright, beautiful, and warm. We got on the train and it was filled with German soldiers who still hadn't changed out of their uniforms into civilian clothes. Among them were soldiers from Yugoslavia, of Croatian nationality. They didn't want to go back to Yugoslavia, because Josip Broz Tito's government there was communist, and these Yugoslavians helped the Germans out in hopes to be freed from it.

As our train got closer to Munich, we came across terrible desolation. Munich's suburbs lays in ruins. Houses were demolished. Scattered about these houses were homeowners and their families, sorting through the rubble, looking for anything still of use. Reaching Munich, the destruction was even greater. I was surprised our train could even get through. Deep pits and demolished roads sat beside us. Old rail lines lay gnarled along our route.

Looking out the window, I admired the Germans, that they so quickly started to pick themselves back up again, all trying to pitch in to fix what was broken. They continued working in silence, and I didn't once spot a tearful woman or child. Nobody impelled them to work. They saw this terrible devastation and tried as quickly as they could to rebuild themselves.

On the train, Roman and I met some Jews, already engaged in some kind of trading. They enjoyed every broken home and laughed, one saying, "If you really needed yourself a Hitler, well here you go, now you have what you deserve."

To the Jews' shouts and cries, none of the German passengers answered.

Some Jews boasted that they were already receiving aid from America and others said they had nowhere to go but Palestine.

"We will rebuild our country! There will be no more violent riots! No more mob attacks! No more concentration camps!"

Some of them had already found yarmulkes and paraded about in them. Some had grown great, long beards as well. We tried talking to them, but they didn't respond to our inquiries politely. They figured we were German youths, and they pushed us about, not letting us get through the train without hostility.

So I said, "Maybe we were in the same concentration camp."

"Why did the Germans arrest you?" one asked.

We told them.

"Two young Ukrainians in a German concentration camp? Why'd they treat you like Jews?"

We responded, but they didn't want to believe us. They were convinced we were lying. An older man overheard our argument, and out of curiosity he asked us about the specifics of the camps we were at. I told him about prison in Lviv, in Krakow, in Breslaw, and then counted all the concentration camps I stayed in up until Landberg.

"Describe Landsberg."

"We initially met a bunch of Jews there who were forced to work at a three story factory being built by the Germans," I said.

"And how about the tunnels?" he asked.

We told them about the bomb shelter tunnels and he admitted, "At first, I didn't believe you. Ukrainians, as German prisoners? But," he turned to the other prisoners, "they're not lying. These are fellow concentration camp prisoners."

Then I showed them the picture I took in Olching after my release. Many were jealous that they too didn't snap a shot.

"So where are you going?" they asked.

We said we were going to take another look at Dachau.

A few then gladly told us the best route, because they had visited too.

"Try to avoid the crematoriums," they warned, "That's were the Germans burned our people."

We thanked them for their guidance and expressed our joy that we met and that we were all living free.

One of them then asked us, "When will you go back to the Soviet Union?"

I told him what camp we were living in and that we weren't given any Soviet liquidation information.

He replied, "I myself speculate whether I should return there or go to Palestine, as my friends are planning. My whole family was taken by the Germans, and I don't know if any of them even survived."

As our friendly conversation with the Jews ended, my attention drew back to yet even more terrible ruins of this city. The train finally set to rest in Munich's main station, which bombs also did not pity, as it also laid in ruins.

As we walked out of the train, we saw scraps of the station already organized and moved into large piles of stones, shattered brick, concrete and iron. Masses of people hurried about. Wherever I turned, I could hear a new language and see a variety of different facial structures and all sorts of garments. The looks on people's faces said, "I hope this is the worst of it," as they walked by still intact walls, waiting to collapse at any moment.

Roman and I walked over to the temporary facility they'd set up and asked an officer when the next train departed for Dachau. He quickly pointed to a nearby train and said, "You better hurry - it should have left already."

So we bolted for the train and jumped on. The train whistle hooooed, and we rolled towards Dachau.

Our train moved slowly and delayed at several more stations, but everywhere we looked was the same: homes in ruins, scattered stone, chunks of cement, and huge piles of bricks. Workers were sprinkled about these ruins and hammered through the cement and sorted it into separate piles.

"Look Stepan," said Roman, "See how conscientiously these Germans work? Quite industrious and disciplined people."

I nodded in agreement, then said, "But it would have been better if their leaders didn't push their country into such devastation. And worse yet, they took down other nations with them."

We talked a bit more and then arrived at a familiar station. As we walked out, pillars held up the same inscription as before:

DACHAU

From the station, we immediately walked to camp. We knew the way. Many prisoners joined us. Perhaps they too spent time locked up here. Or maybe they'd just heard about it. At the camp's main gate, the same inscription hung:

ARBEIT MACHT FREI
(Work liberates.)

Besides our group of prisoners, there were plenty of visitors with organized guides who knew the history and layout of the camp well. They started acquainting people with the grounds and Roman and I tagged along with one of these groups for about an hour, examining the facilities. We passed through the bathrooms which we once thought were gas chambers. We looked over the furnace, in front of it long, tin troughs in which people were placed and slid into ovens. We touched the barbed wire fence and checked out the tower where the guards stood ready with their machine guns. Furthermore, we examined the barracks and passed by number 17. We stayed in that barrack a bit longer.

In the barracks we checked out the triple bunks, toilets, and the yard in which we were so often counted. After some visitors learned that we were former prisoners, we narrated to them about how hungry we were and how often volunteers would go to work disabling bombs just to get breakfast, because we weren't fed otherwise. I explained how barrack number 17 was a transitional barrack that held nearly a thousand prisoners. But I spent most of my time explaining to them what it meant to be Ukrainian, and why we fought against both the Germans and Soviets.

After seeing the camp, including the moat, I once more

touched the barbed wire fence and looked at all the high poplars in front of the barracks.

Then Roman and I walked over to the registration building and ran into some government officials. They were managing the abandoned files of the former camp board. One of the officials took our names and our old ciphers and told us to wait a minute while he went to another room.

I looked back and saw queues of people passing by and marveling at this camp which burned and cremated so many people. And it did so so secretly that even nearby Germans didn't know what was happening behind these barbed wires. Among the passing Germans were also some in short leather pants, hats, and with funny looking hairbrushes. They walked by curiously, joining groups of visitors and ex-prisoners, asking about the details and happenings of what was going on here. They were stunned and couldn't believe that their government was so cruel not only to Jews but also to other nationalities.

The above mentioned officer came back and called us over. He gave both our hands a shake and said, "I'm glad you came out alive. I was also held here. How did the guards treat you as you were taken out of Landsberg?"

We told him how hungry, exhausted and wet we were, being led for three days and three nights, and how that last rainy night we were shoved into a sawmill, locked in, and how the Germans ran off that night.

We then looked over the extracted file brought out by the officer, and all that was written in it were our names and surnames, our non-Ukrainian nationalities, and the last concentration camp we were in. No other information was given. There wasn't a location or reason for our arrest.

Walking out of this registration building, we again carefully soaked up the sight of this monstrous camp. It looked to us very quiet. There was no sense of that former fear we'd felt the first time we were here.

Looking back over Dachau, I turned to Roman and said, "I want to catch up on lost time. As soon as possible, I want to continue my education. To look to the future and forget about the past."

Roman didn't agree: "First, we need to relax and go home."

On our way back to Munich, we sat on the other side of the train to get a new view, but it was the same. Everywhere, even in the suburbs, there lay broken walls of brick and stone. Many of the streets still hadn't been cleared, with passers-by zig-zagging amongst the rubble to find what was left of their homes.

We arrived in Munich and found ourselves with a two-plus hour layover. We decided to take a little stroll down the streets of Munich to see the life of a large city.

Many Germans were still living down in their cellars. Stores and all sorts of urban services also huddled down in basements or cellars, which had been the least damaged by bombing. We stumbled across a kitchen that served all that came hungry for nothing. Plenty of German soldiers stood in these queues, returning back from distant fronts. Roman and I were starving, so we joined them and got a slice of bread and some pretty good soup.

After eating, we went to the nearby pharmacy, which was also located in a basement. There we saw many soldiers obtaining different dressings, bandages, and medicine as well. It was all free of charge, but thankfully, we didn't need anything.

We walked down a street named Dachauer Strasse and soaked in the stunning sight - buildings laid in ruins, with a few homes somehow left in tact. People rushed in and out of the ones still standing. Whichever way we turned, there were hoards of people and all of them were in a hurry. It looked to me like we were the only two who could lazily wander down these streets, observing the bombed out houses and destruction of a world war.

We walked back to the station, boarded our train, and headed back to camp. After a while, the train arrived back at Gerlingen.

We ran into Basil Komar and his wife and told them all about our trip to Dachau. They said that they'd like to go sometime too, but under only one condition - that I went with them. I promised that I would when they were ready. They also complained about lice. Apparently camp was getting pretty dirty.

After listening to our stories, we found more ex-prisoners willing and wanting to go to Dachau. Roman promised them that he'd lead the way.

Just then, a group of Poles were dropped off in camp. They had working with bavors in a small village. Among them was a girl, and Roman fell in love with her at first sight. She spotted this infatuation and latched onto him as well.

It was literally that quick, and since that moment, he stuck to her side and they went to bed together every night. I advised him not to get tied up so quickly, but my tips were unsuccessful. Girls held an important place in his life.

A few days later, a second group went with Roman to visit Dachau. When they got back, Roman told me that he met a Ukrainian Greek-Catholic priest. My interest peaked. With the priest was a young man, and they both said that they weren't returning back to Ukraine.

"I almost got into a fight with them! I thought that they might be collaborating with the Germans and were afraid to go back because they didn't want to be punished," said Roman.

"Roman, calm down. If you were angry, you might have misunderstood them," I said.

But the group he'd gone with felt the same.

I changed the subject by telling them a story about the U.S. Military Garrison. They had arrived earlier that day with German civilian leaders, searching through our barracks:

"They were definitely searching for something, but none of us knew what it was. They didn't say. After the search, they gathered the entire camp and announced that German families were complaining of being terrorized at night. People are robbing them, destroying their vegetable gardens, stealing their chickens... a young calf and a pig were kidnapped too. They asked us if we might know anything about it. But none of us dared to say a thing. Then a former prisoner stood up and said, 'The Germans rob themselves! They just want to assign the blame on us!' One of the U.S. Representatives, who spoke German well, chose three people from our group, me among them! They investigated us individually, seeing if we might know someone in camp whose engaged in these thefts. But none of us broke, and we said that there was no such thing happening here in camp. The American prodded me even more, threatening me and saying, 'If I do find out that someone is stealing here in camp, you'll get no more food here. All of you will suffer.'

"Then, without hesitation, I replied that we are not engaged in such things. After that, he announced to us that from this day onward, he'd personally supervise the happenings of the camp.

"He continued: 'I've been appointed to the village of Gerlingen, and I'm now responsible for its order. I invite you, that if you have any personal problems, to come to my apartment, which is located nearby. And also, it's probable that this camp will soon be eliminated, because your turn has come up to get back to the Soviet Union.'"

After my story about the inspection, the group that Roman took to Dachau went back to their barracks to see if their possessions was overthrown. Roman was about to walk off too, but I asked him, "Do you remember exactly where the priest and his friend were going?"

"The outskirts of Munich, a town called Pasing," he said. "They were talking about a military chaplain of Ukrainian origin who served the American Army. They were going to visit him. But then my companions interrupted and scolded the priest, quarreling a bit. I don't know much else about them. Why do you want to know?"

I didn't want to keep my plans from Roman anymore.

"I've been thinking about whether anybody might stay here in Germany... Roman, I'm scared to go back. I don't want to be arrested by the Soviet police. You can go back safely. You were pulled out of Ukraine for work. You don't have suspicion against you like I do. And when you do return, please send word to my family, if anyone is left alive. And please, don't tell this to anyone."

His feelings lined up with mine and told me that we should get out of camp to make the possibility of staying a reality, rather than just talk about it.

"I feel bad now," Roman repented. "I feel bad that I so harshly responded to that priest. I won't condemn anyone else for staying."

We walked back to the barracks and after a moment he said, "Maybe I should think about whether or not *I'm* going home. My girlfriend told me that the first transports arriving will take people back to the Soviet Union. She said the Polish government came to an agreement with the Allies to send a second transport to Poland..."

This pleased me. If Poland was bringing awareness to the evils of returning back to the Soviet Union, maybe Ukrainians could avoid repatriation as well.

That evening, I met with the Komar family and told them about the priest on the train, about Pasing, and about the Poles being transported separately back to Poland. "This might be our opportunity to avoid returning back to the

Union."

The Komars both were pleased with such information, saying that they were sure that many Ukrainian citizens thought not to return back to Ukraine. But one thing worried us - What if trucks came to deport us as soon as tomorrow? What if they forced us? It had happened before. It can happen again.

I then decided that the next day I'd go to Pasing and find that priest at any price. Komar decided to come and persuaded me to take a third, his good friend who he vouched for. I can't remember his name. Komar, Roman, and I went to visit this man at once to tell him our intentions.

He rejoiced when we told him our plan and immediately said he wanted to come.

"Well you're lucky. Because that's why we came for you," said Komar, smiling.

Just after the sun rose, Basil Komar, his friend and I got up and started our journey for the unknown town, the unknown address, and the unknown chaplain. All we knew hinged on Roman's story - there was a town called Pasing and maybe an American military chaplain of Ukrainian descent was there.

After getting back on the train, we carefully listened to passengers conversations, asking them how far it was to a town called Pasing. We kept asking and asking and asking. No one seemed to know.

But then a man overheard our inquiries and told us that he'll give us a signal when it was time to get off. He did just so, we thanked him, and jumped off the train into the station.

Walking out into the street, we stopped and looked around - *Which way do we go? Who do we ask? And* what *do we ask?* This city was also bombarded, but not as badly as Munich. Then I saw a Latin Church with its tall tower higher than the neighboring buildings. *I could ask a priest about these Americans.*

To our happiness and joy, as we walked up to the church, we spotted an old pastor.

He very politely asked, "Why have you come here? What are you looking for?"

"We'd like to know if any American soldiers are here in town. We have a very important deal to make with their military chaplain," I said.

He curiously asked, "What nationality are you?"

"We're Ukrainians."

"Oh, I already know who you're looking for. Ukrainians looking for an American chaplain? I know exactly who this is. His named is Father Stachiw. Last Sunday he visited our church and served our holy liturgy. He's a very good man. Go to him and he will definitely help you. Many people have come here in search of him. You can get to his offices from here on foot. The buses are still quite infrequent and you're still young. It won't be tough," the priest said.

He wrote down the address and told us how to get there.

We thanked the priest for his guidance and for his warm words. Then we knelt down and earnestly prayed to God for this good fortune.

And even though that priest was quite old, his directions held true. We quickly and easily found ourselves at a house where we'd find a Father Stachiw. Now we just had to catch him at home.

We knocked on the door and an on-duty soldier answered and asked us something that was probably in English, something neither one of us understood. Confused, we began talking amongst each other in Ukrainian and he smiled and then greeted us in Ukrainian. We initially thought that we were going to have to work with this American officer, because at first glance, he was dressed as one. But as the Ukrainian came out of his mouth, I noticed the cross on his collar and realized that this was just the man we were looking for - Father Stachiw.

He led us into his bureau and asked us how we got there. We told him about Roman's train ride and the priest on board who came to visit him.

"That gave us the courage to come find you and ask for advice," I said.

Each of us then briefly described how we ended up in Germany and how we all expect danger if we return back home. We told him with regret that if we weren't actually persecuted, then of course we'd be most happy returning home to our families, as the people of other nationalities were doing. But we didn't know how safe that option was.

"Feel free to make yourselves at home," said Father Stachiw. He laid out some chewing gum for us and then found in his documents the address of an organization.

"Now I can't tell you what to do, but there is a place in Munich for you. You can get there today. Don't be afraid that you don't want to go back to Ukraine or want to stay in

Germany or even go to some other country. Here in Munich, there are a lot of people like you who are afraid to go back. There's a committee there which is in contact with the U.S. Government, and it can issue you a permit which gives you written permission to avoid repatriation, saying that you do not intend to return home because of the danger of Soviet persecution. There will be others there with problems similar to yours. Maybe you'll find some friends there too."

Father Stachiw then pulled out a single piece of chewing gum and began to chew it. "I know the fate of the Ukrainian people well, and I understand your dilemma. I hope that such an evil won't always lurk in Ukraine. And when the Ukrainian people do have their own state, who knows, maybe you'll go back there sometime."

We thanked him and were very happy that our man, an American of Ukrainian descent, was a military chaplain born in America yet still was so well spoken in Ukrainian and most of all, that he helped us in this great adventure. We said goodbye and thanked him again and said that we'd love to meet him again. He told us the way to the Ukrainian Committee and we were off.

From Father Stachiw's place, we happily went back to the same station that we disembarked from and soon thereafter sat down on a train back to Munich. The committee we were looking for was on the street Hohenzollern. So we got to Munich, got off the train, and asked a local man to show us how to get to the street car that led to Hohenzollern. He pointed out our journey, which wasn't far, and two street car rides later, we arrived.

Walking down the street, we met people talking to each other in Ukrainian. We then walked into a building and into the committee room and found all sorts of people being questioned by three officers sitting at tables. People asked questions of finding homes and food, some looking for their friends, and other people sat aside waiting, talking amongst themselves about their war experiences.

The women's stories were the hardest to hear. One woman told a story about the Soviet troops occupying the part of Germany she was taken to, terrorizing everyone, especially the women. She said that they raped not only German women, but women of their own as well. These Ukrainian women were trying to flee west from the Russians, but they ran into drunk soldiers who would yell and scream, "We released you from the Germans and you don't want to have sex with us?!"

These women and girls fought back and wept, but there was nobody around to save them. They were terrorized so much by the Soviets that they'd rather just stay here in Germany to die rather than return to the Union. These stories asserted our want to stay in the west even more.

Our turn came and we got a form from the officers that was printed in German, English, and Ukrainian. It stated that we were refugees, that we can't go back to the Soviet Union, because we'd be prosecuted there. We signed our names and the officers stamped them with government seals. Basil Komar asked for a certificate for his wife and I told the officer about the camp we were in and how it was going to be repatriated soon.

"There are others who don't want to go back. Could you give us a few more forms?" I asked.

He talked to the other officers and gave us five more forms.

After obtaining our certificates, we examined the walls of these rooms and noticed dozens of ads from all sorts of people seeking their families and friends. I stopped at one which stated that the former director of a gymnasium in Lviv, Volodymyr Radzykevych, was organizing a high school for Ukrainian students in a former German school and invited all those that wished to register. It was located on Boschetsrieder in southwest Munich. *A school for Ukrainians?* I walked back over to the officers and asked whether they knew something of this school.

"That announcement came up just a week ago and my son just went and enrolled. They're enlisting an increasing number of students. I think that they'll start class at the beginning of September, or maybe even earlier," he said.

He said told me best way to get there and I decided to go at the next opportunity.

But we didn't have much daylight left and there was nowhere to sleep in Munich. Basil Komar was also delighted about our meeting with Father Stachiw and our obtaining of these permits, so he and his friend wanted to return to Gerlingen to tell their friends about all this as soon as possible. We didn't want the repatriation to happen to the others before we got back.

On the road back to camp, I started planning my trip to that school. I was quite happy, because this day was filled with so many blessings - I have an opportunity to stay here in Germany, but also I get to immediately enroll in a Ukrainian high school, which the officers told me had already received official permission from Germany to open.

At camp, we knew of a few people impatiently awaiting our return who also had no intention of returning back to the Union. But we didn't want too many people to find out, especially those backing Soviet agendas. So all three of us agreed amongst ourselves that everything we'd learned in Munich we'd keep to ourselves and to our most trusted friends. After all we'd been through, we didn't want to end up in the wrong hands once again. There were Soviet political agitators slinking through camps and towns, and we didn't want to run into them.

At that moment, the train stopped and picked up a faction of Poles. These Poles told everyone on board that they were returning back to Poland, after the evacuations for the Soviet Union.

Hearing these stories, we three got our heads together and decided to start a rumor - Ukrainians from Galicia wouldn't have to travel with citizens of the Soviet Union - that they'd be going back on the transports to Poland, because it was more convenient. Why? Because all the other transports would be going to Moscow first. They'd be greeted by Stalin himself and the whole "family." If we were "officially" going on the second transport, then maybe we could avoid flack from those returning to the Union.

Komar told me that he counted nearly twenty people who didn't want to return. He thought we should all stick together as a group so that no one would touch us.

But I thought otherwise.

"Let those who want to stay, stay their course. And let us pretend like it's business as usual. I don't want to bring us any unnecessary suspicion. If we get a big group together, people will notice. They'll ask questions, and they'll probably figure us out," I said.

Basil agreed, "You're probably right. That sounds better."

When we got back to camp, I told Roman about our adventures in Pasing and Munich and jokingly reproached him, saying he caused us all this trouble with his little quarrel with the priest. I showed him my permit and that I also had one for him.

Roman examined mine from all sides and he was on board: "Thanks for thinking of me. And from now on, I'll be able to brag that because of my merit, you won't find yourself back in the motherland!"

However, I had to be further cautious with Roman, because he sometimes liked to drink with big parties that promoted departure to the motherland, and any plans we wanted to keep quiet seemed to leak from his mouth. So I passed him the certificate from the committee of not returning and told him that the Ukrainians from Galicia would be going back with the Poles, not the Soviets. I figured he might spread that rumor for us, but then to *my* surprise, Roman gave me the certificate back.

"Give it to someone else, Stepan. I can do without it. My Polish girl is quite happy. She's told all her friends how happy we are together. I'm going back with her on the second transport," he said. I didn't want to separate from Roman, but I wanted him to be happy too.

This news of the second transport spread fast. It calmed down many of the people who were nervous about returning to their native land. And nobody questioned where this news was coming from. Apparently everyone simply believed our little invention.

Peter the Russian no longer came up to me anymore. He got accustomed to hanging out with all the people returning back to Soviet society, and spent all his days among them. I was glad this was the case, because I didn't want to have to hide my plans of skipping repatriation. I didn't want to look suspicious.

A couple days later, I went back to Munich alone to find out more about this school. *How did it work? What was it's process? Where did they find the teachers?* After two previous visits to Munich already, I'd become quite comfortable with the area.

So I jumped on a tram that seemed headed in the right direction.

"How do I get to Boshatsrider Street?" I asked the German man next to me.

"I'm going there now. You can ride with me," he said. "But make sure you pay attention. It's hard to tell one stop from another, because the bombs destroyed the signs, and nobody's put them back up yet."

So I paid attention to the broken and fallen buildings. They were my new landmarks. A few stops later, the tram stopped, and my German companion gave me a sign. I was off.

The school wasn't far, and, as I walked in, an intense sensation of happiness overcame me. *I would continue my education, which Tato once so earnestly believed in!*

I wanted to tell him, "Thank you for convincing me to stay in school! Your dreams will continue to be fulfilled!"

But then doubt sunk in. I stopped. *Would they accept me without any school records? How much would it cost? I don't have any money.*

Before I'd taken the road that day, I borrowed 25 marks from Basil Komar, just in case. *Would that be enough?*

But my desire to enroll quickly overtook my anxiety, and I boldly dashed up the stairs to the second floor of the former German school. And somehow, this gray, cemented building hadn't been damaged at all by the war.

On the stairs, I met two youngsters, a boy and a girl who were walking down together, speaking to each other in Ukrainian. *Must be in the right place.* But I didn't ask any questions. I wanted to find it all out myself.

So I walked down the hallway, touring several classrooms that made a wonderful impression on me. They had simple, wooden benches for students, huge blackboards hanging off the walls, and desks for teachers to teach from. At last, I walked into an open room with white chalk letters written on a blackboard:

Registration for Ukrainian High School

An older man sat behind a desk. I said hello.

He very politely responded, "My name is Professor Korol. I'm taking registrants for the high school. My subject? Mathematics.

"I'm subbing for Director Radzekevych. He knows that there are a lot of misplaced Ukrainian youth in Germany, so he wants to rebuild our school here."

Professor Korol then spent the next hour asking me questions about my previous schooling, and based on my answers, he assigned me to the eighth grade.

But I was apprehensive: "I haven't taken any Latin, so eighth grade might be too tough."

He assured me: "If you can handle the other subjects, Latin won't be too alien for you. And you probably have your parents here so they'll encourage you to study instead of work."

"I'm alone here," I said. "I did time in the German concentration camps, but my Tato doesn't know where I am right now, because after he got arrested with me, we got separated."

"Hm. I want hear more, Stepan, but there are more registrants," he said. Two other students stood waiting in line behind me.

I thanked him for his good demeanor, and he told me to check out the calendar on the wall for start dates. Walking away from the table, I couldn't truly grasp or imagine what I was actually doing. *Where was I?* Some moments still left me feeling like I was under German command. I shuddered and tried shaking off the fear. Later on, I had nightmares of executioners abusing prisoners, killing prisoners... I'd see Max and Vili standing in the shtubas with sticks and driving out prisoners with their prods. *Could it be that it's all gone?*

Being free, it was hard to me believe that I was actually on my own, and that I didn't have to avoid being hit by a stick...

"No, I'm not there anymore," I kept telling myself. *"I'm looking at my new school calendar and will soon learn from the professors of a Ukrainian high school. And where? In Munich... NOT in a concentration camp."* After that I found myself repeating, *"This time I am free. Free! A prisoner no more!"*

I read and re-read the class schedules and pulled out a pencil and recorded the details. And I didn't have to hurry back to camp, because my train wasn't departing for a few hours, so I hung around for some time in the registration room and again examined the entire building. I also wanted to meet the other two students who spoke with the professor to find out where Ukrainians lived around here.

After some time they both came out of the registration room. They were happy that they both were admitted to the same grade too, eighth.

The girl was cordial, with a beautiful smile, and introduced herself, "My name is Stefa Peretska."

Next to her was a young, slender, and good looking student named Nicholas Plawjuk. Both of them were quite funny and talkative.

"We'd love to talk, but we can't. We're already late for our next appointment," Stefa said.

The three of us walked out together and immediately hopped onto our respective trams. Heading back to the station, I took a good look to avoid accidentally getting out at the wrong stop and kept track to make sure I could get back to the school next time. The landmarks I received from the German on the way to school were quite helpful. I jumped off the tram and took another one to the central station.

Back at Munich's central station, I was so happy. I wanted to tell my most trusted friends all about it. They'd probably ask me things like:

How often will you go to Munich?

Maybe just part time?

Or are you going to leave us and move closer to school?

I got on the train happily and watched sights of broken Germany pass me by on the way back to Gerlingen.

When I got back to camp, I told my friends about my trip. They were happy for me and promised to help me in any way they could.

Roman said, "During the days that you're gone, I'll grab your food for you and hold onto it until you get back." I thanked him. That would do for now.

That night, the field in the middle of camp attracted many people. Nobody had anything to do except wait for departure, grab food in the kitchen, and party in the evenings. Many people took advantage of this chance to amuse themselves, saying that this limbo time wouldn't last forever. And what awaited them on the other side anyway? Job and duties. So the music played and the willing came together, young and old alike.

SEPARATION

I joined them for a while, looking at the musicians and dancers. I stared at the faces that looked as if they were trying to live their entire lives in an evening. They danced, joked, and finished up with songs. And then a Polish group arrived and asked the musicians to play some of their polkas and Polish national dances. So the night went and people rejoiced in being alive.

My eyes then caught a man carrying a red flag. He was followed by others as well. They halted near the musicians and one man preached, "Praise a happy life in the Soviet Union! Praise the invincible Red Army! Praise Stalin! And denounce these German fascists! Let's call for an even greater victory!"

After a few exclamations and the rest of his speech, the music went on and the fun continued. But my not-so-long-ago Russian concentration camp comrades interacted with me less and less, joining the voices that so proudly praised Stalin.

Our Ukrainians from the East and Belarusians gathered together with those Russians as well, playing about with them, but at that moment I didn't see any of them actively campaigning for the return to the motherland. They rather just seemed to be sifting into the stream of the Russians.

Smiles, dances, carouses and singing continued late into the night. But I felt anxious that night and figured I should go to bed soon, though I knew with such cries, it would be hard to fall asleep. As I walked back to the barracks, a Belarusian girl interrupted my thoughts, latched onto me and pulled me along.

But I pushed her away. I looked at her and she looked

quite a bit older than me. I refused her company and then with insult and strife she started berating me. But I paid no attention and went back and laid down in my bed. After seeing what I saw tonight, I wanted no part in any partying.

I thought for a big about tomorrow's possibilities and then fell into a sound slumber.

CHAPTER TWENTY-ONE

REPATRIATION

Up until now, if people partied all night, then early the next morning the camp would be relaxed and quiet. But this morning was different. I was woken up by shouts coming from the yard.

"Trucks are on their way! After breakfast, you'll be loaded and taken out of camp!"

I quickly jumped out of bed, splashed some water on my eyes and rushed over to my neighbor Komar who had just woken up.

"Komar, let's get to the main transport commander and ask him to announce that the only people who depart today are those who were citizens of the Soviet Union before the Second World War," I told him. "Those who were citizens of Poland prior to 1939, will leave on the second transport."

That would legally put us on the second transport, even though we had no plans of taking it.

Basil told his wife where we were going, splashed some water on his eyes, and we were off to look for the repatriation commander.

"What happens if he doesn't want to do what we say?" said Basil.

"He must. He must say that the Poles will go in the next transport. And what would it hurt him to make such a small change? One that could help *us* so much!" I said.

We also agreed not to show him the certificates we received from the Ukrainian Committee in Munich, unless we had no other choice.

I wonder if any representatives of the Soviet government were here? Or would the Americans alone be carrying out our evacuation? I'd heard rumors of such representatives coming to camp, but I still hadn't seen them.

Basil and I approached the tarpaulin covered military Jeep that sat next to a group of American soldiers and several citizens. When we got near, one of the soldiers asked us what we needed. We answered that we wished to speak with whoever headed the repatriation of the camp.

The soldier replied, "Everything is already prepared for the transport. The train is already waiting."

"Yes, we know everything, but we want to ask the commander what we can carry with us."

Then one of the military officers, interested in our questioning, approached us. He spoke to the soldier in a language we didn't understand, probably asking about what we were talking about, and then he turned and asked us, with quite good Polish, "What do you need?"

Good! Polish! Nobody else will know what we are saying.

I asked, "So this transport is only for people who came from the Soviet Union?"

He confirmed, saying, "Yes. A second truck will arrive here later, and it'll go to Poland."

"Could you please clearly announce this to everyone in camp? We've heard many who are returning to the Soviet Union spread rumors that there would be no division in the groups, that we would all go together to Poland and the Union."

This officer listened to us very carefully and suited: "I will."

I then asked him, "Could you please say that those who lived in Poland before World War II, up until September 1, 1939, will return back on the second transport? It would make it more clear."

Our Ukrainian Galicia, where I was from, was under Polish rule before '39.

He wrote this date in his registry and promised us to do so. Basil and I both thanked and praised him that he knew the Polish language so well. At that moment, more transport trucks arrived at camp, and the officer was called to a meeting.

Basil and I rejoiced that we could so easily come to an understanding with the repatriating commander. Most campers were still sleeping, cleaning, or packing, and it looked as though nobody else noticed Basil and I talking to the officer. I was relieved.

We walked back to the barracks and told our friends about the conversation. Some of them were just waking up and couldn't believe that we had figured all this out already. The former fear of a violent repatriation to "the motherland," the fear that haunted them day after day, had melted away. We then asked them to pretend that everything was normal and that we were all getting ready for departure.

Camp people started to rush about, preparing, packing, and finishing up breakfast. Suddenly, an announcement came over the loudspeaker:

"ALL RESIDENTS OF THE CAMP ARE TO APPEAR IN THE MAIN SQUARE."

This announcement didn't need to be repeated. Campers hurriedly gathered to hear the news. Joy was buzzing! Campers were so excited about returning to their families. Poles also gathered on this field, their curiosity circling about whether their return will be mentioned. Among them were also us who would stay.

Roman came near me and warned, "Those who don't return might be threatened by propagandists."

I then told him about my meeting with Basil and the commandant this morning. Roman calmed down a bit and said, "I'll stay by your side. The more of us, the less others will think to attack."

There was another mystery to all this. *How will the Belarusians react?* Before the war, they also partly lived under Polish rule. *What will they do with this later departure? They yearned for their land just as much if not more than the Russians or Ukrainians! Would they split in two?* They made up about a third of all the residents here, so I wondered how sharp their posture would be towards this news. I also wondered if the Russians would catch on to any Belarusian agitation and ask us why we were going back with the Poles.

SEPARATION

After we all assembled in the field, the officers of repatriation drove up in the tiny tarp-covered Jeep. The American officer we first talked to climbed up on the bumper, and he invited up a civilian as well. The officer greeted us all in English, but no one in the camp understood.

Then the civilian translated his words into German and said, "This is the captain of the American Army. He wanted to greet you and to wish you all a happy journey."

And as if they'd planned beforehand, campers cried out "U-S-S-R! U-S-S-R! U-S-S-R!"

The civilian man went on, "The motor trucks will arrive at each barrack, and they shall accommodate you. You can take with you everything you've acquired here in Germany."

"Where is this transport going?" asked a camper.

"To the Soviet Union," he replied.

In response, the crowd again hollered "U-S-S-R! U-S-S-R!" and ceased when the captain came over the loudspeaker. This time he addressed the assembly in Polish and declared that a second transport will travel to Poland soon. His announcement was welcomed by the Poles. I didn't notice any backlash or surprise to this announcement. The captain then pulled out a note and said that the second transport will take everyone who lived in Poland up until September 1, 1939.

We Ukrainians who thought not to go back were very pleased by this announcement. And here, as we assumed, a group of Belarusians inquired the captain, asking him why they have to wait for a second truck.

"Why can't we just go right away?"

The captain listened and agreed, "Whoever wants to ride

in the current transport can do so, and he who wants to return later, do so."

This response excited them, and they all went back to prepare for their departure.

It was all going according to plan. Even better than the plan!

At that moment, trucks drove up to the barracks to pick up individuals and whole families and all their goods. Argument and quarrels arose.

"This is mine!"

"No, mine!"

Others started grabbing chairs and tables.

"You can't take those!" said others.

Whatever could be taken, seemed to belong to somebody, or multiple people. Others started arguing over collapsable beds.

The American soldiers just stood and watched all this silently and probably thought, "When is everything going to be loaded so we can get on with this already?" But they said nothing to anybody.

Whoever wanted whatever they wanted carried it out and put it on the truck.

After several hours, things were loaded and residents settled in on the trucks. They rejoiced at all the things they could fit. But then we heard a shattering of a barrack window. We looked over and people were unhinging doors and flipping furniture. They were cracking walls open and carrying out threats, saying, "Leave nothing for the Germans! Let them know and remember how they treated us during the war!"

At first, the Americans didn't respond to these outrages.

But then smoke started seeping out of a barrack. Once the captain noticed this, he immediately ordered his soldiers to put it out. At that moment, he also gave the signal to get the transport moving down the road. Campers lived it up until the last minute, grabbing all they could and filling suitcases to the brim. I walked amongst everyone, examining the scene. But nobody paid attention to me, because everyone was too busy packing and thinking of home.

After some time, I went inside the barrack and watched through a window, wondering how these campers got so many things. But I was glad and sided *with* them, taking for them whatever was needed for they truly did earn necessary things likes beds and furniture from Germany. And the demolishing of these barracks brought no harm to the Germans. When the second transport leaves, I figured that they would dismantle the rest anyway. They were almost doing the Germans a favor and it was a good way for people to let out their anger.

In such a confusion, no one said goodbye to each other, because most people figured that everyone else was leaving. They looked out for themselves. After the Soviet transport was loaded, the former prisoners looked back and saw that some of us stayed behind and shouted:

"Izmyennikamy!" (turncoats!).

"We'll find you!"

"Why aren't you coming with?" - amongst a variety of other abuses.

I felt sorry for these people, because none of them could even begin to imagine how they would be taken back by their "rodina" (family) in Russia. Looking at this repatriating convoy, I watched the faces of those who I befriended, whom I just spent the last few post-war months with. I wondered what kind of fate was waiting for us who stayed. After saying goodbye without a true hand shake, joy and sadness enveloped me. Joy because I didn't have to go back to Soviet "paradise." Sadness, because I was jealous that I couldn't go back to Ukraine.

At that moment, Roman's girlfriend approached him and said, "Are you sorry that you and the others didn't return home?"

She saw sadness and dissatisfaction in his face.

Roman didn't answer her, but said, "I'll come see you later. I need to be alone."

Roman and I then joined up with the Komar family and consulted to have all the scattered Ukrainians moved into a smaller and more well-kept barrack. It had several rooms inside that once housed separate families. We hurriedly moved over to the barrack before any unknown people might try to move in and by the end of the day, we were settled. To my surprise, another family joined up with us too, one from Eastern Ukraine, who didn't want to return back to the Union either. It was a young couple that always stuck together and kept mostly to themselves.

They told us that they had kept an eye on us and heard of the possibility of not returning back to Soviet Ukraine. Figured they'd do the same as us from Galicia. They didn't return with the others because they were convinced that an awful penalty awaited them.

When we were choosing rooms, Roman asked, "So are you going to stay here in camp or find somewhere to live near the school?"

"Tough for me to say right now," I said, "because I don't know how long the train will continue being free and the winter's coming."

We agreed that we still had time to solve this problem, but in the mean time we picked out a room for both of us, which would fit two beds and adjoined to a small kitchen.

"I like this room," said Roman, "and if you do decide to move out, then my girl will come live with me."

After our move, we Ukrainians all walked about the other freed barracks. Windows were busted out, doors were on the ground, beds were broken, drapes were torn, mattresses cut, and the floor was filled with garbage.

All the kitchen utensils had disappeared. Tables and chairs, except the old and broken, were all gone too. Everything was taken away. Not even a knife or a spoon remained.

The woman who was in charge of the kitchen then approached us. She said that she filed a report to Gerlingen, saying she was no longer engaged in kitchen duties. She said that she had some leftover food for us and more food parcels would be delivered once a week. In order to decide how much food came, we gave her a list of everyone that was still left in camp.

"From this day forward, you cook for yourselves, or you figure out another way to cope with your hunger," she said.

I walked through the barracks and examined them

carefully. Just one day ago, they were noisy, and now suddenly they had become deaf and desolate. Up until now, they were loud and fun and everyone danced. Entertainment was everywhere. But it was as if life had died. The funny musicians would never return.

That night, we stood in groups and reflected on what might happen to us. We were approached by a few Poles and asked why we didn't go home with the others. We told them our fear about suffering persecution. Some of them also replied that they were afraid and that perhaps they might not go back either. They had hope that maybe they could move to Western Europe, or perhaps even further to America.

That night, even with the unknown future, I went to bed with a good and quiet disposition and slept as never before. I was pleased that we managed to somewhat happily part with those reuniting with Soviet Russia. My thoughts led me to sleep.

CHAPTER TWENTY-TWO

UKRAINIAN HIGH SCHOOL IN MUNICH

At last it was August 1945, and it was time for my first day of school in Munich.

The train that morning was crowded, but I found myself a seat. Once again, there was quite a variety of people. Some with bags, others with folders or suitcases. All of them were in such a hurry. Some were in Yugoslavian and Hungarian uniforms. Most of them were Jews. Some of them talked about trade and the black market. Some spoke of travel to America and some to Palestine. I learned about how repatriation to the Soviet Union was going and how the Americans ended the war with Japan. I also heard that the German trains and trams in Munich would soon cease to run for those without tickets. To that moment, my lack of money didn't really concern me. I didn't need it, well, besides when I wanted to grab ice cream near the train station on these hot summer days. Then I overheard a few Jews talking trade.

"I'm selling chocolate and American cigarettes," one told his friends. "I buy them in camp and resell them to Germans for more. Or we trade. There's a demand for chocolate in

Germany right now, so they're paying a good price for it. At the main train station in Munich, traders and brokers barter for chocolate with money or jewelry, including gold."

This all got me quite interested, because the day before I got two large chocolates. I ate half of one and saved the rest for later.

After I got off the train in Munich, I saw people trading goods among the station debris. *Tomorrow, I'll come back with my chocolate and make a deal!*

From the main station, I walked about the city, grabbed some school supplies, and then jumped on the tram and went to school. There I found pupils of all ages. I acquainted myself with them and walked in with my few pencils, two notebooks, and a rubber eraser. The entire high school was assembled into one big room, and we were greeted by the high school Director, Professor Vladimir Radzekevych. He was quite thin, medium height, and slightly hunched over. He introduced himself first and then he introduced the Professor of Ukrainian language and writer Oles Babij, Professor Korol of Mathematics, and Professor Riznyk, who would teach physics and chemistry. The director told us that other professors would be introduced to us as classes were more organized. He seemed very nice and friendly.

"Oh, and please note that we might get transferred from this building to one of the larger camps now being prepared for Ukrainians living near Munich called Karlsfeld. If this happens, there will be enough room for our school *and* for housing, so don't worry. We'll issue you a certificate that says you're students of our high school and then you'll immediately be assigned a place to sleep in camp."

He then shook every professor's hand and wished them success. We students divided up and went off to class.

Our first lecture was with the poet and writer Oles Babii. He approached the 14 of us and inquired each of us about our brief war history. He stayed with me a bit longer when he heard that I was arrested by the Germans and sent to concentration camps. One of his friends was thrown into camps as well. Hearing one story after another of how these 13 other students came together was fascinating. They told stories of how they got to Munich, many of them escaping westward through Hungary, Slovakia, the Czech Republic, Poland, Austria... many just a few steps ahead of Soviet troops. I could listen to these stories for hours.

Oles Babii then started the lecture and spoke about writers. He first chose poet and author Ivan Franko, whom with he had been friends and neighbors. He talked about some of his major works, his life philosophies, about his patriotism, his difficulties, his family life, and at the end of his lecture he added some human aspects of Franko - that part of a famous author's life that is sometimes easy to forget.

"Although Ivan Franko was a great writer, in actual life, he was helpless. His friends always mocked him, saying that they'd be sure some day he'd be trampled on the streets of Lviv like some nobody. He wouldn't even tie the strings of his pants up to keep them clean, lazily dragging them along the streets and getting them dirty," said Babii.

After class, as students walked out of Oles's lecture, we talked and bragged and argued over which of us knew most about Franko. Then one of the students said, "Oles Babii, though also a well known writer and poet, seems like he sins by the same nature as Ivan Franko. A black tie hung around his neck that might have been knotted before the *first* world war!"

All of us students laughed at his remark. Young people sure do have quite the imagination.

Over the next three weeks, I studied in Munich. New students came joined our class every week, and Director Radzykevych divided us into sections. All our classes were in Ukrainian and German, and English was a separate subject.

When we weren't learning, many of us students were still very interested and tied to what was happening in Ukraine and the Soviet Union.

After lectures, I would hang out at the main train station and do homework amongst the broken pieces of cement. And because of the Director's announcement that we'd be moving soon, I didn't ask the other students where they were living or whether there was room for another.

The next day, I took all my chocolate to the train station black market. Step by step I got closer to the traders and closely observed how they bartered, because I had no idea what I was doing. After seeing a couple trades, I figured out the system and saw how the buyers all mutually warned each other when there were German or American police in sight. Apparently, if they were caught by the police doing underground trades, they'd get all their goods and money confiscated and get chased away from the station. With all this and the fact that I had to be at school soon, I decided to sell my chocolate as soon as possible.

One trader approached me and asked me what I needed.

"I have chocolate for sale," I said.

"Show it to me," he said.

I did. He went off to his accomplice, and they both agreed to something. He then came back and said, "It's quite expensive chocolate. I'll pay you 120 German marks for it."

At the time, that was a lot of money. I agreed.

He stretched out his hand and said, "Let me have the chocolate first, and I'll give you the money."

"I don't believe you. Pay me first," I said.

He then began to complain in some language I didn't know and pulled out a wad of money from his pocket and counted it all in front of me. In the meantime, he also called over his friend.

He paid me 20 marks, and said, "Now do you believe me that I'll pay? Give me the chocolate or I'll find someone else."

I needed to get to school soon and the rest of the money was right there in his hands.

So I gave him the chocolate.

But then his big friend appeared and the first guy turned away from me, saying, "That's all you get."

I was dumbfounded. Cheated. But both of them were healthy looking and were ready to put up a good fight against my 5'2" frame. I then regretfully and angrily left, only somewhat satisfied by the 20 marks. *At least I got 20.*

I didn't tell anybody at school that day and only told

Roman when I got back to camp that evening.

He looked at me confidently and said, "Tomorrow, we will go to Munich together. I'll teach them how to deal with honest people."

"No, no, we don't have to do that," but he insisted and I could by no means convince him otherwise.

"But I don't have any more chocolate," I said, figuring that would end the conversation. I really didn't want to mess with those black market traders again.

"My girl still has one. We'll go sell it for her," he said.

I ended up agreeing in the end and figured that maybe he would reconsider after a night's sleep.

But I was wrong. The next morning, when I got up, Roman already was up and ready, so I didn't argue and we went together to Munich.

At the Munich station, we walked over to the traders. Buyers approached us and asked us what we had for sale. But Roman refused and wouldn't sell it to anyone besides those two who I dealt with the previous day. Then I spotted one of those crooks up ahead of us.

I pointed him out to Roman, he spotted us, and said, "He probably recognizes me and wants to escape."

The man slowly started to creep away.

But Roman insisted on waiting until the second man appeared too, and then he alone would approach them. I couldn't believe Roman's confidence. But then the crook moved a little further and further and then started sprinting away. We ran after him but lost him and our search ended fruitlessly.

"They won't be back," said Roman.

After a short standstill, Roman called one of the traders to him and asked him whether he'd like to buy a chocolate. This trader saw Roman and me and didn't seem like in much of a hurry to deal. He looked at us like maybe we were going to cheat him. However, the giant piece of chocolate in Roman's hand convinced him otherwise.

The trader went off to his friend, came back, and offered 150 marks for it.

"I want 200," said Roman.

"180."

Then Roman put out his hand, and they shook on it. He pulled out the 180, gave it to Roman, and Roman gave him the chocolate.

I stood there in wonder. *How different this was from yesterday! This is what a trade looks like with honest people!* Those thieves had exploited me.

Roman then gave me 120 marks that I needed for school and for his girlfriend he kept the other 60.

I was so appreciative of Roman, because this money would help me pay off my school fees.

CHAPTER TWENTY-THREE

STARTING ANEW IN KARLSFELD

It was early September 1945, and our high school had moved from Munich to Karlsfeld, where several thousand Ukrainian people now lived. Even the camp council was Ukrainian. The police standing at the gates, who preserved the order in the camp, were all Ukrainian. The camp kitchen was led by Ukrainian women. In the administration building, there was a medical care facility with Ukrainian doctors.

In some buildings, there was space allocated for temporary churches, which served the everyday needs of believers. There was even a sports club named Lions. A choir was organized. There were youth groups similar boy scouts called Plast and Cym(pronounced soom), a trade school, a drama group, and still other organizations. Performances were held by Ukrainian musicians like Vladimir Blavatsky and Yosyf Hirniak. And the religious and cultural events were all organized quite majestically as well. A large hall was re-built that could hold several thousand people. In the past, this hall was used to house the German army.

The barracks were all two stories tall. The buildings were

in good condition, some housing entire families and some housed single people. The whole camp was covered in greenery and was quite close to the forest. Many people took strolls through the trees, looking for personal space or intimate getaways. My eighth grade class grew to 120 students and had to be divided up into three different classes. And a dozen more prominent professors including Vasilij Stetsyuk, Fedusevych, Tofan, Vaskovych, Hayda, Stepanenko, Syrotunsky, Antonovich, O. Tarnavetsky, and still others joined the school.

And through all this, I had a difficult time parting with my dear friend Roman and the other good friends that flanked my sides after the war. As I was getting on the train from Gerlingen for what seemed to be the last time, they gave me a big farewell, like I was truly one of their own brothers. They promised me that if I needed anything, they would still be in Gerlingen, so I could return whenever I wanted to. I promised them that when I knew anything else about opportunities to emigrate to other countries, I'd inform them immediately.

After that, I only returned from Karlsfeld to Gerlingen once more, because the trains began to cost money. I found that Roman had been getting double rations from my food card for a while. The last transports for Poland were also sent out and shortly thereafter the camp in Gerlingen was completely dismantled and given back to the Bavors to raise crops.

In Karlsfeld, I was assigned to live in the student building, which was housed in the first block, where students were broken down by individual classes. I was assigned to a room with Paul Kohut, his brother Nicholas, Basil Shuja, Nicholas Plavyuk, Janoslaw Trakalo, Roman Stawowyj, Eugene Wagner, Miroslav Stec, Ihor Kostecki, Ivan Shumylo, and William Tkachuk.

Nicholas Plavyuk and I had several disputes about the UPA, but after about half a year, I learned to enjoy our conversations, eventually sharing meals together and sleeping in the same bunk, him below me.

Another memory also sticks out because of our reformation of social classes. Since I got out of prison, I didn't really have a chance to buy new clothes. Half of mine were still military leftovers. And I didn't want to steal. But these military clothes were worn out and weren't even my size to being with. So I went over to the social care section of camp, which received used clothes from America, and very politely told them my problem and asked for help. But no one would listen. Nobody showed me any empathy for the fact that all my clothes were taken from me because of the war. The only response I could get was that the pupils in the lodging would all get the same clothing, so that we could be identified as students.

I went back to my barracks with a little hope. But then the next day my roommate walked in with new clothes from that exact same office that assured me we'd all get the same clothes.

So I returned back a second time to that "social care section" and the doors were shut on my face, and the employee said, "All the apparel was distributed. We don't have any more." I left discouraged.

On holidays, such as Christmas and Easter and others, I had to borrow clothes from William Tkachuk, so I wouldn't stand embarrassed with ragged and over-sized clothes.

And once camp settle a bit, the camp was divided into groups of different privileges, and the leaders of these groups quarreled about regional and religious views.

It was at that time that I decided that I would never put myself in a position to ask for help from anyone.

Within half a year, delegates from Soviet Union arrived under the supervision of American police. They tried to persuade the inhabitants of Karlsfeld to return back to the "motherland."

At first, these delegates created a panic and fear that the American Army would appear and help these Soviet officials forcefully repatriate all the former nationals to the Soviet Union. But none of the camp inhabitants listened. They didn't believe the propaganda, but rather ridiculed it and whistled, yelling:

"We know all your lies well!"

"If Soviet Russia is so good, then you yourself go live with your god in Siberia!"

"We will not be slaves in order to feed you!"

They tried coming again and again, but the inhabitants started threatening them:

"Don't come back if you value your *precious* life!"

At the camp gates, police were set up and didn't let the propagandists in anymore. However, many of these Soviet delegates somehow wandered in anyway and spread fear amongst the residents. And the fear came from this - the Allies, who themselves fought against Germany, signed a document that said all former Soviet citizens had to return back to the Soviet Union, and where the need be, force would be used. Several camps began to be liquidated with American-approved force back to their "native land."

Desperation to avoid Soviet life skyrocketed. In protest, dozens of people committed suicide by throwing themselves and their children into rivers to drown.

Seeing this, the Western Powers quickly came to their senses and in short time abandoned this forceful repatriation.

In late Autumn of 1945, Karlsfeld was completely full. Two of my friends from Uherci, Ivan and Peter Kantsyari, as well as their friend Shport of Stodilok, showed up alive and wanted to live in Karlsfeld, but there was no place for them. They were sent to a camp called Frayman in Munich.

During my stay at Karlsfeld, I contributed quite heartily to the Ukranian community, including attending high school, joining the youth organization PLAST, and becoming a leader amongst the eighth graders. I recited by heart many important Ukrainian works such as the "Tower of Bernadine" by Oles Babij, on the holiday of Andrey Sheptytsky I did Theodore Kurpity's "Large Metropolitan," and in the academy, in honor of Taras Shevchenko, Ukraine's most well-known writer, I recited his "Dream (Mountains of Mine So High)."

Indeed my joy in camp Karlsfeld was great. However, I just couldn't seem to share this joy with others, because none of them were family.

I wanted to share my accomplishments with my Tato and my Mama, who had so much hope for me, who had encouraged me so that I could have a better life than they did. I wanted to tell them how I passed my final exams and graduated from the high school with the best grades in the entire eighth grade.

But they weren't there. I never saw my Mama or my Tato ever again.

CHAPTER TWENTY-FOUR

Epilogue :: What happened to my family?

My second trip with my wife to Ukraine ended July 19, 1994. That day we flew by plane from Kiev Boryspil International Airport to John F. Kennedy Airport in New York. On the plane back to America, I had a good opportunity to quietly remind myself once again of all those events of my arrest in 1944.

This trip gave me the chance to talk to my sister Maria, my brothers Michael, Oles, and Volodymyr, as well as my cousin Michael Burbura and my friends from before I was arrested, Stephan Chornenky and Stephan Korobchak. Chonenky's dad was the village leader before my Tato. They helped me remember what had happened. I hadn't seen some of them since 1944.

Of Stephan Chornenky's huge family, only his youngest sister Mary was still alive. She somehow survived with her twin sister Irka after fleeing from a transport that was headed for Siberia after Tato and I were arrested. They spent years hiding in fields, forests, and neighboring villages, often being chased by the KGB and its loyal supporters. During the winter, the sisters slept in open fields as close as they could to fresh piles of manure to stay warm. Hunger, cold, and fear was such a common companion that their minds often raced, wondering if it would not be easier for them to get exported to Siberia instead of escaping and wandering.

I decided to go back to Lontsky Prison in Kiev, a place that supplanted in me such a strong image that to this day, I still can't get it out of my head. I still hear the click of the iron locks, the knocking of the heavy German boots, the sounds of the prison guards striking prisoners, and the groans of prisoners being interrogated.

That day, when I visited the prison, I still felt the same terror from when I was seventeen. When I entered the main doors of the prison, the military guard stopped me and asked what we needed there. My brother Oles and his son Stephen were also with me.

"We'd like to see the inside, especially the second floor," I said.

He replied politely, "Why are you interested in *this* building? And why the second floor?"

I explained to him that I had come from America and I was arrested by the Germans and detained here in 1944. The guard told us to wait as he went over to talk to his superior.

The head of the military guard came out and asked, "What do you need here?"

I explained that I was writing my memoirs about my arrest by the Nazis and wanted to remember a bit more about the inside of the prison. I showed him my picture from Olching, still wearing my striped prison rags. This chief then gave me his hand and said that we were welcome to go where we needed. I thanked him and he showed us the way to the second floor.

Walking up the steep, winding, and squeaky wooden stairs, I didn't see the iron partitions that once stood at the openings of the floors. The prison corridors looked to me just as long but not as wide. And being so long, it was tough for me to guess which chamber I was once held. They were all closed at the moment too. But I did get into one room where there were several secretaries and a few open windows so that I was able to look out into the prison yard, where we once were led out to walk. This yard, for some reason, looked a lot smaller than I remembered.

We had no supervisor to tour us around the prison, so we couldn't request to get into any chambers. All the officers seemed very busy, either hurriedly disappearing off somewhere or explaining cases while surrounded by people.

Maybe because of a great fear in my subconscious, I had no courage to hang out any longer in this prison and ask for more information from the officers. That same day, I went outside and looked at the prison Brygidky that was located on the former Kazymyrivska Street, now Horodetsky. The doors to that prison were locked and the main gate was as well. Some of the windows were busted and covered with a strongly fastened plywood. I couldn't tell if the prison was still in use today or not. However, its appearance didn't make such a depressing impression like visiting Lontsky, maybe because I wasn't there as long.

Throughout this trip, I questioned my siblings about what happened to them after my arrest, but I spoke mostly with my sister Maria, because she was the oldest of us and she remembered the most. We spent a lot of time talking together.

She told me that several months after our arrest, the Soviet Army returned. She also told me about my friends, some who were still alive, some who had disappeared, and some who went on further to study. As for our family, it was difficult to survive without Tato and me.

She talked about who of our extended family helped them the most and how the war finally ended between the Soviets and the Germans. She told me that the family looked for me and Tato even before the end of the war.

During that time after the war, whole transports of former Soviet citizens who'd been forced to work in Germany returned back. Among them were Jews and prisoners of war. Some of them returned voluntarily. Some were caught and were forced to return to "The Motherland."

Watching these prisoners come back, our whole family impatiently expected the return of Tato and me. But then people began circling rumors that some of those who gladly returned to The Motherland, were instead deported to Siberia. Among them were former soldiers of General Vlasov*.

My family hoped that Tato and I actually lived and would return back, because they had apparently gotten my one letter

I had sent from camp Heinkel, where I wrote that I lived and worked. They also received a similar letter from Tato. Those were the only letters they got from either of us, because by that time, the German front had already retreated west onto Polish land.

So time soon turned over and the war ended and many returned, but Tato and I did not. The transports from Germany began to bring less and less people, and then finally stopped.

Mama and the rest of the family began to worry. Each subsequent day, they shed a layer of hope for our return, and they thought that maybe both of us ended up dead. So passed the summer and Tato and I did not return.

*the German collaborator who was mentioned earlier in the book on the first day of the death march

Maria explained that the postwar year in Ukraine was very difficult. Many lands were left unused. Many things went missing. There was little food, little clothing, and meager stores of coal and wood to heat up houses. Mama paced around with melancholy and wondered how her family could cope like this and survive during such a difficult time of year.

Then, all of a sudden, in November 1945, a military truck arrived in the village. In it was Tato, with a young boy who spent time with him in a German concentration camp. The boy came from a village, which lay near the town of Rudky, where our brother Michael drove him the next day in the cart.

The commander who brought them both into our yard,

with admiration for Tato, told our family and neighbors about Tato's experiences. The villagers gathered around the commander's car, greeted Tato and asked him many different questions.

Apparently Tato had returned so late because when the other detainees and prisoners were brought back from Germany, he was very ill and enfeebled by hunger. When he finally did become healthy, he himself voluntarily went to the British forces and requested that they sent him to the zone occupied by the Soviet Army, which he thought would get him closer to Ukraine. On the border, he was joyfully welcomed by authorities and provided transport home.

Unspeakable joy enveloped the whole family to see Tato alive. They felt sorry for him too and told the neighbors to give him a little rest and to come later or the next day to talk to him.

"Give us first the opportunity to spend time with him," requested Mama. Tato was one of the most giving and active members of the village, so many of the people wanted to see him.

So curious villagers came in for the next several days and asked Tato about his stay in Germany. Maria said there was no end to the questioning! Tato told everybody several times about his severe experiences that he suffered in the Germany concentration labor camps.

The Soviet KGB agents even came to hear his story to make sure he wasn't a threat, but they were convinced that all Tato spoke of were the evil German prisons, so they left him alone. In their presence, he said that after the war he went nowhere else besides the hospital, and that he knew nothing else. After listening to his stories, they praised him and were most convinced that he survived a great tribulation in Germany.

After several days and some rest, the family and some neighbors began to get more courageous with their curiosity and were eager to learn why he came back without me. He was not very happy to report, and even when he spoke he became very sad and uncertain.

He said that he sometimes doubted whether I lived, because he saw firsthand how many prisoners were unable to survive until the end of the war. He assumed that if I was alive, that I would come back home.

Tato also said that while in the camps he felt close to moving on to the next world. In camps, his work was very hard - he worked long hours and received minimal food. He carried stones, working on roads, loading coal, carrying debris to clear out bombed buildings, and digging trenches against airstrikes. He always went hungry, had no medical care, and once he got sick, he figured he wouldn't live much longer. He often didn't even have the power to move.

So another day, another two, he figured he would share the fate of the others who couldn't withstand the conditions, who daily were taken to a joint grave. But he kept on. During the final few days of the approaching front, all the Germans gave them was warm water. The Germans wanted to get rid of them.

When the war ended, they were so starving, thin, and weak, that a few British soldiers delivered him and others straight to a hospital, where Tato weighed in at 55 pounds. At that time, even the end of the war didn't please him.

The British took care of him in the hospital. He and his fellow patients were nurtured in the hospital like young children, and gradually, many of them became healthy.

Tato continued his story, counting out the camps where he was held. The first one was Gross-Rosen, where he parted with me, because I got a high fever and was moved to a special barrack.

From there, he was moved to Buchenwald and then to Oranienburg. In Oranienburg, he met a Polish prisoner who stayed with me in the isolated barrack. This prisoner told Tato how in a few days I got healthy and was taken out somewhere else to other camps.

"I knew that he had survived his coma, but what happened to Stepan after that, I heard nothing and didn't know," he said.

From Oranienburg, he was sent to another camp, Bergen-Belson, then later to Hamburg and was released by the Brits from camp Neuengamme.

After he was released, he was held in the British military hospital for more than four months. Some prisoners healed quicker and were released and returned back to their lands. They were prisoners from Western Europe, especially French, Belgians, Dutch, and some of them were Poles. The prisoners who hailed from the Union were detained the longest.

"With our return to health, we were dressed in white hospital clothes and given light chores in the hospital. We eventually all felt better and became healthier. Then, one day, it was announced, that Soviet transport vehicles with a military garrison arrived under the hospital gates. The hospital staff told us to gather and said that the British authorities had agreed with the Soviet authorities to deport us back to our homes. I was glad that I could finally see my family again and that I was healthy. But some of those former prisoners were already accustomed to the new circumstances and didn't think to return. But at that moment, no one officially inquired whether we had a choice," said Tato.

An Uherci villager then chimed in: "There are camps in Germany full of people who fled west before the arrival of the Soviet troops. They were considered deserters, so they feared a return to the Soviet Union."

Tato said, "I haven't heard of such camps, so I know nothing."

He then told our family that he cleared his name on the Eastern border of Germany, so his Underground transgressions against the Germans were written off. He then returned home.

Some time after returning home to Uherci, Tato resolved that it was time to disassemble the old house and build the new one. Most of the materials needed were already purchased before his arrest.

Also, at that time local authorities pushed him to immediately re-join the village council as the political head of the village, but he refused, saying that after all he endured as a German prisoner, somehow before his very eyes, he survived and his first move was to forget it all.

"This will be my best vacation, that I get permission to re-build our family a house, because the old one is beyond repair and won't last," apologized Tato. For some time, he was left in peace.

But he couldn't stand aside long after hearing the active members of the Ukrainian Underground paint patriotic images of freedom. Former associates of his came to him during the night multiple times, asking him to again take on his previous post as the District Executive of the Underground in Uherci (along with the head of the village).

Fights between the KGB and the Ukrainian Underground movement had revived throughout Ukraine. The Bolsheviks sought to destroy all the manifestations of Ukrainian patriotic revival and aspirations awakened during the war.

In the forests lay small groups of UPA insurgents spread out in different parts of Ukraine, waiting for orders from central leadership, about what their next move should be. The Soviet KGB didn't sleep either, treacherously trying to destroy the resistance of the Ukrainian people.

At that time, the Ukrainian Underground Army represented a great power and waged struggle in various parts of Ukraine. And most jarring for Tato, were that high officials were abusing power over peaceful people, especially in our Galicia, Volhynia, and Carpathia as well.

It was safe to say that Tato's patriotism wasn't fully cooled off. It wasn't important to him which Ukrainian party led this fight. To him, importance lied in the Ukrainian patriotic movement that advocated human rights, freedom of people, and the independence of Ukraine. Tato even said that he wouldn't mind to see communists lead this fight, but independent Ukrainian communists, who could forever separate Ukraine from Russia.

After some deliberation, memories of his beatings and the concentration camp punishments didn't change Tato's conviction and he gave his consent to continue engaging in Ukrainian Underground work.

After obtaining permission to build a new house, Tato bought yet more material and using local building experts and families help, he happily finished the structure. That house was built with brick and covered with a tile roof. Tato did indeed have time to build the house he wanted, but he simultaneously worked no less for the Underground movement.

As he was building his house, he labored in the smithy, and he also belonged to the Underground contingent. The Underground obliged Tato to deliver food, clothing, footwear, as well as weapons. These weapons were hidden in the gardens of the peasants, which they had kept there since the Germans attacked Ukraine in 1941.

Farmers then collected these weapons and rubbed them with vaseline and buried them in wooden bundles in underground storages. They had to be hidden there until they were needed for self-defense or when there would be a commitment to the armed forces of an independent Ukraine.

Organizing and juggling all this was hard on Tato. Also, in these dangerous times, unknown informer agents called "jumpers" appeared. Local traitors gave them information and these werewolves reported back to the KGB about life and all the movements happening in the village.

To add to that, the city councilman of Horodok came to our yard and ordered Tato to go with him back to Horodok.

Mama, seeing this car with unknown people, immediately got scared. "Who are these people? And what do they need?"

Tato calmed her down saying, "They're asking me to help the village council."

"He'll be back soon," they assured mama. "We just need to fix some matters."

Tato and the officers left the house together and drove to the village office. There, in the company of the village council, he was told about the death of the village head and the reason why they brought him there.

"We are appointing you to village head in place of the deceased one," they explained. "We've already given you enough time to rest and you've built your house. You have no excuse not to be head of the village council."

Tato was initially struck by the sudden death of the head of the village. He then tried asking the officers to appoint someone else and he gave them the choice of several other candidates, considering how immensely busy he was.

However, they didn't want anyone else. They reminded

him that he was once head of this council when the Red Army initially "liberated" western Ukraine.

"Why would you give up this position, when now you'll have a much easier time fulfilling it? We have no intention of teaching anyone else how to do this."

So now along with being the Underground District Lead, he was being asked to be the head of the village.

Tato's further refusals brought no success. The council then started to threaten him that if he refuses, that they would re-examine his arrest case and challenge why he was sent to the German concentration camps. Immediately hearing such a threat, Tato agreed to the position but requested they give him a week's time so that he could better get ready. They agreed to this, because they were convinced that he would do it and that in a week he wouldn't change his mind.

During that week, a few members of the Organization of Ukrainian Nationals (the Underground) visited Tato, and he told them about how the local council basically forced him into being head of the village council. These Underground members pointed to the double danger of his situation, but they also saw a great benefit for the Underground and opportunity to learn about the intentions of the KGB and their informers.

"As the head of the village, you'll soon learn if any danger exists in the village, and you can quickly inform the Underground leadership," they said.

For Tato, it must have been difficult to re-expose his entire family to the danger of this double work. He knew well that if he was caught and found out that he works with the

Underground, his whole family would probably be ripped apart or killed. So for him, it must have been very difficult to agree with such circumstances.

But his patriotism and his love for his people and the Ukraine was so strong that he made his decision to continue this fight, a fight for which so many victims had already suffered in Ukraine.

Tato tried consulting more with the Underground, seeing if it would be advantageous for someone else to take over as the organization's District Executive. But they decided that Tato should continue to lead both obligations, as the chairman of the village and the District Executive of the Underground.

The guide from the Underground told Tato that there were others leading these dual lives, and it was useful because it weakened the KGB's stronghold, which may even lead to their elimination.

Even after the war was done, rumors spread of it still reappearing. Communist Russia seemed not at all satisfied with her victories and her control of only half of Europe. Their slogan, "Workers of the World, Unite!" still to them seemed possible to achieve.

The Comintern, or Communism International, increasingly gained more propaganda throughout the world, from China to France to Italy, and it even had some support in America. In Soviet propaganda, voices of criticism of England and America grew more frequent as well. They loudly cried accusations and complaints that the west did not come in time to help with the war on Germany, and therefore, the Soviet Union suffered such huge losses in materials and people. The Soviets more and more often repeated their slogan that "Communism and the Soviet Union destroyed Germany, not England or America."

There were almost no words, at that time, to describe the intensity of the Communist Red Army's ideologies that were glorified in Soviet Russia. They said it would prevail first in Europe and then onto the liberation of all proletarians of the world, including America.

"We've heard that England and America intend to replace the Polish government to as it was in pre-war bourgeois Poland. We will not allow this because we have a strong army and life in our union is better than in any other country! Where there's an established communist regime, it will remain forever. We'll help the communists of every country, so that we could bring communism into their lands!"

The Ukrainian Underground closely followed the communist propaganda and the more intense events of the world. They were convinced at this time, in case of war, it would receive full support from the west, who also wasn't interested in a communistic system.

Some Underground members, who were passing news, said that the British government sent its agents into Ukraine to work with the formation of the UPA and her leadership and were preparing joint plans for the future, as well as contingency plans should a new war arise. So the Underground took a look at these worldly events, and the

Ukrainian side adjusted to them by continuing to expand their UPA and fight and hope for an independent Ukrainian nation.

At that time, my sister Maria left the family home and moved to teach in the next village called Cherlyany. She was happy with this position, because the village of Uherci was filled with senior teachers and there was no room for her to teach. She didn't want to work any longer in the farm system, knowing that in a short time, the communist government would introduce the collective farm system that didn't seem appealing to be a part of, so she went to a teacher seminar and obtained a teacher degree. In the meantime, she still further hoped for similar work in Lviv.

In the spring of 1947, elections were appointed to the Ukrainian Soviet Republic. To assure that all the "happy" people of Ukraine would take part in elections, the Soviets sent military units to the villages who "encouraged" people to vote.

A military detachment was sent and spread throughout our entire village in order to delegate duties to the farmers. However, the situation was not so simple. The Ukrainian Underground urged the peasants not to vote, and to instead protest the Soviet regime. So the farmers were posed a contradiction: if we don't vote, we'll be marked as opponents to the government, but if we do, we'll be an opponent of our own nation and Underground.

On election day, a military commander came to the village and told Tato that they would both, along with a protection unit, stroll through the village so the villagers would see them and feel safe to go vote. After their walk, they would go to the school, where the voting would take place. Tato didn't want to but what choice did he have?

Following these roads of the village, they saw none of the villagers. The village looked dead. No one came out of their houses. Seeing this, the military commander ordered his guards to go into every house and demand that all the people go out and vote.

Somehow, at that very moment, one of our neighbors who was hiding, sneaked out of her house and crouched down to take care of a "natural need." She was noticed by a guard who was passing by, and he ran over to her and shouted, "Why aren't you voting?"

She began to rebuke him.

The guard, with his rifle in one hand and our neighbor in the other, tried to force her toward the school in mid pee. But she wouldn't have it and ripped herself away from him. In this confusion, he unintentionally pressed the trigger on his rifle and shot a bullet which pierced through his leg.

He cried out with pain. Hearing this cry, a second soldier, who knew nothing of what happened, shouted that in the village barns, Bandera insurgents are hiding. So they started firing. More guards appeared and they all together started shelling neighborhood barns.

In a short time, several of the barns caught fire, along with our family's as well. The shooting continued further, but it was only heard from one side - the Soviet troops. This whole event was witnessed by my brother Michael.

After some time, Tato and the commander came running and asked what happened. The soldiers yelled and explained that there were Bandera's Underground hiding in the barns that started shooting and that one of them wounded our soldier.

Hearing such a lie, my brother Michael ran out of the house to Tato and denied their accusations. He argued that nobody was shooting from the barns. Then he explained the whole story of how one of the soldiers tried to convince a neighbor that she should go vote, and that in his hand he had a ready rifle and that through his own carelessness, he shot himself. He said that while the other soldiers heard a shot and the cry of a wounded soldier, they immediately thought it was shooting and mistakenly blamed Bandera's bandits and started shooting.

The Commander did not like Michael's point of view and he ordered his immediate arrest, figuring that the arrest of Michael would protect his military unit in front of his superiors, and that his arrest would hide this whole thing and it would remain a mystery. Michael at the time was still in his early teens.

But Tato spoke up and said that Michael was his son, that he was still young, and that he didn't know what he was saying. The commander then agreed to forget the whole matter and Michael was released.

"Don't dare speak about this to anyone else," the

commander told Michael.

And he threatened Tato, saying, "If he further slanders us, he'll be put under our arrest, whether he is your son or not. No one will protect him then."

The village elections ended without any other obstacles. However, only a few villagers voted that day and the military unit departed from the village.

Even though the military left, more unknown individuals began appearing in the village, these so-called "jumpers," or communist spies. They were reported to Tato by other members of the Underground.

Slowly, their presence began to bother and scare some of the more active members. At the same time, groups of UPA warriors came at night in small groups to pass on communication. These warriors were starting to get noticed by the jumpers, who were snooping around the village at night.

Tato warned the members of the Underground to be very careful with such jumpers, not to cause any suspicion or provocation, but this was not always possible.

One of the crucial members of the organization in our village was Vorih, Tato's assistant, thought that one of these jumpers noticed him as he went through the village with an unknown man, who was an Underground member as well.

He then nervously entered into unnecessary controversy with the jumper. One thing led to another and the Communist agent/jumper in strife called Vorih one of

Bandera's bandits. Vorih denied it.

The agent replied, "If you aren't a Bandera, well you sure do talk like all the other Banderas. Speaking like this, you could easily be arrested."

Vorih then replied, "You yourself could be a Bandera speaking this way and sneaking through our village!"

They both parted in strife and from that moment on, Vorih began to follow the movements of this jumper in our village.

One evening, Vorih went to Tato, a move which was previously discussed as too risky. Tato told Vorih that they would no longer meet together in order to avoid unnecessary suspicion of cooperation. But this time, Vorih dared to go to Tato, so Tato immediately realized the immediate danger of the situation.

So Vorih told him that he wanted to get rid of this jumper, because he looked to be quite suspicious and dangerous. Tato advised him not to spontaneously do anything, because any radical movements could bring our village even more oppression. He assured Vorih that the very next day, he would talk to him, because he, as the village leader, was entitled to know all people wandering through the village. Tato also said that he would go to nearby Horodok and verify exactly who this man was, and ask that they take him away from the village, because there are rumors about him being engaged in theft. Vorih agreed on Tato's proposal, saying it was better than anything he'd thought of.

The next day, Tato was unable to meet with the jumper. Another week passed and he was no longer seen in the village.

Tato was pleased with such a solution and thought that he must have gone off somewhere else. Thus passed a few more days.

Then, the KGB police arrived in the village and started asking villagers for a man who, according to their description, looked exactly like the jumper whirling through the village. They said they were looking for him because there was an accusation that he might be an anti-state spy.

Earlier, the same police also came to Tato and asked him if there were any other dangerous people in the village who might be working against the Soviet government. They asked him if in the village sometimes Bandera bandits move through, because they are now in almost every village. They also asked him who would be their leader.

Tato claimed that there are no such people in Uherci, that in our village is peace and that he does not think there is a possible sabotage to the detriment of the Soviet power.

"If there was, someone would have already reported this to me," he said. "In such a case, I would have told you all this already."

Tato explained that the farmers are not engaged in politics, for they know well that for such work, they'd be arrested and deported to Siberia.

Then they hinted to Tato, that maybe he just can't see or know everything, because they already have some accusations and they already know a few names suspected in the village. They ordered Tato to come to Horodok the next day, so that maybe he could tell them more.

Tato warned the local members of the Underground. He

impatiently waited for the next day and then went out in the morning to meet the head of the KGB in Horodok. But this head however, was not found for he had already left. No one else working there could tell him the reasons for why Tato was called there. Tato returned home sad and troubled.

The next day, the same police appeared in Uherci.

They announced to Tato that they came to arrest two people and ordered him to assign a man to take the guards into their homes.

"Who?" Tati asked.

"District Executive Vorih and Denisiv Bohdan."

Although Vorih was a part of the Underground, it was indeed Tato who was the District Executive.

Tato asked the village secretary to lead the guards into the two houses and the men were both arrested and taken to jail in Horodok. Tato felt sorrowful for those arrested because he himself figured out that this jumper had left not to flee, but to go to the KGB and tell them about Vorih.

Tato hoped that these would be the only two arrested. He knew Vorih really well and believed that even if he had to die, he wouldn't betray anyone. But this time, it happened differently than Tato expected. And Vorih could not foresee it either.

On August 1, 1947, about a week after Vorih and Bohdan's arrest, this very same KGB police returned to our family's yard. They announced that they were arresting 22 additional people, men and women. They gave Tato the list of people and a command that he should prepare the wagons and send all of them to Horodok. He was ordered to show the KGB where all the villagers lived.

This was probably the hardest and most depressing order that Tato ever had to comply with. Every person on the register belonged to the Underground, for which he was the District Executive for. They all knew Tato and his obligations to the movement.

He also wondered if his fellow Undergrounds thought that he gave them up to save himself. He also wondered why the letter held all of the village activists, but he alone was left out. He was confused but had no other choice. He had to go along with this all, or immediately cast suspicion upon himself.

The armed KGB police followed Tato into the designated houses, and they took in turn each of the suspicious people. There was great panic throughout the village. Nobody had predicted that so many of the best leaders would be arrested at once and taken from the village.

Tears, regrets, and fear gripped the entire village and none of the detainees could even say goodbye. Then, after they were all rounded up, they told Tato to raise his arms up to be searched and he was arrested as well.

A little later, Mama and the rest of the family found out that Tato was arrested along with the others. The news soon spread throughout the entire village. Mama couldn't believe it. No way was her husband being arrested again.

She lamented that Tato had just recently returned from the German prisons, and the same officials from Horodok who appointed him village head... how was it that these same officers arrested him? Poor Mama didn't know that after returning back from Germany, Tato had agreed to cooperate again with the Underground.

Tato's arrest troubled the entire family and our neighbors as well. They came to Mama and tried to comfort her in whichever way they knew, all while hoping that they too wouldn't be arrested, because such arrests were spreading through many villages.

From the day of Tato's arrest, my younger brother Michael started spending nights away from home. It seemed that he had a presentiment that something more would happen and that something was wrong. He told my Mama that he would sleep at Aunt Petrychyhy's so that he wouldn't let the police catch him when they'd come looking for him to take him to Siberia.

At that time, on the railway station at Horodok, there was a train waiting which was rumored to soon deport our Ukrainian people to a distant and alien Russian Siberia. And in a very short time, this reality appeared more cruelly than expected.

On October 21, 1947, a man came to Mama and said that he had very important business to relay from the Ukrainian Underground. Mama explained that she did not know what he was saying, that she doesn't know about some Underground organization, and that she didn't want to know about it.

That man however, further insisted that the news was

linked to Tato's arrest.

"I have to help your husband, so you need to tell me whom I should turn to," he said.

Mama then crossed her arms and said, "Get out of the house! I already have enough problems and don't know a thing!"

And she didn't know with whom Tato kept ties.

Then this man began to beg Mama to help him, to help meet up with her son Michael. "I have to meet with him, because what I have to relay, it will not only help your family, but also the entire village. I've long been familiar with Ivan. I met him in the village Zavydovych. He doesn't drink or smoke and he was in German concentration camps and I must now help him."

He pleaded and persuaded and finally convinced the unhappy Mama. She believed him and said that Michael had been sleeping at Aunt Petrychyhy's and explained to him where her house was. "It's still early, so you should be able to find him there."

This man at once ran off to my aunt's and told her that he must speak immediately with Michael Fedenko. "His mother said he was in your house, spending the night."

Our aunt, too, immediately believed this man, because Mama sent him over. So she sent him to the barn and told him, "That's that where you'll find my son Hrynio and Michael. They're both still sleeping in there."

This man went into the barn and woke them both up. He ordered Michael to dress and follow him.

Michael immediately recognized that this was an ambush

against him, and looked to escape from the barn. Michael ran towards the back door, but the man drew a pistol and ordered him down off the hay. Two more men entered the barn and took our brother Michael.

A few days before that event, a village boy started visiting our house. He had already tried to persuade our sister Maria to marry him. But his proposition wasn't convincing to Maria, and they only met up as good friends. After Maria left to teach, this boy came to our house and asked for her multiple times. Mama asked him why he needed to know where she is. He said that he seriously thought about it and wanted to marry her.

Mama took it for a joke and said that he could choose a lot of other girls:

"You talk about it to her, not me."

One night he came to Mama and said, "You are left all by yourself. They took your husband, and I can be a helping hand. Who knows how long they'll take him for? You know that I like Maria. We're both well suited for each other. Let me talk to her."

And Mama apparently believed his words because he was a village boy and she saw him once with her. "But how come you don't know that she's teaching?"

He excused himself, saying he was very busy with work and was unable to keep contact with her.

Mama then told him that she teaches in a nearby village called Cherlyany. He thanked Mama and said that he will see her soon and that maybe they can come back together and visit her.

So on that same day that Mama told a strange man where Michael was sleeping, she watched with amazement, as Michael was being led to the house by three men, among them the one who she had told where to find Michael. Mama could not believe that this once flattering man could so cunningly deceive her.

One man from the group leading Michael, perhaps their chief, ordered the whole family out of the house.

He announced, "You are all being deported. You've got 15 minutes to pack up your things, only that which you precisely need. You are being taken to Siberia."

"Mama! You betrayed me!" Michael berated her.

These words wounded her even more, so much so she shattered into pieces, not even knowing what to take with her. In a panicked stupor, she picked up a pair of new boots and instead of putting them on her feet to wear, she walked out the house carrying them.

One of these KGB men took these boots away from her and turned her back into the house. Mama then managed to take a small bag of beans and tried to look for something more to take. But the 15 minutes was quickly up. She had to leave for the car.

In the meantime, Michael managed to bring a bag of flour and a bag of potatoes and loaded it up into the truck and drove over to the train station in Horodok. There, in the station, a transporting train was already waiting and they were already loading arrested people up for deportation.

They drove our family all the way up to the train, as if they would still try to escape somewhere. They immediately ordered them inside the train. The guards who brought them let Mama take the bag of beans into the train, but they made Michael leave the flour and potatoes in the truck.

The guards mocked them saying, "Where you're being taken, you won't need such things."

The guards probably took them for themselves.

Michael grew pale and angry. He quarreled with them and said that other families took all they brought with them into the train. But they didn't listen to him anymore and walked away to take whatever they wanted from other Ukrainians.

Fortunately for the family, Aunt Potyuchka found out about their arrest. She immediately milked out her cow and took the milk in a jug and two loaves of bread and she somehow managed to run up to the train station and pass it all to Mama.

That same day, October 21, 1947, when the KGB took Mama and our whole family into trains, a KGB officer arrived to a school during a lesson in the village of Cherlyany. That officer called yes, my sister, over for a conversation. Maria saw the principal and another teacher with him.

The officer said to Maria, "You're not returning to class. You're assigned for deportation."

Maria was very sorry to learn this, although she had heard from some of her students that some families were being deported from Cherlyany that day. She requested to enter her apartment so she could take necessary supplies with her. However, the KGB officer refused to do so and immediately ordered a guard to deliver her to the police.

She requested of these guards that on their way, they could stop at her Mama's place to tell her that she is being deported to Siberia. But this request was not allowed either. They brought her immediately to the police who had already assembled a good number of people for deportation from Ukraine.

After more than two hours of waiting and watching the KGB arrest more people, all of them were then taken to the train station in Horodok.

In Horodok, Maria saw just how many families were already gathered for exile. There was a long train and each car was filled with people. She sought out for some familiar faces to convey the news to her Mama about her deportation to Siberia.

She looked around at all the crying, poor people, young children even, and elderly grandparents. They were all abandoned and resigned to crying, embracing and saying goodbye and wondering whether they'd ever see each other again.

This removal of empty-handed Ukrainians to Russian Siberia resembled exactly to her what such deportations happened when the Germans had just five years ago done this to the Jews, taking their innocent families to the German concentration camps.

Maria then decided to look into more wagons to check whether there she'd see anyone from the village of Uherci. She did not have to go far. In the third wagon, she found her shambled, crying Mama and standing by her were her brothers Michael, Oles, and Volodymyr. The brothers all at once started asking how she ended up here.

They were not happy to have met her, for they hoped that she at least might remain in Ukraine. They hoped that they could get help from her back home.

Our Mama pulled our sister close and they collapsed into each other crying. She asked her if she brought anything for the road. Sister said that she didn't bring anything because she was taken straight from school and wasn't allowed to stop at home.

Where our Tato was at that time, no one knew. Mama still looked and thought that since Maria was brought to them, maybe Tato would appear here as well. But he never showed.

Other families in other train wagons had similar experiences, full of tears and complaints for their unhappy fate. Many of these villagers assembled here for deportation had never even left their village or surrounding area.

How difficult it was for them to leave! To leave their threshold, their relatives, their poor houses, their native village and go to someone else's cold, unknown country... the distant stranger Siberia.

A few more families were added from the village of Uherci, among them the family of our Uncle Ivan Burbura, as well as the family of former head of the village Dennis Chornenky, Vorih, and his 85 year old father Bilyk.

Women continued to wail and their small and frightened children cried with them. This sadness and fear enveloped every train car.

On both sides of the train, armed guards strolled showing hostility to those prisoners nervously waiting for when the train would finally depart on the road.

The crying children and their mothers did not phase these guards. They probably had performed this function of such Ukrainian deportation to distant Siberia repeatedly, so they didn't speak or show any sympathy to anyone.

Finally, just before nightfall, the guards shut the wagon doors, settled themselves, and the train went along its journey. It was a very long journey. Every day, the train stopped in uninhabited places. Prisoners in need were allowed to exit the train and empty themselves.

Once a day, the train would stop and each passenger got a bowl of some potato soup or cereal. This soup was usually cold, but not a person refused.

At the very border of Ukraine and Russia, the train stopped again. KGB guards checked every wagon and if there were any sick or old, they chased them out of the train and left them without any care at the border.

"Russia doesn't need these people and they themselves don't deserve such a privilege to go there," they told them.

The 85 year old grandfather Bilyk was thrown from the train in one of these uninhabited places, realized he couldn't bear the family separation, and died on the spot.

So after two weeks of hardship, crying children, lamentations and groans of elders and sleepless nights, the train drove into the city of Prokopyevsk, which was halfway into Russia and about 3000 miles from Lviv, Ukraine. It was announced to the deportees that this would be the place where they would live out their lives. At that time, each family was separately called and demanded to give their "voluntary" signature that they found this new place suitable to live out their lives here. No one dared to protest such signatures.

All the exported were totally perplexed, that they had no other choice... either sign the document or immediately be annihilated. After this signature, all the deportees were ordered to form groups and funneled into the city bath by the armed KGB guards.

At that time, the local population was already notified in advance that there would be a transport of people arriving from Ukrainian Galicia. On both sides of the rows of incoming deportees, local teenagers ran up and shouted the most hostile and meanest words.

"You scoundrels, you Bandera bandits - where are you hiding your horns?"

Others simply said, "Lo and behold they look just like us."

This is how the local population was prepared by Soviet Russian authorities to accept their "brothers" who, simply for their patriotism and love of Ukraine, had to endure such abuses, outrages, and blasphemy.

In the baths, they were lined up one by one and ordered to take off their clothes and give them up for de-licing and sterilization. Men had to go to a separate washroom, women to another. All the clothes were mixed together and put through dry, hot steam.

When they were released in groups from the baths, they

had to find their clothing mixed up among others and go to their assigned seats. The prisoners shouted and disagreed in confusion.. Some unconscientious people changed their clothes with others, picking what they liked best.

Police had to intervene to reconcile these people and somehow get everyone's clothing back to their owners. Among them were frightened wandering children, having no idea who to cuddle. Should they look to their parents, to angry strangers, or to the armed guards?

Coming out of the baths, Mama had trouble finding her clothes. She looked and looked, but couldn't find her shirt. Mama went and asked the other women if some of them might have accidentally taken it.

No one responded to her. So she was left in Siberia without a good, strong, linen shirt. And in Prokopyevsk, it was so needed. It was October, and the average high was 7 degrees fahrenheit. She was frozen, and any food they brought with was quickly consumed. Those people that had a little left over from the road were not allowed to keep it.

After their baths, the prisoners were sent to the so-called currently in-construction temporary shelters scattered a bit further outside the city. Each of these shelters had its own oven which held enough coal to heat the shelter, even in the winter. But in those shelters, lice like those in Breslau multiplied by the many and the prisoners couldn't get rid of them.

After several days, local craftsmen from the nearby

factories came to the shelters and chose all the talented people for different jobs. Those selected were issued a food card valued at 300 grams per day. For the seniors, children, and those not picked, they received 200 grams. Also, because winter was coming, all workers were issued tights, some cotton pants, and work boots.

Our sister Maria and brother Michael were assigned to a mechanical plant, and Oles and Vlad were still too young to work in the factory, so they were left in temporary housing with Mama. Since Maria was marked as a teacher in the registry, she was appointed at work to be a "timekeeper." Her task was to develop a card file on each worker stating where he had to work in the shop and at what time. After a month working the cards, she was approached by the head of the plant who ordered his deputy to take her out of work. He said that she does not deserve such a function and that she should be doing dirty work. Our sister was then taken inside the plant and put into stall work as a lathe turner. She'd never worked on such a machine before. The master who was supposed to show her how to use the crank-operated machine refused to do so. He called her a Banderivka and said, "You're so smart, so guess yourself how to do it. And your daily production should not falter."

Maria then observed others on similar machines and in this way somehow became successful in her endeavor.

Then one day returning back from the factory with the other workers, with whom she lived in the dugouts, from behind a bush jumped a group of young boys and attacked her with sticks, beating her up and breaking her nose. They only ceased to beat her when out of nowhere an old man stood up to them and drove them away screaming.

He loudly scolded them, saying, "Your crime is worthy of punishment! These Banderas, whom you so viciously mock, suffer and long for their own native lands! What have they done to you? What gave you such permission to beat them here as they suffer punishment from their motherland!"

Only then did the young boys listen to the grandfather and walked away irritated. On the appeal of the beaten, none of the local council responded and the case went unresolved.

So passed the first month of work in Siberia.

The next month, my family received food vouchers. Mama carefully laid the vouchers in a tiny burlap sack, because a she didn't have a bag or a purse. These stamps were supposed to feed our family for a whole month, and they could barely live off of it at that. The next day, Mama went to the consumer store, hoping the line would be short so she could end up with first choice in goods.

However, there was already a long line when she got there, so she got in line with the second group. After she finally got through the line, she asked the clerk for the price of several products. Mama said that she had five people in her family. The clerk answered, telling her the price and then asked mama for her cards. Mama put her hand down into the bag, poked around a bit and it was empty. She shoved her hand all the way down and her hand went through - someone had apparently stood next to her in line, carefully cut out the bottom of her bag, and stole all her coupons.

Unfortunately, these cards were not issued with names on them, so they couldn't be verified. Mama cried out and ran throughout the store, complaining that her whole family would die of hunger because someone in line stole all of her food cards. But no one paid any attention to her weeping. These people who were waiting in line just looked on, knowing now that they will move up in line sooner because my mama didn't have anything to buy food with.

The on-duty policeman tried to remove mama from the queue so as not to delay the others in line.

"Get out of line! You're only causing a ruckus!" the policeman said.

Mama didn't pay attention to the policeman's threats. She still thought that she could somehow get paid appropriately, because she didn't have the courage to go back to her four hungry children with nothing.

To somewhat appease my mother, the chief salesman promised her that she could remain until the store closed, and then he would allow her to grab what was left from the table. So she waited the entire day, as it crept on, watching person after person get their rations.

After everyone got their turn and when the shop began to close, the chief salesman called her over. He told her to collect all that was left on the table. At that moment, Mama thought that she'd get her rations. She looked at the table, but then saw nothing of use that remained, nothing to actually feed a family. All that was left were bread crumbs, a few candies, and some scattered grains. She began to cry. This table had enough food on it for one good meal. And her rations were supposed to last a month.

"Please, please, anything. I have four children. What's left on your shelves?" Mama said.

But it was all in vain.

"Take what you want from the table, and if not, begone, because we're closing shop. There are plenty of people like you, quite common," the chief salesman said.

Mama realized that they didn't believe or didn't want to believe that someone had stolen her coupons.

When the doors were finally being closed, she quickly swept all the crumbs from the table and the store clerk ended up giving her five more potatoes. In despair, she returned back to her dugout and breathlessly told her children how she was robbed. They had been waiting hungry all day for her.

The whole family cried. They shared the crumbs brought home by mama with looks of concern - how could they continue without food? Who could they go to for help?

Mama then began to look for something in their dugout. When she found it, it was a a sewing kit, and she took her bag that someone had stolen food cards from and began to sew it back up. She also sewed her long belt into it to act as better handles.

Then, with great difficulty, she said, "Tomorrow I will go ask for charity." That is, she was going to beg the local villagers and hoped that from them she could obtain something. "Maybe we'll still meet some good people, who might somehow be able to help."

This was a great embarrassment to my brothers and sister,

and they pleaded, "Mama, please don't do it."

But none of them had a better solution or a back up plan. And even in this sad situation, theft was not an option.

Mama tried to cheer everyone up, saying, "When I go into town, the first thing I'll do is ask for a temporary job."

A droplet of hope for a dire situation.

The next day, Mama got up early to beg. My youngest brother Volodymyr offered to help and Mama couldn't deny that he'd probably be of good help, because people would see a hungry child. So they went together.

But it wasn't so easy for them to get anything from these villagers. People met them with anger and resentment and chased them from their yards, shouting, "Don't ever come back!"

Some even sent their dogs.

After a day of begging, all they came home with was a carrot and a turnip and a little slice of bread. Vlad ate the bread and gave Mama a bite too.

That night, Mama made turnip and carrot soup and shared it with her kids, but she took nothing.

The next day, she and Volodymyr begged further. That day, not embarrassment, not swearing, not even the dogs slowed them down because the family had to somehow stay alive. To make matters harder, Volodymyr got mad at Mama, telling her he couldn't go any longer. But his sorrowful feeling seeing Mama kept him going and he continued to walk with her. After hearing their story, an older man found some compassion for my brother Vlad and told him to look after his cow. For this work, he gave him a tin of milk and a bread roll.

Mama and Vlad were overcome with great joy.

The next day, Vlad went to this man's house when he was still asleep. The man had no idea Vlad was coming, but Vlad cleaned his stable. When the man woke up and saw the stable, he was surprised that Vlad took it upon himself to do so.

Therefore, at the recommendation of several of his trusted neighbors, Vlad began grazing their cows and he became so very pleased with his exceptional work. He just kept cleaning and cleaning around people's homes, even without people telling him to.

For this behavior, the old man told him that when it gets colder and freezes over and the snow falls, he will teach Vlad how to skin animals and make shoes. This man was a shoemaker by profession.

Vlad's work untied a big knot of the family's hardship. Mama gradually stopped going to beg. They lasted the rest of the month, got their coupons, and this time they held on to them tight.

Amongst rumors starting to swirl that some people had escaped, running off to China where they openly took fugitives, after some time, in Prokopyevsk, all the exported were told that every Saturday, after work, they had to volunteer in the command's headquarters.

On Saturday, when my sister Maria went to volunteer at the command headquarters, she met the head of the command and was called into his office. He was very polite with her and ordered her to volunteer with him the next day at 8pm. Maria was skeptical and worried about this challenge and told Mama about it.

Mama told this to the entire family who at this out-of-the-blue news, tried to guess what she was guilty of or why the head would choose her. Such people had been called by this commandant, and they were often arrested and taken away to another place.

The next day, Maria went to the head at the appointed time. In the counselor office, there was an armed police officer. Maria immediately thought that he was there to arrest her.

The commandant then turned to her very politely and asked, "Are you satisfied with your work here? Are you satisfied with your living arrangement with your family?" He asked her more and more questions and surprisingly, at the end ordered her to write his biography.

"Now go home and come back again tomorrow evening at 8," he said.

She did so and the next night she found herself alone with the commandant in the counselor office. He immediately began asking her more questions.

"Are you married? Do you have children? I have much easier work for you than writing my biography and easier than what you're doing now. We need you here to better understand the camp's circumstances," he said.

He continued, "We need someone here, like you, who knows a lot about the imported visitors... someone who they all respect and trust. So we've chosen you to be our employee. You'll get a different name, one that no one will know but me. You will be our mystery collaborator. You're going to talk to the other men and women and find out all they have to say about the local environment, about us leaders, whether they plan on spoiling or sabotaging any of our factories here, or whether any of them plan to escape. All these facts you will deliver to us."

Maria immediately replied, "I'm not available for this work. Give me the dirtiest and most difficult job here, but do not tell me to be a police informant. You arrested me, took me far from Ukraine and into Siberia, and now you expect me to be your informer? You're ruining me. What am I even guilty of?"

He replied to her, "I've already thought about this quite thoroughly. Here you need to survive, you and your family. Doesn't your family long for a sweeter life? We can send you to school here. You're still young. You'll have access to special food stores. We'll give your family a cow, and anything else you'd need here. Your entire family will get better work, which will lead to better accommodations."

"No. I am unfit for such work," she said.

The head warned her and said, "You better think this over before you give me your decision. And secondly, you better not tell a word of this to anyone. All of this that I just said is to remain untold."

The head noticed my sister's agitation and that his request this evening was not successful.

"Go back to your shelter and again come here tomorrow

at 8 o'clock."

My sister did so and the head maybe ten times or more repeated these same demands to her as the night before. He gave her these promises again and their conversation lasted at least two hours. But she stood pat and again gave the same answers.

This got on the head's nerves and he ordered her to come to his office every night for a whole month.

Every night, at each of these meetings, the head's flowery words of a nicer life turned to swearing and threats. He'd thunder both his fists on the table, terrorizing her and yelling at her, saying that she would forever regret not working with him.

Maria often went home crying to Mama and the rest of the family, scared that they all yet may suffer.

Finally, the head himself realized that my sister wouldn't ever give in to his suggestions and gave up. One last time, he clearly stated that if she told anyone about this, then she'd regret it for the rest of her life.

Then he pulled out a form: "Your signature states that you will never tell anyone that you came here and from this night on I won't call you. To me you are unneeded. In your place I can find many willing, maybe even one of your good friends."

He handed the form to my sister and showed her where to sign.

My sister was so happy that she signed the document without even reading it. She was sure that he'd finally leave her in peace.

A little less than a month later, after our family ended up getting a nicer shelter and had even got some of the locals to come together nightly after work to pray, without a priest even, the local council sent a young boy to Maria to make her see the newly appointed camp commandant.

She thought that maybe she'd been called because of her help in orchestrating the religious celebrations and prayers. So she went to the commandant calm, not anticipating anything bad. Once she got to his office, they greeted each other in a friendly manner and he asked her to sit down.

"How's your family's health? Good, good. I wanted to let you know that I'm quite pleased that you agreed to be a collaborator for the administration. You probably don't regret your act, I'm sure," he said.

My sister was so taken back that she didn't know what to say.

The head then picked up a paper, lifted it up in front of my sister and she recognized that it was the document she'd signed with the last head.

"Is this your signature?" he asked.

"Yes."

"Well right here you signed with the previous commandant, stating that you voluntarily will become an informer for us," he said.

My sister started crying and told him that this wasn't true in every way and she tried to explain to him why she signed the paper.

"He deceived me! He told me that if I signed this paper that I wouldn't be an informer. I believed him so I didn't read what I signed."

The head however did not accept my sister's explanation. He was even more cruel than the last head and berated her:

"So why, if you're so wise, do you not read what you sign? You signed it with the previous captain! *Now* you're rethinking this after he gave you a new home?! You cheater! How will my mentors see me if I let you get away with this? I hope your conscience gnaws at you and pities you for what you have done!"

He lined up to hit her but then grabbed a wooden chair and slammed it on the ground with all his force, cracking it into pieces.

"You will not lie to me here. And soon you will pay," he said, red as a beet and he stormed all over the room. "Get to breakfast. And tomorrow evening get back here!"

That next evening, this new menacing head with his even greater threats couldn't persuade my sister to work. Afterwards, she headed back to her family with a huge burden on her heart, but decided, "Let them beat me down and kill me, I will not cooperate with them."

Unbeknownst to her, Tato was taking the same stance a few thousand of miles away.

The next night, Maria again had to report to the chief. She figured that they wanted to break down the exported in every way possible, that they had time, and that they wouldn't hurry. If this commander didn't get someone to cooperate with them, they'd find someone else.

So again, my sister went to these meetings, with curses and threats amongst further promises of better living if she cooperated. After every meeting, she had to sign a paper that she had been there.

At the end of another month of meetings with the chief, he called two armed soldiers into one of their meetings and ordered them to lock her up for two weeks, on the account that she had lied. Without any sort of trial, my sister was escorted by the guards to a nearby prison.

She was handed off to the prison foreman and after reading the note from the chief, he explained to my sister her sentence.

"I'm putting you in here to clean and wash the guard's rooms and sweep and clean the prisoner's corridors as well. This won't be too bad of a punishment for you. If however, you speak at all to anyone about what has just happened to you, you'll be sentenced not to 15 days but 15 years. Your family from that moment will never find peace and you'll have the label 'liar' attached to you for life."

Those 15 days went pretty much according to plan and Maria was released back to the family. Mama cried with joy in seeing her.

Oles, during that time, was also put to work. He worked at a wood lathe and Michael ended up welding iron. When Vlad was finished herding cows, the shoemaker took him under his wing to treat leather.

The cobbler was so impressed with Vlad's skill and love for the work that he soon taught Vlad how to sew shoes and boots and made them even better and faster than the shoemaker.

For this, he was able to make much needed money for the family. My sister Maria also got her old job back.

But everything wasn't back to normal when she returned. The religious practices she helped put together were banned by the Camp Board, and they also forbade the prisoners from gathering at all in groups.

Getting used to these new conditions in Siberia, although it was very primitive, families started to consult each other as if they were going to stay for the long term. They also were well aware of what life they "voluntarily" signed up for. Which also signified that they'd remain in Siberia forever without any possibility of return back to Ukraine.

Paradoxically, the Siberian Russian Communist Government urged the rest of the world that the Ukrainians had volunteered for sustainable resettlement where they'd get more work, higher wages, and better housing. The Russians were gradually destroying what was left of the Ukrainian people and telling the rest of the world that it was our choice.

So our family accepted these conditions and also went through a lot of changes. Maria grew fond of a boy who was also taken to Siberia named Dmitri. They married in 1950. My brother Michael married in 1952 and Oleh in 1953. Lastly, my brother Volodymyr got married and he most was happy because a special visitor was able to make it.

On March 5th, 1953, Joseph Stalin died. This news brought hope of improving the deported's conditions in Siberia, but the change didn't happen immediately. And a little later that year, a partial amnesty was declared for some prisoners arrested under Stalin, which sprinkled through countless camps around the Union.

Then 1955 rolled around and a second amnesty released another round of prisoners. Tato had initial difficulty getting amnesty, because he had signed a letter which said he was part of the Ukrainian Underground. But after some immense effort and interrogations by the amnesty commission, he persuaded officials that he had simply signed it to save his own life.

"What would you do if you were given the choice to either get beaten every day until the day you died in prison or sign a sheet of paper saying you were part of the Underground and sit in prison?" he pleaded.

They didn't answer this question but told him he was free. Originally, Tato had been sentenced to 25 years in camp, of which 10 years he'd already served. But the Moscow general prosecutor issued his release with a passport, which said he could go back to Ukraine.

But upon learning that his entire family had been deported to a permanent settlement in Prokopyevsk, Siberia, which was East of the camp he'd been banished to in Baikal Lake, he asked the government to not send him home to the west, but to them in the east.

The government allowed him to as long as it was also on

the same terms as our family had taken, namely a permanent settlement and death in Siberia.

So in 1956, 10 years after they last saw him, Tato got to Prokopyevsk to my family and their joy was immeasurable. Mama cried with joy to the point of getting sick the moment she and Tato were reunited. The family, besides me, was back together again.

Yet they did have a few extra. Maria had given birth to two sons, Igor and Ivan. My brother Michael had one son named Bogdan, and Oles had a son named Stepan. Vlad wasn't far behind, and he married in 1956 shortly after Tato arrived. Mama and Tato then moved in with Oles and his family.

Tato's presence made the family warmer and made their lives in Siberia much easier to accept.

In 1956, eleven year after I last saw them, I finally decided to write home. But instead of trying to get a hold of my family, because I didn't want to cause any additional worry or stir up any Soviet supporters, I wrote to my uncle and asked him to let my family know that I was alive. His son, Hrynio, agreed to be my correspondent to my family. That way, I'd steer clear of any Soviets scouring America, as well as keep my family safe in Siberia.

Later that year, I dared myself to write that postcard to my family and only gave them my name and the name and address of my bride, Anna Drohomeretski. I told them that I am healthy, I study at university, and that I am glad they survived war times and are all alive.

At that time, Polish immigrants came with news to Tato and Mama that their eldest son Stepan, who was arrested and taken to Germany with his father, was alive and had emigrated from Germany to America.

To confirm this rumor, a short postcard arrived from me in America, written to Mama's side of the family in a village called Zavydovych, to my Uncle Evstah Matsiovski. What a surprise it was too! At that time, almost none of the other immigrants tried to get in touch with their family in Ukraine. Everyone who left Ukraine didn't want the Soviets to know anything about them, because they feared that even in America or somewhere abroad, the Soviets would still find them. Many emigration newspapers and magazines warned about the Soviets, telling immigrants that they be careful with their correspondence, and especially warned them against visiting because of the chance to be flipped by Soviet spies.

So I dared not to ask them anything about why they were in Siberia or how long they'd be there. I also knew that Tato was separated from them and spent nine years in others camps.

As later described to me by my sister, Tato was the first to get the letter and shared with our whole family and friends the exceptional news and comfort that his son was also not destroyed by the German concentration camps! Maria said she'll never forget that day and the joy felt by our parents.

At that same time, an agreement was signed between America and the Soviet Union, that parcels were allowed to be sent into Siberia, with some restrictions on product and weight. The first pack I sent the family, at that time by borrowed money, was in the late autumn of 1956. My sister Maria, to this day, has kept this first kerchief that I sent her.

The second letter I sent was in December of that same year in which I told the entire family that I was getting married. Although I was the oldest son of all the brothers, I married last. I honorarily invited all of them to my wedding day on February 23rd, 1957. I had asked a Ukrainian lady's hand, who came from middle Berezivka, Anna Drohomeretski. And not to cause any suspicion to any Siberia authorities, because my family was linked to the Underground, we sent the rest of our packages under her maiden name. I'd only slipped up once and put my own last name. Tato addressed me back, saying not to do so as not to cause any unnecessary harm.

From grandparents to grandchildren, my whole family often huddled at my parent's home. They recalled as they once lived in Ukraine, of how beautiful it was, about the family that remained there, and the possibility of once again visiting.

Tato took awhile to open back up to his experiences in the Nazi concentration camps. But after some time he calmed down and started to give more details about his arrest, especially about the second one. He, at that point, admitted to Mama that he had rejoined the Underground movement when he came back and how impossible it was not to fight for

Ukraine's freedom.

"The arrest of all Greek-Catholic bishops, priests, conscious Ukrainian leaders... the famine... the dictatorship... these affairs forced me to rejoin the fight, and I, once again, became the District Leader of the Underground. And at the same time, the Soviet government had appointed me as the head of the village, the same Soviet government who'd arrested me 18 months later."

He continued: "It started with Vorih and Dennis Bogdan - they were arrested and both taken to Horodok. The Soviets kept them there for some time and beat them and humiliated them and interrogated them. But Vorih and Dennis wouldn't say a word. They bravely and courageously held on, with no beating or threat breaking them down. They didn't betray anyone and were ready to give their lives to Ukraine.

"After failing time and time again, the investigators decided to try something new and sent them in a truck to Lviv, with two men manning machine guns on top and two KGB members in a lead car ahead. But as they were heading through the Oboroshensky Forest in the dark, a faction of the Ukrainian Povstanski Army attacked the small convoy. They fired at the lead car and killed the KGB members. In this unpredictable swoop, they jumped on top of the truck and killed the armed guards as well before they could react. All four of the Nazis were thrown into the woods and the UPA took the convoy into the forest.

"The UPA members explained that they'd been watching the Soviet truck movement from the woods and were glad that they could help them. 'We're ambushing and liberating our people in different towns and cities and thank god when we took yours, we didn't lose a man.'

"After a short ride through the forest, they jumped out of the machines and hiked to their hideout. Inside, there were a few soldiers, among them one of the captains of the UPA, and he immediately recognized Vorih and greeted him. The captain originated from the village Drozdovychi and his pseudonym was 'Raven.'

"They all exchanged familiar names to grow more accustomed to each other, and then Raven sat them down and asked them how they were doing. Both prisoners rejoiced as there was no way they could have expected such a quick rescue. After a few more niceties, they got down to business.

"Raven said, 'The KGB will probably know about your escape soon and will immediately go back to your village to look for you. But we've got another village for you where you'll be completely safe.' Vorih thanked him.

"One of the soldiers then asked them how was it that only the two of them got arrested in their village. 'Why are there so few of you working in the Underground there?'

"Vorih explained that they were the only two arrested because an informer - a jumper - was sent to the village and didn't have enough time to find everyone else out because he had left suddenly. The soldier asked, 'So you're the District Leader in your village?'

"'No,' Vorih replied. 'I'm only the deputy. Our District Leader just happens to be our village chairman appointed by the Soviets too. No one suspects him because he's already under the Soviet's watch. He'd also already been arrested by the Germans, sat concentration camps, so definitely no one suspected him.'

"'Oh, you're speaking of Ivan Fedenko (Tato),' replied the Raven. 'He's quite wise.'

"'Well only because his deputy does all the work,' Vorih replied, smiling.

"Raven sympathized with him and asked him how many villagers helped the Underground with his work. Vorih named them and praised them, saying that they are all good people and that they can all be counted on for good work.

"Raven rejoiced and praised Vorih and his exceptional assistants in the organization for their good work towards the Ukrainian cause. 'I'll address Fedenko and tell him about your release. Go ahead and write him a note for us so that he recognizes your handwriting and trusts the message.' Vorih wrote that they're free and that they'll soon meet up and put down his signature. Dennis Bogdan didn't really participate in these talks, because he didn't know as much about the affairs.

"As soon as their conversation finished, Raven got up and then howling sirens came from outside. 'Maybe it's those cars we took from the KGB,' one soldier said. However, suddenly, the Underground hideout was raided by the KGB and they greatly outnumbered the Undergrounders and quickly won the battle. Vorih and Bogdan were arrested again. They were returned back into prison in a small town and thrown into a basement, where there sat a man they knew named Dmitri.

"Dmitri asked them what happened and after listening he said, 'Well that sounds like it was deliberately constructed. What did you talk to them about?'

"Vorih vehemently rebutted and said, 'No! They were our guys. I know the Raven well!'

"'That's fine,' said Dmitri, 'but have you heard that some of the Underground has been exposed and they're now working for the Communists? I was tricked this way by my own uncle.'"

Tato continued: "And it just so happened this way. On August 1st, 1947, 22 members of the Underground organization in Uherci were arrested and brought to the city of Horodok. I was officially arrested again and searched and then interrogated by the head of the KGB in Horodok.

"When my turn came up, the investigator was ill and furious. And the investigator next door apparently recognized my voice and came in too. He just happened to be the KGB member who'd forced me to be the head of the village. He told everyone else to leave the room and started to lecture me:

"'You lied to me! You tried to deceive Soviet power! You did prohibited Underground work! I trusted you and made a mistake. Someone even told me that you might be Underground, but I didn't listen. I thought that after the Nazi concentration camps that you'd no longer be involved in politics.'

"I told him that I was innocent and didn't know what he was talking about, or who made such slander.

"He replied, 'I am sorry for your body and the beating which awaits you. You better confess soon, because your friend, Vorih, already sang at the top of his lungs about all you do for the Underground. And now that he's in prison, he'll tell us more. But now comes your turn. You can no longer live outside this charge, so tell us everything. Choose which road you want to take and see what happens. Otherwise, you'll have a great chance to compare which methods of interrogation work best for us Germans. You'll quickly be taken to prison in Lviv and you'll explain all the work that led you into the Underground. And Vorih will be your first witness, which I'm sure he'll spill out the rest. Also, think hard about your decision, because it will impact the fate of all the prisoners with you.'

"Then he pulled out a document for me to read. This document was a calculated report on all 22 people who were just arrested in the village and confirmation that I was the District Underground leader.

"I didn't sign it initially and after several days of life in prison in Horodok, we were taken to Lviv's Lonstky, my second time there, where they kept me for three months.

"Vorih was so disappointed that he was so easily deceived by these vile traitors and that he unintentionally exposed all Uherci's Underground members, that from that time on he didn't say a word. He'd rather die than speak another word. No death, suffering, or tricky promises had any more influence on him. He never spoke again.

"So after three months of interrogations, I realized that I couldn't reject my connection with the Underground anymore. I admitted that I was the District leader and took all the blame for the Underground activity in the village. I said that I alone was the only member of the Underground in my village, the only one who sympathized with the Underground.

"But that wasn't even the toughest part. *That* was when they asked me about my communication with the Underground leadership. Who was my superior? Who was my contact? I told them that I didn't know, that they'd always come with pre-arranged nicknames. I didn't know them personally and didn't know where they were. This kept the organizations strong and less able to break.

"But the KGB didn't believe me. They told me it was impossible. I told them that the first Underground member who came to me went by the nickname 'Under.' He urged me to work and that no one else would know about my work, that 'Under' would be in charge of communication upward. I told the KGB that's all this man told me.

"After further interrogations and beatings and getting nothing more out of me, I was sentenced to 25 years in Tayshet Camp at Lake Baikal in Siberia. On the way there, I fell off the train and broke my arm.

"Vorih had sat in the same prison Lontsky with me, but we were never together. He was also sentenced to 25 years. The rest of the prisoners were sentence to 10 and sent to camps in Siberia. And after the amnesty was signed, they were released with a clean record and sent home to Ukraine.

"Vorih returned but not to Uherci. He settled in a village near Lviv. There he married and eventually died."

When Tato was freed, he found out about our family in Siberia and went there.

And after Stalin's death, rumors circled about possible

return to Ukraine. There were changes in Soviet leadership, laws, and power. News came of the Poles protesting the Soviets and the Soviet troops retreating back to The Motherland.

News also broke of the U.S. And the Soviet conflict, specifically their standoff involving Cuba and their back and forth threats. All this news brought light to the evil ways of Soviet communism.

Then finally, the rumors became fact and those taken to Siberia were allowed to make requests to return back to Ukraine. Our brother Michael was the first of the family to dare to make such a request and received permission to return to Galicia.

But many of the returnees weren't allowed back in their old homes, which had been taken by the Soviets. Some couldn't even go back to their villages. It may have been the policy of the Soviet authorities to send people all over to keep us confused and keep as much of their control as they could.

Michael managed to get to Horodok, the closest town to Uherci. With the help of a local family, he quickly built a makeshift home and was employed in Horodok and made enough connections to get the rest of his own family back to Ukraine as well.

Back in Siberia, families had a hard time finding willing buyers for their homes. Similar homes would cost three times as much to build in Ukraine for what they got in Siberia.

The next family to get back to Ukraine was my sister's. She was lucky enough to be placed in Horodok, and with time came my brother Oles's family with Mama. Tato stayed in

Prokopyevsk to try and help Vlad get back while also was waiting for retirement money. Vlad took longer to return, because he initially thought he might quicker make himself a happy life in Siberia, because at the time he had no home or money in Ukraine.

Tato wrote letters pleading the village of Uherci so that they'd sent him a certificate that he'd been the village leader, hoping he could get some money. At that time, the house that Tato built in Uherci stood empty and was intended for sale. The school across the street used it most often.

Tato hoped to get his house back and to live the rest of his days in it but someone else ended up buying it first before any movement could be made on Tato's behalf.

Meanwhile, Mama's separation from Tato and return to Ukraine was not a happy one. She didn't want to bear a third separation from Tato. But at his request, she still agreed to go. Tato assured her that he would return as soon as he could get adequate pension and convince Vlad to come back. He couldn't, with good conscience, leave Vlad in a foreign country.

Tato's retirement money finally came in. But they nullified his nine years in prison and also most of the time he spent as the head as well. He ended up getting 18 rubles and three pennies, which was almost nothing.

After that awful news, Vlad agreed to come back, so Tato was in the end pleased. They, along with Vlad's wife, returned to Ukraine on October 27, 1965. Later that same year, they both settled in Horodok with the help of Michael and his friends in the city.

Tato was pleased enough to be this close to his village home, because many of his friends were relocated much further from their homes. But Tato and Mama didn't live in Horodok long. They decided to live with my brother Oles who had found work in Lviv. Some time went by and everyone found their feet underneath them with homes and jobs and life finally settled.

After hearing the story about my family's return to Ukraine, I was reminded of a letter my sister Maria had wrote to me about one of Tato's friends inviting him over and them singing songs from 26 years ago together. When they had gotten back, apparently they'd sang so much that they couldn't even talk. I wondered how, at that age, they could still remember songs from so long ago.

The letter also spoke of Tato's final return to Ukraine. She said that when they were reunited, Mama couldn't hold back her tears. Mama asked God that they'd never separate again. And thank God, after three times separated, they were no longer bothered.

At 82 years of age, Tato died of natural causes on January 31, 1984. News of his death somehow spread amongst his friends and they made sure that his funeral was held in Uherci, where his journey began. A bus load of people traveled to Uherci just for this event. Others road trains and some even drove cars. Family and friends from the village Zavydovych, the town Drozdovych, from Horodok, Lviv, Zymha Voda and other places came too. To transport his coffin to the cemetery, the family was even given a transport car.

But that day, the car was never used. So many people came to the funeral that they carried the coffin from Horodok to Uherci, a good five miles.

His spouse, my Mama, Fevronia Fedenko, died on September 26, 1990. She was 88 years old.

In my chest to this day remains a great love, a pride, a respect, and a sincere prayer to God for them, and in my solitude, I will have quiet and endless conversations with them that will be with me until the end of my life.

I'll remember you forever!

In 1994, I visited Ukraine and Uherci, the village where I was born, the place where I grew up happily, where we children played, where we sang and danced... but this old field where we used to play was covered with wild weeds, obstructed by a fence. In my old garden, there simply sat a pear tree.

Our noisy house, where farmers once listened to the broadcasts from the only radio in our village, or where they heard Tato read the news, was no longer there.

What remained, as a lonely witness of the past, was just a deep well from which all the neighbors were still getting water and still called her "Burburovoyu," as our family had always called it too.

CHAPTER TWENTY-FIVE

GLOSSARY

Red army :: the army and air force of the USSR from 1918-1946.

NKVD :: closely associated with the Soviet secret police, this was Joseph Stalin's law enforcement agency known for its political repression.

Yaroslav Stetsko :: a Ukrainian patriot and leader of the OUN from 1968 until 1986 as well as the leader of the Ukrainian government during the Nazi invasion of the Soviet Union.

Stepan Bandera :: a Ukrainian political activist who declared Ukraine's independence during WWII, with the hope of Germany as an ally against the Soviets. Instead, the Germans arrested him and his newly formed government and sent them to camps in Germany.

Andrii Melnyk :: a Ukrainian military and political leader during WWII. He led the OUN until Stepan Bandera and his faction broke off and started their own organization.µ

The Underground :: a generic term for the OUN.

UPA :: the Ukrainian Povstanska Army, which was the OUN's army, which translates best to the Ukrainian Insurgent Army.

OUN :: the Organization of Ukrainian Nationals, which was the entire movement of Ukraine fighting for its freedom.

Stepan's journey by location (spoiler alert - don't read before reading the story):

Uherci :: Stepan's village, south of Lviv and southeast of Horodok. It's now called Uhry.

Horodok :: a small town northwest of Uherci and southwest of Lviv.

Lontsky Prison :: a prison in Lviv, Ukraine. This was Stepan's first prison.

An unnamed prison :: Krakow, Poland. Stepan stayed here for one night after being saved by a Nazi.

Breslau Prison :: a prison in Breslau, Poland, which is now called Wroclaw. Stepan spent a night in the basement/cavern of this prison.

Gross-Rosen Concentration Camp :: a concentration camp in modern day Gross-Rosen, Poland, which at the time was occupied by the Nazis. Stepan's first camp. His Tato was beaten here, and Stepan was separated from him after falling into a four day coma.

Sachsenhausen Concentration Camp :: a concentration camp in Oranienburg, Germany. Stepan witnessed the Red Cross investigate the camp.

Sub-camp Heinkel :: a sub-camp of Sachsenhausen. Here Stepan was held here in a youth barrack until a boy went missing.

Dachau Concentration Camp :: a concentration camp located in Dachau, Germany. Stepan spent a few weeks here.

Baumenheim factory :: a German factory which housed the Messerschmitt fighter jet company. Stepan spent the most time in this camp and survived a bombing here.

Landsberg Concentration Camp :: a camp in southwest Bavaria, Germany. Stepan didn't spend much time here, because the Allies were close and the Nazis sent him on a three day death march. Hitler wrote Mein Kampf while incarcerated here in 1924.

Olching :: a city in Bavaria, Germany, 12 miles northwest of Munich. This was Stepan's first village of freedom after his ~30 mile death march.

Gerlingen :: a town in Ludwigsburg, Badn-Wurttemberg. Stepan stayed in a displaced prisoner camp here.

Munich :: the capital city of Germany and its third largest city. Stepan went back and forth out of Munich to organize his new life of freedom.

Karlsfeld :: a municipality in the district of Dachau, in Bavaria, Germany. It was a sub camp of Dachau during WWII. The story ends with Stepan going to high school here and restarting his life in this displaced prisoner camp.

CHAPTER TWENTY-SIX
ABOUT THE AUTHOR

Stepan Fedenko was born January 3rd, 1926 in the Ukrainian village of Uherci, now Uhry, southwest of Lviv. He studied there up until fifth grade and spend sixth and seventh grade in the nearby town of Horodok. After that, he studied for two years (1942-1944) in craft school in Lviv. During April 1944, he and his father were arrested by the Germans. In 1946, after gaining his freedom, he finished high school in a camp for immigrants in Karlsfeld near Munich in Germany. In 1950, he immigrated to the US. In 1951, he joined the American army, where he served for two years. From 1953 to 1956, he studied mechanical engineering at Wayne State University in Detroit. In 1956, he became a partner at Cylectron Corporation. In 1957, he married Anna Drohomeretska and they had two daughters - Mary and Donna. Mary married Alex and had two children - Damian (this book's translator) and Christine. Donna married Markian Fedorowycz and had four children - Olenka, Levko, Lys, and Kalyna. In 1993, Stepan retired and he now lives in Warren, Michigan, outside of Detroit. At 89, he's still an active member of the choir and will always hope for peace in Ukraine.

If you would like to reach Stepan or Damian, please email Damian at dnoflows@gmail.com.

www.ingramcontent.com/pod-product-compliance
Lightning Source LLC
Chambersburg PA
CBHW021131090426
42740CB00008B/742